DATABASE MANAGEMENT

Introduction to

DATABASE MANAGEMENT

A Practical Approach

Gerry M. Litton
University of San Francisco

Wm. C. Brown Publishers
Dubuque, Iowa

Book Team

Editor *Nicholas Murray*
Developmental Editor *Nova A. Maack*
Designer *Mark D. Hantelmann*
Production Editor *Gloria Schiesl*
Photo Research Editor *Shirley Charley*
Permissions Editor *Carla D. Arnold*
Product Manager *Linda M. Gorchels*

wcb group

Wm. C. Brown *Chairman of the Board*
Mark C. Falb *President and Chief Executive Officer*

wcb

Wm. C. Brown Publishers, College Division

G. Franklin Lewis *Executive Vice-President, General Manager*
E. F. Jogerst *Vice-President, Cost Analyst*
George Wm. Bergquist *Editor in Chief*
John Stout *Executive Editor*
Beverly Kolz *Director of Production*
Chris C. Guzzardo *Vice-President, Director of Sales and Marketing*
Bob McLaughlin *National Sales Manager*
Marilyn A. Phelps *Manager of Design*
Julie A. Kennedy *Production Editorial Manager*
Faye M. Schilling *Photo Research Manager*

To Poco and Tomasina, who were merciful to the manuscripts

Contents

Chapter Two

Using a Database Management System   25

Chapter Three

Data Storage Devices and Data Formats   47

Chapter Four

Chapter Five

Chapter Six

Chapter Seven

Chapter Eight

Chapter Nine

A Conceptual Database Design for Jellybeans, Inc.   245

Chapter Ten

Relational Database Systems   273

This book is intended to be used as a text for an introductory course in database management. Its main focus is the combination of practical database design principles with hands-on experience in the computer laboratory. The text may be used for a full semester course, or the first part of it may be used for a shorter course. An accompanying workbook is designed to furnish material for the laboratory portion of the course. Students using this book as a full semester text should have had some degree of prior exposure to computers. A course in programming is a desirable, but not essential, prerequisite.

Rationale for This Text

In the last few years, two significant trends have produced a noticeable gap in the textbook literature dealing with database management. First, the availability of database management as an everyday tool has increased at an incredible rate, due to rapid advances in microcomputer hardware and software. This growth has far outrun the general ability to use the available database tools effectively. Second, there has been a growing tendency for colleges and universities to acquire significant numbers of microcomputers for educational purposes.

The net result of these two factors is that large numbers of students now have the opportunity to learn about database management by combining theoretical textbook material with practical laboratory work. Unfortunately, few texts exist to address this situation. Furthermore, most textbooks dealing with database management pay little, if any, attention to the impact that microcomputers have had on the field. This book is the outcome of those deficiencies. It contains practical information concerning database design principles, presented in a way that applies equally well to mainframe and microcomputer environments. The accompanying laboratory workbook is designed to acquaint students with the practical aspects of designing and working with databases. The vehicle used is dBASE III®, the most popular of all database management systems.

Structure and Scope of the Text

The book is divided roughly into two sections. The first of these, consisting of chapters 1 through 7, contains introductory material, presented at a relatively low level; database design is introduced using a fairly intuitive approach.

This first section, plus associated workbook material, may be used to form the basis of a shortened or simplified course, because they contain all of the material necessary for an introduction to database management.

The second part of the book, chapters 8 through 14, contains more advanced material, including a well-structured approach to database design.

Chapter 1 is a general introduction to the subject of database management. It traces the development of data processing, and discusses the advantages of the database approach.

Chapter 2 develops the basic concepts of designing and implementing a database by introducing a case study that runs throughout the entire text: Jellybeans, Inc., a wholesale distributor. This introductory material is placed early in the text to give students an immediate feeling of the richness inherent in database management.

Chapters 3 and 4 deal with data storage devices and file structures. In courses where students have adequate background, this material may be either briefly covered or entirely skipped.

Chapter 5 discusses standard searching and reporting techniques for single-file databases.

Chapter 6 presents material normally not encountered in a text on database management: the role of programming in the database environment. The program examples are kept as simple as possible, and students with some programming experience should be able to grasp the principles illustrated by these examples.

For simplified courses designed for students with no prior programming experience, this chapter, plus parts of chapter 7, may be omitted without interfering with the flow of the book.

Chapter 7 takes the topic of database management beyond the realm of single-file processing, by introducing an extension to the simple database developed in prior chapters: a two-file database for Jellybeans, Inc. Again, the programming examples may be omitted if necessary.

Chapter 8 begins the advanced material of the book, a methodical approach to the design of complex databases.

Chapter 9 utilizes the principles introduced in chapter 8 by developing a fairly complex database design for Jellybeans, Inc.

Chapter 10 introduces relational database systems, showing how the relational approach follows naturally from the design principles introduced in chapter 8. In addition, these principles are further developed, generating techniques for optimizing database designs. These techniques are illustrated by applying them to the Jellybeans, Inc. database design developed in chapter 9.

Chapter 11 discusses various aspects of relational database systems. A fairly extensive discussion of relational query languages is presented.

Chapter 12 covers issues related to database security and protection.

Chapters 13 and 14 deal with database systems other than relational, emphasizing the network and hierarchical models. Chapter 13 supplies the technical background for understanding the types of systems presented in chapter 14.

Learning Aids

Each chapter of the text contains the following features to help students master the material:

- **Introduction** shows the relation of chapter material to the preceding chapters.
- **Summary** provides a convenient review of the topics of the chapter.
- **Review Questions** help students check their mastery of the material.
- **Problems** challenge students to apply what they have learned.
- **Key Terms** provide another convenient reviewing device to help students learn the vocabulary of the subject. These terms also appear in a glossary at the end of the text.

In addition to these features for each chapter, an **Appendix** contains a comparative survey of various categories of commercial database software – a valuable overview of current products.

Supplementary Materials

- **Laboratory Workbook** contains instructional material, plus a large number of exercises intended to lead students through the various steps of designing and working with dBASE III databases. This workbook is designed as a "do-it-yourself" guide, and the student should need minimal instructional assistance. In the latter part of the course, the student can use the knowledge gained through this workbook to practice some of the advanced design principles developed in the main text.
- **Tutorial diskette** is to be used in conjunction with the laboratory workbook. This contains many database and program examples to help students as they progress through the workbook.
- **dBASE III program diskette (educational version)** contains one of the most popular database management systems. A copy of this diskette is made available to instructors using this textbook.
- **Instructor's manual** contains the following material for each chapter:
  - A list of key objectives to be achieved within the chapter, in terms of concepts and ideas to be developed
  - Lecture outline, in the form of (1) chapter outline, (2) suggestions for topics to be given special emphasis, and (3) additional examples to supplement the text material
  - Suggestions for coordinating the exercises in the laboratory workbook with the text material
  - A set of transparency masters for each chapter.
  - Answers to problems at the end of the chapter
  - A test bank of multiple choice and true/false questions

- **wcb GradePak**, a computerized service, offers instructors assistance in maintaining lists of student scores, and in computing various statistical quantities, such as class averages.

Acknowledgments

Many people have contributed to the development of this text, and I am grateful to all of them for their individual and collective support: Nick Murray, for his constant patience and fund of ideas; Nova Maack, for keeping it all together; Carol Schwamberger, for her never-ending encouragement, and for her help in reading countless proofs; Karen Doland, for her meticulous and thorough editing; Mark Hantelmann, for his design work; Gloria Schiesl, for jumping in at a difficult time; Carla Arnold, for her help with permissions; Shirley Charley, for photo research; Bob Stern, whose faith got the project off the ground; and, finally, to the following people for reviewing the material and contributing to its reshaping:

James E. Benjamin *Southern Illinois University–Edwardsville*

A. Faye Borthick *University of Tennessee*

Douglas L. Cashing *St. Bonaventure University*

Dennis Geller *CNR, Inc.*

Jon L. Huhtala *Ferris State College*

Arthur B. Kahn *University of Baltimore*

James A. Larson *Honeywell Computer Sciences Center*

J. C. Peck *Clemson University*

Christopher W. Pidgeon *University of California–Irvine*

Darlene M. Wall, CDP *Lower Columbia College*

Michael Wang *University of Texas–Austin*

Chapter One

An Anatomy of Database Management

Introduction

We live in an age of information processing. The explosive growth of computer usage during the last twenty years is unrivaled by any other type of human expansion in recorded history. Although attributable to many factors, this remarkable change has fundamentally been brought about by rapid technological developments in computational hardware. These have in turn generated equally rapid computer software developments in many areas, including operating systems, programming languages, and user-oriented software packages such as database management systems. It is the purpose of this text to explore the latter.

The impact that database management has had on modern information processing can best be appreciated by glimpsing the way things were in the early, pre-database days. As we shall see, some aspects of data processing have remained somewhat the same, while others have undergone significant changes.

Early Data Processing

In the early days of data processing, only a handful of experts were able to communicate with the formidable machines known as digital computers. These devices were very large and expensive. They would reluctantly yield results of questionable value, but only after endless hours of frustrating effort by dedicated programmers. The end-users of that era, that is, people who hoped that their particular problems might be successfully solved by the machines, normally communicated via the professional programmer, who in turn "spoke" to the computer. Each problem was dealt with in an individual manner, requiring its own programs and data files. Not surprisingly, a great deal of time elapsed between the conception of a problem and the final generation of computer results.

1

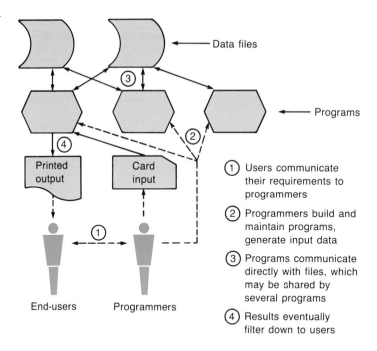

Figure 1.1
Early file processing.

Eventually, as computers began to find their way into commercial use by large organizations, the day of the individual programmer flourished. Some of the principal elements that were involved in a data-processing environment of this time are discussed in the following paragraphs and illustrated in figure 1.1.

- **End-users** were the prime movers in the early days of data processing, generating problems that required computer solutions. In a large organization, a typical end-user might have been the payroll department, with a requirement for monthly tallying of time cards and production of salary figures. Another end-user might have been the president of the organization, requesting a statistical breakdown of a particular aspect of the operation. Regardless of who the end-user was or the nature of the particular problem, (s)he needed the services of:

- **Programmers.** Computers needed to be spoken to by experts. This was an elite group, being bilingual in a very special way. They spoke the languages both of humans and machines, translating the specific requirements of the former into instructions that could be carried out by the latter. These instructions were grouped into packages, each of which was designed and constructed specifically to perform a certain task. These packages made up the organization's:

- **Programs.** When it was necessary for the computer to perform a specific task, the appropriate program was run, or *executed*. Typically, a program was designed to operate on a specific set of **input data**, with the intent of generating a desired set of **output data**. Input data was usually on punched cards, and outputs were on either printed paper or magnetic tape. For example, input for a particular program might have been a set of monthly time cards, and the output might have consisted of (1) a revised set of values for YEARLY_SALARY_TO_DATE; and (2) a set of values for MONTHLY_SALARY_PAID_OUT. Because some output data would be needed as input at a later time, either by the same programs or by others, it was stored in machine-readable form on:

- **Data files.** Information to be processed by one or more programs was often stored on magnetic tape or disk and divided into logical groups, called **files.** For example, basic personnel data would be stored on one file and salary-history information on another. The data files and their associated programs were "matched"—data on each file was stored in a particular format, and each program accessing that file had to be written to match the details of that format.

Problems with Early Data Processing

Large organizations often had many end-users, and each of these end-users had a variety of jobs for the computer, such as the generation of a report, or the processing of a particular set of data. Each of these jobs required that one or more programs be written, and each program interacted with one or more files. Although quite productive in many ways, this situation was also frustrating and unsatisfying because there was frequently a long time delay between the inception of an idea and the final result. Programs often took weeks or even longer to write and debug (fix all the errors). Even a simple job, such as the generation of a short report, could involve many hours of programming.

The need for change was a constant source of difficulty because files and programs were tightly locked into each other, and any type of design change often generated a lengthy domino effect. For example, suppose that a particular data file contained information on employee names, addresses, and salaries. In addition, assume that several different programs interacted with this file, each program performing a particular function such as a report generation or a file update. Suppose that for some reason the head of the personnel department decided to add NUMBER_OF_CHILDREN to the data for each employee. In order to accomplish this, the following tasks would have to be done:

- A program to update the file, adding the required data on the number of children for each employee, would have to be written.
- Every program that accessed the data file would have to be rewritten so that each one could read the re-designed file.

Since writing new programs was time-consuming, and modifying existing ones even more so, changes to a data system were approached with a good deal of caution.

Figure 1.2
Data processing before
the days of database
management.

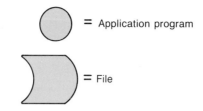

= Application program

= File

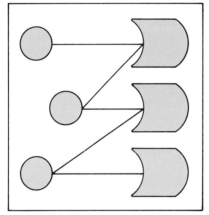

Payroll
dept.

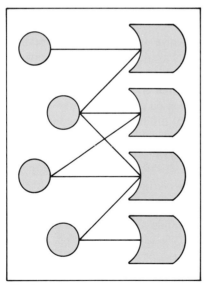

Employee-
relations
dept.

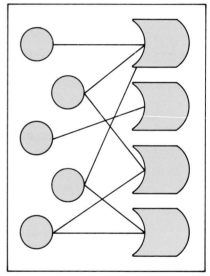

Personnel
dept.

As computer usage within an organization grew, different departments tended to carry on their data processing activities independently of each other. One consequence of this was the generation of a great deal of duplicate information, which in turn led to many secondary complications. For example, suppose that within a particular company, the computer was utilized by the payroll, employee-relations, and personnel departments, and each maintained its own data files and related programs, as illustrated in figure 1.2. Each department kept data on individual employees, which meant information was duplicated in each of the department's files. This had several implications: (1) extra effort was required to input the duplicate data, and (2) additional computer storage was needed to store the duplicate data, usually on magnetic tape.

Another important consequence of the data duplication was the possibility for data inconsistencies, which could take many forms. For instance, each department would probably have its own conventions for data formats, resulting in difficulties with matching or locating particular data (is J. Jones the same employee as Jones, J.?). Data inconsistency had the strongest effect when it took the form of data simply *not* being duplicated at all. For instance, suppose that employee J. Jones terminated employment with the organization. It is possible that although the data on Jones was deleted from the PERSONNEL department files, the other departments were not informed of Jones' departure (possibly because of a misplaced memo). The immediate result would be inconsistency within the data files of the organization. The long-term results could range from comical to disastrous: Jones would continue to receive periodic notices about how to get along with his associates, or worse yet, he would continue to receive monthly paychecks!

The Database Management Approach

A database management system is a collection of prewritten, integrated programs. Its major function is to assist users in all aspects of data manipulation and utilization. For simplicity, we shall often use either the term *database system* or the acronynm DBMS for database management system. Within the framework of database management, the previously discussed relationships among end-users, programmers, programs, and data are significantly altered, as illustrated in figure 1.3.

One of the important changes illustrated in this figure is that programs no longer interact directly with data files. Instead, they communicate with a DBMS (the middleman, so to speak), which in turn controls the flow of information to and from the files. At first glance, this may seem to be adding an extra layer of complexity to the situation (compared with figure 1.2 for example), and in a sense this is true. However, not only is this complexity invisible to the user, but it also serves to enhance the user's ability to interact with the data. An analogous situation is moving from an automobile with a manual transmission to one with automatic drive. The latter is much more mechanically complex, yet to the driver, the result is considerably less effort.

Figure 1.3
The database
management
environment. (a) A
multiple-user system;
(b) a single-user
system.

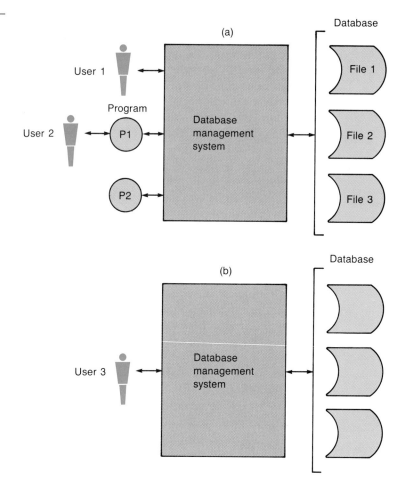

Figure 1.3 shows a set of data files grouped together into a common **database.** This illustration shows the real significance of the term *database:* a collection of *integrated* data that is under the control of a database management system. The various ways interactions may occur within a database are also illustrated in figure 1.3(a). User 1 is working *directly* with the DBMS, which in turn manages the data—no externally-written programs are utilized. Instead, the user issues various **commands** (instructions) to the DBMS to access and manipulate information. User 1 is working **interactively** with the DBMS. User 2, on the other hand, is working interactively with the DBMS, but through an **application program** written by a programmer to perform a particular function not directly available with the DBMS. The term *application program* refers to a program written for use in a database environment. Finally, the figure shows Program 2 executing without the presence of a user. Programs of this type are known as **batch programs** and they are used for a variety of purposes, such as the generation of periodic reports.

As suggested by figure 1.3, users 1 and 2, as well as program P2, may all be interacting simultaneously with the DBMS. User 3, shown in figure 1.3(b), illustrates an innovation that is entirely new to the field of data management—a single user having exclusive and total use of a computer. The machine is a microcomputer, on which a piece of DBMS software is executing, managing a database designed solely for the user. Amazingly enough, although the situation represented by User 3 is relatively new, it already represents by far the most common use of database management.

Database Features

In this section, some of the important features that differentiate database management from ordinary data-processing are outlined. The list of features is by no means inclusive, nor do all DBMS's have all of these characteristics. In general, however, most of the features that are outlined below will exist in some form or other on the majority of database systems.

Operation Modes

The interaction between a user and a DBMS can occur in one of three ways, depending on the capabilities of the DBMS and the needs of the user. These modes of interaction are: **command driven, menu driven,** and **program driven.** Some database systems have capabilities for all three modes, while others are built around only one.

Command mode. In this mode, a user interactively gives commands to the DBMS. This type of interaction is frequently employed by users with some technical experience, because it allows for the most flexible use of a database system. The command mode of operation is not popular with those who wish to use a DBMS casually, because a fair degree of study and practice is required in order to become familiar with the commands.

Typically, if a DBMS has a command mode, there may be dozens, or possibly hundreds, of commands at the disposal of the user. For this reason, learning to use a large DBMS can be a time-consuming process.

Menu-driven systems. This mode of operation is generally utilized by users with limited and clearly defined data-storage applications. Menu-driven systems are also popular with users who have little or no technical background. The big advantage of this type of system is that a user may generate and use a database with virtually no effort, because all necessary instructions are displayed on the screen. Database systems that operate only in the menu-driven mode have limited capabilities compared to those that also offer the command mode of interaction.

Program mode. Often, user needs are very complex, requiring the assistance of one or more application programs. As discussed earlier, programs may run either in **batch** mode or interactively. Sizeable database applications typically involve significant amounts of data processing, including data inputting and report generation. These are often best accomplished by running batch programs.

Smaller database systems place comparatively little emphasis on program-driven operation because of the expertise needed to write the programs. On the other hand, most large DBMS's have both program and command mode capabilities.

Data Access

One of the strongest features of most database systems is the ease with which data can be accessed. This includes adding new data, modifying existing information, searching a database for specific information, and generating reports from particular parts of a database. Usually all of these operations are easily accomplished in both command-driven and menu-driven modes.

Interactive data entry is particularly useful because input data can often be checked for validity, with immediate feedback given to the user if data errors are detected. The term *data modification* is used to describe both the process of altering existing data and the deletion of database information. Modifications may be done one record at a time, or they may be done **globally,** that is, to many records at once. It is possible, for example, to delete an entire subset of database records with a single command—a useful but dangerous feature.

Interactive searching of a database is a powerful feature of many DBMS's, especially when combined with accompanying reporting capability. These features give the user the opportunity to find certain data of interest within a database, and to then obtain output of the data in a particular format. The interactive aspect to this activity is especially useful because of its spontaneous and creative nature.

Help Facility

Many DBMS's have adopted a feature that has found its way into many types of modern software packages—the on line help facility. This feature allows a user to obtain help at any time during interaction with a DBMS by entering a few keystrokes. Help facilities come in various forms. Often, the system notes which part of the software is being accessed when help is requested, and a list of helpful suggestions is displayed. Other systems may require the user to specify what type of help is desired. Regardless of the form it takes, a help facility can be a great time-saver, frequently taking the place of an extensive search through a users' manual.

The terms *database* and *database management* have come to apply to widely varying situations, ranging from extremely large and complicated data systems to small applications for the individual. There are database management systems for virtually every computer in existence, and they vary in price from a few dollars to hundreds of thousands of dollars. However there are enough commonalities to justify pulling them all under the common heading of database management.

Mainframe Database Systems

The first database systems came into being in the late 1960s. They were designed to run on large computers generally known as **mainframes,** in conjunction with COBOL programs designed to manage information for sizeable companies. These very large database systems have continued to evolve since then, developing more sophisticated techniques and features in response not only to improvements in hardware and software, but also to evolving data management ideas.

In general, these database systems are characterized by the following features: (1) they are used for highly complex information-system applications; (2) they are very expensive, some of the more elaborate ones costing well over $200,000; and (3) they require the expertise of full-time professional programmers, who are devoted either to developing programs for new applications or to modifying existing programs to fulfill changing requirements.

Database management is invariably an integral part of a large organization's information system. Extremely large organizations may even maintain several separate but interrelated databases, each representing a particular segment of information. Typically, one or more databases form the very heart of an information system, being regularly accessed by many individuals within the organization.

Another type of large database is used by public-access information retrieval systems. These databases contain information of interest to a broad range of public users, who may access the data via public dial-up lines. Examples of this type of database are Lockheed's Dialog system and Compuserve, each of which maintains many different databases on a wide variety of topics.

Microcomputer Database Systems

The emergence of microcomputers and associated software packages has radically altered the meaning of database management. Microcomputer-based database systems have been used for an enormous range of applications that were unthinkable just ten years ago. Typically, these applications are oriented around either individuals or small companies, and the total investment in both hardware and software is usually in the range of $2,000 to $25,000. The *initial* technical level of micro users is usually very limited, although in many cases the amateur rapidly turns into a skilled technician. Because of the nonprofessional orientation of these users, micro-based DBMS's tend to be relatively easy to use, requiring in some cases only a few hours of study, even for a complete novice.

Until quite recently, microcomputers had very limited **primary storage,** that is, the memory where programs reside during execution. As a result, micro-based DBMS's have tended to offer far fewer features than mainframe database systems. On the other hand, microcomputer DBMS's offer much better value than their larger counterparts in terms of features per dollar. This is due primarily to the enormous market that exists for microcomputer applications, coupled with the limited financial resources of each user within this market.

Recently, there has been a huge increase in the amount of primary storage available for microcomputers, particularly those that are IBM PC-compatible. Database systems that will take increasing advantage of these memory developments are beginning to appear, and users can expect more and more features that had previously been available only with far more expensive systems. These features will come at little cost to the user because of the competitiveness within the microcomputer DBMS field.

Another interesting aspect to micro-based DBMS's are the many innovations that they have generated in the database-management field; these innovations have eventually found their way into mainframe software. This is partly because the microcomputer database systems arrived relatively late in the game, long after larger systems had become well-established. Designers of the micro-based systems were able to build on the experiences of their larger predecessors, without having to carry along the extra baggage that inevitably exists within systems that have gone through many changes.

Like most microcomputer software, DBMS's offer a tremendous amount of computing power per dollar. The general trend continues in this direction, with dramatic increases in value occurring regularly. The database capability that cost $100,000 ten years ago is available today for less than $10,000.

Network Systems

A trend just beginning to become popular is that of microcomputer networking. A **network** consists of two or more microcomputers connected together for the purposes of sharing common resources such as magnetic disks, printers, software packages, and even databases. The process of **multi-user access,** in which two or more users share a database at the same time, requires specialized software to be incorporated into a DBMS. As networking is becoming more dominant in the microcomputer arena, the trend in DBMS software is also toward multi-user database access.

The term *database management* is used to describe a large variety of software, ranging from mainframe systems costing over $200,000 to $49.95 software packages for the tiniest microcomputer. Because of this enormous variety, it is worthwhile to categorize the different forms that database management takes.

File Managers: A Special Case

There is general agreement within the data processing industry that a "true" DBMS is one that is able to manage a database consisting of many different types of interrelated data. Most DBMS's divide information into files, each of which contains a specific type of information; a database may consist of several files of related information. For example, a company database might consist of information dealing with customers (one file), orders (another file), and shipments (still another file). The information in the different files is clearly interrelated since customers submit orders, receive shipments, and so on.

File managers are distinguished from true DBMS's in that each database may consist of only a single type of data, that is, a single file. In a sense, a file manager acts as a kind of electronic filing cabinet, with built-in indexing and report-generation capabilities. Even with the one-file-per-database restriction, file managers are extremely useful for a wide variety of applications, such as maintaining lists of individuals, companies, and events.

File managers are primarily aimed at the microcomputer market, and all have several common characteristics. Because they are at the lower end of the price range of data-management software, and are designed for the technical novice, they are extremely "user friendly". Often, file managers are menu-driven, which means that a user is continually guided along, presented at every step with a set of choices (a menu) or other detailed instructions. Figure 1.4 illustrates typical steps in using this type of system. Figure 1.4(a) shows an initial menu, offering a user the option to create a new file, search a file, add more data, and so on. The choice of "Create a new file" leads to the next screen display, which gives the user sufficient information to define a new file (figure 1.4(b)).

The strong points of file managers are the ease with which a user may (1) search a file for particular subsets of information, and (2) generate reports based on the results of a search. For example, a company might maintain a file of information about all of its customers. With a few simple operations, the user could create a report that would list only those customers whose address was in California.

File managers have been ideal for those users with (1) limited and well-defined data-storage needs, (2) limited financial resources, and (3) little or no technical background. The days of the simple file managers are probably numbered however, because true DBMS's are becoming both easier to use and less expensive, offering the simplicity of file managers for the novice, as well as additional complexity for the advanced user.

Figure 1.4
(a) A typical opening
menu for a menu-driven
file manager; (b) display
shown in response to
"Create a new file."

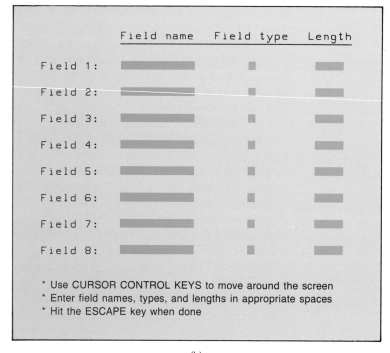

```
        What would you like to do?

   1. Create a new file
   2. Enter data into an existing file
   3. Modify existing data
   4. Search a file
   5. Create a report
   6. Delete a file
   7. Modify the design of a file

        Please enter your choice (1—7):
```

(a)

```
                Field name   Field type   Length

Field 1:        ▆▆▆▆▆▆        ▪            ▆▆▆

Field 2:        ▆▆▆▆▆▆        ▪            ▆▆▆

Field 3:        ▆▆▆▆▆▆        ▪            ▆▆▆

Field 4:        ▆▆▆▆▆▆        ▪            ▆▆▆

Field 5:        ▆▆▆▆▆▆        ▪            ▆▆▆

Field 6:        ▆▆▆▆▆▆        ▪            ▆▆▆

Field 7:        ▆▆▆▆▆▆        ▪            ▆▆▆

Field 8:        ▆▆▆▆▆▆        ▪            ▆▆▆


* Use CURSOR CONTROL KEYS to move around the screen
* Enter field names, types, and lengths in appropriate spaces
* Hit the ESCAPE key when done
```

(b)

Integrated Packages

Integrated packages combine database management with other popular features such as word processing, spread-sheeting, telecommunications, and graphical output. They are usually oriented around microcomputers, and because of their complexity, tend to be relatively expensive.

Integrated packages are particularly useful when various capabilities such as word processing and database management must be used on the same set(s) of data on a regular basis. The advantage of this type of system is that commands for accessing and manipulating data tend to be uniform, giving users somewhat of an advantage in learning to use the package effectively.

The biggest disadvantage of these systems is that many of the individual capabilities (word processing, for example) tend to be somewhat inferior to dedicated packages (Wordstar, for example). This is very much the case for the database management features of integrated packages. They may be sufficient for those applications that could be handled by a file manager, but are poorly equipped to deal with complex database needs.

Data Models

As mentioned earlier, a "true" DBMS is one that can manage databases consisting of many different types of interrelated data. The particular way in which information is subdivided and managed within a database is referred to as the **data model** used by the DBMS. Each DBMS is based on a specific data model, and a user must choose a DBMS with a model that is appropriate for the specific application.

For example, some database systems are oriented around textual information, such as books or journals. For these, a common model of data is either the paragraph, chapter, or some other arbitrary subdivision of text.

The data model used by most DBMS's is one in which database information is grouped into files, with each file containing groups of **records.** Within a particular file, each record contains information about a particular object or event, and all of the records within a file represent similar objects or events.

For instance, a pet shop might maintain a database consisting of information dealing with its animals, as illustrated in figure 1.5. One file called ANIMALS contains a group of records, each of which contains data for a particular animal, such as name, type, and age. Another file called VET_VISITS, contains information about visits by the local veterinarian. Each record contains the data for a particular visit, such as date of visit, which animals were examined, the accompanying diagnoses, and so on. The data in these two files have strong interrelationships because each veterinarian visit (one record) deals with several animals (another type of record).

Figure 1.5
A pet shop database.
The database consists
of two files: ANIMALS
and VET_VISITS. Within
each file are records
containing data of
similar nature.

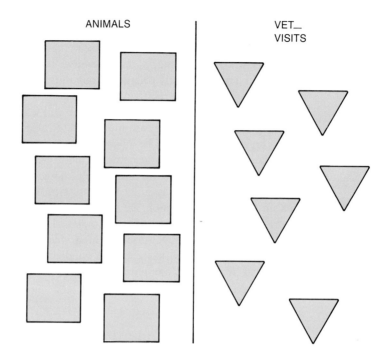

The exact way in which a DBMS connects related information for the benefit of the user represents another level of data modeling. In this respect, there are three commonly-used models: the RELATIONAL, NETWORK, and HIER-ARCHICAL. Most DBMS's that divide data into files and records belong to one of these three data models. Of the three, the RELATIONAL is the most common, and it is the model used throughout most of this text.

Advantages of the DBMS Approach

The use of database management systems offers several levels of improvement over earlier forms of data processing, including the introduction of many types of features that were previously nonexistent.

Reduced Data Redundancy

Early file processing systems often suffered from excessive data redundancy, which was accompanied by problems such as excessive memory requirements and data inconsistencies. Because a database consists of an *integrated* set of files, data redundancy tends to be minimized, especially when a database is well-designed. As a result, there is far less likelihood of data inconsistencies and their associated problems. Thus, in a typical database for a company, the name and address of each employee is stored only once, with access to this data available to all departments. When an update is made to an employee record, the changes are automatically available to all interested parties.

A centralized database within an organization offers several other advantages related to minimization of redundancy, such as the promotion of data standards. For example, because there is only one copy of vital statistics on employees, there is automatically agreement among the departments as to the exact form of the various data items, such as name and address.

Reduced Programming Effort

Database systems are designed to easily perform many standard functions frequently required by users, such as database searching, creation of reports, and adding data. In many cases, a user's requirements can be met by the built-in capabilities of the DBMS, *without the need for any additional programming.* This has been particularly helpful in the case of micro-based systems because of the nontechnical background of most of the users.

Many applications do have requirements beyond built-in DBMS capabilities however, and in these cases programming is required. Invariably, the amount of necessary programming is considerably less than it would be in the absence of a DBMS.

Faster Response Time

Because programming effort is often reduced or even eliminated in DBMS's, end-users tend to get desired results relatively quickly. Frequently, users become familiar enough with a database system to be able to make their own interactive queries, essentially eliminating the middleman (i.e., the programmer). Faster response times generally promote more of a feeling of flexibility, and end-users have a stronger sense of continuity between what is needed and when it can be obtained.

Data Independence

One of the primary functions of database systems is to free the users and/or programmers from the responsibility of knowing the *physical* details of data storage. Since the database system assumes this task, users may concentrate on the *logical* content of the data. For example, suppose that a file consists of CUSTOMERS records, each of which contains the data items NAME, ADDRESS, and TELEPHONE. The DBMS must know precisely: (1) where each record resides in memory; (2) the exact length of each record and of each of its data items; and (3) the exact physical arrangement of data in each record. On the other hand, a user must only know the logical structure of the data—namely that the CUSTOMERS file contains records, each of which contains particular pieces of information. In fact, the user may have only a vague idea of what actually constitutes a file or a record.

Figure 1.6
Physical and logical
views of a database
record.

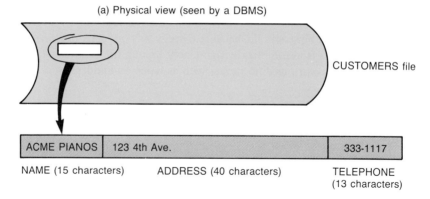

(a) Physical view (seen by a DBMS)

CUSTOMERS file

| ACME PIANOS | 123 4th Ave. | 333-1117 |

NAME (15 characters)   ADDRESS (40 characters)   TELEPHONE (13 characters)

The DBMS must know: (1) The exact physical location of the record
(2) The precise physical structure of the record

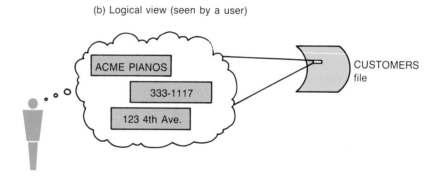

(b) Logical view (seen by a user)

CUSTOMERS file

The user knows only that a record (whatever that is) for ACME PIANOS
exists somewhere in a file (whatever that is) called CUSTOMERS.
Moreover, the record contains values for the company's name, telephone
number and address.

The physical and logical points of view are illustrated in figure 1.6. Their separation is called **data independence.**

Suppose that a user wishes to access the data for "ACME PIANOS" from the file. Often, one or two simple commands such as the following would be sufficient to obtain the result:

> USE CUSTOMERS
> DISPLAY FOR NAME = "ACME PIANOS"

It is the responsibility of the DBMS to locate the desired record, then to display it for the user.

Figure 1.7
A program segment
illustrating the
independence from
physical data
structures. The
program accesses the
file from a *logical* point
of view, so that many
types of design
changes to the file may
leave the program
unaffected.

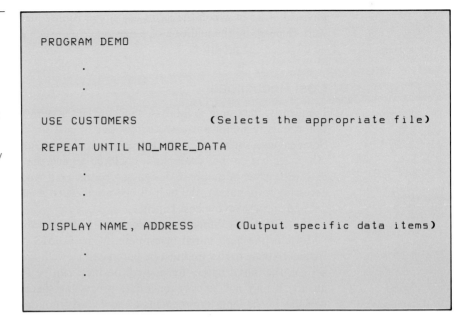

```
PROGRAM DEMO

          .

          .

USE CUSTOMERS              (Selects the appropriate file)

REPEAT UNTIL NO_MORE_DATA

         .

         .

DISPLAY NAME, ADDRESS     (Output specific data items)

         .

         .
```

The Ability to Change

Database management systems often give users freedom to make database design changes with comparatively little effort. For example, consider the file of CUSTOMERS described in the preceding section. Each record contains information on a customer's name, address, and phone number. Suppose that at some point in time, we decide that an AGE data item should be included as part of each customer's record. With many DBMS's, this change could be made with minimal effort, requiring only a few simple instructions. In contrast, making the same type of change in a non-DBMS environment would involve a considerable amount of programming.

Even with complex database applications involving many applications programs, design changes may often be made with little trouble. Many times, a particular change can be effected without requiring any modifications to related programs—a situation quite unlike that existing in pre-DBMS days. This is due to the data independence inherent in database systems, and the fact that application programs are written with an orientation towards the *logical* structure of a database.

Figure 1.7 illustrates this principle, showing a small segment from a program that accesses NAME and ADDRESS data items from the CUSTOMERS file. In this simple example, the program refers only to the logical content of the file; it is unconcerned with details such as the exact size of the data items, or the physical order in which the items are stored. Consequently, if the file structure were changed by the addition of a new data item such as AGE, there would be no effect on the program.

Cost Reductions

Frequently, the use of a database management system for a particular application results in significant cost savings, due in part to factors already discussed. Some savings, such as the reduction in required programming, are obvious, while others are less so. For example, it could be argued that because of the relative ease with which a database design can be changed, and because of the ease of accessing information, the overall operation (such as a business) is enhanced, with an accompanying cost benefit.

It is sometimes difficult to appreciate the dollar value of a database system because of the high initial investment. Many DBMS packages are costly, and frequently new hardware must be purchased as well. Even for a microcomputer system, the initial outlay for a small business can be $10,000 or more. Consequently it may not be easy for a data-processing specialist to convince a businessman of the long-term benefits to be reaped from database management.

Information Protection

The security and privacy of information is vital to the success of a database; in fact, a database is only as valuable as the degree to which it is protected. Data must be safeguarded against any conceivable type of damage, whether from system failure, human error, or intentional mischief.

Different DBMS's offer varying types of information protection, and to widely-varying degrees. Because it is automatically presumed that every database will sooner or later suffer fatal damage due either to a hardware or software failure, or from user error, several techniques are used to facilitate recovery following a fatality.

Making periodic **backups,** or copies, of a database is one level of insurance that can be done even without the aid of a DBMS. **Logging** is another aid offered by some of the more sophisticated DBMS's. With this technique, every change to a database is recorded separately on a **log,** which is maintained on a separate memory device from that on which the database is stored. Following a database fatality, the log can be used to reconstruct the database. Logging is particularly important in situations where the loss of any data whatsoever is unacceptable, such as banking and airline reservations systems.

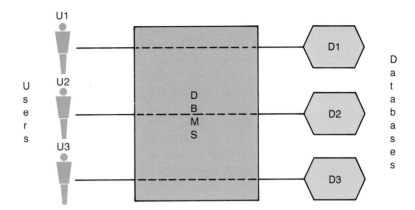

Figure 1.8
A multi-user DBMS.
Each user interacts with
a separate database in
this example.

For various reasons, information must often be kept confidential. Many DBMS's offer various levels of protection for maintaining the privacy of sensitive information, the most common being the use of **passwords.** With this device, a user is granted access to particular parts of a database only if (s)he enters the correct password. Often, a single database may be subdivided, with each piece being accessible only to a particular password.

Multi-user Support and Distributed Processing

Larger database systems are designed to interact simultaneously with several users, a process referred to as **timesharing.** The largest systems can handle thousands of users at once. In some cases, each user accesses his or her own database, as shown in figure 1.8. In other situations, a DBMS allows several users to access the same database simultaneously (figure 1.3(a)). Here, the DBMS must exercise **concurrency control**—the ability to deal with situations in which several users attempt to modify the same data at the same time.

Some computing systems allow users to interact **remotely,** that is, from a location physically removed from the computer facility. Usually, the connection is made with ordinary telephone lines and sometimes satellite links as well. This **distributed processing** ability is a great asset for database systems that support multiple users, and in many cases, such as airline reservation systems, it is indispensable.

Database Applications

Database management systems have found their way into many types of applications, ranging from simple personal lists to complex information management systems involving multitudes of data types and the full-time support of many programmers.

Individual Users

The greatest number of databases lie in the hands of individuals, either for personal use or in connection with a small business. The common types of applications deal with various types of lists, indexed in different ways. These lists may be used for maintaining information about members of organizations and clubs, to generate mailing labels, and so on. In general, these types of applications are handled quite well by file managers rather than a more sophisticated type of system, and individuals usually have little trouble learning how to set up and maintain their own applications.

Computer applications strictly for home use have been highly overrated, and most personal computers that are not used in connection with a business or organization have eventually found their way into the attic. The reason for this is that most individuals do not have enough data in any particular area to justify the time required to maintain that information in a database. Contrary to popular advertising, it's really considerably easier to maintain a checkbook manually rather than with a file manager.

Small Businesses

Database systems are used by small businesses in a variety of ways. Often, a simple file manager may be used to maintain lists of clients, appointments schedules, and so on. For this type of application, the DBMS is used as a tool for assisting with very well-defined sets of data.

Some small businesses have chosen to build information systems in which all of the major operational data is maintained in a fully-integrated database. Typically, information would be kept on customers, orders, shipments, stock-on-hand, accounts receivable and payable, and more. In this type of application, the database has become an integral part of the business operation.

Data systems of this kind require the services of competent data-processing professionals, who generally install one of the following types of software:

Off-the-shelf packages. Many fully-developed packages are commercially available for managing typical small-business information. These packages, which are sets of prewritten programs, often based around a commercial DBMS, are specifically designed to fit the information processing needs of a typical small business.

The advantage of these packages is that they are ready to use, having already been tested and debugged. Their main disadvantage is that they may not satisfy the specific needs of a particular business. If this is the case, then either the business must compromise on its requirements, or the package must be modified by a professional programmer.

Customized software.   A competent programmer may use a DBMS as the basis
for developing a system geared to the particular needs of a company. While this
approach is more likely to result in a tailor-made system that better suits the
requirements of a business, it has the disadvantage of being much more expensive
than a comparable off-the-shelf package because of the high cost of programming.

Regardless of the route taken, the incorporation of a fully-integrated database
into a small business is a relatively costly undertaking, requiring a good deal of
planning and investment in time and money. Often, the system must be able to
support several users, requiring either a multi-user DBMS or a local area network. The total outlay may be in the range of $10,000 to $25,000, possibly even
more. If the system is well conceived and implemented however, the benefits to
the organization usually justify the investment.

Large Organizations

As organizations grow, so does the amount of information that must be handled,
and in fact, database management is considered a necessity for large organizations. Typically, the computers are in the medium-to-large range, which translates into a value equal to the better part of $1,000,000. This type of application
invariably involves larger DBMS's, and therefore requires a great deal of programming and program maintenance. Usually, a separate data-processing department exists for this purpose.

Invariably, large company databases are multi-user-oriented, often with distributed use over large distances. In some cases, users are spread across conti-
nents, with communications taking place via telephone lines and satellite
connections.

Choice of Database Management Systems

Each database in existence has required that somebody decide which DBMS to
use. Rarely is the choice a simple one because for each specific application there
are invariably a great many systems that may be suitable. The major factors
involved in any decision usually involve: (1) cost; (2) ease of use; (3) features
available; (4) potential for application growth.

Cost is invariably a significant factor, whether the data application is a personal list of acquaintances or a multi-million dollar industrial database. Whatever the intended use, cost must be balanced against other factors.

Although it may be easy to assess present database requirements, it is much
more difficult to predict the needs in six months or two years. For example, you
may choose a minimal-cost file manager for maintaining customer lists. As time
passes, the system seems so convenient that you may wish to incorporate data on
customers' orders as well, only to find that the file manager cannot easily do so.

Your initial "savings" has become a double-edged sword, because in order to expand you must now abandon the file manager, starting over with a more flexible database system.

By the same token, systems that are initially very easy to use may also prove to be inadequate for later requirements. For example, menu-driven systems are quite attractive because they literally lead the user along at every step. However, a totally menu-driven system has very severe limitations compared to systems that are command-driven, and the features that seem initially attractive may turn into a straightjacket.

Generally, the choice of a database management system should occur only after a long and serious look has been taken at the present *and* projected future requirements, even though the latter may be difficult to assess.

For complex database applications, whether for micros or large computers, the final choice of both hardware and DBMS should be delayed, if possible, until the design of the database has reached an advanced stage. In this way, the hardware and software requirements can be better anticipated.

Database design is a complex subject. A design for file managers is straightforward, since it is limited to one file at a time. For databases involving many different types of information however, good initial design is crucial to the overall success of the database. For this reason, the latter part of this text is directed toward database design.

Summary

Database management has had a significant impact on the way computers are utilized. The use of DBMS software packages has greatly increased not only the types of data management applications that can benefit from computerization, but also the type of person who can directly interact with the computers. Only a few years ago, computer interaction was limited to a few highly-skilled programmers and technicians working with large machines. Much of today's database management software is accessible to anyone with basic reading and writing skills.

Database management software offers many advantages to both data-processing specialists and casual users, and a variety of ways exist for utilizing this software. Direct interaction between users and the DBMS is often adequate for many database applications. On the other hand, professional programming support may be required for complex database applications. In either case, the use of prewritten DBMS software offers a great deal of flexibility in the way information can be manipulated.

As the use of microcomputers increases, database management, along with word processing and spread sheets, will continue to be commonly-used types of applications.

Terminology

application program	end-user
backup	file
batch program	file manager
command driven	integrated package
DBMS	interactive
DBMS command	mainframe
data independence	menu driven
data model	network
database	program driven
database management	record
distributed processing	timesharing

Review Questions

1. Outline the shortcomings of conventional file processing in the light of data-processing requirements. For each item, how has database management improved matters?
2. Discuss the basic difference between user/data interactions in: (a) conventional file-processing; and (b) the database management environment.
3. What is meant by an *integrated* set of data?
4. Discuss each of the three ways in which users may interact with a **DBMS**.
5. Can you think of an example in which an application program would be useful, in the context of database management?
6. What type of applications are best suited for a file manager?
7. What differentiates a file manager from a "true" database management system?
8. Why are programs often unnecessary in the DBMS environment?
9. From a database management point of view, what is the biggest disadvantage of integrated packages?
10. What are some of the features of database systems that are particularly "user-friendly"?
11. List five significant advantages offered by the DBMS approach.
12. Suppose that you own a small business and are thinking of computerizing. You plan to begin by building a list of current customers, and eventually hope to expand to much more extended use of the computer. How would you go about selecting a DBMS and a computer?

Chapter Two

Using a Database Management System

Introduction

Database management is a valuable tool for manipulating computerized information, and with the aid of this tool, the processes of storing, retrieving, and modifying data are greatly simplified. This chapter will explore the basic concepts of using database management systems. To help understand these concepts, we will present a simple case study in the form of a jellybean distributor, Jellybeans, Inc., and explore the initial steps involved in establishing and using a simple database. We shall first describe the process of setting up this database using a DBMS. This discussion will help to clarify exactly what constitutes a database. We shall then illustrate some typical methods of entering data into the database, followed by techniques for modifying and retrieving this data. In later chapters, the same case study will be expanded in order to explore more complex features of database management.

The context, or setting, of the example in this chapter is in terms of a microcomputer-system. That is, it is assumed that the Jellybean, Inc., database is being installed and used on some type of microcomputer. This setting is chosen primarily because of the current widespread use of microcomputers.

Although much of the thrust of this text is oriented around microcomputers, it is important to realize that the basic concepts apply equally well to database management in environments associated with minicomputers or mainframe machines. In fact, a few of the ideas which will be discussed later are applicable only to larger computers. When this is the case, it will be clearly pointed out.

Historical

We will consider the hypothetical situation of a small business, Jellybeans, Inc. For the first year or two, there wasn't very much business; customers were few and far between, orders were small, and cash flow amounted to little more than a trickle. As a result, it was easy to manually keep track of what little information there was. Recently, however, business has improved and the amount of paperwork has become a significant problem. There are now many customers, each of whom places orders with the company on a regular basis. Many customers have paid all of their bills, while others have not. Some customers are given considerable amounts of credit, while others are given very little. Because there are so many orders from customers, and because jellybeans are perishable, it is difficult to estimate the supply of jellybeans to keep on hand at any given time. Consequently the number of jellybeans shipped from the manufacturer to Jellybeans, Inc. often does not keep up with the demands of the moment.

Consultation with a professional data-management expert has produced the following suggestion: the business is basically sound and healthy, with an excellent chance for growth; but its potential for expansion is suffering because of the inability to access appropriate information in a quick and accurate manner. On the advice of this expert, a plan has been made for methodically computerizing the data associated with the operation of the business. The plan calls for this process to proceed slowly, so that familiarity with the computer can be gained at a comfortable pace, without causing a sudden and traumatic disruption to daily operations. To achieve this, a microcomputer system has been purchased.

The Computer System

This computer system consists of a microcomputer, associated peripheral devices (for moving data in and out of the computer), and a database management system. Figure 2.1 shows a schematic of the system, and each component is described in the discussion that follows.[1]

The microcomputer is, of course, the heart of the system. It consists of several components, all of which are closely interrelated. The main ones are the **central processing unit,** usually abbreviated to **CPU,** and **primary storage,** sometimes called **main storage** or **main memory.** The CPU is where most of the major activity of the computer takes place. Here, the instructions of a running program are executed. These instructions can involve arithmetic operations, data transfer from one area to another, and other types of processes.

---

[1]This discussion is brief, since some fundamental knowledge concerning the basic components of a computer system is assumed. If this is not the case, it might be appropriate at this point to do some supplemental reading from any of a number of excellent introductory textbooks on the subject.

Figure 2.1
Typical microcomputer
setup.

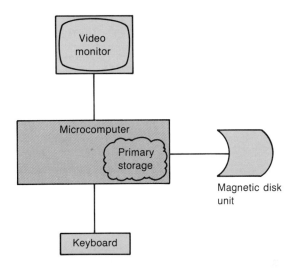

The primary storage of the computer has two major functions. It is here that the instructions constituting a program are stored during the execution of that program. Secondly, primary storage is used to store part or all of the data being handled by the executing program. Normally, during the execution of a program data is transferred between primary storage and other devices, such as the keyboard or the disk unit, which are described later.

The primary storage cannot be used for long-term retention of information for two reasons. First, data stored here is **volatile;** that is, if the power supplied to the computer is interrupted, even for an instant, the data is irretrievably lost. Secondly, the amount of data that can be stored in this area is a tiny fraction of normal data-storage requirements. Consequently, other devices, such as the disk unit must be used for this purpose.

The **keyboard** is the principal device by which users communicate with the computer. It is used for entering instructions and commands, entering data into the computer, making queries of this data, creating reports based on portions of the data, and many other purposes. The **video monitor,** or **display screen,** is used by the computer to communicate with a user. Normally, a dialog between a user and the computer consists of the user entering commands or data into the computer via the keyboard, and the computer displaying appropriate responses on the monitor. The **printer** is used to obtain **hard copy** from the computer. For example, in a database application, a typical output to the printer might be a report made by the DBMS in response to a user request.

The **disk unit** is the device used for long-term storage of information. Under the control of an executing program, data is transferred between the disk unit and the computer, where it is held temporarily in primary storage for use by the program. Both data and programs are stored on the disk unit.

Table 2.1

Preliminary List of Items for the CUSTOMERS File

Item	Comments
Customer name	Name of an individual or a company
Address	Should contain street, city, state, zip code
Phone number	Should include area code
Credit limit	Upper limit on customer's credit (dollars)
Outstanding balance	Amount currently owed to Jellybeans, Inc.

The database management system is itself a program, or a set of integrated programs, stored on the disk unit. When a user wishes to access a database, (s)he calls the DBMS into operation. This is usually a two-step process. First, the computer copies the DBMS programs into primary storage. Secondly, the program begins to **execute,** and a dialog begins between the DBMS and the user. This dialog consists of **DBMS commands** issued one at a time by the user, followed by appropriate responses from the DBMS.

An Initial Database Design

Because computerization will be a totally new experience for the company personnel in our case study, the database will be introduced in small steps, so that the personnel have the opportunity to work into the computerization gradually. As a starting point, we will begin by designing a single-file database to consist of information pertaining specifically to the customers of the company. Note that the complete design of a database for an organization such as Jellybeans, Inc. is in fact a complicated process, involving many interrelated factors. In chapter 8, we will present an integrated methodology for dealing with complex designs.

Design Data

In order to begin the design, we must first select the information to be included in the database for customers. Our criterion will be to establish a list of data items that (1) relate *directly* to a customer; and (2) will be used on a regular basis by the company staff. This list is compiled by studying the operation of the company, including interviews with appropriate personnel. The result of this study is the list of data items shown in table 2.1. Note that information required by the staff on an infrequent basis has been excluded from the list. Examples of this would be the type of car a customer drives, or the name of a customer's bank. (From time to time, a bank name might in fact be needed, but not frequently enough to justify including it in a database design.)

Figure 2.2
A file of CUSTOMERS
records. Each record
represents data about a
particular customer.
Each field contains a
single value,
representing something
about that customer.

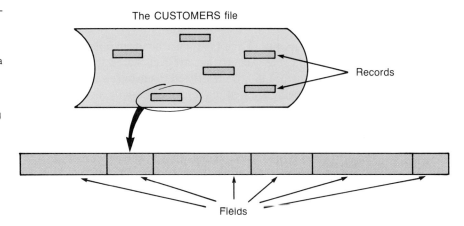

The list in table 2.1 will be used as a starting point for the initial database design. Later, if it seems appropriate, other items can easily be added.

The CUSTOMERS File

In this initial design, the database will consist of a single file that contains the customer data. This file is arbitrarily named CUSTOMERS. In general, a database may consist of several files of interrelated data. In later chapters, the Jellybeans design will be expanded to include additional files.

A note on syntax and terminology. Many of the examples used in this and subsequent chapters are based on dBASE III® syntax and concepts. However, because many of the ideas presented in this text go beyond the limitations of any particular DBMS, occasional examples will deviate from dBASE III. Furthermore, many micro-based DBMS's such as dBASE III tend to confuse the terms *file* and *database,* often using the terms interchangeably. The distinction should be made clear: a *database* is a collection of one or more *files* of related information.

Records and Fields

When the database is implemented, the CUSTOMERS file will eventually contain many **records,** each of which contains data for a particular customer. The term *record* is a technical term that refers to a logical grouping of information about a particular real-world object or event. Figure 2.2 schematically illustrates the CUSTOMERS file, containing a few records.

A CUSTOMERS record will consist of a group of items, each of which contains a particular value. These items are called **fields** in database terminology, and they are chosen to represent items such as those listed in table 2.1.

dBASE III® is a registered trademark of Ashton-Tate.

The file design process begins by specifying the following details for each field:

Field name. Each field must be given a name. Usually, each DBMS will have certain rules about what are considered to be valid names. For example, each field name might be restricted to ten or fewer characters, with only the characters A–Z being allowed in the name. Usually, field names are chosen to represent as closely as possible the actual real-world items. For example, the field name for a telephone number might be PHONE.

Field type. Recognizing that a user may wish to treat different types of data in different ways, database systems also differentiate between various types of data. Therefore, the **type** of each field must also be specified. Different DBMS's allow different choices of field types, and table 2.2 lists some of the more common ones.

Field length. For some field types, such as those containing alphanumeric data, the length of the field must be specified. For example, the length of the customer NAME field might be chosen to be 35 characters on the assumption that this is large enough to accommodate any possible name.

The File Design

The design of the CUSTOMERS file will be limited to the two most common types of fields, CHARACTER and NUMERIC. Normally, a CHARACTER data field can contain a value consisting of any combination of alphanumeric symbols, such as upper and lower case letters, digits, and special characters. The general rule is that if it's on the keyboard, it can be used in a character field, with the exception of special function keys such as ESCAPE and RETURN.

| Table 2.2 | Commonly Used Field Types |

Commonly Used Field Types

Field Type	Comments
ALPHANUMERIC	Contains textual data. Allowable characters include most of those found on keyboards
NUMERIC: integer NUMERIC: decimal	Integer values do not contain decimal points, whereas decimal values do. Many DBMS's do not distinguish between these two types
DATE	Usually in a form such as MM/DD/YY
LOGICAL or BOOLEAN	Limited to values of *true* and *false*

NUMERIC fields, on the other hand, contain only numeric quantities. Data in these fields can be used in various types of computations, such as summations, averages, and so on. Usually, the only allowable characters in these fields are the ten digits, a decimal point, and plus and minus signs.

Table 2.3 lists the fields for the initial design of the CUSTOMERS file. As much as possible, field names have been chosen to represent the corresponding real-world data items. Field lengths have been chosen to accommodate the largest expected values. Furthermore, the fields CREDIT and BALANCE have been specified as NUMERIC types because they each represent dollar amounts, and will very likely be involved in various computations. Each of these two fields has been given a total length of 8 in order to accommodate a maximum amount of 9999.99 (six digits, a decimal point, and possibly a minus sign).

Four fields have been chosen to represent a customer address. These choices are dictated by considering the different ways in which the address information might be used. For example, we might wish to list all of the customers residing in a particular city, or within a particular zip code. These considerations make it logical to divide the address into the separate fields STREET, CITY, STATE, and ZIP, with reasonable lengths chosen for each.

| Table 2.3 | Initial Design for the CUSTOMERS File |

Data Item	Field Name	Type	Length
Customer name	NAME	C	25
Address	STREET	C	25
	CITY	C	15
	STATE	C	2
	ZIP	C*	5
Telephone number	PHONE	C	13
Credit limit	CREDIT	N	8,2**
Outstanding balance	BALANCE	N	8,2

C → CHARACTER
N → NUMERIC

*This field could have been specified to be numeric, since zip codes ordinarily consist of only digits. However, fields are usually specified to be numeric only if they are to be used in arithmetic operations.

**The first digit specifies the *total* field length, and the second digit specifies the number of places to the right of the decimal point.

It is important to recognize that the file design represented by table 2.3 is only provisional. As we begin to use the file and explore its capabilities, other possibilities may begin to emerge, some of which may suggest changes to this design. For example, we may find that a length of 25 is too small for some customer names. Moreover, it may prove to be useful to add other fields to the design.

One of the advantages of working with a modern database management system is that it is often possible to make changes to a file design, even when a considerable amount of data is stored in the file. We will see, in fact, that changing the design is often an integral part of working with a file. Knowing that the design at any moment is not a permanent commitment, and that it can be changed with relative ease, helps to make the process of working with database files a relaxing and creative process.

It should be pointed out that with many older types of DBMS's, it is quite difficult to change a database design. This is because of the intimate connection between a particular design and the associated programs, usually written in FORTRAN, COBOL, or PL/I. Each design change may necessitate many corresponding changes to the related programs. In contrast, the modern approach in database management systems is to move away from this strong dependency between a particular database and its related application programs so that ideally, changes to the design of a database require no modifications whatsoever to related programs. This concept is embodied in the principle called **data independence.**

Entering the File Definition

Having worked out a preliminary design for the CUSTOMERS file, as shown in table 2.3, we can now illustrate the process of entering this information into the DBMS. During this process, the DBMS saves the information about each field, and it constructs an internal picture of the file. This picture is called the **file definition,** and it becomes a permanent part of the file. It serves as a guide, or template, for the DBMS to use in all subsequent operations involving the file, such as data entry, data retrieval, and so on.

There are several different methods of entering a file definition and each particular DBMS has its own style. The particular method used in the following example is representative of that employed by most microcomputer-oriented DBMS's. It is simple and straightforward, and it should give a clear picture of the overall process. We will assume that the computer has been suitably activated, and that the DBMS has been called into execution. The user is now in

Figure 2.3
Screen setup for
entering the file
definition of the
CUSTOMERS file, using
the full-screen editing
mode. Shaded areas
indicate where user
may enter information.

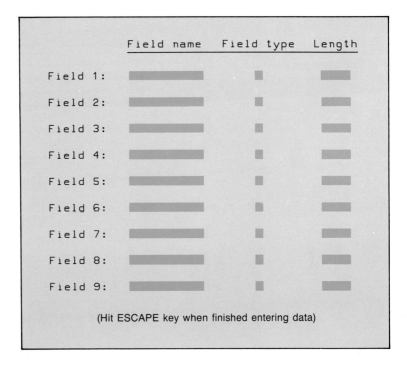

(Hit ESCAPE key when finished entering data)

direct communication with the DBMS, and as a first step a DBMS command is issued that specifies that the structure of a new file is to be defined. This command might take the following form:

CREATE CUSTOMERS

The verb CREATE is the DBMS command, and CUSTOMERS specifies the name of the new file whose structure we wish to specify. The DBMS will normally respond to this command by entering a **file definition mode.** In this mode, the DBMS prompts the user to enter the details of each field that is to become part of the file definition.

Figure 2.3 is an example of how the screen display might appear in response to a file creation command. This figure typifies what is known as the **full-screen mode**—the DBMS establishes specific areas on the screen into which the user may enter values for field names, lengths, and types (in the figure, these are the shaded areas).

Figure 2.4
The same full-screen
display shown in figure
2.3, but with the data
entered.

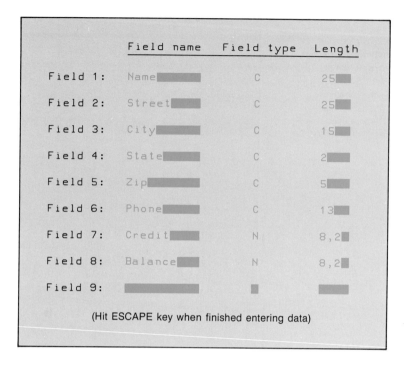

	Field name	Field type	Length
Field 1:	Name	C	25
Field 2:	Street	C	25
Field 3:	City	C	15
Field 4:	State	C	2
Field 5:	Zip	C	5
Field 6:	Phone	C	13
Field 7:	Credit	N	8,2
Field 8:	Balance	N	8,2
Field 9:			

(Hit ESCAPE key when finished entering data)

When the user is finished entering file-definition information, the screen will appear as shown in figure 2.4. An appropriate command from the user then causes the DBMS to store the information as a permanent part of the new CUS-TOMERS file.

Entering Data into the File

As a first step in developing a feel for working with database information, the process of data entry will be illustrated. In order to do this, the user issues DBMS commands such as the following:

USE CUSTOMERS   *{Specifies the name of the file to be accessed}*
APPEND   *{Specifies that data is to be added to the file}*

Figure 2.5
Screen display to
accept data for a new
CUSTOMERS record.

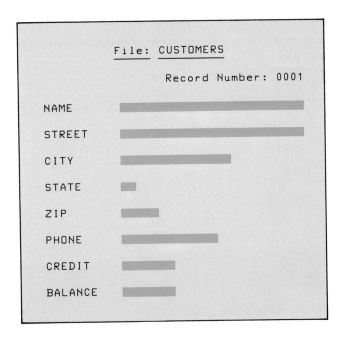

File: CUSTOMERS

Record Number: 0001

NAME

STREET

CITY

STATE

ZIP

PHONE

CREDIT

BALANCE

The Full-Screen Data-Entry Mode

The DBMS will respond by entering a **data-entry mode.** Again, the exact nature of this mode will depend on the particular DBMS. We will illustrate the process by assuming that the DBMS uses full-screen data-entry. Figure 2.5 illustrates how the screen might appear.

In constructing the screen shown in figure 2.5, the DBMS has used the file definition in two different ways. First, the name of each field is listed exactly as it was entered during the file definition. Secondly, the length of each field is indicated by the length of the corresponding shaded areas into which data can be entered. Notice also that in the upper right-hand corner of the screen is an entry "Record Number: 0001". This represents a common practice—as each new record is added to a file, the DBMS assigns it a unique **record number.** The reasons for this will become apparent as we explore the uses of the DBMS.

Figure 2.6
The screen display
shown in figure 2.5 after
a CUSTOMERS record
has been entered.

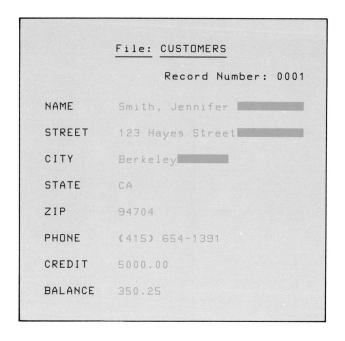

File: CUSTOMERS

Record Number: 0001

NAME   Smith, Jennifer ▮▮▮▮▮▮▮

STREET   123 Hayes Street▮▮▮▮▮▮

CITY   Berkeley▮▮▮▮▮▮

STATE   CA

ZIP   94704

PHONE   (415) 654-1391

CREDIT   5000.00

BALANCE   350.25

NAME	STREET	CITY	STATE	ZIP	PHONE	CREDIT	BALANCE
Smith, Jennifer	123 Hayes St.	Berkeley	CA	94704	(415) 654-1391	5000	0.00
Harris, Peter	19 Taraval St.	Oakland	CA	94620	(415) 565-1985	1000	155.75
James, Jesse	39 Trout Gulch	Newark	CA	95061	(818) 232-3987	5000	532.87
Norman, Samuel	339 40th Ave.	Oakland	CA	11123	(415) 565-3492	0	0.00
LaRue, Elaine	7244 52nd St.	Berkeley	CA	94169	(415) 654-9641	1000	955.00
Clark, Kent	7 Hidden Way	Pittsburg	CA	94882	(408) 974-2581	1000	395.15
Gregory, Robert	357 Mission St.	Berkeley	CA	94704	(415) 654-0127	5000	1857.32
Drue, Ellen	55 Pork Place	Albany	CA	94666	(415) 335-9741	10000	3527.98
Smith, Alfred	18 Center St.	Oakland	CA	95543	(415) 853-1596	1000	0.00
Andersen, Tim	9532 Clark Place	Albany	CA	94661	(415) 335-9264	5000	327.13
Baker, James	1 Cyle Road	Berkeley	CA	94704	(415) 654-4826	10000	125.15

Figure 2.7   Contents of the CUSTOMERS file.

When the data for the first customer has been entered, the screen will appear as shown in figure 2.6. Upon suitable command from the user, the data will be stored in the file, which will then contain one record.

Normally, many records would be entered at one time, especially during the initial phases of building a file. For the sake of the following discussions, we will assume that a few records have been added to the CUSTOMERS file. The contents of these records are tabulated in figure 2.7.

Figure 2.8
A sample of data entry
in which the DBMS
prompts the user for
each field value of a
new record. DBMS
prompts are in
boldface.

```
CUSTOMER:      Smith, Jennifer

STREET:        123 Hayes Street

CITY:          Berkeley

STATE:         CA

ZIP:           94704

PHONE:         (415) 654-1391

CREDIT:        5000.00

BALANCE:       350.25


ANOTHER RECORD? (Y_N)

CUSTOMER:      Jones, Martin

STREET:        456 Peters Street

CITY:          Oakland
                    .

                    .

                    .

                    .
```

Other Data-Entry Methods

Various data-entry techniques are employed by different DBMS's, in addition to the full-screen mode already described. One of the common ones involves the process of **prompting.** With this technique, a dialog occurs between the DBMS and the user—the DBMS asks the user to enter a value for each field of a record, and the user responds by doing so. Figure 2.8 illustrates an example of this kind of dialog. In the figure, the boldface entries are the DBMS prompts, displayed one at a time. The other entries are user-supplied responses to the prompts.

One other common method of data entry involves the use of **batch mode.** With this method, data for many records is assembled in some type of machine-readable form, such as magnetic diskette or tape. The accumulated data is submitted to the DBMS as a batch operation, in which the DBMS reads the group

RECORD NO.	NAME	STREET	CITY	STATE	ZIP	PHONE	CREDIT	BALANCE
01	Smith, Jennifer	123 Hayes St.	Berkeley	CA	94704	(415) 654-1391	5000	0.00
02	Harris, Peter	19 Taraval St.	Oakland	CA	94620	(415) 565-1985	1000	155.75
03	James, Jesse	39 Trout Gulch	Newark	CA	95061	(818) 232-3987	5000	532.87
04	Norman, Samuel	339 40th Ave.	Oakland	CA	95123	(415) 565-3492	0	0.00
05	LaRue, Elaine	7244 52nd St.	Berkeley	CA	94169	(415) 654-9641	1000	955.00
06	Clark, Kent	7 Hidden Way	Pittsburg	CA	94882	(408) 974-2581	1000	395.15
07	Gregory, Robert	357 Mission St.	Berkeley	CA	94704	(415) 654-0127	5000	1857.32
08	Drue, Ellen	55 Pork Place	Albany	CA	94666	(415) 335-9741	10000	3527.98
09	Smith, Alfred	18 Center St.	Oakland	CA	95543	(415) 853-1596	1000	0.00
10	Andersen, Tim	9532 Clark Pl.	Albany	CA	94661	(415) 335-9264	5000	327.13
11	Baker, James	1 Cyle Road	Berkeley	CA	94704	(415) 654-4826	10000	125.15

Figure 2.9 Display of the CUSTOMERS file in response to the command **DISPLAY ALL**.

of records into the specified file. This mode of data entry is especially suitable to those types of situations in which data is collected over an extended period of time.

For interactive data entry, the full-screen mode is preferable, because the user has the option to make corrections to any errors before the data is added to the file. However, regardless of which data-entry method is used, errors are bound to occur, and the following section describes methods for reviewing and modifying the information in a file.

Displaying the File Contents

Most DBMS's offer a variety of methods for examining file contents. In fact, one of the most powerful features of a typical DBMS is the flexibility with which information can be accessed. In this section, we shall illustrate some simple examples of how data in the CUSTOMERS file can be displayed.

Standard Display Modes

Ordinarily, a DBMS will have at least one or more simple commands for displaying the entire contents of a file in a standard mode, which displays the contents of each record in a way that is comprehensible to the user. For example, suppose that we wish to view all of our CUSTOMERS records. Commands for doing this would look similar to the following:

USE CUSTOMERS   {*The file to be accessed*}
DISPLAY ALL   {*Display the entire contents of the file*}

RECORD NO.	NAME	STREET	CITY	STATE	ZIP	PHONE	CREDIT	BALANCE
05	LaRue, Elaine	7244 52nd St.	Berkeley	CA	94169	(415) 654-9641	1000	955.00

Figure 2.10 DBMS display in response to the command DISPLAY 5.

Figure 2.9 shows how the response of the DBMS might appear on the screen. In this example, we assume that the DBMS is kind enough to label each column with the name of the field. Note in figure 2.9 that the unique record number assigned by the DBMS is displayed as part of each record.

Record Keys

Often, one may wish to display a particular record. In order to do this, the record must be identifiable in some easy and unique manner. A common method of providing this identification is to assign each record a unique value called the **record key.** In some cases, as in the current example, a DBMS automatically assigns to each record a unique value as the key. In other cases, the user is responsible for supplying values for the keys. In either case, record keys are indispensable for easy access to records.

In order to display a particular CUSTOMERS record, a command such as the following would be given to the DBMS:

DISPLAY 5

This instructs the DBMS to display the contents of the record whose key value is 5 (see figure 2.10).

Other Display Modes

The contents of a file can be examined in different ways. For example, we may wish to display only those records satisfying a particular set of criteria, such as all of the customers living in a particular city. A set of DBMS commands to accomplish this would look similar to the following:

USE CUSTOMERS
DISPLAY ALL FOR CITY= "Berkeley"

Figure 2.11 illustrates how the DBMS reponse to these commands might appear.

As another example, we might wish to examine those records for which the balance due is greater than a particular amount. The command for accomplishing this would look similar to the following:

DISPLAY ALL FOR BALANCE > 500

Figure 2.12 shows a typical DBMS response.

As an example of the power of database manipulation, we illustrate how the above two queries could be combined to form a more complicated one, in which the DBMS is instructed to display all of the records for customers who live in Berkeley *and* who also have an outstanding balance of $500 or more. The single command to accomplish this would look something like the following:

DISPLAY ALL FOR CITY = "Berkeley" AND BALANCE > 500

Figure 2.13 illustrates the response.

Ordering the Display

Often, when records are displayed it is convenient to display them in some particular order. For example, we might wish to view the entire contents of the CUSTOMERS file listed alphabetically by customer name. Alternatively, we might wish to see the records ordered by city, or perhaps by decreasing value of the outstanding balance. As an example, the commands for displaying all of the CUSTOMERS records ordered by the customer name might take the following form:

USE CUSTOMERS
DISPLAY ALL, ORDER BY NAME

The first part of the DISPLAY command instructs the DBMS to produce a list of all of the data in the CUSTOMERS file. The second part of the command instructs the DBMS to list the records ordered by the contents of the NAME field. Thus, the display would be similar to that shown in figure 2.14.

The ORDER BY NAME clause in the above command is an example of a **command option,** which is an extension of a regular DBMS command that details special conditions to be carried out as part of that command. Ordering output according to a particular criterion is a particularly useful and common option, and there are many others.

RECORD NO.	NAME	STREET	CITY	STATE	ZIP	PHONE	CREDIT	BALANCE
01	Smith, Jennifer	123 Hayes St.	Berkeley	CA	94704	(415) 654-1391	5000	0.00
05	LaRue, Elaine	7244 52nd St.	Berkeley	CA	94169	(415) 654-9641	1000	955.00
07	Gregory, Robert	357 Mission St.	Berkeley	CA	94704	(818) 654-0127	5000	1857.32
11	Baker, James	1 Cyle Road	Berkeley	CA	94704	(415) 654-4826	10000	125.15

Figure 2.11 DBMS display in response to the command DISPLAY ALL FOR CITY= "Berkeley".

RECORD NO.	NAME	STREET	CITY	STATE	ZIP	PHONE	CREDIT	BALANCE
03	James, Jesse	39 Trout Gulch	Newark	CA	95061	(818) 232-3987	5000	532.87
05	LaRue, Elaine	7244 52nd St.	Berkeley	CA	94169	(415) 654-9641	1000	955.00
07	Gregory, Robert	357 Mission St.	Berkeley	CA	94704	(415) 654-0127	5000	1857.32
08	Drue, Ellen	55 Pork Place	Albany	CA	94666	(415) 335-9741	10000	3527.98

Figure 2.12 DBMS response to the command DISPLAY ALL FOR BALANCE > 500.

RECORD NO.	NAME	STREET	CITY	STATE	ZIP	PHONE	CREDIT	BALANCE
05	LaRue, Elaine	7244 52nd St.	Berkeley	CA	94169	(415) 654-9641	1000	955.00
07	Gregory, Robert	357 Mission St.	Berkeley	CA	94704	(415) 654-0127	5000	1857.32

Figure 2.13 DBMS response to the command DISPLAY ALL FOR CITY= "Berkeley" AND BALANCE > 500.

RECORD NO.	NAME	STREET	CITY	STATE	ZIP	PHONE	CREDIT	BALANCE
10	Andersen, Tim	9532 Clark Pl.	Albany	CA	94661	(415) 335-9264	5000	327.13
11	Baker, James	1 Cyle Road	Berkeley	CA	94704	(415) 654-4826	10000	125.15
06	Clark, Kent	7 Hidden Way	Pittsburg	CA	94882	(818) 974-2581	1000	395.15
08	Drue, Ellen	55 Pork Place	Albany	CA	94666	(415) 335-9741	10000	3527.98
07	Gregory, Robert	357 Mission St.	Berkeley	CA	94704	(415) 654-0127	5000	1857.32
02	Harris, Peter	19 Taraval St.	Oakland	CA	94620	(408) 565-1985	1000	155.75
03	James, Jesse	39 Trout Gulch	Newark	CA	95061	(415) 232-3987	5000	532.87
05	LaRue, Elaine	7244 52nd St.	Berkeley	CA	94169	(415) 654-9641	1000	955.00
04	Norman, Samuel	339 40th Ave.	Oakland	CA	95123	(415) 565-3492	0	0
09	Smith, Alfred	18 Center St.	Oakland	CA	95543	(415) 853-1596	1000	0
01	Smith, Jennifer	123 Hayes St.	Berkeley	CA	94704	(415) 654-1391	5000	0

Figure 2.14 Display of the CUSTOMERS file in response to DISPLAY ALL, ORDER BY NAME.

Modifying Data

There are many reasons why it may be necessary to modify information within a file. First, the data-entry process is normally accompanied by a certain percentage of errors; these are due either to incorrect data on the source documents, or to the accidental hitting of wrong keys during data entry. (In fact, a good standard procedure to develop is to proof all data after it has been entered into a file.) A second reason for modifying data is that facts represented by the data may change over the course of time. People's addresses change, credit limits may vary, and so on.

Regardless of the motivating reasons, it is necessary that a DBMS offer easy methods by which information within a file can be modified. These changes might be simple ones, such as the correction of misspellings. Others might be the changing of values in specific fields; still others might be the removal of entire records. Some simple examples will illustrate how such changes might be effected.

If we scrutinize figure 2.9, we see that there is a typographical error in record number 08. A typical command sequence for correcting this error might be the following:

> USE CUSTOMERS
> EDIT 08

Once again, we assume that the DBMS uses the full-screen mode for this process so that a display similar to that shown in figure 2.15 appears. The value "Pork" would be changed to "Park" by the user, and then the ESCAPE key would be hit, as indicated by the instructions in the display. This would cause the original record number 08 to be replaced by whatever values were currently displayed on the screen.

Deleting Records

It is usually a simple matter to remove a particular record from a file. Again, the existence of a record key facilitates the task, which can be accomplished by a simple command such as the following:

> DELETE RECORD 05.

Often, the DBMS will give the user a chance to verify that the correct record number has been entered. This is done by issuing a message such as:

> DO YOU WISH TO DELETE RECORD 05 (Y/N) ?

```
┌─────────────────────────────────────────────────────────┐
│                                                           │
│           Modifying Record Number: 0008                   │
│                                                           │
│                                                           │
│     CUSTOMER:      Drew, Ellen                            │
│                                                           │
│     STREET:        55 Pork Place                          │
│                                                           │
│     CITY:          Albany                                 │
│                                                           │
│     STATE:         CA                                     │
│                                                           │
│     ZIP:           94666                                  │
│                                                           │
│     PHONE:         (415) 335-9741                         │
│                                                           │
│     CREDIT:        10000                                  │
│                                                           │
│     BALANCE:       3527.98                                │
│                                                           │
│     Move the cursor to the desired field(s),     ⎤        │
│        then make the necessary changes           │ Instructions │
│                                                  │ to the user  │
│     When you are finished, press the ESCAPE key  ⎦        │
│                                                           │
└─────────────────────────────────────────────────────────┘
```

There are usually many different possibilities for changing or eliminating records in a file. For example, one may wish to delete all records for which the credit limit is zero and for which the outstanding balance is less than a certain amount. The command for doing this would be similar to the following:

DELETE ALL FOR CREDIT = 0 AND BALANCE < 25

Alternatively, one may wish to increase all credit limits by 25%. This might be done as follows:

REPLACE ALL, CREDIT WITH (1.25 * CREDIT)

This instructs the DBMS to replace each value contained in the field CREDIT with a value which is equal to 1.25 times the current value.

The possibilities for modifying data are virtually endless, and the flexibility of a particular DBMS in this area is a very important measure of its usefulness.

Summary

In this chapter, we have used Jellybeans, Inc., to illustrate a few of the basic ways in which a typical DBMS can be used for storing and manipulating information. The creation of a database file consists of two steps: (1) the file definition process, in which the structural details of the file are defined to the DBMS; and (2) the adding of records to the file. A file consists of a group of records, each of which in turn consists of a group of fields. Each field has a name, type, and length.

Data entry to a file consists of adding records, one at a time. This may be accomplished using the full-screen data-entry mode, or by other methods. Records may be accessed in many different ways for the purposes of display or modification. Each record has a unique record key, by which it can be directly accessed. This key is assigned either by the DBMS or by the user, depending on the particular system.

The examples in this chapter of DBMS commands are but a small fraction of the capabilities of a typical database system. In later chapters, additional DBMS features will be explored.

Chapter Review

Terminology

batch mode	full-screen mode
central processing unit (CPU)	hard copy
command option	primary storage
DBMS command	prompt
data modification	record
field	record key
file definition	record number

Review Questions

1. What are the main components of a microcomputer system?
2. What are the basic steps involved with designing a database?
3. What are the basic components of a database? A file? A record?
4. What are the fundamental characteristics of record fields?
5. How many different types of data can you think of that could be handled by database systems?
6. What is the term for the basic process of entering the structure of a file into a DBMS?
7. What is the difference between entering a file definition and entering data?
8. What are the basic methods for entering data into a database file?

Problems

1. Can you think of any additional fields that might be added to the list in table 2.3? Explain each item that you list.
2. Suppose that you wish to create a file to contain information on your friends and acquaintances.
   a. Make a list of the significant data items that you would like to include for each person.
   b. Using the above list, construct a table similar to that shown in table 2.3. Choose appropriate names to represent the data items. Justify your choice of field types and lengths.
3. Referring to the data shown in figure 2.9 and using the examples in the text as guides, construct DBMS commands to display the records for each of the following:
   a. Customers whose outstanding balance is greater than $1000.
   b. Customers who live either in Berkeley or Albany.
   c. Customers whose outstanding balance is greater than their credit limit.
4. Write a DBMS command to delete CUSTOMERS records for each of the following:
   a. The record whose number is 09.
   b. Customers who live in Berkeley.
   c. All records in the file.

Chapter Three

Data Storage Devices and Data Formats

Introduction

In the previous chapter, some of the general concepts dealing with databases were introduced. We saw how the process of database definition could be accomplished, and how information could be added to a database and subsequently manipulated. In this chapter, we will go one step further and describe the various secondary-storage devices used for storing database information, including descriptions of the physical layouts of data on these devices.

In order to understand how these machines are used for data storage, we must have a clear picture of the nature of the data itself. Consequently, the first part of this chapter is devoted to a brief discussion of the structural components of a database, namely files, records, and other related quantities. Following this discussion, we will describe each of the more commonly used types of storage devices, with special emphasis placed on the strengths and weaknesses of each type, with respect to database management. Finally, some possibilities for future developments in storage devices are examined.

Figure 3.1
The structure of a
database.

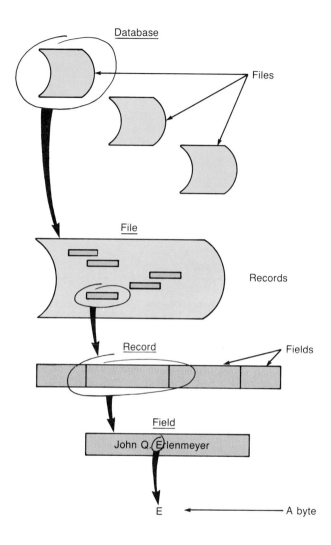

From Databases to Bytes . . . and Further

Files, Records, and Fields

One of the most commonly-encountered database structures is illustrated in figure 3.1. As discussed in chapter 2, a database consists of one or more files, each of which contains a group of records. Each record contains information about a particular real-world object or event, and all of the records within a single file represent objects or events of the same type. Each record consists of several fields, each of which contains a particular piece of data about the represented object. Every record within a single file has the same **structure,** that is, specific grouping of fields. For example, with reference to the CUSTOMERS file discussed in the last chapter, every record contains the fields NAME, PHONE, and so on.

Figure 3.2
A CUSTOMERS record
showing its precise
structure in terms of its
fields.

Field names

NAME	STREET	CITY	STATE	ZIP	PHONE	CREDIT	BALANCE
John K. Abercrombie	123 Haste Street	Berkeley	CA	94704	(415) 849-0473	5000.00	255.22
(25)	(25)	(15)	(2)	(5)	(13)	(8)	(8)

Field lengths

Bytes of Data

Fields themselves have structure, in that each field consists of a particular number of **bytes,** or characters. Often, it is convenient to measure database records in terms of their total length, expressed as the number of bytes. Usually, the total length of a record is the sum of the lengths of its fields. (There are some exceptions, in which records contain system-type information in addition to that contained in the fields themselves.) Figure 3.2 depicts a CUSTOMERS record in terms of its fields. The total length of the record is 101 bytes.

The byte is often considered to be the fundamental unit of information in the computing world (there is even a popular computing magazine whose title is BYTE). The byte is used to express the lengths of database fields and records, and the total size of a database is often given in terms of either **kilobytes** (one thousand bytes) or **megabytes** (one million bytes). Recently, data storage capacities increased to the point that a new term, the **gigabyte,** has been coined to represent one billion bytes, or one thousand megabytes. Many other quantities are often expressed in terms of bytes. For example, the data-storage capacities of the devices described in this chapter are usually measured in terms of kilobytes or megabytes.

Bits of Bytes

Each byte itself has structure, consisting of a set of magnetic **bits,** usually eight bits per byte. Each bit has one of two states: *magnetized* or *nonmagnetized,* and each byte has a unique combination of magnetized/nonmagnetized bits. Since each bit has two possible states, magnetized or nonmagnetized, it may be thought of as a **binary digit,** having either a value of 0 or 1. Carrying this one step further, the unique combination of bits for each byte can be represented by an eight-bit binary number.

As an example, suppose that the set of bits for the character Z is represented by the eight-bit sequence 00011000. This sequence could be represented by the **octal** number 30, and also by the **decimal** number 24. (If you do not understand octal numbers, you may happily ignore the last remarks.)

Standard Codes

Two nationally accepted standards have been developed for character codes stored on magnetic media. They are known as ASCII and EBCDIC. Virtually all data-storage devices maintain data as sets of 8-bit bytes, using one of the two standard codes. Note that using eight bits per byte, there is room for 256 possible characters in the set. Most microcomputers store alphanumeric data internally using one of these codes. In fact, the first popular microcomputers were "8-bit machines" because 8-bits-per-byte had become an accepted standard, and the word size of these machines was chosen to be large enough to hold exactly one byte. (A computer **word** is the smallest unit of data storage that can be referenced by the computer.)

Data Storage Media: An Overview

One of the most important features of a modern computer system is the ability to store and retrieve large amounts of information. In fact, the explosive increase of computer usage has been possible partially because of the rapid developments in various information-storage devices. These developments have involved technological achievements both in the magnetic media for storing the data and in the physical devices for manipulating these magnetic media.

It is important to distinguish between the two fundamentally different types of information storage associated with a computer—primary and secondary storage.

Primary Storage

Built into every computer is a memory area where information can be stored and retrieved extremely rapidly. This area is referred to as **primary storage.** It is where an executing program resides, and it is also where data is temporarily stored when it is being manipulated by an executing program. Although the primary storage of modern machines may be quite large, it is usually hopelessly inadequate for storing the amounts of information required by contemporary users. Also, as was mentioned earlier, primary storage is volatile, which precludes its being used for long-term retention of information.

Secondary Storage

Most computers have attached to them one or more **secondary-storage** devices, also referred to as **data-storage devices,** for storing comparatively large amounts of data. These machines have neither of the disadvantages mentioned with regard to primary storage—they can retain information indefinitely, regardless of whether

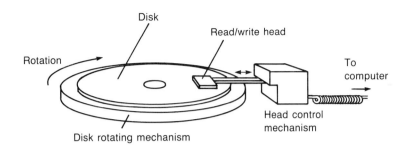

Figure 3.3
Schematic of a disk
drive showing the head
mechanism.

or not electrical power is supplied to them, and they have very large storage capacities. Although there are many different types of secondary-storage devices, those that utilize magnetic disks or tapes as the storage media are used in nearly all database applications. The following sections introduce the basic concepts of magnetic disk and tape-storage media.

Magnetic-Disk Devices

Secondary-storage devices utilizing magnetic disks as the storage medium are the most common for database applications. Their outstanding advantage over other popular forms of secondary storage is that they are **random access** (also called **direct access**) devices. This means that if a database is stored on a disk device, any particular part of that database can be accessed in a very short time. By contrast, magnetic-tape devices do not offer random access to data, a fact that limits their database uses to certain auxiliary, but nevertheless important, functions.

General Description

A magnetic-disk drive can be described in terms of two basic parts—the disk itself, which contains the stored information; and the mechanism for storing and retrieving data from the disk. The disk consists of a circular substrate that is coated with a magnetic material, onto which information can be **written,** that is, recorded. Information written onto the disk remains there permanently, or until it is **overwritten** by new information.

Data can be written onto the surface of a disk as follows. The disk rotates at a constant speed, usually several hundred revolutions per minute. As the disk spins, a **read/write head** is positioned over a blank part of the disk, and as the disk rotates under the head, the data is recorded one byte at a time onto the disk by the head. Reading data from the disk is essentially the same process, except as the disk rotates under the head, the data is read from the disk, one byte at a time, and transmitted to the computer. This process is analogous to the way in which a high-fidelity record is "read" by a pickup stylus. Figure 3.3 illustrates the basic components of a magnetic-disk drive.

Fixed and Removable Disks

Disk drives may be categorized according to whether the disks (platters) are removable or fixed. When the disks are fixed, they are an integral and permanent part of the drive. As the name implies, removable-disk units are built so that the the disk can easily be removed and replaced with another. The advantage of devices with non-removable disks is that they can be sealed off from the environment, thus making data storage considerably more reliable; a single speck of dust can ruin a significant portion of data on a disk. However, the chief disadvantage of these devices is that they have a fixed data-storage capacity—once the disk is filled with data, no more can be added until room is made for it by deleting existing information.

By contrast, the chief advantage of removable-disk devices is that they offer virtually unlimited data-storage capacity—when one disk "fills up," it can be removed and replaced with a fresh one, ready to record more data. However, the ability to remove a disk also implies the ability to mishandle it in such a way that the data can be damaged. In general, some care must be exercised in handling removable disks.

Hard and Floppy Disks

Magnetic disks may be categorized according to whether they are **hard** or **floppy.** Hard- and floppy-disk devices are both extremely popular and have found widespread use in database management. Each has particular advantages and disadvantages, and the following section discusses both types of devices.

Floppy-Disk Devices

The floppy-disk drive is by far the most popular type of secondary-storage device used with microcomputers. The reasons for this are: (1) floppy drives are quite inexpensive but nevertheless surprisingly reliable; and (2) they offer a virtually unlimited amount of data storage, because the disks are removable. Some microcomputers are produced with built-in floppy units, whereas others require connections to separate floppy-disk drives. Figures 3.4 and 3.5 show these two different types of devices.

Figure 3.4
The Apple Macintosh.
This machine contains
a built-in 3½ inch disk
drive. (Courtesy of
Apple Computer, Inc.)

Figure 3.5
An Apple II computer
with an external disk
drive. An ordinary
television set is being
used as a monitor.
(© Bob Coyle)

Table 3.1

Typical Storage Capacities for Floppy Disks

Disk Description	Storage Capacity (Approximate)
8″	1,000,000
5¼″, single-sided	100,000–200,000
5¼″, double-sided	400,000–1,000,000
3½″	800,000

Physical description.   Floppy disks are extremely flexible and therefore quite susceptible to damage. Each disk is enclosed in a heavy jacket, which offers some degree of protection from dust and accidental injury. As is the case with many areas in computing, the sizes of floppy disks (and their associated drives) have shrunk rapidly in a very short period of time. The earliest floppy disks in use were 8 inches in diameter, and these were followed shortly by a smaller 5¼ inch version. The 8 inch size is still in use to some extent, but mainly on older machines.

In 1984, the first microcomputer containing a built-in 3½ inch "floppy-cartridge" disk drive was marketed. This new type of floppy represents a significant improvement because the disk is enclosed in a rigid cartridge and is therefore well-protected from accidental damage. Figure 3.6 illustrates two different sizes of floppy disks.

Storage capacities.   The data-storage capacity of floppies varies a great deal, as indicated by the summary shown in table 3.1. This variation is due to the following factors:

- **Recording Surfaces.** Floppies are rated to be either **single-sided** or **double-sided,** referring to whether one or both sides can be used for recording data.
- **Recording Density.** Data may be recorded onto a disk at different **densities.** The density refers to the amount of data that is recorded per unit surface area of disk. Most floppies are rated as **double-density,** which is a holdover from the past, when many disks were rated as only **single-density.**
- **Hardware.** In general, the maximum capacity of a disk is determined not only by the physical limitations of the disk itself, but also by the hardware used to write on the disk. Some disk units are capable of using only one recording surface, whereas other devices can make use of both. In addition, the density at which data is recorded is hardware dependent.

Thus, we see that the capacities shown in table 3.1 represent hardware limitations as well as constraints imposed by the disks themselves.

Figure 3.6
(a) A 5¼ inch floppy disk. The data-storage capacity of this disk varies from 160 Kbytes to 1.2 Mbytes, depending on the read/write hardware. (James Shaffer) (b) A 3½ inch floppy disk. This disk is mounted in its own protective container and fits nicely into an ordinary pocket. (Courtesy of Apple Computer, Inc.)

(a)

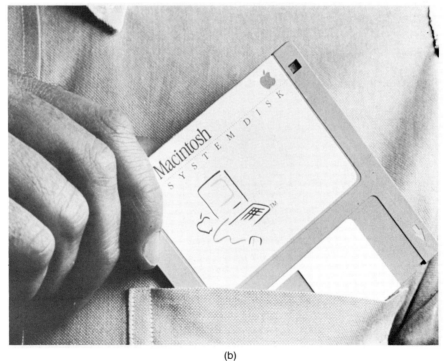

(b)

Figure 3.7
Drawing of a multiple
platter hard-disk unit.

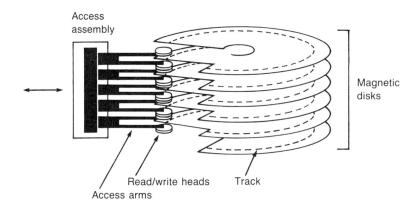

Access
assembly

Magnetic
disks

Read/write heads   Track
Access arms

Pros and cons of floppies. Floppies are an extremely convenient form of data storage, possessing a number of strong points. They are portable, allowing convenient transfer of data from one computer system to another. They are quite inexpensive, and because they are removable they offer virtually unlimited data-storage capability at a very reasonable cost. In fact, floppies offer the least expensive way to store data on disk. It usually requires about two floppies to store a megabyte, at a cost of $1.50 to $10.00, depending on disk quality and type.

Floppies suffer from several disadvantages, one of the biggest being their "floppiness." It is quite easy to mishandle them, resulting in folding, spindling, or mutilation. This particular problem has been solved to a large extent by the rigidity of the 3½ inch floppies, a fact that greatly enhances their attractiveness.

Data-transfer rates for floppies are relatively slow, and for many applications these speeds are considered unacceptable. Also, although floppies do offer unlimited data storage, the capacity of an individual disk is limited. This effectively limits the size of databases that can be conveniently managed with these devices.

Even as technology is improving the data-storage capacity of floppy disks, their days of dominance are numbered. Other types of disk storage are rapidly preempting the lead of floppies, and the time is not far off when floppies as they now exist will play a minor role in secondary storage.

Hard Disks

Hard-disk drives are quite different from their floppy counterparts in several important aspects. First, much higher data densities and data transfer rates are possible with hard disk devices, primarily because the disks are quite rigid. This rigidity allows the use of so-called **Winchester technology,** in which the read/write head is positioned extremely close to the disk surface, riding as it were on a narrow air cushion. This close proximity between the head and disk surface

Figure 3.8
(a) An IBM hard-disk
drive for medium and
large computers; (b) the
removable disk pack for
this drive. (Both,
courtesy of International
Business Machines
Corporation)

allows a higher, more concentrated magnetic flux to be generated, which in turn allows data to be recorded more densely. Finally, the Winchester technology incorporates much higher rotational speeds, again increasing data-transfer rates.

The extremely small distance between the disk and the read/write head makes it much more critical that any foreign matter, such as dust particles, be excluded from the environment. Therefore, hard-disk drives must be designed to isolate the rotating disk and read/write heads.

Another difference between hard- and floppy-disk technologies is the fact that floppy-disk drives work with only one disk at a time. In contrast, a typical hard-disk drive consists of two or more platters all of which are rigidly mounted on a common, rotating central shaft. Figure 3.7 illustrates a schematic drawing of a typical hard-disk drive, showing several platters and the read/write heads. Each surface has its own head, but all of the heads are mounted on a common moving mechanism.

Fixed and removable hard disks. Some hard-disk devices are constructed in such a way that the disks are permanently built into the drive, whereas other devices allow rapid disk removal by a user. Both types of devices are available for virtually every type of computer.

Figure 3.8 shows a hard-disk drive used with a medium-sized computer. The heart of the device is a removable **disk pack,** which consists of several platters mounted on a common shaft. Typically, a disk pack such as that shown in figure 3.8 has a capacity of approximately 500 megabytes.

Removable hard-disk drives are also used with microcomputers, but these are much smaller than that shown in figure 3.8, and have a much smaller storage capacity. These machines are just beginning to penetrate the microcomputer

Figure 3.9
A Bernoulli Box (Iomega Corp.). This device is used with a variety of microcomputers. It utilizes removable disk cartridges, each of which has a 5–10 Mbyte capacity. (Courtesy of Iomega Corporation)

market, and their future is uncertain. Figure 3.9 illustrates a typical device of this type. A single removable platter has a storage capacity of between 5 and 10 megabytes.

Data-storage capacities. Although the physical size of hard-disk drives has been shrinking, corresponding data-storage capacities have increased. Naturally, there is still a strong correlation between the size of a disk drive and the amount of data it can store, but the trend has been one of incredible increase in the amount of information that can be packed into a physical volume.

In general, maximum disk capacities are somewhat tied to the size of the related computer. Thus, mainframe devices generally have much higher storage capacities than those for microcomputers, although the gap is narrowing rapidly. For example, a typical mainframe disk unit would contain approximately 500 megabytes, whereas the average storage capacity for micro-oriented hard disks is approximately 20 megabytes as of this writing. It has been estimated however, that this latter figure will double each year during the next few years.

All of the above figures are for fixed-disk devices; for removable disks, the figures are considerably lower, particularly for micro-based devices. In general, disk capacities are increasing at such a fast rate that during the time it has taken to publish this text, the figures quoted here will undoubtedly have become obsolete.

Figure 3.10

The ultimate in hard-disk size reduction: a 20 Mbyte disk mounted on a card that fits into a regular IBM PC slot. (Courtesy of Plus Development Corporation)

The trend towards integration. Until the middle of 1983, hard-disk devices generally were built as separate physical units. These machines were rather large and cumbersome, and both their size and high cost were sufficient to limit their use mostly to larger computers. This situation has now changed dramatically. Recent technological improvements have significantly reduced the physical space occupied by disk drives, and prices have dropped exponentially.

These trends have had particular impact in the microcomputer area. Whereas a few years ago it was unthinkable that an individual would acquire a hard-disk device, today the situation has almost reversed—one of the major decisions facing a potential owner of a microcomputer is whether or not to include a hard disk in the purchase.

The size reduction in hard-disk technology has been amazing, to put it mildly. Many microcomputers are now being designed with built-in hard-disk drives with a disk storage capacity of 30 megabytes. Even more unbelievable is the fact that you can buy a 20 megabyte hard disk mounted on a standard plug-in board for a PC (figure 3.10).

Comparing Hard and Floppy Disks

For large-computer database applications, hard disks are virtually the only data-storage devices in use. However, in the context of microcomputer applications, it is important to compare the relative merits of hard and floppy disks, because both are in common use. The two most outstanding differences between hard disks and floppies are data-storage capacity and data-transfer rates. Hard disk devices have relatively huge on-line storage capacity. The term *on-line* refers to the data that can be accessed *at any instant* by the computer. Thus, at present the largest capacity of a commercially available standard 5¼ inch floppy disk is approximately 1 megabyte, a figure that dwindles in comparison to the tens or hundreds of megabytes available with hard disks. For many database applications, on-line storage-capacity requirements are so large that a hard disk is a necessity. Often, the crucial question is whether or not an entire database can fit on a single floppy disk. If it cannot, then a hard disk is likely to be appropriate data-storage medium.

Hard disks also have significantly higher data-transfer rates than floppies. Typically, rates for hard disks are two to four times higher than those for floppies. Again, this difference may be important for many database applications.

The major disadvantages of hard disks as compared to floppies are (1) lack of data portability and (2) sensitivity to shock and vibration. Portability of data is an important factor in assessing the desirability of various devices. Again, with respect to microcomputers, until recently floppies were the only practical means of transferring information from one machine to another. To some extent, this has changed with the introduction of removable hard-disk devices. Engineering developments have helped to reduce the mechanical reliability problems of sensitivity to shock and vibration of both fixed and removable hard-disk devices, but they must still be treated with somewhat more care than floppy devices.

In general, the advantages of hard-disk devices greatly outweigh their negative features, and it is inevitable that in the near future they will become the primary data-storage medium for all types of computers.

Physical Data Formats

For the vast majority of database applications, information is divided into files and records. These occupy space on a disk surface, and the physical arrangement of data is fundamentally the same for all types of disks. In this section, we shall describe the physical layout of data within a disk device. Emphasis will be on the *structure* of data, rather than on the technical details of exactly how the data is written and read.

Figure 3.11
The subdivision of a
disk surface into tracks.

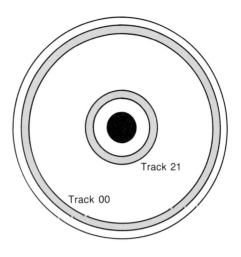

Track 21

Track 00

Tracks, Sectors, and Blocks

A disk surface consists of a uniform distribution of magnetic material. For the purpose of data storage, this surface is subdivided into separate areas, each of which contains a certain amount of data. The primary subdivision of the surface is into a number of **tracks,** as shown in figure 3.11. The tracks are numbered sequentially, and the total number of tracks on a surface depends on the particular device. The surface of a large hard disk, such as those used with medium and large computers, contains several hundred tracks, whereas the surface of a 5¼ inch floppy usually contains less than 50 tracks. Tracks are created by the positioning of the read/write heads when data is recorded onto the surface. In other words, a head has a number of set positions at which it can be located for reading or writing.

On some disk devices, tracks are subdivided into **sectors,** as shown in figure 3.12. Identifying information giving sector number and track number is written at the beginning of each sector.

The most common subdivision of data on a track is the **block.** Normally *the block is the smallest unit of data that is directly accessible on a disk.* With devices that utilize sectors, each block consists of a fixed number of sectors. For devices that do not divide tracks into sectors, each track is divided directly into a number of blocks, the latter being numbered consecutively from zero. In some cases, the specific size of blocks, in terms of number of bytes, is fixed by the hardware. In other cases, the user may specify the block size. This is often advantageous, since the block size can sometimes significantly affect system performance for a particular application. For a given disk, all blocks are the same size.

Figure 3.12

The subdivision of a disk into tracks and sectors.

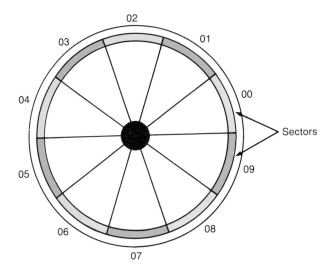

Each block contains a **block header** and a number of database records. The header contains identifying information, such as the block number, that may be used by the system when searching for a particular block. The number of records contained within a block is determined by the block and record sizes; usually, a small portion of each block is unused. Figure 3.13 illustrates the subdivision of a track into blocks, along with the block structure itself.

Disk Addresses

Blocks are located by means of their **physical disk address,** which specifies the exact location of the block on the disk. Physical addresses are expressed in several ways, depending on the hardware and software. For floppy disks, an address consists of a track number and a sector number. In other words, given the track and sector number of a particular block, the disk device can move the read/write head to that location and search for the block. When a disk device consists of multiple surfaces, the address specification is somewhat different, consisting of **track number, cylinder number,** and **block number.** In this case, the track number specifies the *surface,* and the cylinder number indicates the exact radial position of the read/write head. The block number specifies the block on that particular track.

Figure 3.13
(a) A track divided into
sectors and blocks.
(b) A track divided into
blocks and records.

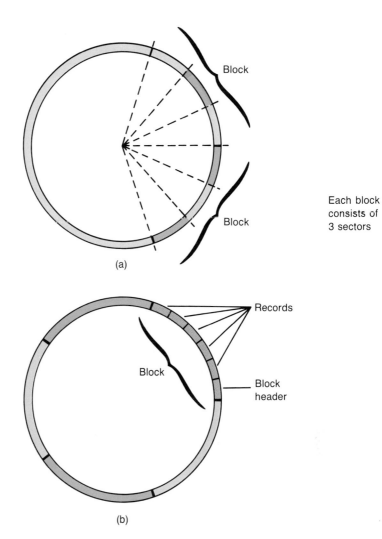

Block

Block

Each block
consists of
3 sectors

(a)

Records

Block

Block
header

(b)

Figure 3.14
A file of records, along
with its associated
directory. The numbers
in parentheses are
cylinder numbers and
the underlined numbers
are block numbers. On
each track, blocks are
numbered
consecutively, starting
with 00.

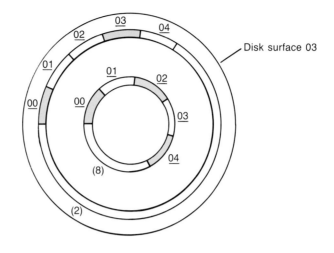

File directory	
Relative block number	Physical disk address
00	030800
01	030802
02	030804
03	030200
04	030203

Often, when working with files of records, it is convenient to specify the address of a record in terms of its **relative disk address,** which is defined as follows. Each file consists of a number of blocks, which may grow as the file expands with the addition of records. These blocks may be scattered about the disk, but each one is assigned a relative block number. Thus, the first block of the file is assigned the number 0, the second block the number 1, and so on. These numbers are referred to as the relative disk addresses of the blocks. The operating system maintains a **file directory,** which contains the physical disk address for each block of the file. Figure 3.14 illustrates the directory for a file of records that are contained within a group of blocks distributed over a disk surface.

When a program, such as a DBMS, needs to access a particular record, it supplies the relative disk address of that record to the operating system, which in turn converts the relative address into a physical disk address. This is sent to the controlling hardware and software of the disk, which positions the read/write head over the correct track and then reads in the appropriate block. The block is transmitted back to the DBMS, which locates the desired record within the block.

The process of writing a database record on a disk is somewhat the reverse of that for reading. The DBMS sends the new record to the operating system, which in turn determines the physical disk address of a block that contains sufficient vacant space to hold the record. The relative address of this block is returned to the DBMS, which makes a permanent record of that address. In addition, the operating system sends the physical address and the new record to the disk device, and the record is written into the block at the specified address.

The preceding description of reading and writing of records is somewhat of a simplification of the actual processes involved. However, it does illustrate the basic concept that is important for database management applications: a database record occupies a specific physical area on a disk, which is identified by a disk address. If that address is known to the DBMS, then that record can be *directly* accessed by the operating system.

Data Access Modes

Random Access

From the preceding discussion, it should be clear that database information on disks are stored as random-access files; any record may be directly accessed with very little searching. In addition, any record may be modified by the process of **rewrite-in-place:** the record is read into primary storage, modified as necessary, and then rewritten to the same disk location. Finally, new records can be added directly to a file, without the need for extensive file manipulations.

Sequential Access

Files can also be maintained on disk devices in **sequential access** mode. They are called **sequential files,** and their chief characteristics are the following: (1) the order in which records are written to the file is the only order in which they may be read; and (2) new records may be added only to the end of the file.

Sequential-access disk files play a major role in many areas of data-processing, including database management. Often, input data is collected on sequential files, prior to its being added to a database in a batch operation. A more detailed discussion of sequential files is given in chapter 4.

Performance Characteristics

One of the major advantages of disk devices is the speed with which data can be located and sent to the requesting program. This speed is determined by the following three factors:

- **Seek Time.** A data request to a disk device includes the physical disk address at which the data is to be located. In order to access the data, the read/write head must be moved to the proper cylinder. The time required for this depends on how far the arm must move. This can vary from zero (no movement) to the time it takes to move from the outermost to the innermost cylinders. The performance of a disk device is quoted in terms of the **average seek time,** a figure usually supplied by the manufacturer. For larger devices, this time is on the order of 15 ms (milliseconds); for micro-based hard disks, it is usually between 30 and 100 ms. For floppy devices, it is even larger.

- **Rotational Delay.** After the read/write head has been correctly positioned, the disk must rotate until the proper block is under the head. The delay may be anywhere from 0 seconds to the time required for a complete revolution, and the **average rotational delay** is equal to the time necessary for one-half of a revolution. It may be calculated as follows. Suppose that the disk device rotates at **RPM** revolutions per minute. Then if A is the average rotational delay, it may be expressed as:

$$A = (1/2) \times \frac{60,000}{RPM} \text{ ms}$$

- **Data-transfer time.** The speed at which data is transferred depends on several factors. For a single block of data, it can be estimated by using the following formula to calculate the data-transfer rate, expressed in bytes per second:

$$\text{Data-transfer rate} = \frac{RPM}{60} \times (\text{number of bytes per track})$$

If the size of a block is known (number of bytes), then the time to transfer that block can be calculated using the results of the preceding formula, as follows:

$$\text{Block-transfer time (ms)} = \frac{\text{bytes per block}}{\text{data-transfer rate}} \times 1000$$

The total time to transfer a block of data is given as the sum of the above three quantities:

$$\text{Transfer time} = (\text{seek time}) + (\text{rotational delay})$$
$$+ (\text{block-transfer time})$$

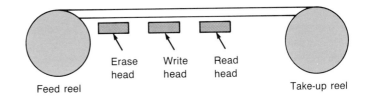

Figure 3.15
Schematic drawing of a
magnetic tape device,
showing the tape
passing by the various
heads.

Magnetic-Tape Devices

The first medium to achieve popularity as secondary storage for digital computers was magnetic tape. For many years, it was the principal means by which large amounts of data could be stored for extended periods of time. Because data on magnetic tape can be accessed only sequentially, these devices play only secondary roles in database management. Nevertheless, these roles are vital ones, so the current status and future development of these devices is of interest in this text.

General Description

Many different types of magnetic-tape devices exist, but the basic principles of operation are the same for all of them. These principles are probably familiar to most readers due to the popularity of cassette-tape devices used for music reproduction.

The tape itself consists of a strip of flexible material, coated on one side with a material that has magnetic properties, such as iron oxide. In a magnetic tape drive, the tape is fed from one reel to another, and in transit the tape passes across a set of read/write heads. These heads can either record data on the tape or read previously-written data from the tape. Figure 3.15 shows a schematic of the process.

Magnetic-tape devices are built to serve a wide variety of needs. At one end of the scale are the large machines (see figure 3.16), which utilize 12-inch reels. These devices are most often used with larger computers, primarily because of their relatively high cost. Data **density,** which is the number of bytes stored per linear inch of tape, ranges from 1600 to as high as 6400. The corresponding total storage capacity of a single 2400-foot reel can be as high as 200 million bytes.

For use with microcomputer systems, smaller machines known as tape cassette or cartridge devices have become quite popular. A single tape cartridge, used in a device similar to that shown in figure 3.17, can hold up to 80 megabytes.

Figure 3.16
An IBM magnetic
device for medium and
large computers. This
device uses full-size
tape reels, each of
which may contain
approximately 100
million bytes. (Courtesy
of International
Business Machines
Corporation)

Figure 3.17
A pair of magnetic tape cassettes, shown next to an Apple II computer. (Courtesy of Apple Computer, Inc.)

Figure 3.18

Bytes of data on a magnetic tape. Each byte occupies a tiny slice of tape, approximately 0.001″ in width.

this is a sequence of characters on tape. It goes on a

Figure 3.19

Data structuring on magnetic tape.

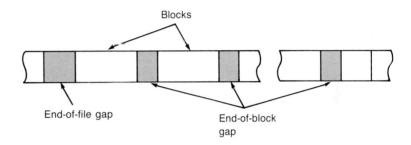

Physical Data Formats

Data on a magnetic tape is arranged sequentially, one byte placed after the next on the tape, as illustrated in figure 3.18. This data is subdivided in much the same way as it is for magnetic disks—each reel of tape may contain many data files, each of which consists of several blocks. Each block contains one or more records, and the records have the usual structure of fields and bytes. Each file ends with an **end-of-file gap,** and each block within a file terminates with an end-of-block gap. Figure 3.19 illustrates this structure.

The block is the smallest unit of data that can be transferred to or from a tape. The gap at the end of each block informs the tape drive that the end of that block has been reached, and it allows sufficient time for the tape to stop moving, following the read or write of a block. Typically, a block gap is approximately ½-inch in length. Within each file, all blocks are the same length, and this length is set by the software that writes the file.

In the simplest picture of a magnetic tape data file, each block contains exactly one record. However, if each record contains a fairly small number of characters, the amount of tape occupied by the end-of-block gap will be much larger

Figure 3.20
Record blocking on
magnetic tape. (a) For
very small blocks, most
of the tape is in the
end-of-block gaps;
(b) for larger blocks,
most of the tape is
used for data.

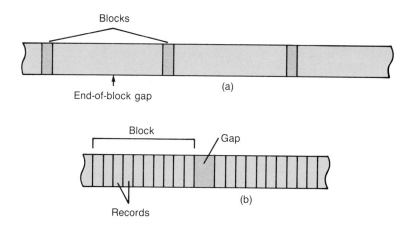

than that occupied by the records themselves. Obviously, this is a waste of tape, and the alternative to this is to make the size of the block large enough to hold several records so that only a very small percentage of tape is used for the gaps. Figure 3.20 illustrates these two situations.

The Sequential Nature of Magnetic Tape Input/Output

Unlike magnetic disks, tape devices cannot operate in a random-access manner. Instead, they are restricted to the sequential-access mode of operation, described earlier in this chapter. This is because of the way in which tape devices function. It is very difficult to position a tape to any part of a file other than its beginning, and it is even more difficult to write over part of an existing file while at the same time guaranteeing that adjacent data will not be accidentally erased.

Database Uses for Magnetic Tapes

Because of the sequential nature of magnetic-tape devices, they are unsuitable for the kind of direct data access that is required of database interactions. Nevertheless, tapes play an important part in modern database management, particularly in the areas of **backing-up** and **archiving.** Most databases are backed up routinely. In this process, a copy of a database is written onto magnetic tape. This copy is referred to as a backup, and it is safely stored away, usually at a considerable distance from the computer. If the database on disk becomes corrupted or destroyed, the backup can be used to restore the database to the disk.

Long-term storage of database information is an important part of modern practice. Magnetic tapes are the ideal choice for archiving, because they are quite inexpensive and have a life expectancy of many years.

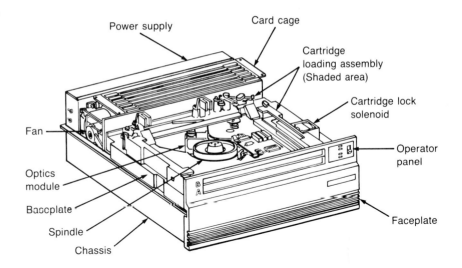

Figure 3.21
Schematic of a laser
optical-disk drive
(Provided by the
Shugart Corporation,
Sunnyvale, California.)

Power supply   Card cage

Cartridge
loading assembly
(Shaded area)

Cartridge lock
solenoid

Fan

Operator
panel

Optics
module

Baseplate

Faceplate

Spindle

Chassis

Some hard-disk devices are manufactured with a built-in cassette tape re-corder, which may be used both for backing-up disk information and for gen-erating archival tapes. These combination devices are extremely convenient because they usually contain software for performing easy backup and retrieval of selected portions of the disk.

Laser Optical Disks

One of the newest developments in secondary storage devices is the laser optical-disk drive. These devices have several important advantages over magnetic re-cording devices, such as recording capacity and durability. This recording tech-nology is just emerging and it is difficult to predict what kind of a long-term impact it will have in the database field.

General Description

The laser-disk drive has many similarities to magnetic-disk drives. The disk itself is a removable platter, and the most common sizes are 5¼ and 12 inches. When a disk is placed in an operating drive, it is rotated on a spindle at a constant speed. Information is written onto the disk with an **optical head** which emits a highly focused laser beam. The focal point of the beam is at the recording layer, which is slightly below the surface of the disk. This layer is protected by a thin film which is transparent to the laser beam, thus giving the optical disk extremely high durability and resistance to normal wear factors such as abrasion and dust. Information is recorded when the beam physically alters the recording surface in some manner. Common techniques include burning holes, creating bubbles or pits, and inducing phase changes in the surface material. Figure 3.21 shows a schematic of a laser disk drive.

When a disk is read by the drive, a laser beam is again directed by an optical head to the recording surface but this time at a greatly reduced intensity. The laser light is reflected from the surface back to the optical head, and then converted to electronic signals. The amount of reflected light from a given spot on the disk depends on whether or not that spot was previously "altered," and the difference in reflected light from "altered" and "unaltered" spots is enough to differentiate between them. Some devices use different heads for the processes of reading and writing; others use the same head for both.

Comparisons with Other Technologies

The laser-optical disk technology has several significant advantages over that of both magnetic disks and tapes, the biggest one being the enormously higher data capacity. This is due to the ability to focus the laser beam very precisely, thus producing a very high data density on the disk. At present, these densities are on the order of 100 times greater than those possible with magnetic disk devices. These high densities open the door to many possibilities, such as the ability to keep extremely large databases online.

The ability to remove an optical disk from its drive is another advantage of this technology, and it is again due to the fact that the laser beam can be very highly focussed. This allows the head to be placed several millimeters away from the recording surface, thus facilitating a design that allows for easy disk removal. By contrast, the Winchester technology for hard magnetic disk drives requires that the head be extremely close to the disk surface. In this case, it is quite difficult to design a device with a removable disk.

As mentioned, the laser disk is highly resistant to abrasion, heat, dirt, and general sloppy handling. Since data is recorded by inducing physical changes in the surface of the disk, it is virtually permanent.

These qualities of laser disks, coupled with their low cost, make the laser disk extremely attractive for use in the archiving of large databases. In contrast, magnetic tape slowly deteriorates, even in the most carefully-controlled environment. It is fairly susceptible to heat and dirt, and highly susceptible to even a modest amount of abusive handling. Above all, the data storage capacity of magnetic tapes is inferior to that of laser disks—one 12-inch laser disk can hold the equivalent of several full-size, high-density tapes.

Ironically, the laser disk's biggest advantage from one point of view is its biggest disadvantage from another—the permanency of the recorded data. Information recorded on a disk is there forever, at least with currently available technology. Consequently, if a database needs to be updated, a new disk must be written. Obviously, this is not suitable for applications in which a database changes frequently, so that currently available laser technology does not pose a threat to the use of magnetic-disk drives for the vast majority of database applications.

Another disadvantage of current laser-disk technology is the relatively slow access time. Whereas current hard-disk drives can seek out a particular record in a few milliseconds, laser drives require between 100 and 500 milliseconds.

Data Formats and Capacities

The logical arrangement of data on a laser disk is similar to that for magnetic disks. A disk surface is subdivided into tracks and sectors, and recorded data is logically divided into files, records, and so on. From an operational standpoint, the difference between using laser and magnetic disks should be imperceptible to a DBMS, except for the previously-noted permanency of recorded data.

As mentioned above, the precision with which a recording head can be focussed leads to the ability to store very high data densities on a laser disk. This is true not only in the linear bit density (number of bits per linear inch), but also in the track density (number of tracks per radial inch). The result is a total data density which is approximately ten times that available with hard-disk systems. Translated into numbers, this is equivalent to approximately one thousand megabytes, or one gigabyte, on a single 12 inch disk. This is equivalent to approximately one-half a million pages of word-processor output, or considerably more than the equivalent of a full-size textbook. Another point of comparison is that one laser disk surface holds the equivalent of each of the following: (1) ten full-size high-density magnetic tapes; (2) more than ten large microcomputer-based hard disk drives; (3) two thousand double density, single-sided floppy disks.

Future Trends

Currently available laser-disk technology precludes the rewriting of a disk, which makes it untenable for those database applications that require frequent data updating. However, technology for erasing and rerecording laser disks is available in the laboratory, and the expectation is high that this technology will eventually reach the commercial market. If and when this occurs, and assuming that such technology follows the rest of the industry in terms of ever-decreasing costs, then one would expect to see a revolution in secondary storage devices.

It is anticipated that optical drives will evolve along lines similar to those of magnetic-disk devices. That is, size reductions will occur along with increases in data storage capacities. The 5¼ inch and 3½ inch magnetic disks have become standard, and optical disks will undoubtedly follow similar patterns. At the same time, projections indicate that disks of this size will have capacities on the order of 500 megabytes.

Proponents of the optical-disk technology foresee a bright future for its applications, even for the write-once-only disks, and there are many applications which could benefit from these devices. One of the most promising areas deals with the ability to access very large databases. At present, a private individual, or even a small organization, has such access only by using commercially-available on-line retrieval services. Normally, a user accesses one of these services by making use of an ordinary terminal and modem and the telephone communication lines. Once connected to the service's database of interest, the user can search through it, usually at a cost of $25 to $100 per hour of connect time.

It is possible that soon a frequent user of a particular database may be able to purchase a copy of it stored on a single disk. The initial investment in a microcomputer and optical disk reader would reap long-term savings, in terms of the money not spent on retrieval services. In fact, some of these services see this as a very real possibility and are reorienting their activities to meet this possible change in the use of large databases.

As mentioned earlier, the archiving of user-generated databases could eventually be dominated by laser disks, due to the combination of extreme longevity, resistance to damage from physical abuse, and large data capacity. Many databases change sufficiently slowly that it is necessary to archive them relatively infrequently, for the purposes of backup and historical retention.

Like so many other areas in the computer world, however, changes in the field of laser disk technology are happening rapidly; and any predictions concerning future sizes, capacities, or applications will more than likely prove to have been inaccurate.

Summary

A variety of data-storage devices are used for secondary storage. Of these, magnetic tape and disk machines are the most common. Magnetic-disk devices are particularly useful for database applications because of their random-access nature, which allows rapid retrieval of any record within a database.

Various types of disk devices are in common use, including floppy and hard-disk units. These devices may also be categorized according to whether the disks are removable or permanently fixed. Each particular type of device has its advantages. Floppy units offer unlimited data storage in principle, although too many floppies may lead to practical difficulties dealing with storage and retrieval. Hard disks are faster than floppies, and they offer a great deal more on-line data storage. Although each fixed-disk unit has an upper limit on data storage, the limits are rising rapidly. Hard-disk devices are currently being sold with capacities approaching 100 megabytes.

Removable hard-disk devices have been common on mainframe computers for many years, and they have recently become attractive for micros as well. They offer the potential of unlimited data-storage capacity, coupled with the speed and environmental isolation associated with fixed hard-disk units.

The 3½ inch floppy cartridge is another recent development in the microcomputer world that also offers significant advantages over 5¼ inch floppies, including improved resistance to both environmental hazards and mishandling.

Data-storage capacities of all types of magnetic-disk media are increasing rapidly due to explosive technological advances. There seems to be no end in sight with regard to both cost and size reductions.

Magnetic-tape devices continue to be a mainstay of secondary storage in the computer industry. Because their only data-access method is sequential, their main uses in database applications are information backup and archiving. Nevertheless, these functions are extremely important, and modern cassette tape devices are becoming a standard tool in microcomputer database environments.

The laser optical disk is the newest entry into the secondary-storage market, and its enormous data-storage capacity and resistance to physical damage offer great potential for database applications. At present, these devices are commercially available in the write-once/read-only mode, limiting their general usefulness. If and when they become available as read/write devices, they could significantly alter the face of microcomputer secondary storage.

Chapter Review

Terminology

archive
ASCII code
average rotational delay
average seek time
backup
bit
block
block header
byte
computer word
cylinder
data density
data storage device
direct access
disk drive
disk pack
double-sided disk
end-of-block gap
end-of-file gap
file directory

fixed disk
floppy disk
gigabyte
hard disk
kilobyte
laser-optical disk
megabyte
on-line storage
physical disk address
random access
read/write head
relative disk address
removable disk
secondary storage
sector
sequential access
sequential file
tape cassette
track
Winchester technology

Review Questions

1. Describe the structure of a typical database, in terms of records, and so on.
2. What are the most common measures of data-storage capacity?
3. What is the smallest unit of data storage that can be referenced by a computer?
4. List the advantages of hard disks. Of floppy disks.
5. Distinguish between the two types of hard disks. What are the advantages of each?
6. List typical data-storage capacities for the various types of magnetic-disk devices.
7. What is the basic advantage of disk storage over tape, with reference to database applications?
8. What uses does magnetic-tape storage have in database management?
9. What are the fundamental differences between a *random-access* file and a *sequential* file?
10. Describe the way data is physically subdivided on the surface of a disk.
11. What is the smallest unit of data that is directly accessible on a disk?
12. What is the difference between a *physical disk address* and a *relative disk address?*
13. What constitutes a physical disk address for a multiple-surface disk device? A floppy disk?
14. What is the purpose of a file directory?
15. Describe the organization of data on a magnetic tape.
16. What are the pros and cons of laser-optical disks?

Problems

1. A particular disk drive consists of a single surface, and it has the following characteristics:

   Number of tracks on the surface: 40
   Number of sectors per track: 40
   Number of bytes per sector: 256
   Number of sectors per block: 5

   a. What is the total data-storage capacity of the disk?
   b. How many blocks are there on each track?
   c. What is the size of the largest single data record that can be stored in a block?
   d. Show how the physical disk address of a block is specified.
   e. A sequential file of 50 records is to be written to the disk. Each record requires a total of 500 bytes. How many tracks are required to store the file?

2. A disk drive has the following characteristics:
   Total number of recording surfaces: 15
   Number of tracks per surface: 1,500
   Number of bytes per track: 50,400
   Number of bytes per block header: 25
   a. How many cylinders make up the entire unit?
   b. What is the total data-storage capacity of the drive?
   c. Suppose that a file consisting of 260-byte records is to be stored on the disk, and the DBMS has set the block size at 500 bytes (including the block header).
      (1) Assuming that a block cannot be split between two tracks, how much space on each track is wasted, that is, unusable for data storage? (Note: space used by headers is not considered to be wasted.)
      (2) Assuming that a record must fit *entirely* within a single block (a record cannot be split between two blocks), how many records can be written on each track? How much track space is wasted?
      (3) Choose a larger block size that would result in less wasted disk space.
3. The following operating characteristics apply to the preceding disk device:
   Average seek time: 50 ms
   Rotational speed: 1200 RPM
   Suppose that 500-byte records have been written to the disk, using 5025-byte blocks.
   a. What is the smallest number of records that can be read from the disk with a single access?
   b. What is the total *average* delay time when reading a block?
   c. What is the average total time needed to read in a block from the disk? (Time begins at the moment the device begins to devote its energy to finding a piece of data.)
4. A particular disk device consists of several recording surfaces. Each track has a capacity of 5000 bytes and is subdivided into 5 blocks. A file of database records has been written to the device on surface number 04, starting with cylinder 00 and going to consecutively higher cylinder numbers. The file consists of a total of 9 blocks, each block containing 3 records.
   a. Tabulate the contents of the directory for this file.
   b. List the relative disk addresses of the first 8 records in the file.

Chapter Four

Standard File Structures

Introduction

The previous chapters were primarily concerned with laying the groundwork for the fundamentals of database usage. Chapter 2 was devoted to a survey of some of the more commonly used methods for creating and using simple databases. Chapter 3 then described the main devices used for storing database files and also the manner in which information is physically stored on these devices. This chapter is devoted to a discussion of the nature of the various types of files utilized by database management systems.

The casual database user can get by with only a vague idea of the meanings of file, record, and so on. However, the more sophisticated user must have a deeper concept of what is going on inside the little black boxes that store the information. It is all very well for a user to toss together a database design, trusting that the hardware and software will make it all work. When limits are reached, however, or when it is vital to get more out of a system because things are taking too long, a deeper understanding of the nature of files, records, and other database concepts is essential to obtaining improved utilization of database management tools.

We shall continue to use the fundamental concept of a file as a collection of records, each of which consists of a number of fields. Furthermore, it will be assumed that all records in a particular file have identical structure, in terms of field lengths, types, and so on. A consequence of this assumption is that the discussions will be in the context of files of **fixed-length records,** a type of structure that is extremely common among many types of computer systems and database management systems.

Fixed-length records are by no means universal. A small number of database systems use variable-length records, and a few of these systems do not even use records as a unit of data storage. However, fixed-length records are by far the most common unit of database management storage. Consequently, most of this book will be oriented around that method of data subdivision. As a final introductory note, the file types discussed in this chapter are utilized in many data-processing applications other than database management. As mentioned in chapter 3, files fall naturally into two basic categories: sequential and random-access. To review, the records in a sequential file can be read *only* in the order in which they were originally written to the file, beginning with the first record of the file. Consequently, accessing a particular record in a sequential file is often a very time-consuming process.

By contrast, any record within a random-access file may be *directly* accessed—the read/write mechanism of the storage device can be directly (or nearly so) positioned at the physical location occupied by the record. This seems like a perfectly reasonable way to access records in a database environment, and in fact all databases are constructed using some type of random-access file.

Sequential Files

Characteristics

A sequential file has special qualities that distinguish it from other types of files:

- **Order.** Records in the file have a logical order, which is precisely the order in which they were originally written to the file.
- **Access.** The file may be read only from the beginning, and only in the logical order. Consequently, if a particular record is to be accessed, the file must be searched, starting at the beginning. There is no way in which part of a sequential file can be quickly skipped over in order to locate a particular record.
- **Updating.** If a record in the file must be modified, or if a new record must be added between two existing records, the entire file must be rewritten. For example, suppose that *file1* is a sequential file, consisting of four records, written in the order A, B, C, D. If record C were to be modified, the following sequence of I/O (input/output) operations would be necessary, resulting in the creation of a new file, *file2:*

1. Read A and B from *file1*
2. Write A and B to *file2*
3. Read C from *file1*
4. Modify C
5. Write C to *file2*
6. Read D from *file1*
7. Write D to *file2*
8. Delete *file1*
9. Rename *file2* to *file1*

A similar sequence of operations would be required if a new record were added to the file.

Sequential File Applications

Sequential files are well-suited for applications in which all of the file records are processed at the same time. For example, a payroll file might hold the records for all of a company's employees, with each record containing the fields EMPLOYEE NAME, MONTHLY_SALARY, SALARY_PAID_TO_DATE, and other information. Each month, the file would be processed sequentially, with the SALARY_PAID_TO_DATE of every record updated to reflect the current monthly wages earned.

As mentioned in the previous chapter, sequential files are also important for the purposes of storing database archives and backups. The process of backing up databases is a vital one, and it will be discussed in chapter 12.

For many types of applications, the operating characteristics of sequential files are unacceptable. For example, consider a file of bank account records, each one containing a person's NAME, CURRENT_BALANCE, and other information. If this file is used in an on-line system, then different records will need to be accessed at different times. Tellers, for example, perform updating of CURRENT_BALANCE information as deposits and withdrawals are made. For this system to be effective, each record must be accessible in (at most) a few seconds. If the records were stored on a sequential file, the average access time would be on the order of *minutes,* rather than seconds. Clearly, another type of file is needed for this mode of data access.

Sequential File Storage Devices

Virtually any type of secondary-storage device can be used to maintain sequential files. The most common forms of storage are magnetic tape and disk devices. Sequential file maintenance with each of these is described in the following discussion.

Magnetic Tape

Magnetic tape is distinguished from other types of storage media in that tape is *by nature* sequential (imagine what it looks like). To write a file, the tape is first positioned either to its **load point** (by rewinding), or to the end of the last file written to the tape. Records are then written onto the tape grouped into blocks as described in the preceding chapter. The file is terminated with an **end-of-file gap.** Several files may be written to the same tape, one following immediately after another. Figure 4.1 illustrates the physical layout of files on a magnetic tape. In order to read a particular file, the tape must be positioned at its beginning by skipping over all preceding files. Many tape devices have provisions for rapidly moving to the beginning of a specified file.

Figure 4.1
Data storage on
magnetic tape.

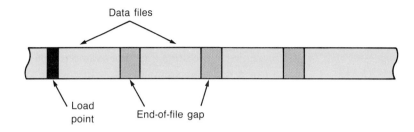

Data files

Load
point

End-of-file gap

Figure 4.2
Layout of a sequential
file on a disk. In this
example it is assumed
that no other files are
on the disk surface.

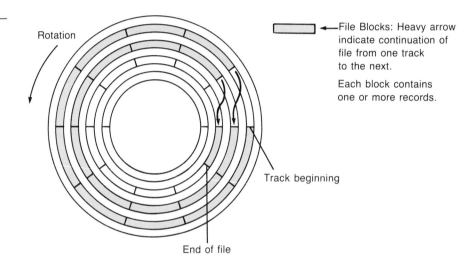

Rotation

File Blocks: Heavy arrow
indicate continuation of
file from one track
to the next.

Each block contains
one or more records.

Track beginning

End of file

Magnetic Disks

Magnetic disks are frequently used to store sequential files. This is an inevitable consequence of two facts: (1) disks are by far the most common secondary-storage devices for virtually all types of computers; and (2) sequential files are used for many types of data-processing applications.

If the surface of a disk is devoted *exclusively* to a single sequential file, the process of writing records to the disk can be pictured as follows. The records are first grouped into blocks, as described in the previous chapter. The blocks are then written one after the other onto the first track of the disk, each block being placed immediately adjacent to the preceding one. When as many whole blocks as possible have been written to the track, the read/write head moves to the second track, and the writing continues. This process goes on until all of the records have been written. An example of this type of file layout is shown in figure 4.2. In order to read this file, the read/write head must be positioned at the beginning of the first track, and it then proceeds to read from block to block, and track to track, until the end of file is reached.

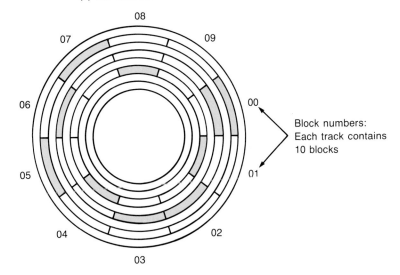

(a) The distributed records

08

07   09

06   00

Block numbers:
Each track contains
10 blocks

05   01

04   02

03

Figure 4.3
A sequential file
distributed over the
surface of a disk.
(a) The distributed
records; (b) the file
directory. The file is
distributed on the first
three tracks of the disk.

(b) File directory*

```
030801
030808
010800
020806
020803
010807
010805
020800
020802
030804
```

*Addresses consist of cylinder number + surface number + block number

Unfortunately, this simple example is rarely the way in which sequential files are actually written because many different files may reside on the disk at the same time. Each of these files may require varying amounts of disk space as records are added and deleted. From a space management point of view, the most efficient way to allocate disk space to a file is on an *as-needed* basis. As a consequence, the records in a sequential file are usually distributed over the disk surface. The following paragraphs describe a more realistic way in which space is managed for sequential files.

When a file is created, it is allocated a portion of disk space equal to that of a single block. After this space has been filled with records, another block of space is allocated, *wherever space happens to be available on the disk*. This process continues until the entire file has been written. Figure 4.3 illustrates the distribution of a sequential file on a disk surface.

File directory. The various blocks that contain records for a specific file are linked together through its **file directory,** which is maintained by the operating system and used for all file operations. The directory contains a list of addresses of all file blocks, as well as other information necessary for file maintenance. When the file is read, the order in which the blocks are accessed is determined by the entries in the directory, and the order of these entries corresponds to the order in which the blocks were originally written. Thus, although the file is randomly distributed about the disk, it is treated in a sequential manner.

Figure 4.3(b) shows the basic directory information for the file illustrated in figure 4.3(a). It is assumed that the entire file is on surface number 08 of the disk device.

Random Access Files

For many types of data processing applications, records in a file must be accessed in a random manner, rather than sequentially. For example, consider the data associated with a computerized airline reservations system. In this situation, it is important that any particular record be accessible in a few seconds. As stated earlier, sequential files cannot be used for this type of application because of the length of time needed to locate a particular record.

Random-access files permit speedy record retrieval. For example, with a random access file containing 50,000 records, any particular record can be found in a few seconds. Typically, the access time is so quick that a user would hardly notice the difference between working with a file containing 10 records and one containing 100,000!

Many types of files come under the general heading of random-access, and each represents a different solution to the following problem: given an identifier which is unique to a particular record, retrieve that record from the secondary storage device in a short time. Although the word "short" is obviously subjective, we can state that in general, a random-access file is considered to be working reasonably well if a record can be retrieved in no more than one or two seconds.

This chapter will concentrate on three of the most commonly used types of random-access files. **Indexed files** make use of auxiliary indexes in order to locate quickly one or more records. **Indexed-sequential files** are a special case of indexed files, achieving many of the benefits of both random-access and sequential files. **Direct files** use algorithms to convert a record identifier, or name, directly into an address. In order to investigate the workings of the various types of random-access files, however, the concept of a record key must first be understood.

Figure 4.4

The basis of random access. The details within the box depend upon the type of random-access file used.

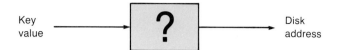

Key value → **?** → Disk address

Record Keys

To explore this idea, we begin with an analogy. Suppose that you have a filing system containing information dealing with different companies. A separate folder exists for each company, and the folders are arranged alphabetically by company name. Obviously, if you wish to retrieve data for a particular company, you must know the name of the company. This may seem trivial, but it is in fact the crux behind an important concept: *if you wish to locate a record in a random-access file, its identifier must be specified.* This identifier is technically called a **record key.**

The way in which keys are used in conjunction with random-access files is illustrated in figure 4.4. If the value of a record's key is known, it may be supplied to the DBMS, which *converts* the value into the disk address at which the record is located. The question mark in the figure indicates that several methods exist for doing the conversion, depending on the type of random-access file.

If a particular key value locates only a single record, the key is said to be **unique.** On the other hand, a **nonunique key** may correspond to several records.

Primary and Secondary Keys

Usually, a file must have at least one unique key, whose value specifies the principal "name" of each record. This is called the **primary key** of the file. If a file has more than one unique field, the one chosen to be the primary key would be that whose values seemed best suited as the record "names." Any keys other than the primary key are called **secondary keys.** A secondary key may be either unique or non-unique.

The simplest type of primary key consists of a single field within each record, often referred to as a **key field.** In some situations, the database designer specifies to the DBMS which field is to be the primary key; in other cases, the DBMS itself creates a special primary-key field.

Figure 4.5

A simple file design for
payments to
Jellybeans, Inc.

```
┌────────────────────────────────────────────────────────────┐
│                                                            │
│    Field name                  Contents                    │
│   ─────────────────────────────────────────────────────    │
│   CUSTOMER_NAME          Name of customer                  │
│   AMOUNT_PAID            Money received by Jellybeans, Inc. │
│   DATE_RECEIVED          Date payment received (mm/dd/yy)   │
│   PAYMENT_TYPE           Check, money order, cash, etc.     │
│                                                            │
│                                                            │
│   Primary key: CUSTOMER_NAME + DATE_RECEIVED               │
│                                                            │
└────────────────────────────────────────────────────────────┘
```

Concatenated Keys

A key may be formed by combining two or more fields. For example, consider a simple file for holding data on customer payments to Jellybeans, Inc. The definition for this file is shown in figure 4.5.

If we assume that there may be more than one customer with the same name, then there is no unique field in the file. However, if a *combination* of two fields is unique, it may be used as a primary key. For example, it is unlikely that a customer will submit two payments on the same day. Therefore, the combination of CUSTOMER_NAME and DATE_RECEIVED is unique, and it may be used as a primary key. This type of field combination is called a **concatenated key,** and it is expressed as:

CUSTOMER_NAME + DATE_RECEIVED

Each key value is generated by literally connecting, or concatenating, values from the two fields together. For example, suppose that a particular record in the file contains the following values:

CUSTOMER_NAME: "Jones, Ltd."
AMOUNT_PAID: 125
DATE_RECEIVED: "11/25/85"
PAYMENT_TYPE: "MO"

The concatenated key for the record would be:

"Jones, Ltd.11/25/85"

Any type of field, or combination of fields, may be a key. Regardless of the composition of the key, the process represented in figure 4.4 is valid because any type of key may be used to generate an address.

Figure 4.6
An example of
searching an index.

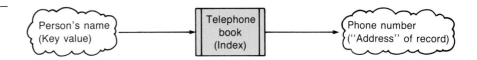

Indexed Files

One of the most commonly used methods for gaining random access to a file is the creation of one or more **indexes** on that file. The basic idea behind an indexed file is quite straightforward, although in practice there are many complex variations on this simple theme.

Suppose that a random-access file exists on a disk, with records randomly scattered about the disk An index on this file could be described as a two-column table of values: the first column contains record key values, and the second contains disk addresses. The success of using the index rests on the fact that the *keys are arranged sequentially*. Thus, any particular key value can be quickly located. A good analogy to an index is a telephone book. The people are analogous to records, and their names in the phone book are the keys. If you wish to find a particular record (person), you locate the appropriate name in the book, which gives you that person's address (street and telephone number). The fact that the names are arranged sequentially enormously simplifies locating any particular entry. Figure 4.6 illustrates the process.

Example of an Indexed File

Suppose that for the CUSTOMERS file described in chapter 2, we wish to be able to locate any record by means of its RECORD_NUMBER. One way to accomplish this is to maintain an index based on the RECORD_NUMBER field. In this example, we shall describe the process of building the file of CUSTOMERS records. This will include: (1) the addition of records to the file; and (2) the concurrent building of the index. Because RECORD_NUMBER is assumed to be the primary key of the file, the index is called the **primary-key index.**

Adding records to the file. When the CUSTOMERS file is first opened, it is allocated a block of disk space by the operating system. As records are added to the file, they are written into this block, and when the block is filled, another is allocated, wherever disk space is available.

As each CUSTOMERS record is written to the disk, an entry is made in the RECORD_NUMBER index, consisting of the following:

1. Key value for the record, that is, the value of RECORD_NUMBER
2. Block number into which the record is written. This is referred to as the relative address, or simply the address, of the record

In effect, the index may be thought of as a table consisting of two columns: RECORD_NUMBER and ADDRESS, as shown in figure 4.7(a).

Figure 4.7

(a) An index for the CUSTOMERS file using RECORD_NUMBER as the key; (b) a set of directory entries for the blocks in the RECORD_NUMBER index; (c) the process of searching the index.

Key value (RECORD NUMBER)	Relative address
01	01
02	01
03	02
04	02
05	03
06	03
07	04
08	04
09	05
10	05
11	06

Because RECORD NUMBER is unique, each value has a single corresponding address

Two records fit into each block

The relative addresses are equivalent to block numbers assigned to the index. The physical disk addresses of these blocks are contained in the directory for the index, shown below.

(b)

Relative address	Physical disk address
01	030204
02	030205
03	030114
04	031211
05	031212
06	030102

Searching the index. Suppose that a particular CUSTOMERS record is to be located, perhaps in response to a user request. The index is searched for the entry that contains the specified value of RECORD_NUMBER. When that entry is located, the associated address is used to locate the desired record. Note that this is a *relative* address; the physical disk address must be obtained from the file directory, shown in figure 4.7(b). Figure 4.7(c) depicts the retrieval of record 04, using the process via the RECORD_NUMBER index.

Figure 4.7 [*Continued*]

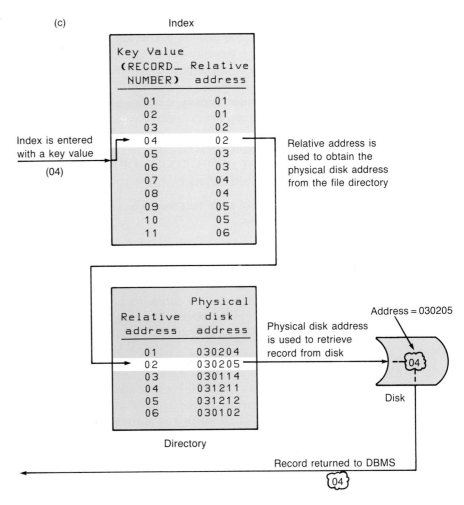

(c)

Because the index entries are ordered sequentially by RECORD_NUMBER, as shown in figure 4.7, a particular entry may be located quickly by any of several methods that take advantage of the ordering. Some of these methods are discussed later in the chapter.

It is important to note that the relative placement of the records on the disk is immaterial. That is, records can be written to the disk in any way that is convenient for the operating system.

Another important point is that RECORD_NUMBER is a unique key, and consequently no two records have the same value for this field. Therefore, the index will contain only one address for each key value, so that each search of the index will produce only one record.

Using an index for sequential record-access. One of the most important uses of an index is to allow access to a file of records in a particular sequence. This sequence is determined by the order in which records are referenced by the index, namely in **key-sequence.** For example, the RECORD_NUMBER index would permit the entire file of records to be listed sequentially by RECORD_ NUMBER values. Usually, a DBMS has one or more commands for performing this type of access. For example, consider the following set of DBMS commands:

> USE CUSTOMERS
> SET INDEX TO RECORD_NUMBER
> DISPLAY ALL

The sequence of steps that would be performed by the DBMS could be represented as follows:

---

1. Go to the first entry of the index
2. Do the following until NO_MORE_RECORDS:
   a. Retrieve and output the record whose address is in the current index entry
   b. Go to the next entry in the index

If it is known that a file must be accessed frequently in a particular order, an index can be created on the appropriate field or fields. The cost in required disk storage may be well worth it in terms of the savings in searching time.

Adding another index. Suppose that the CUSTOMERS file will be queried frequently on the basis of the CITY field. Each of these queries would take the form of something similar to:

> "Display all CUSTOMERS records that have a value of 'city' for the CITY field".

Ordinarily, this query would be carried out by a **sequential search** of the file— each record in the file would be examined, and if the CITY field contained the value "city", the record would be returned to the DBMS for display.

Because a sequential search involves many disk accesses, a great deal of search time can be saved by creating an index on the CITY field. Again, this index can be represented as a two-column table, as shown in figure 4.8. The first column contains all of the values for CITY contained in the file, and the second column contains corresponding relative addresses. As before, the key values are arranged sequentially.

```
Key value
   (CITY)     Address

ALBANY          04
ALBANY          05
BERKELEY        01
BERKELEY        03
BERKELEY        04
BERKELEY        06
NEWARK          02
OAKLAND         01
OAKLAND         02
OAKLAND         05
PITTSBURG       03
```

The CITY index differs from the RECORD_NUMBER index in one very important respect: for each particular value of CITY, there may be *several* corresponding records. By contrast, the RECORD_NUMBER index contains exactly one address for each value of RECORD_NUMBER. For example, in figure 4.8 there are 4 entries corresponding to the value "Berkeley," which means that four records in the CUSTOMERS file have a CITY value of "Berkeley."

Because the field CITY is the basis of a separate index, it is said to be a key. Furthermore, because CITY is a nonunique field, it is a secondary key. Finally, the index based on CITY is called a **secondary index,** which is a term used to describe any index other than that based on the primary key.

In the preceding example, we have tacitly assumed that more than one index may be associated with a file. This is in fact the case, and there could conceivably be as many indexes for a file as there are fields in each record. In fact, if concatenated keys are used, there could be more indexes than fields.

Index Maintenance

The responsibility for the maintenance of indexes is a complicated issue, since it depends on the particular system in use. One thing is happily clear: it is *not* the responsibility of the user, except that (s)he must specify that an index on a particular key is to be created and maintained. In the context of a database environment, the DBMS is usually responsible for the maintenance of all indexes. In practice, the details of index maintenance are usually of little concern to the user, who needs only to understand the concept of what an index is and how it may be utilized.

Many methods exist for searching an index for a particular entry, and the objective of each method is to locate the desired entry using the fewest steps possible. The particular search method used in a given circumstance depends on the structure of the index, and because indexes may be built in many different ways, many searching techniques exist.

The particular structure used for a given index depends on many factors, such as the size of the index and the type of hardware on which it will reside. In this section, the more common types of index structures will be mentioned, outlining popular searching techniques for each.

An index exists as a separate disk file, and like any other type of data it must be read into primary storage before it can be used. If an index is too large to fit completely in primary storage, then it must be used *piecewise,* with different pieces being read in as needed. Consequently, small indexes can be structured quite simply, while large indexes require complicated structures so that the search time remains reasonably short.

A simple index structure. The simplest type of index structure imaginable is one in which all of the index entries are stored contiguously on a disk. For simplicity, we will refer to this type of structure as **tabular,** because its entries can be thought of as though they were successive entries in a simple table. A telephone book is an example of a tabular index. If an index is sufficiently small, it may be built in tabular form, and some very straightforward searching methods can be used to quickly locate any desired entry.

Sequential searching. The simplest way to search a tabular index is to start at the beginning and inspect the entries sequentially, until the desired key value is located. On the average, this method will require that one-half of the index entries be examined for each search. Although this simple technique is not too slow for reasonably small indexes, it may consume a considerable amount of CPU time for larger ones. In general, therefore, sequential searching is best used as a point of reference for studying better strategies.

Binary searching. A method far superior to the simple sequential search is the **binary search.** You may very likely use a method similar to this when using a telephone book. As an example of this technique, we will demonstrate a search of the index shown in figure 4.8, looking for the entry with a value of "Pittsburg." Essentially, this search works by successively dividing the table into pieces of approximately equal size. At each step, a determination is made as to which piece contains the desired entry.

In this example, the index is first divided into half, as shown in figure 4.9(a). Note that the *last* entry of the upper half shows a key value of "Berkeley." Since the entries are ordered sequentially by key values, it can be deduced that the desired value, "Pittsburg," is in the lower half. In the next step, the lower half

Figure 4.9
A binary search of the index shown in figure 4.8. The desired entry is "PITTSBURG." At each step, the table is divided into two pieces: the last entry of the top piece and the first entry of the bottom piece are used to detemine in which piece the desired entry is located. That piece is again divided, and the process continued.

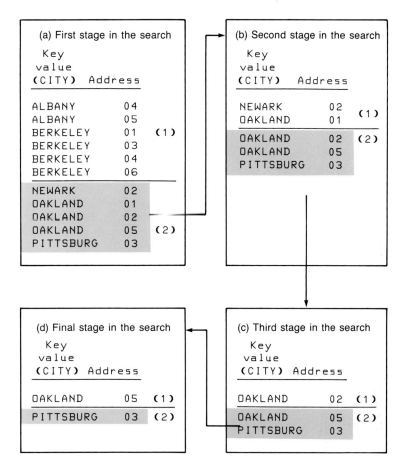

is divided approximately into two pieces, as shown in figure 4.9(b). Again, it can quickly be determined which piece contains the desired entry. In this case, it is the lower one. Eventually, the desired entry is isolated, as shown in part (d) of the figure.

Index-searching methods are an integral part of database management systems. Moreover, different search techniques are used by different systems, depending on the size of the index, the speed requirements, and in some cases, the personal preferences of the system designer.

Index Complications

The simple model of a tabular form is adequate for small indexes with perhaps a few hundred entries. However, for indexes associated with larger files, this model is inadequate. In order to understand the reasons for this, we must examine the different ways in which large data files are used.

File searching. Searching for records in an indexed file often involves the search of an index for a specific key value. When an index becomes large, the sequential and binary search techniques previously described become ineffective because a large index will occupy many blocks on the disk, each of which requires a separate disk access. The significance of this problem lies in the fact that disk accesses are costly, in terms of both the real-time involved and the degradation of system performance.

In the case of single-user systems, such as most small microcomputers, the real-time involved is the significant issue—disk accesses are time-consuming. A search of an index that involves many disk accesses can seem interminable, especially when floppy-disk drives are used. Even with the use of hard disks, the real-time needed for a single index search may amount to many seconds. This is a great nuisance for an on-line user making many searches, and it could be intolerable for a batch program making hundreds or thousands of searches.

For multi-user systems, not only is the real-time issue a problem for the user doing the searching, but in addition, overall system degradation becomes significant. Whenever a disk is being accessed by one process, it is unavailable to other users, and a process requiring many disk accesses can significantly reduce the availability of the disk. As a result, overall system performance deteriorates.

File updating. As records are added and deleted from an indexed file, the associated indexes must be updated to reflect the current condition of the file. For example, suppose that a new record has been added to the CUSTOMERS file, containing a CITY value of "Colfax." The CITY index in figure 4.8 must be updated in order to make room for the new entry, as illustrated in figure 4.10.

Because the index in this figure is small, only a few entries need be moved to accomodate an addition. However, suppose that the index were to contain 50,000 entries instead of a dozen. In that case, an average of 25,000 entries would need to be physically relocated in order to make room for each addition. This process would consume a significant amount of CPU time, and it would also require a great many disk accesses. Again, the issues of real-time cost and degradation of system performance would be significant.

File reorganization. The size of a random-access file usually changes over a period of time, as records are added and deleted. When a record is deleted, an empty spot or "hole" is left in the file. Because of the way in which some operating systems function, it may not be possible to use this hole for further data storage without a **file reorganization.** This is a function performed either by the DBMS, the operating system, or a combination of both. When it is performed, all of the records in a file are physically reorganized so as to eliminate the holes. As a result of this reorganization, all record addresses in the file are altered, and any associated indexes must be completely rewritten. If many indexes are attached to the file, this process can be quite lengthy, and while it is taking place, the computer may be effectively out of commission as far as any other activity is concerned.

Figure 4.10

Adding an entry to the
index shown in figure
4.8. The shaded entries
must be moved down
to accommodate the
new entry.

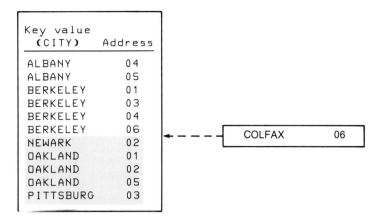

Key value (CITY)	Address
ALBANY	04
ALBANY	05
BERKELEY	01
BERKELEY	03
BERKELEY	04
BERKELEY	06
NEWARK	02
OAKLAND	01
OAKLAND	02
OAKLAND	05
PITTSBURG	03

COLFAX 06

Having described the types of index problems that can occur in connection with various file activities, we will now discuss some of the more popular methods devised for building indexes with structures that minimize the effects of these problems.

Minimizing Index Complications

Symbolic addressing. We will first consider a type of index that helps reduce the amount of effort involved with the reorganization of a file. Consider the two indexes for the CUSTOMERS file shown in figures 4.7 and 4.8. Note that the first of these (RECORD_NUMBER) is the primary-key index for the file. Suppose that for the other (CITY) index, we remove the values in the "Address" column, and in their place we substitute the corresponding RECORD_NUMBER values from figure 2.9, which shows the original CUSTOMERS data. The result of this substitution is shown in figure 4.11(a), in which the "Address" column has been relabeled "Symbolic address." This implies that each value in this column does not contain an address but instead contains information which can be used to find the address. Thus, the symbolic address of a record is its primary key.

In order to find a particular record using this modified CITY index, a two-step process is necessary. As an example, figure 4.11(b) illustrates the process of finding the records corresponding to the city of Newark. The first step is to search the CITY index for the correct entries, using perhaps a binary-search technique. In this particular case, there is only one entry, and the value in the symbolic address column is 03. *This value is then used as a search item in the primary-key (RECORD_NUMBER) index.* This search, which again might be done using a binary-search technique, produces the record address 02.

Note that in the second step, only a single record will be found from the index search, because the search item is a primary key.

Using this indexing method, a search of the CITY index now requires additional steps, because both the CITY index and the primary-key index must be

Figure 4.11
Using symbolic
addresses. (a) The CITY
index with symbolic
addresses replacing
relative addresses;
(b) searching the CITY
index.

(a)

Key value (CITY)	Symbolic address
ALBANY	08
ALBANY	10
BERKELEY	01
BERKELEY	05
BERKELEY	07
BERKELEY	11
NEWARK	03
OAKLAND	02
OAKLAND	04
OAKLAND	09
PITTSBURG	06

The symbolic address of each record is its primary key, shown in figure 2.9

(b)

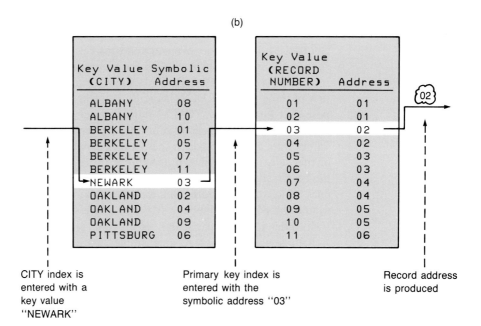

CITY index is
entered with a
key value
"NEWARK"

Primary key index is
entered with the
symbolic address "03"

Record address
is produced

searched. Why have we gone to this trouble to make things more tedious, when our objective was the opposite? The answer is the following. Assuming that primary key values are sacred (never changed), then when a file reorganization takes place, the CITY index does not have to be changed because it no longer contains physical addresses. The primary-key index is the only one that must be rewritten.

To emphasize the significance of this point, suppose that there was a total of ten indexes attached to the CUSTOMERS file, including the primary-key index, the CITY index, and eight others. Furthermore, assume that all but the primary-key index contained symbolic addresses. Finally, assume that a file reorganization occurs. In this situation, only the primary-key index must be rewritten. In other words, the use of symbolic addresses would eliminate 90% of the disk activity involved with index reorganization.

We must still consider the fact that with symbolic addressing, index search time is doubled. In practice, this is offset by the fact that indexes are constructed so that a search involves very few disk accesses. As a result, doubling the search time still has minimal effect on overall system performance. Nevertheless, many systems do not use symbolic addressing, and instead take the time needed to do the occasional file reorganizations whenever necessary.

Multi-level indexes

A common approach to the problem of dealing with large indexes is to build them in **levels.** Each individual level is essentially an index to the next lower level, and each level is organized into a number of **buckets.** A bucket simply consists of one or more blocks, the size being chosen in such a way to minimize the number of steps needed to carry out a search. Each bucket contains a number of **entries,** each of which contains the following:

- **Pointer:** Contains the address of a bucket on the next lower level. (In general, the term *pointer* refers to a data item containing an address.)
- **Data value:** Contains the *highest* data value in the entries of the bucket pointed to by **pointer.**

An example will help clarify these ideas. Figure 4.12 illustrates a three-level index in which the key values correspond to LAST_NAMES. The top level of this index contains a single bucket with four entries, and the lowest level of the index contains addresses of the actual records. The entries in each bucket are ordered sequentially according to the data values, that is, the actual values of LAST_NAME.

Suppose that this index is to be searched for an entry with a value of "Pierce." We begin by scanning the top level, looking for an entry greater than "Pierce." We begin with the lowest value, "Harris." The search ends when an entry is found that contains a value greater than "Pierce." In this case, it is the second entry, which contains the value "Prince." This entry in turn "points" to the appropriate bucket on the second level. This bucket is retrieved and searched, again looking for the first entry containing a value greater than "Pierce." This turns out to be

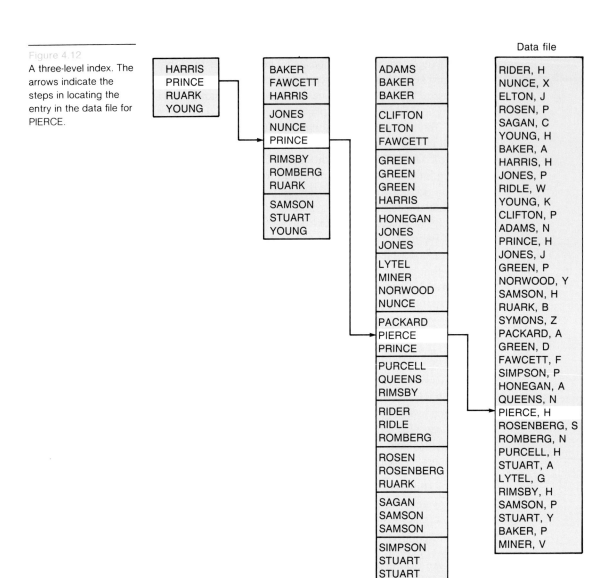

Figure 4.12
A three-level index. The arrows indicate the steps in locating the entry in the data file for PIERCE.

the third entry, which in turn points to another bucket on the next level. This bucket is retrieved and searched, and its third entry is the desired one. Because this entry was retrieved from the lowest level of the index, the pointer contains the address of the actual data record corresponding to the name "Pierce."

Bucket searching. Note that in this example, three different buckets were successively read into primary storage and then searched for a desired entry. Any convenient search algorithm may be used to locate a particular entry within a bucket. One of the most common is the binary search technique described earlier.

Disk accesses. If we assume that in this example each bucket consists of a single block, then only three disk accesses are needed to locate the address of any particular record, even though the entire index consists of a great many blocks. This is true in general: an N-level index requires the retrieval of N buckets in order to locate a particular record address, *independent of the total size of the index.*

Updating a multi-level index. When records are added or removed from a file, any related indexes must be modified. Recall that on the average, one-half of the entries had to be physically moved to accommodate the change for the simple tabular-type index. For a multi-level index, far less work is involved. A bit of analysis will reveal that when an entry is added to, or removed from, the index, only a small number of entries at only the lowest levels will need to be changed. Again, a well-designed index will minimize the number of required changes.

As an example, suppose that a record with a primary-key value of "Rawson" is to be added to the file whose index is shown in figure 4.12. Assuming that a bucket may contain a maximum of four entries, then only the lowest level of the index must be altered. The modified index, including the new entry, is shown in figure 4.13.

Incorporating symbolic addressing. It is possible to make use of symbolic addressing with multi-level indexes. This would occur at the lowest level, where the pointers to the actual data records would be replaced by symbolic addresses. Again, the object would be to reduce the overall time needed for file reorganization.

Index design. The design of a multi-level index is quite complicated, with many factors to be considered. For example, the fewer the number of levels, the fewer disk accesses are needed per search. On the other hand, in order to minimize the number of levels, the number of buckets on each level must be relatively large, which means that the bucket size must be relatively large. This latter conclusion follows from the fact that each bucket on level X points to a group of buckets on the next lower level, Y. Consequently, if there are more buckets on Y, then each bucket on X contains more pointers and is therefore larger.

Figure 4.13

Adding a new entry, RAWSON, to the file and index.

| HARRIS |
| PRINCE |
| RUARK |
| YOUNG |

| BAKER |
| FAWCETT |
HARRIS
JONES
NUNCE
PRINCE
RIMSBY
ROMBERG
RUARK
SAMSON
STUART
YOUNG

| ADAMS |
| BAKER |
BAKER
CLIFTON
ELTON
FAWCETT
GREEN
GREEN
GREEN
HARRIS
HONEGAN
JONES
JONES
LYTEL
MINER
NORWOOD
NUNCE
PACKARD
PIERCE
PRINCE
PURCELL
QUEENS
RAWSON
RIMSBY
RIDER
RIDLE
ROMBERG
ROSEN
ROSENBERG
RUARK
SAGAN
SAMSON
SAMSON
SIMPSON
STUART
STUART
SYMONS
YOUNG
YOUNG

Data file

| RIDER, H |
| NUNCE, X |
| ELTON, J |
| ROSEN, P |
| SAGAN, C |
| YOUNG, H |
| BAKER, A |
| HARRIS, H |
| JONES, P |
| RIDLE, W |
| YOUNG, K |
| CLIFTON, P |
| ADAMS, N |
| PRINCE, H |
| JONES, J |
| GREEN, P |
| NORWOOD, Y |
| SAMSON, H |
| RUARK, B |
| SYMONS, Z |
| PACKARD, A |
| GREEN, D |
| FAWCETT, F |
| SIMPSON, P |
| HONEGAN, A |
| QUEENS, N |
| PIERCE, H |
| ROSENBERG, S |
| ROMBERG, N |
| PURCELL, H |
| STUART, A |
| LYTEL, G |
| RIMSBY, H |
| SAMSON, P |
| STUART, Y |
| BAKER, P |
| MINER, V |
| RAWSON, X |

On the other hand, as bucket size increases, the number of disk accesses needed per bucket also increases. Thus, a smaller total number of levels, which implies fewer disk accesses, requires larger bucket sizes, which implies more disk accesses! If all of this seems complicated, it is, and the choice of values for the various design parameters is an interesting and complex problem.[1]

Although the use of a multi-level index drastically reduces the number of disk accesses needed for a given search, there is a price to pay in the form of additional disk space needed to store the extra index levels. A single-level index would correspond almost exactly to the lowest level of the index shown in figure 4.12. The higher levels all represent additional data which must also be stored on the disk. Nevertheless, when large indexes are involved, the price is happily paid because of the benefits gained from multi-level indexes.

Indexed-Sequential Files

A special type of indexed file is that in which the records are physically stored on the disk in groups. Within each group the records are stored *sequentially by primary key*. When each group corresponds to a physical subdivision of the disk, such as a track, the file type is known as **ISAM** (Indexed Sequential Access Method). In addition to the sequential arrangement of the records within each track, a separate primary-key index is also maintained. Records within an ISAM file may be accessed in two fundamentally different ways. First, the entire file can be read sequentially, just as though it were an ordinary sequential file, with the records physically sequenced by key. (Throughout this discussion, the term *key* refers to primary key.) Alternatively, records may be accessed via the index, which functions like any other type of index: the index is entered with a key value, the address is located within the index, and the record is retrieved.

ISAM files are used primarily in situations which (1) require random access to the file records using the primary key as the search key, and (2) require frequent access to the file in primary-key sequence. In general, ISAM files are most frequently encountered in larger-computer applications. The following section gives a brief description of indexed-sequential files.

File Structure

An ISAM file is similar to other types of files in that records are stored on a series of tracks. However, ISAM files differ in that each track that is allocated to the file is used *exclusively* by the file. Furthermore, the records on each individual track are arranged *sequentially by key*.

For example, figure 4.14 schematically shows the layout for a small ISAM file, as well as the associated index. (To simplify this discussion, we assume that all records are on the same disk surface.) Each entry in the index contains two

---

[1]Martin gives a very good overall picture of issues involved with the design of multi-level indexes. Martin, J., *Computer Data-Base Organization,* 2d ed. (Englewood Cliffs, N.J.: Prentice-Hall 1977).

Figure 4.14
A small ISAM file.
(a) The data file; (b) the
file index.

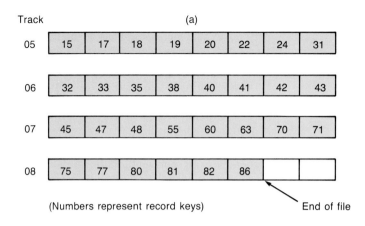

Track   (a)

(Numbers represent record keys)   End of file

(b)

Track	Highest key value
05	31
06	43
07	71
08	86

values: the track number and the value of the highest key on that track. Because the records on each track are arranged sequentially, *only one index entry is needed for each track.*

Record Retrieval

To illustrate how the file shown in figure 4.14 is used, suppose that record 60 (that is, the record whose key value is 60) is to be retrieved. The index is searched, starting at the top, for an entry whose key value is greater than or equal to 60. In this case, it is the third entry, which points to track 07. This track can then be searched for record 60.

File Maintenance and Overflows

In order to accommodate record additions and deletions, the simple picture described above needs to be augmented. Suppose that record 23 is to be added to the file illustrated in figure 4.14. Where can it be put? It should be written onto track 05, but this is not possible because the track is filled. The record cannot be written to any other existing track, because it would then be out of order. The most common solution to this problem is to incorporate an **overflow area** into the file design. This is a section of the disk into which records may be written as a

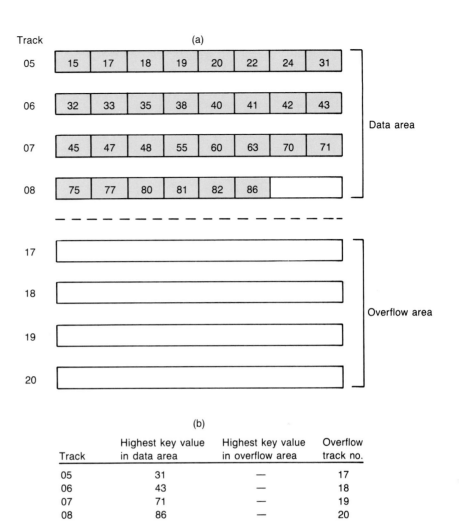

Figure 4.15
(a) ISAM file with an
overflow area; (b) the
file index.

Track   (a)

| 05 | 15 | 17 | 18 | 19 | 20 | 22 | 24 | 31 |

| 06 | 32 | 33 | 35 | 38 | 40 | 41 | 42 | 43 |

| 07 | 45 | 47 | 48 | 55 | 60 | 63 | 70 | 71 |

| 08 | 75 | 77 | 80 | 81 | 82 | 86 | | |

Data area

17

18

19

20

Overflow area

(b)

Track	Highest key value in data area	Highest key value in overflow area	Overflow track no.
05	31	—	17
06	43	—	18
07	71	—	19
08	86	—	20

result of new records being added to the file. There are many techniques for implementing overflow areas, and we shall describe one of these here. Figure 4.15 shows the file of figure 4.14, but with the addition of several **overflow tracks.** Each regular data track is assigned one overflow track.

Because of the existence of the overflow area, additional information must be kept in the index, as shown in figure 4.15(b).

We now reconsider the problem of adding record 23 to the file. The index is searched, and it shows that record 23 should be written to track 05. However, this track is filled, and in order to accommodate the new record, all of the records starting with record 24 are physically moved. The last record on the track, record 31, is "pushed off," since there is no longer room for it. As it is deleted from the track, it is copied to the associated overflow track, and the appropriate entries are made in the index. Figure 4.16 shows the situation in the file and the index after record 23 has been added.

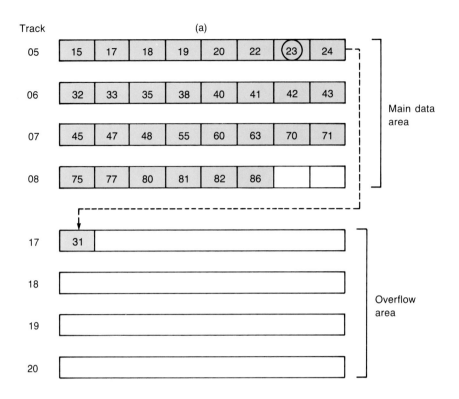

Figure 4.16
(a) The addition of a record to the file, as shown in figure 4.15; (b) the file index. As record 23 is added, record 31 is pushed into the overflow area.

Track (a)

05 | 15 | 17 | 18 | 19 | 20 | 22 | (23) | 24 |

06 | 32 | 33 | 35 | 38 | 40 | 41 | 42 | 43 |

07 | 45 | 47 | 48 | 55 | 60 | 63 | 70 | 71 |

08 | 75 | 77 | 80 | 81 | 82 | 86 | | |

Main data area

17 | 31 |

18 | |

19 | |

20 | |

Overflow area

(b)

Track	Highest key value in data area	Highest key value in overflow area	Overflow track no.
05	24	31	17
06	43		18
07	71		19
08	86		20

If additional records are subsequently added to track 05, more records will be pushed off into the same overflow track. With this type of approach, when any overflow track fills up, the entire file must be reorganized before any more records can be added.

For very active files, overflow tracks will fill up frequently, necessitating many file reorganizations. Because these reorganizations are time-consuming, other overflow schemes are preferable to the one described above.

One popular overflow method establishes a common overflow area in which any empty location may be used to store overflow records. Thus, a particular data track could have as many overflows as necessary, and as long as there was vacant space anywhere in the overflow area, overflow records could be accomodated. In order to implement this type of method, overflow records from a particular data

Figure 4.17
An ISAM file with
overflow records.
Records are shown for
one data track and its
overflow. Arrows
indicate connections via
a linked list.

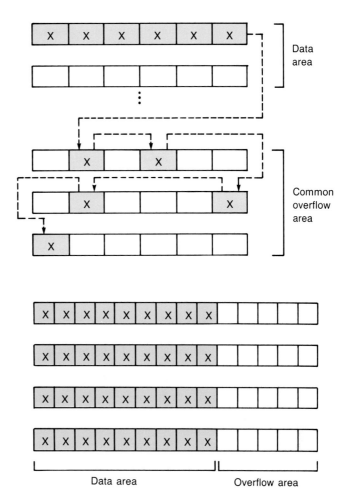

Data
area

Common
overflow
area

Figure 4.18
An ISAM file with
distributed overflow. A
portion of each track is
reserved for additional
records.

Data area   Overflow area

track would have to be connected by pointers. Figure 4.17 schematically illustrates the process. Techniques for using pointers are discussed at length later in the text.

Still another approach to overflow is to intersperse overflow areas within the data tracks themselves. With this method, a certain amount of space is left blank at the end of each track, as shown in figure 4.18. When a record is written to a particular track, it is placed in its proper key-sequence by moving records that are already on the track. The overflow space at the end of the track accommodates the movement. The advantage of this scheme is that the extra bookkeeping and file searching associated with a separate overflow area is eliminated: all records for a particular track are on that track rather than in a physically separate part of the disk. This method has its limitations because as soon as any track fills up, the entire file must be reorganized before further records can be added.

Sometimes, a combination of methods is used for dealing with overflows in order to take advantage of the best features of each. For example, a file could be built in which each track contains a certain amount of overflow area. In addition, a general overflow area could be used to handle overflows from tracks whose individual overflow areas were full.

Pros and Cons of ISAM Files

An ISAM file is a design compromise. Records may be accessed either sequentially (in key order) or randomly. Because of the design of the index, it is considered smaller than an ordinary index, and it may be rapidly searched for a particular entry. However, locating a particular record requires that an entire track (and possibly its overflow records) be read. Thus, on the average, more disk accesses are needed than for the case in which an ordinary (i.e., non-ISAM) index is used to locate a record.

The index of an ISAM file may be based *only* on the primary key. Other secondary indexes may also be maintained for the records of an ISAM file.

Direct Files

A different approach to relating primary record keys to record addresses is to use some type of computational algorithm to transform primary-key values directly into addresses. This approach has the advantage of being very fast and also of eliminating the space needed to store indexes. It also has several disadvantages, which will be discussed later.

The basic idea behind the use of a direct file is as follows. When a particular record is to be written to the file, the value of its primary key is transformed, using some type of simple numerical computation. The result of this computation is an integer, whose value is equal to the record address. This conversion process is illustrated in figure 4.4. In this case, the question mark in the figure represents a numerical computation. Usually, the result of the computation is a relative address, which may be converted to physical disk address via the file directory.

When access to that same record is desired, its primary-key value is put through the *same* computation. The address that was generated in the first place (when the record was written to the disk) is again generated, and the record can thus be retrieved. In other words, whether a particular record is to be written or retrieved, its key value is put through the same computation, which produces the same record address.

Many different types of computational techniques have been devised for use with direct files, and in the following section, two of the more common ones will be described.

(a)

RECORD NO.	NAME	STREET	CITY	STATE	ZIP	PHONE	CREDIT	BALANCE
01	Smith, Jennifer	123 Hayes St.	Berkeley	CA	94704	(415) 654-1391	5000	0.00
02	Harris, Peter	19 Taraval St.	Oakland	CA	94620	(415) 565-1985	1000	155.75
03	James, Jesse	39 Trout Gulch	Newark	CA	95061	(818) 232-3987	5000	532.87
04	Norman, Samuel	339 40th Ave.	Oakland	CA	95123	(415) 565-3492	0	0.00
05	LaRue, Elaine	7244 52nd St.	Berkeley	CA	94169	(415) 654-9641	1000	955.00
06	Clark, Kent	7 Hidden Way	Pittsburg	CA	94882	(408) 974-2581	1000	395.15
07	Gregory, Robert	357 Mission St.	Berkeley	CA	94704	(415) 654-0127	5000	1857.32
08	Drue, Ellen	55 Pork Place	Albany	CA	94666	(415) 335-9741	10000	3527.98
09	Smith, Alfred	18 Center St.	Oakland	CA	95543	(415) 853-1596	1000	0.00
10	Andersen, Tim	9532 Clark Pl.	Albany	CA	94661	(415) 335-9264	5000	327.13
11	Baker, James	1 Cyle Road	Berkeley	CA	94704	(415) 654-4826	10000	125.15

(b)

Relative block number	Physical disk address	Record keys	
0	030514	01	02
1	030515	03	04
2	030516	05	06
3	030600	07	08
4	030601	09	10
5	030602	11	12
6	030615	13	14
7	030616	15	16
8	030708	17	18
9	030709	19	20

Figure 4.19 (a) The CUSTOMERS file and (b) file directory. Note that the values listed in the last column are not part of the directory; they are included to indicate which records reside in each block.

Linear Addressing Methods

Linear addressing methods are commonly used with direct files, particularly in microcomputer applications. The basis for this method is establishing a *simple linear relationship* between primary-key values and relative disk addresses.

To illustrate a simple linear addressing technique, consider the file of records shown in figure 4.19(a). The directory for this file is illustrated in figure 4.19(b). Note that "relative block number" is equivalent to "relative address." For the sake of discussion, we assume that each record is 200 bytes in length and that block lengths are 512 bytes. Figure 4.20 illustrates the placement of the first few records of the file in their blocks. (In the figure, each record is represented by its primary-key value.)

Figure 4.20

Records and blocks of
part of the file shown in
figure 4.19. Blocks are
represented by large
rectangles, block
numbers are in
parentheses. Each
block contains a small
amount of unused
space.

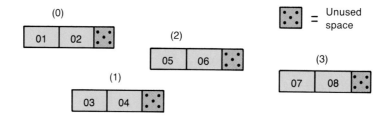

We shall assume that the RECORD_NO field is the primary key, with numeric values automatically assigned by the DBMS in sequential order as each new record is added to the file.

If the primary-key value of any record is known, its relative address is computed as follows:

$$\text{Relative address} = \text{TRUNC} \left\{ \frac{key\ value - 1}{recs\text{-}per\text{-}block} \right\}$$

Where: *key-value* = primary-key value
recs-per-block = number of records that fit in each block
And: TRUNC |*num*| = smallest integer less than or equal to *num*

For example, suppose that we wish to find the relative address of the record with a key value of 15. The calculation is as follows:

$$\text{Relative address} = \text{TRUNC} \left\{ \frac{15 - 1}{2} \right\} = 7$$

The physical disk address may then be found from the file directory, as shown in figure 4.19(b).

Deleting records. When a record is deleted, a vacant space or "hole" is left in that particular block of the file. Usually these holes cannot be conveniently reused by the DBMS and are left vacant.

Eventually, the file may become permeated with so many holes that a file reorganization must be done. This is accomplished by a system program that moves records around, filling all of the holes.

The need to reorganize this type of file periodically creates a problem. Because each primary-key value corresponds to a unique relative address, records that are moved must be assigned new key values during the reorganization. For example, suppose that record 05 is deleted in figure 4.21. This hole will remain until a reorganization takes place, the results of which are shown in figure 4.22. Many of the records have been assigned new key values.

The problem lies in the fact that because primary-key values change, it becomes difficult to use them as a means of locating records. For example, consider

Figure 4.21
A record is deleted
from the file shown in
figure 4.20. The arrow
indicates the empty,
unusable space created
when the record is
deleted.

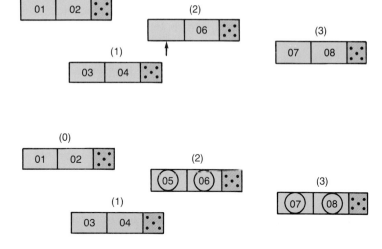

Figure 4.22
The file shown in figure
4.21 is reorganized.
Records that have been
moved during the
reorganization are
circled.

record 06 in figure 4.21. After the reorganization, it has become record 05, a fact that may not be known to the file users. The analogy to this situation would be for several people to change their names and then tell *only* the telephone company. When the new phone book was published (file reorganization), these people could no longer be located in the book because all of their acquaintances would be looking up the old names!

How, then, can users access specific records if the names of the records change? One possiblity is by using other fields as a basis for searching. For example, a secondary index could be created on the NAME field of the CUSTOMERS file. In fact, even if there are duplicate values of NAME in the file, the index may still be useful inasmuch as other data fields can usually help to differentiate one record from another.

Another way to quickly access records when the primary key is not available is to create another unique field as part of the file definition. For example, each customer could be assigned a unique identification number, placed into a CUS-TOMER_ID field. An index created on this field would then always yield a single record for a given ID number. This practice is quite common in many types of data-processing applications, even though the users must bear the responsibility for assigning unique identification values.

One other possibility for locating records with changing primary keys is to maintain an up-to-date list of records and their primary keys, renewing the list after each file reorganization.

In spite of its shortcomings, the linear addressing method is used by many DBMS's. One of the main advantages of the method is the speed with which a particular record may be accessed. When used in conjunction with secondary indexes, it is a powerful method for dealing with random-access files.

Hashing Methods

One of the oldest and most popular techniques for converting primary-key values into disk addresses is that of **hashing.** This is quite different from the direct-addressing approach, in that record addresses are not in any sense linearly related to key values. On the contrary, one of the basic requirements of hashing is that the calculated address be a random function of the key. A file of this type is often referred to as a **hashed file.** The following example will illustrate the method.

Suppose that a group of 1000 records are to be stored in a hashed file. The primary key for these records is a RECORD_NUMBER field, which contains 6-digit numbers. A distinctive feature of a hashed file is that *the entire disk space must be allocated for the file before any records are written to the file.* This means that the entire file directory is set up before any records are added to the file. Furthermore, for reasons to be explained later, the amount of allocated space must be somewhat larger than that necessary to hold 1000 records; consequently, we shall assume that space for 1400 records has been set aside.

The hypothetical situation is summarized below:

1. Total number of records to be written to the file: 1000
2. Total file space reserved for file (measured in records):   1400
3. Range of primary-key values: 0–999,999

For the sake of simplicity, it will be assumed that one record fits exactly into one block. (If this were not the case, the arithmetic would be slightly more complicated.) Therefore, the total disk space allocated for the file consists of 1400 blocks, each of which is assigned a relative-block number (relative address) ranging from 0000 to 1399. Again, as before, the relative address is easily transformed to a physical disk address by using the file directory.

Fundamentally, a hashing technique is based on a simple algorithm that maps the primary-key values into the range of the addresses, namely the integers [0–1399], as depicted in figure 4.23. Furthermore, for reasons soon to become clear, the mapping process should be a random one so that the records are evenly distributed among the 1400 addresses.

A simple hashing algorithm. It happens that the following simple algorithm for converting keys to addresses is one of the most effective:

$$ADDRESS = Remainder(key\_value / file\_size)$$

Where: *file_size* = total record capacity of the file.

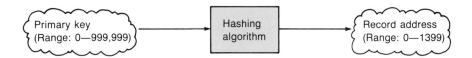

Figure 4.23 The mapping of primary key values into addresses. The hashing algorithm transforms each key value into a specific address.

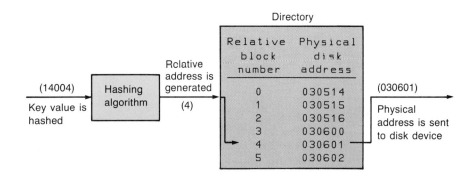

Figure 4.24 Writing a record to a hashed file.

This algorithm is sometimes known as a **division method.** It is popular because it is quite simple and it generates a reasonably uniform distribution of addresses, provided that the key values are not biased in any particular way.

Adding records to the file. Suppose that a record with a key value of 14,004 is to be added to the file. The above formula yields the following calculation:

$$\text{ADDRESS} = \text{Remainder}(14{,}004/1400) = 4$$

Thus, the record would be written to the block with relative number 4. Figure 4.24 illustrates the steps involved in writing the record to the file, including the transformation of the relative address into the corresponding physical disk address.

Collisions and clumping. The method just described would be perfect except for one significant complication. Given that 1,000,000 possible key values are being mapped into a total of 1400 addresses, there is high probability that as records are being written, more than one key value will map to the same address. In fact, each address corresponds to over 700 different key values! Amazingly, this does not invalidate the method, but some additional cleverness must be generated in order to deal with the situation.

Figure 4.25

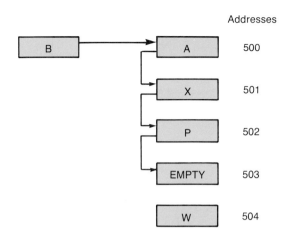

Addresses

Dealing with a collision
in a hashed file. Record
B maps to address 500,
which is occupied.
Successive addresses
are examined until an
empty one is found.
Eventually, the record is
written to location 503.

Suppose that during the process of adding records to the file, record A is written to location 500. At some later time, record B is to be written to the file, but its key value also maps to location 500. Because record A already exists at this location, record B must be written somewhere else—we say that a **collision** has occurred, or that B is a **collision record.**

Rather than simply throwing record B away without telling anybody, the system inspects the next address, 501. If this location is unoccupied, it may be used to store record B. On the other hand, if location 501 contains a record, then location 502 is inspected, and so on, until a vacant address is eventually found and record B is written to that address. Figure 4.25 illustrates the process in which a total of four disk accesses are necessary in order to find a vacant address in which to write record B.

We can now understand the need for having the records distributed as evenly as possible within the blocks of the file, and for making the file considerably larger than the number of records to be stored. Both of these conditions are necessary in order to minimize **clumping,** a situation in which records tend to be grouped together. If clumping is high, then on the average many disk accesses will be needed for each record to be written.

Clumping is minimized when records are distributed as randomly, or uniformly, as possible. Clumping is also affected by the **packing density,** which is the ratio of the total number of records in a file to the maximum record capacity of the file. Figure 4.26 illustrates two files, one with a high packing density, and the other sparsely populated. Clearly, the average number of accesses per write will be higher for the highly packed file than for the other one.

Consider what would happen if the size of our 1400 record file was reduced to exactly the maximum number of records to be written, namely 1000. When the very last of the 1000 records was about to be written to the file, the probability is that 500 disk accesses would be needed in order to find the last vacant address. In fact, even when 50 vacant addresses remained, many accesses would be needed for each new record added.

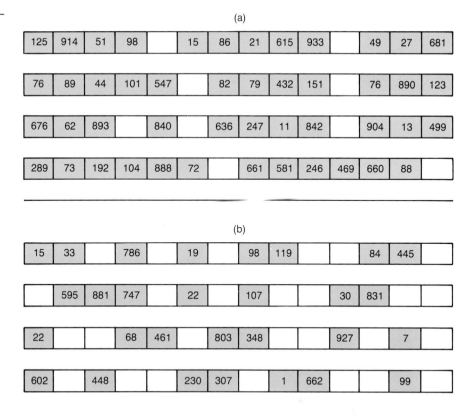

Figure 4.26
(a) Densely and
(b) sparsely packed
files. Disk addresses
are indicated by
rectangles, occupied
locations are indicated
by primary key values.

Figure 4.27 shows the results of an exercise in statistics, illustrating the average number of disk accesses needed to write a record to a file as a function of the packing density of the file. These results are based on the assumption that the hashing algorithm generates a perfectly random set of addresses. From this figure, we can see that beyond a packing density of approximately 0.7, the average number of accesses increases rapidly. Interestingly enough, even with a packing density of 0.7 (70% of the file is filled), less than 4 accesses are needed (on the average) to find an empty location. The data in figure 4.27 can be helpful in designing a direct file so that the system performance does not degrade significantly under normal file usage.

Record retrieval.   The same hashing algorithm that is used for writing records is also used for retrieval. To locate a record, the algorithm is applied to the key value of the desired record. The result is the address from which the record can be read. Note that this process assumes that the key value of the record is known, but this is nothing new. If we wish to retrieve a particular record using *any* random-access method, we must know its key value. (Remember the telephone book analogy?)

Figure 4.27
Average number of disk
accesses needed to
locate a vacant
address, as a function
of packing density.

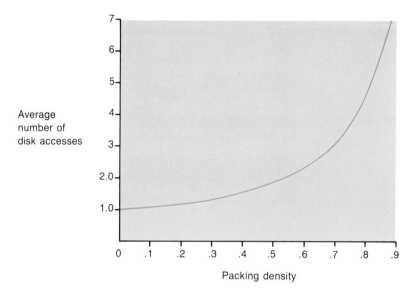

Average
number of
disk accesses

Packing density

The retrieval process is complicated slightly by the existence of collisions. For example, suppose that at some time after many records have been added to the file, we wish to locate record B (the same one used in the previous example, figure 4.25). When the algorithm is applied to the key value of record B, the address 500 is generated. When this address is inspected, record B is found not to be there (recall from the previous example that record A is there). However, by examining those locations immediately beyond 500, record B is eventually located. Figure 4.25 may be reinterpreted to illustrate the retrieval process: beginning with the address generated by the hashing algorithm, successive locations are inspected for the desired record.

Defining empty records. From the discussion, it should be clear that the system must be able to distinguish an empty location in the file from one that contains a record. In order for this to be possible, each location on the disk must contain a special "flag" byte. This byte may take on one of two values: filled or empty, which denote either the presence or absence of a record. When the file is established, the flag byte of every location is set to empty. When a record is added to the file, its flag byte is set to filled, and when a record is deleted from the file, the byte is set to empty.

Using nonnumeric keys. The simplest kind of keys to which hashing algorithms can be applied are those containing numeric values. However, algorithms can easily be devised to handle nonnumeric keys as well, because all data is in reality stored as binary information in the computer. For example, consider a group of nonnumeric characters that make up the value of a NAME field. Each

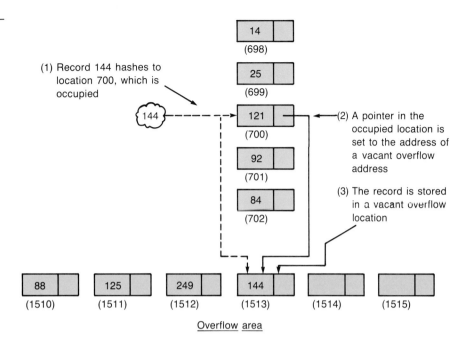

(1) Record 144 hashes to location 700, which is occupied

14
(698)

25
(699)

121
(700)

92
(701)

84
(702)

(2) A pointer in the occupied location is set to the address of a vacant overflow address

(3) The record is stored in a vacant overflow location

88
(1510)

125
(1511)

249
(1512)

144
(1513)

(1514)

(1515)

Overflow area

of these characters is in fact stored as a separate binary number, and the concatenation of all of the characters in the field produces a single binary number. For instance, the value of "Boston" is equivalent to the following binary number:

$$01000010010011110101001101010100010011111101001110 .$$

The equivalent decimal number is 667983847978, which can be hashed just like any other numeric key. The trick is to get the computer to agree to look at the same piece of data in two different ways (alphanumeric and numeric). This is nearly always possible for the determined programmer.

Other hashing algorithms.   Many different schemes have been tried for hashing a set of key values into a specific range of numeric values. The simple division method already discussed, along with various minor modifications, seems to be about as good as any other.

Alternative methods for handling collisions.   Several methods have been used to handle the problem of collisions, in addition to the method previously discussed. One of the more popular techniques is to establish an overflow area, which is used for storing collision records. Figure 4.28 illustrates the process, which works in the following way.

Suppose that record 144 is to be written to a hashed file, and further suppose that its key value hashes to location 700, which is already occupied by record 121. A vacant location is found in the overflow area (assume that it is location 1513), and record 144 is written there. In addition, a pointer to location 1513 is

Figure 4.29
Storing an additional
record to the file shown
in figure 4.28.

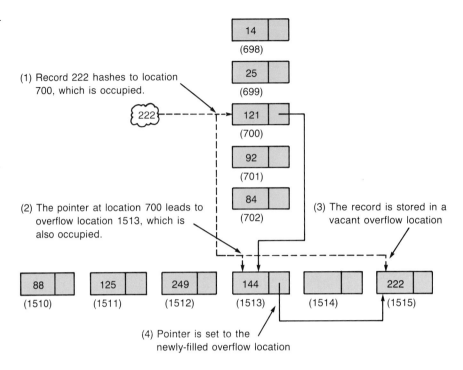

(1) Record 222 hashes to location
700, which is occupied.

(2) The pointer at location 700 leads to
overflow location 1513, which is
also occupied.

(3) The record is stored in a
vacant overflow location

(4) Pointer is set to the
newly-filled overflow location

stored in a special field in record 121. This pointer contains the actual address of location 1513, which may be used in subsequent retrievals of record 144.

Let us further suppose that at some later time, record 222 is to be written to the file, and that its key value also hashes to location 700, as shown in figure 4.29. As before, this location is occupied, so record 222 would also be written to a vacant overflow location (assume it to be 1515). In addition, a pointer to this address would be stored in the pointer field of record 144. These steps are summarized below:

1. Record 222 hashes to location 700, which is found to be occupied.
2. The pointer in location 700 leads to overflow location 1513, which is filled. This latter location is noted, meanwhile:
3. A vacant overflow location is found, into which record 222 is written. The address of this location (1515) is then written into the pointer at location 1513.

If, at a later time, either record 144 or 222 must be retrieved, the record can be located by duplicating the paths established when the records were stored. For example, suppose that record 144 is to be retrieved. As before, its key value is hashed, which leads to location 700. Upon examination, it is seen that record 144 does not live there. However, the overflow pointer in location 700 points to address 1513, where record 144 is found.

If record 222 must be retrieved, the above process is duplicated, with one final necessary step: location 700 is first examined, leading to overflow location 1513, which in this case does not contain record 222. However, its pointer leads to location 1515, where record 222 is finally located.

The group of records and pointers described above is called a **linked list.** Structures of this type are extremely useful, and they will be discussed in more detail later in the text.

Many variations on the the hashing techniques discussed above have been implemented. One of the most common is to associate a bucket with each hashing address, which is large enough to contain several records. This approach tends to reduce the average number of disk accesses needed to find a vacant spot into which to write a record.

Summary

Sequential files allow rapid retrieval of a file of records, but only in the specific order in which records were originally written to the file. On the other hand, any record within a random-access file may be retrieved rapidly, regardless of its position in the file. The two main types of random-access files are indexed and direct. An Indexed Sequential Access Method (ISAM) file is a special type of indexed file.

A record field, or combination of fields, that is used as the basis for any type of random-access method is called a key. Keys may be unique or nonunique. Keys may also be either primary or secondary. A file may have only one primary key, which is the basis for giving unique "names" to the records of the file. Any key other than the primary is called a secondary key, and any number of secondary keys may be defined for a file. Primary keys, which must be unique, are the basis of both direct and ISAM files; secondary keys are the basis for any other type of index.

The objective of each type of random-access file is the same: to convert the key value into the disk address of one or more records, which may then be retrieved.

Indexes may be either unique or nonunique, depending on the nature of the field(s) used as the basis for the index. A file may have many associated indexes, depending on the needs of the user. An index on a particular key has two main purposes: (1) to gain random access to file records on the basis of that key; and (2) to access all of the file records in the sequence based on the key. Each index carries a cost in terms of the additional storage space required.

ISAM files are a special type of indexed files, combining some of the best features of both sequential and indexed files. An ISAM file significantly reduces the amount of required disk space for the index, by maintaining records in key-sequence order on each track of the file. A primary key is the basis for the construction of an ISAM file.

Any number of secondary indexes may be defined on an ISAM file, in addition to the main ISAM index.

Direct files, which are based on primary keys, offer the fastest way to retrieve individual records. The most common types of direct files use either hashing or linear addressing methods. These files do not allow retrieval of records in any particular sequence; consequently, secondary indexes are frequently used in conjunction with them.

Files that use linear addressing tend to use the least amount of extra disk space of any random-access method because there is a one-to-one correspondence between each record key and a disk address. Also, these files can grow to any size, within the limits of available disk space. The biggest disadvantage with linear addressing files is that primary key values are usually assigned by the DBMS, and these values change whenever the file is reorganized, often imposing extra bookkeeping on the user. File reorganization must be done periodically to free up space left vacant by record deletions.

Direct files that utilize hashing methods have the advantage of allowing any type of data elements to be defined by the user as the primary key. In addition, these values may remain unchanged during the life cyle of the file.

The size of a hashed file is fixed at the time the file is created, and that disk space must be reserved at that time. If the packing density of a hashed file grows beyond a certain limit, a completely new, larger file must be defined, and the records transferred. There is always a certain amount of wasted space associated with a hashed file in order to maintain reasonably short record access times. Although this waste may amount to over 20%, it is still significantly less than the amount of space required by most types of indexes.

Table 4.1 lists the more important merits of the various types of random-access methods.

All of the random-access methods described in this chapter are normally carried out either by the operating system, the DBMS, or a combination of both. The user of a set of database files is often unaware of the techniques being employed on his or her behalf. Nevertheless, for the user who has more than a casual interest, an understanding of these methods can be extremely valuable in using a database management system to its fullest potential.

Table 4.1

Comparison of Different File Types

	Sequential file	Indexed* file	ISAM file	Hashed file	Linear addressing file
Allows RANDOM ACCESS to records	No	Yes	Yes	Yes	Yes
Allows SEQUENTIAL ACCESS to records	Yes	Yes**	Yes**	Yes**	Yes**
Uses PRIMARY KEYS as the basis for record access	No	Sometimes	Yes	Yes	Yes
Uses SECONDARY KEYS as the basis for record access	No	Sometimes	No	No	No
SECONDARY INDEXES may be used with this file type, in addition to the major access method	No	Yes	Yes	Yes	Yes
Relative speed of random access to records	—	Fast	Moderate	Very fast	Very fast
Amount of **additional** disk space required by the access method (indexes, etc)	—	May be very high	Moderate	Moderate	Minimal
File size may grow as required	Yes	Yes	Yes	No	Yes

*The term *indexed file* is general: *any* type of random-access file may also have secondary indexes. An ordinary index may be based on either a primary or secondary key.

**In sequence by key value.

Terminology

binary search
bucket
clumping
collision
collision record
concatenated key
direct file
disk access
file reorganization
fixed-length record
hashed file
hashing
index
indexed file
ISAM file

key
linear addressing
multi-level index
overflow area
overflow record
packing density
pointer
primary key
random-access file
secondary index
secondary key
sequential file
sequential search
symbolic address

Review Questions

1. Discuss the basic differences between sequential and random-access files.
2. What types of secondary-storage devices are used for sequential files? For random-access files?
3. Give some examples of real-life situations in which rapid response time from random-access files is important.
4. Review the various ways in which record keys are categorized.
5. What types of keys can be used as the basis of an index? Are there any types of keys that cannot be used?
6. Explain how an index works in conjunction with a file directory to generate the physical disk address of a record.
7. What is the basic difference between an ordinary index and the primary index of an ISAM file?
8. What is the difference between the two types of direct files: hashed and linear addressing?
9. What is the biggest advantage of direct file that uses linear addressing?
10. When and why must linear addressing files be reorganized?

Problems

1. A sequential file contains 150 records, each of which is 200 bytes long. They are to be written to an empty, single-surface disk device with the following characteristics:

> Track capacity: 5000 bytes
> Block length: 1000 bytes
> Block header: 25 bytes

Data is written to this disk starting with track 00, then 01, and so on.
   a. How many blocks will the file occupy?
   b. How many tracks will the file occupy?
2. Outline the contents of the directory for the file in problem #1.
3. A file containing student data has the following fields:

      STUDENT_NAME, CITY,
      STUDENT_ID, STATE, STREET, ZIP

   a. What choices are possible for a primary key? Justify each of your suggestions.
   b. Give some examples of possible secondary keys for this file, including at least one concatenated key.
   c. Under what conditions might CITY + STATE be a more reasonable choice for a secondary key than CITY by itself?
   d. If CITY + STATE were chosen as a concatenated key, give an example of a value for this key (be very precise).
4. Using the CUSTOMERS file discussed in this chapter, outline the contents of an index based on the STATE field.
5. Again referring to the CUSTOMERS file, suppose that you plan to output reports on a regular basis, containing the following data: a list of all customer names, sorted first by state, then by city, and finally by customer name. Design an index to facilitate the generation of these reports.
6. Suppose that a simple tabular index exists with exactly 100 entries.
   a. If sequential searching is used to locate individual entries, on the average how many entries must be examined in order to locate a particular one?
   b. Suppose, instead, that binary searching is used to locate entries. Estimate the average number of entries that must be examined to locate a record. Calculate this estimate by using the binary search method for each of the following situations, counting the number of necessary examinations in each case. Then average your results.
      (1) A record at the end of the index
      (2) A record at the beginning of the index
      (3) A record in the middle of the index
7. Suppose that a multi-level index is to be designed for a file that contains 10,000 records. Each index entry (key value plus address) occupies exactly 10 bytes. Each disk block has a capacity of 1000 bytes of data (excluding the block header).
   a. If each bucket is designed to contain up to 10 entries (a key value plus address).
      (1) How many index levels are required?
      (2) How many buckets are required on each level?

b. Suppose that the bucket size is changed to accomodate up to 200 entries. In this case, What is the answer to each of the questions in part a?

8. How many disk accesses are needed to locate the address of any particular record in parts a and b of the above problem?

9. Suppose that the CUSTOMERS records are written to an ISAM file. For this file, each primary-key value requires 6 bytes, and each relative address occupies 4 bytes. The file contains 10,000 200-byte records. Each track can hold a total of 20,000 data bytes, or 100 CUSTOMERS records. Each data track has a corresponding overflow track. Estimate the amount of space occupied by the ISAM index. Compare this result with the amount of space needed for the index in problem 7.

10. A file that uses linear addressing consists of 100 byte records. The block length of the disk device is set at 2000 bytes, of which 25 are for the block header. Assuming that the primary-key values are sequential, starting with 1,2,3, and so on, what is the relative address of the record with a key value of 225?

11. A direct file is to be established, using hashing. Each record will be 250 bytes in length, and the maximum number of records in the file will be 500. The primary key field is a 4-digit integer.
    a. Approximately how much disk space must be reserved for the file?
    b. Devise a hashing algorithm for this file, assuming that the primary key values are more-or-less randomly distributed.
    c. Using the algorithm from part b, calculate the relative address generated for a key value of 1255.
    d. Suppose that for the first few hundred records in the file, the keys are assigned sequential values, starting with 1. What relative addresses will be generated by your hashing algorithm? Is this satisfactory? Explain your answer.
    e. Devise an alternate hashing algorithm for the situation in part d.

12. Referring to the file in question 11, suppose that 250 records have been written to the file. What is the average number of disk accesses that will be needed to write each of the next few records?

13. The database management system dBASE III uses the DELETE RECORD n command for deleting a particular record from a file, where n is the primary-key value. Even after this command is issued, record n may still be accessed, although a *deleted* flag is set for the record. When a PACK command is issued, two things occur: (1) all deleted records are gone forever; and (2) many records have their RECORD NUMBER values changed. Speculate on the type of random-access technique employed by dBASE III.

Chapter Five

Searching and Reporting

Introduction

A great deal of the power and usefulness of database management derives from the flexibility with which data may be searched. The result of exploring a database, often referred to as the **search result,** might be a single record, or it could be an entire database, depending on the specifications chosen for the search.

Many database inquiries are conducted on line, being initiated interactively from a terminal or microcomputer. A user interested in finding specific data would make a very specific query. Alternatively, a user might wish to "browse around" in a database, making a number of fairly general queries in an attempt to zero in on some vaguely specified information. A large database might require a great deal of searching in order to obtain the desired information.

In contrast to on-line explorations, batch programs are frequently the source of a large number of repetitive, often related queries that are made against a database. These programs are frequently run on a routine basis, producing a variety of results for many different purposes.

The other side of the search coin is the ability to view a search result in different ways. This is commonly termed **database reporting.** The degree of flexibility in this respect is also a measure of the power of a DBMS. A simple report might amount to no more than a crude display of the raw data resulting from a database search. On the other hand, a sophisticated report could be a carefully massaged digest of a search result, presented in a thoughtful and interesting manner.

In general, a **report** is any type of display of a search result. It might appear on the screen of a terminal or computer, or it might be a hard-copy printout. The report could consist of a simple field-by-field display of each record in the search result, or it could be the output of a carefully designed program. Often, this type of program will involve the reformatting of the search result into information which is of direct interest to the user. For example, HOURLY_WAGE_RATE data might be combined with HOURS_ON_THE_JOB data to produce WEEKLY_PAY information, which would be used by the payroll department to generate weekly paychecks.

Figure 5.1
The process of
searching and
reporting.

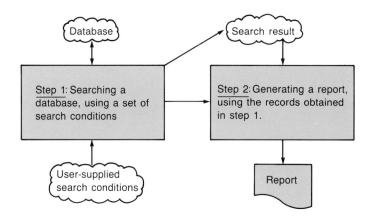

The relationship between database searching and reporting can be described in terms of a two-step process, as illustrated in figure 5.1. The first step is the search itself, which produces a search result consisting of those records satisfying a specified set of **search conditions.** The search result usually contains one or more database records. However, if the search conditions are too stringent, no records may be found and the search result is empty.

Regardless of how information is displayed, the same general concept applies: a report is a set of output based on a search result, and the search result is in turn the outcome of a query made against a database.

Although database management systems vary in their strengths and weaknesses in searching and reporting, most of them have at least a fair degree of power in both respects. In this chapter we will explore the various ways in which databases may be searched and reports generated.

In order to illustrate the various ideas pertinent to database searching and reporting, many examples are used in this chapter, and most of these are based on dBASE III syntax. Those examples that do not conform to dBASE III will be specifically noted. It is important not to miss the forest for the trees while studying the various examples in this chapter. The main purpose of these is to illustrate the types of searching and reporting operations that are possible with database systems— the fact that dBASE III syntax is used is incidental.

As a final note, the reader should recognize that the examples in this chapter are representative only. Searching and reporting capabilities vary a great deal from one DBMS to another, and the examples presented here by no means include all of the possibilities available with various DBMS's.

A **database search** may be defined as any type of probe or inspection of a database. It is carried out in response to a user-generated query command that normally contains the following parts:

1. The name of the file to be searched
2. The **range** of records to be searched, that is, which records within the file are to be accessed. This is often the entire set of records in the file. It may, however, be a subset of these
3. The **search conditions** to be used. This is a set of conditions that must be met by each record that is to be included in the search result

Search results may be generated in two entirely different ways, depending on the nature of the particular DBMS and the type of search request made. One type of search generates the entire search result at one time, usually as a set of record addresses. After this set has been generated, the report is produced, manipulating the entire set of records in whatever way is necessary for the purposes of the report. Figure 5.1 directly applies to this type of search, which is generally used when a good deal of record reformatting is needed for a report.

The second type of search deals with each record individually. That is, as each record is located during a search, it is formatted if necessary, and then immediately output. This type of search is most common when simple types of reports are required.

A great deal of database searching is done in the interactive mode, usually with a user making queries at a terminal or microcomputer, and this mode will be the focal point for our discussions. Searching in the batch mode will be discussed in chapter 6, which deals with programming in the database environment.

In this section, we shall examine the various types of searches that are most commonly used. We begin with a description of simple sequential searches, and then proceed to the use of indexes. Complex searches will also be discussed.

Sequential Searching

Sequential searching is one of the most common types of searches. It often (but not always) starts at the beginning of a file, and each record in the file is in turn examined. If it meets the set of search conditions specified by the user, it is included in the search result.

NAME	STREET	CITY	STATE	ZIP	PHONE	CREDIT	BALANCE
Smith, Jennifer	123 Hayes St.	Berkeley	CA	94704	(415) 654-1391	5000	0.00
Harris, Peter	19 Taraval St.	Oakland	CA	94620	(415) 565-1985	1000	155.75
James, Jesse	39 Trout Gulch	Newark	CA	95061	(818) 232-3987	5000	532.87
Norman, Samuel	339 40th Ave.	Oakland	CA	11123	(415) 565-3492	0	0.00
LaRue, Elaine	7244 52nd St.	Berkeley	CA	94169	(415) 654-9641	1000	955.00
Clark, Kent	7 Hidden Way	Pittsburg	CA	94882	(408) 974-2581	1000	395.15
Gregory, Robert	357 Mission St.	Berkeley	CA	94704	(415) 654-0127	5000	1857.32
Drue, Ellen	55 Pork Place	Albany	CA	94666	(415) 335-9741	10000	3527.98
Smith, Alfred	18 Center St.	Oakland	CA	95543	(415) 853-1596	1000	0.00
Andersen, Tim	9532 Clark Place	Albany	CA	94661	(415) 335-9264	5000	327.13
Baker, James	1 Cyle Road	Berkeley	CA	94704	(415) 654-4826	10000	125.15

Figure 5.2 Contents of the CUSTOMERS file.

A Simple Search

Consider the file of CUSTOMERS records shown in figure 5.2, and suppose that we wish to generate a search result consisting of records for all customers who are located in the city of Oakland. Also, we would like to have the entire search result displayed on the computer monitor. The following database commands accomplish this:

(1)

> USE CUSTOMERS
> DISPLAY FOR CITY = 'Oakland'

The first command specifies the name of the file to be searched. The second command serves two different purposes. First, it specifies the search conditions to be used: the CITY field must contain the value 'Oakland'. The DISPLAY part of the command indicates that the search result is to be sent to the standard output device, usually the screen or printer. Note that implicit in this command is the fact that the *entire* file is to be searched.

The DISPLAY command is especially useful because it serves both to find a particular set of records and also to output them. Many DBMS's have a similar type of search-and-output capability. With this type of command, each record is displayed as soon as it is located. However, the user has little or no control over the format of the output. When more control is required, such as for sophisticated types of displays, other types of commands must be used.

Complex Search Conditions

The preceding example uses a search condition involving only a single field, namely CITY. It is possible to specify more complicated search conditions that involve several fields. In the following examples, we shall omit the USE command, focussing instead on the commands that specify the search conditions.

Suppose that we wish to find the records for those customers living in Oakland and who also owe more than $500. This could be accomplished by performing two separate searches, one on the CITY field (CITY = 'Oakland') and the other on BALANCE (BALANCE > 500). The two search results would then be compared and the common records extracted. This would be a time-consuming process, and it is usually unnecessary because of the ability to specify complex search conditions. The following *single* search command accomplishes our goal:

(2)   DISPLAY FOR (CITY = 'Oakland') .AND. (BALANCE > 500)

We could extend the search for delinquent customers to include those who live in the city of Berkeley as:

(3)   DISPLAY FOR (CITY = 'Oakland') .AND. (BALANCE > 500)
.OR. (CITY = 'Berkeley') .AND. (BALANCE > 500)

This command specifies that records satisfying either of the parenthesized conditions are to be included in the search result.

Boolean and relational operators. The preceding two examples of search conditions each makes use of **Boolean** and **relational operators,** which form the backbone of complex search conditions. Although the formal names for these operators are a bit intimidating, they can be used quite easily with a little practice.

Boolean operators are used to form complex search conditions by combining simpler ones. They are **.AND., .OR.,** and **.NOT.** With some DBMS's, they are written simply as **AND, OR,** and **NOT.**

The meanings of the .OR. and .AND. operators are best explained by examples. Consider the search command shown in (2). It has the following precise meaning: display a record only if *both* of the following conditions are met:

    The CITY field contains the value 'Oakland'
and
    The value of the BALANCE field is greater than 500.

On the other hand, consider the following search command:

(4)   DISPLAY FOR (CITY = 'Oakland') .OR. (BALANCE > 500)

In this case a record will be displayed if *either* of the following conditions is true:

    The CITY field contains the value 'Oakland'
or
    The value of the BALANCE field is greater than 500.

When using combinations of the Boolean operators, parentheses should be used liberally in order to eliminate possible ambiguities. There is no penalty for using extra parentheses. It is also important to make sure that the search condition as written truly describes what is wanted. For example, consider the following search command:

(5)
$$\text{DISPLAY FOR CITY} = \text{'Oakland' .OR. CITY} = \text{'Berkeley'}$$
$$\text{.AND. STATE} = \text{'CA'}$$

Because the search condition is written without any parentheses, it could be interpreted in two ways:

(6a)
(CITY = 'Oakland').OR.(CITY = 'Berkeley'.AND.STATE = 'CA')

or

(6b)
(CITY = 'Oakland'.OR.CITY = 'Berkeley').AND.(STATE = 'CA')

If (6a) represents the correct interpretation, the search result would consist of all records for which either (1) the city is Oakland *or* (2) the city is Berkeley and the state is CA. On the other hand, if (6b) represents the correct interpretation, the search result would be those records for which (1) the city is either Oakland or Berkeley *and* (2) the state is CA.

Which is the correct interpretation? The answer is that *we cannot know,* because different DBMS's will interpret the command in (5) differently. Therefore, parentheses must be used to guarantee that the search condition clearly expresses what is actually desired.

The **.NOT.** operator is used when it is convenient to express a search condition in terms of **negation.** For example, suppose that we wish to find all of the CUSTOMERS records for those customers who do not live in Oakland. This can be most easily done by making use of the .NOT. operator as follows:

(7)
DISPLAY FOR .NOT.(CITY = 'Oakland')

The presence of the .NOT. operator in a condition reverses the sense of whatever is inside the parentheses immediately following the operator. The .NOT. operator is particularly useful when the logic of a situation tells you exactly what is not wanted. For example, suppose that you want to display the records of all delinquent customers living in any city except Oakland or Berkeley. The search condition for finding the reverse situation, namely any customer that does live in either Oakland or Berkeley, is written as

(8)
DISPLAY FOR (City = 'Oakland') .OR. (CITY = 'Berkeley')

Table 5.1

The Family of Relational Operators

Operator Symbol	Interpretation
=	Is equal to
<>	Is not equal to
<	Is less than
>	Is greater than
<=	Is less than or equal to
>=	Is greater than or equal to

Consequently, we can find those not living in either city by negating the condition in (8):

(9)
$$\text{DISPLAY FOR .NOT.((CITY = 'Oakland') .OR.}$$
$$\text{(CITY = 'Berkeley'))}$$

It is important to parenthesize the entire search condition in (9) to ensure that the sense of it is exactly reversed.

The search conditions used in (2) and (3) make use of the ">" operator to express "greater than." This **relational operator** is one of a family of six, which are extremely useful in developing search conditions. Table 5.1 lists all of these operators.

Relational operators may be used alone to form simple search conditions, or in conjunction with Boolean operators to form complex conditions. For example, the following search command could be used to locate all delinquent customers:

(10)
$$\text{DISPLAY FOR BALANCE} > 500$$

As an example of a more complex condition using both relational and Boolean operators, suppose that we wish to produce a list of all of the customers living in Oakland with an outstanding balance between \$100 and \$500. We can develop a search condition by first noting that each record must satisfy both of two *independent* conditions—one deals with the CITY field, and the other with the BALANCE field. Thus, the query can be written in outline form as follows:

(11)
$$\text{DISPLAY FOR} \quad \text{[Condition involving CITY]}$$
$$\text{.AND.} \quad \text{[Condition involving BALANCE]}$$

The next step is to expand on each of the two conditions. The CITY condition is straightforward and is written as:

(12)
$$\text{(CITY = 'Oakland')}$$

The BALANCE condition is more complicated, involving two subconditions. It can be written in many ways, one of which is as follows:

(13a)

$$(BALANCE >= 100) .AND. (BALANCE <= 500)$$

Notice that this condition involves the two relational operators "$<=$" (less than or equal to) and "$>=$" (greater than or equal to). Another possibility for writing the condition is the following:

(13b)

$$(BALANCE > 100) .AND. (BALANCE < 500)$$

which is a slight modification of (13a). Which is correct? The answer depends on whether the search result is to include records whose BALANCE field contains exact values of either 500 or 100. If we choose to include those records, then the condition in (13a) should be used. Otherwise, (13b) should be used. The final search command is constructed by substituting the conditions in (12) and either (13a) or (13b) into (11):

(14)

DISPLAY FOR (CITY = 'Oakland') .AND.
((BALANCE $>=$ 100) .AND. (BALANCE $<=$ 500))

Although relational operators are most often used in conjunction with numeric fields, they can also be used with nonnumeric fields. For example, consider again the problem of finding all of the records for customers who do not live in the city of Oakland. One search command to accomplish this is given in (7), but the same result can also be obtained using the following query:

(15)

DISPLAY FOR CITY $<>$ 'Oakland'

The relational operators "$=$" and "$<>$" are the ones most frequently used with nonnumeric data. The other operators may also be used with non-numeric fields, but with a great deal of care. We will not discuss their use here.

Many DBMS's place few, if any, restrictions on the degree of complexity that may exist in a single search command. Conditions may be constructed using virtually any combination of the Boolean and relational operators, and often there may be several ways to write the same query.

Processing an Entire File

Frequently, we may wish to list the entire contents of a file. This is easily done with some DBMS's by simply not including a search condition in the basic search command. For example, the complete CUSTOMERS file could be output with the simple command:

(16)

DISPLAY ALL

The FOR phrase has been omitted to indicate that no search condition is to be used, and the ALL phrase specifies that all records in the file are to be scanned.

Disadvantages of Sequential Searching

The use of complex search conditions combined with sequential searching is a powerful tool, and it can be used to retrieve virtually any desired subset of records. With large files, however, the searching time may prove to be quite lengthy because a great many disk accesses will be needed to process the entire file. For example, if a floppy disk file contained 1000 100-byte records, it would require several minutes to read the entire file. Often, the use of indexes can significantly reduce the search time. The next section deals with this subject.

Indexed Searching

Indexes may be of great assistance in file searching and in this respect they have two primary uses. First, and most significantly, an indexed search is often enormously faster than the equivalent sequential search. The second use of indexes is to generate reports in which the records are sequenced with respect to the values of one or more fields. For example, we may wish to display the contents of the CUSTOMERS file in sequence by customer name. This could be accomplished with the use of an index.

In this section, we shall explore the various ways in which indexes are used for database searching and reporting.

Index Creation

Often, a good deal of judgment must be exercised in deciding whether or not to create an index for a particular application. In making this decision, the user must balance the benefits of improving the response time during searches against the amount of additional disk space needed to store the index. Each of these factors is discussed in the following paragraphs.

Estimating the size of an index.   Indexes occupy disk space, and it is important to be able to estimate the extent to which an index affects the total amount of available space. For example, in one situation the creation of a particular index may have a negligible effect on available disk resources. In another situation, the presence of an index could mean the difference between whether or not there would be room to store additional data records.

As an example, consider the CUSTOMERS file shown in figure 2.7. Referring also to figure 2.3, we find that each record occupies a total of 100 bytes. If we assume that the file contains 1200 records, then the entire file occupies approximately 120,000 bytes of disk storage. Let us also assume that this file is stored on a 5-1/4 inch floppy disk, with a total data-storage capacity of 190,000 bytes. Suppose that we wish to create an index on a NAME field, which is 25 bytes long. As a very rough first estimate of the size of the index, we assume that it is in simple tabular form, as discussed in chapter 4.

Each entry in the NAME index consists of a KEY value and a pointer, the latter being either a relative or physical address. The size of each index entry is then given as:

(17)

$$\text{Entry length (bytes)} = \text{KEY length} + \text{ADDRESS length}$$

Typically, an address occupies two bytes, and the KEY value contains a value from the NAME field, which in this case is 25 bytes long. Consequently, each entry in the index occupies 27 bytes. Since the file contains 1200 records, the total size of the index is given as:

(18)

$$
\begin{aligned}
\text{Index size} &= |\text{\# records in file}| \times \text{entry length} \\
&= 1200 \times 27 = 32{,}400 \text{ bytes.}
\end{aligned}
$$

This estimate is inadequate because indexes are invariably built in multi-level structures, as illustrated in figure 4.12. As a first approximation, the size of a multi-level index can be taken to be twice that of the equivalent simple tabular index. Therefore, the total size of the NAME index calculates to 2 x 32,400, or approximately 65,000 bytes.

Since the CUSTOMERS file itself occupies approximately 120,000 bytes on the disk out of a total of 190,000, then the addition of the NAME index would come close to filling up the disk. Because of the approximate nature of the calculations, it might be necessary to build the index to see exactly how much space it occupies and at the same time determine whether the remaining disk space, if any, is sufficient for anticipated needs.

As a contrasting example, suppose that this same file contains another field, STATE, which is 12 bytes long, and we wish to create another index on this field. Since STATE occupies only two bytes per record, then each entry in the index would consist of only 4 bytes (2 for the STATE value plus 2 for the ADDRESS). The total size of the index is then estimated as follows:

$$
\begin{aligned}
\text{Index size} &= 2 \times |\text{\# records in file}| \times \text{entry length} \\
&= 2 \times 1200 \times 4 = 9600 \text{ bytes.}
\end{aligned}
$$

The addition of a STATE index would put much less of a strain on the disk resources than would the NAME index.

When an index may be created. Many DBMS's allow the ad hoc creation of an index at any time during the life of a file. Others allow the specification of indexes only at the time the file is first created. When the latter applies, a great deal of thought must be given to which indexes are to be created, since it may be difficult to change this decision later.

A system that allows the ad hoc creation and deletion of indexes gives the user a good deal of flexibility, in that indexes may be created temporarily as needed.

For example, suppose that we wish to do extensive searching on the CUS-TOMERS file using the CITY and BALANCE fields. Indexes for these two fields could be created just prior to the searching process. At the conclusion of the search, the indexes could be destroyed.

The ability to create indexes at any time gives the user the best of both worlds. The indexes provide the advantage of reduced searching time, yet may exist only when needed, thus reducing the overall requirements for disk storage. In fact, a DBMS clever enough to *automatically* build temporary indexes as needed during a search is conceivable.

The ad hoc creation of an index frequently involves only one or two DBMS commands which must specify three items:

1. The fact that an index is to be created
2. The name of the field or fields to be indexed
3. The name of the file in which the index is to be stored

Consider the following commands:

USE   CUSTOMERS

INDEX   ON NAME TO NAMEINDX

(19)

The command INDEX specifies that an index is to be created. The identifier NAME specifies which field is to be indexed; and NAMEINDX specifies the name of the file to contain the index. Obviously, there can be many variations on this syntactic theme, and any particular syntax that can be imagined has probably been adopted by at least one DBMS.

Timing considerations. The amount of time required to create an index for a file is considerably greater than that necessary to simply do a sequential read of the entire file. This is because the creation of an index involves many tasks in addition to reading the file. As each record is read, an entry for it must be placed in proper sequence in the index. Also, the growing index resides on disk, and many disk accesses may be necessary as each new entry is made to the index. Thus, whereas a sequential read of a particular file may take one minute, the building of an index on the file could take many times longer.

Suppose that we wish to do a number of similar searches of a particular file, and we wish to decide whether or not building an index to assist in the searches will result in a net savings of time. The following analysis will help answer this question. We begin with the following definitions:

(20)

N_S = Approximate number of searches to be made

T_S = Average time required for a particular sequential search

T_X = Time required to build the index to assist in the searches

The quantity T_S is essentially equal to the time needed to do a sequential read of the file because the CPU time required to process each record is negligible compared to the time needed to read the record. Therefore, making the following additional definitions:

(21)

$$T_{RR} = \text{Average time to read one record from the file in sequential mode}$$
$$N_R = \text{Number of records in the file}$$

then:

(22)

$$T_S = N_R \times T_{RR}$$

In order to justify the building of an index, the net time for building the index must be less than the total time required to do all of the searches. That is,

(23)

$$T_X < N_S \times T_S$$

Incorporating (22) into (23),

(24)

$$T_X < (N_S \times N_R \times T_{RR})$$

As a first approximation, the time required to build an index is proportional to the number of records in the file:

$$T_X = T_{XR} \times N_R$$

where:

$$T_{XR} = \text{Average time needed to add one record to the index}$$

(25)

The quantity T_{XR} is not truly a constant since it depends to some extent on the actual number of records being indexed. In fact, it may be found by experimenting with the DBMS by measuring the time needed to build indexes for files of different sizes. Substituting (25) into (24), and solving for N_S, we obtain the expression for the conditions under which it is advantageous to build an index to assist in a set of searches:

(26)

$$N_S > T_{XR}/T_{RR}$$

The quantities T_{XR} and T_{RR} may be found experimentally for any particular system.

As an example, consider a file containing 5000 records. Average times have been measured for reading and indexing records, as follows:

$$T_{RR} = 0.1 \text{ seconds per record}$$
$$T_{XR} = 0.6 \text{ seconds per record}$$

Using the values in (26), we obtain

$$N_S > 6$$

Thus, if we plan to do fewer than 6 searches of the file, creating an index will not be particularly helpful.

Using Indexes

Invisible indexes. There is a growing trend among many of the more sophisticated DBMS's to allow the user to treat indexed and non-indexed searches exactly the same. That is, the user specifies what (s)he wants, in terms of a general search-command syntax. It is up to the DBMS to decide how best to obtain the search result—if an index exists that could assist in a particular search, the DBMS recognizes the fact and makes use of the index in the best possible way. This approach is advantageous to the user, who must learn only one type of search syntax.

Specialized commands for indexed searches. The degree of sophistication described in the preceding paragraph has not yet penetrated the majority of DBMS's, most of which have separate commands for indexed and non-indexed searching. The commands needed to affect an indexed search must contain the following information:

1. The name of the database file to be queried
2. The fact that an indexed search is to be carried out
3. The set of search conditions to be used

For example, a set of dBASE III commands for performing an indexed search of the CUSTOMERS file is:

(27)

```
USE   CUSTOMERS
SET   INDEX TO CITY
FIND 'New York'
```

The first command specifies the file to be accessed. The second command "attaches" the CITY index to the CUSTOMERS file. The last command defines the search condition, namely (CITY = 'New York'). By contrast, the equivalent commands for a sequential search would be:

(28)

```
USE       CUSTOMERS
DISPLAY   FOR CITY = 'New York'
```

Figure 5.3
The steps in an indexed
search, using dBASE III
to find all entries with a
value of "BERKELEY."

```
                            Key value        Address

                                 .               .
                                 .               .
                            ANAHEIM            1243
                     ①⇥ →   BERKELEY           3329
                         ⤷   BERKELEY           3947
                     ②⇥ →   BERKELEY           2947
                         ⤷   BERKELEY           0274
                         ⤷   BERKELEY           5924
                            COLUSA             9872
                            COLUSA             9756
                                 .               .
                                 .               .
```

① First entry in the index
   is located by the DBMS
   index-searching strategy

② Successive entries fol-
   lowed until end of ap-
   propriate entries is
   reached

The type of search result that is generated by an indexed-search command depends on the nature of the DBMS. For example, the set of dBASE III commands shown in (27) finds only the first record in the file that satisfies the search condition. The following group of dBASE III commands would be needed to display all of the appropriate records:

(29)

USE	CUSTOMERS
SET	INDEX TO CITY
FIND	'New York'
DISPLAY	NEXT 999;
	WHILE CITY = 'New York'

As discussed, the first three commands serve to locate the first appropriate record by searching the index. The last command instructs the system to examine successive records *in the order dictated by the index,* displaying each record until one is found that does not satisfy the search criteria.

To recapitulate, the CITY index is used in two different ways by the commands in (29), as illustrated in figure 5.3. First, the FIND command initiates a search of the index, in order to locate the first appropriate record. Secondly, the DISPLAY NEXT command causes the outputting of records pointed to by successive entries in the index. The logic of these commands is quite different from that of the non-indexed-search commands shown in (28).

It is worth noting that in executing the DISPLAY command in (29) the DBMS is exhibiting a degree of intelligence by noting that the CITY index has been accessed. Therefore, the DISPLAY command is used in conjunction with the index, rather than simply accessing the file sequentially, as it would do in the absence of the index.

The method described for performing the indexed search in (29) is by no means universal. With some DBMS's, the type of command sequence shown in (27)

Figure 5.4

An index based on
STATE and NAME
fields. Each key value is
the concatenation of
values from both fields.

```
        Key value              Address

                "
                "
        CAAndersen, Tim          2211
        CABaker, James           3322
        CAClark, Kent            6654
                "
                "
```

would generate a search result consisting of *all* records satisfying the search condition. The advantage of this approach is that fewer commands are required to locate the desired records.

Generating Sequential Lists

Frequently, it is desirable to produce a list of all or part of the records in a database file, arranged sequentially by a particular field. An index on that field may be utilized to specify the order in which each record in the file is accessed. For example, suppose that we wish to generate a list of all of the CUSTOMERS records arranged by NAME. The following commands would accomplish this:

(30)

```
USE       CUSTOMERS
SET       INDEX TO NAME
DISPLAY   ALL
```

Again, the fact that the NAME index is attached to the CUSTOMERS file causes the records to be accessed in the order dictated by the index.

Indexes Based on More Than One Field

Many database systems permit the construction of an index to be based on two or more fields. Again using the CUSTOMERS file as an example, suppose that regular reports are to be made, sequenced first on the value of STATE, then on the NAME field. That is, all customers within the state of Alabama would be listed first, then those for Arizona, and so on. Within each state, the customers would be listed alphabetically.

Since an index may be used to display the records within a file in a specified order, the following commands could be used to create the appropriate index:

(31)

```
USE       CUSTOMERS
INDEX     ON STATE+NAME TO SNDX
```

Figure 5.4 illustrates a sample of the contents of the index. Each entry consists of the concatenation of values from the STATE and NAME fields of a record.

A Comparison of Indexed and Non-indexed Searching

Almost without exception, the use of indexes for conducting file searches is enormously more efficient than searching the file sequentially. This is true of both the required search time and the overall system performance.

As an example, we shall analyze the performance of both types of searches for finding all records whose NAME field contains the value 'Smith'. Consider first the indexed search, initiated by the following commands.

(32)

```
USE     CUSTOMERS
SET     INDEX TO NAME
FIND    'Smith'
```

Assuming that the CUSTOMERS file is quite large, many records may satisfy the search condition. We can break up the process of generating the search result into two parts:

1. The steps needed to find the address of the first record that satisfies the search condition
2. The steps needed to find the remaining addresses satisfying the search condition

We shall consider these in order. A typical multi-level index for the NAME field is illustrated in figure 4.13. Assuming that the index is built in N levels, then N disk accesses will be needed to find the first entry corresponding to 'Smith'. Because entries in the index are arranged *sequentially by key,* the remaining entries for 'Smith' will be immediately adjacent to the first (in the lowest index level). In other words, after the first index entry has been found, the remaining ones are immediately accessible. If there were many entries in the index for 'Smith', one or two additional disk accesses might be necessary to read all of them. The sequence of events is roughly illustrated in figure 5.3.

Additionally, one disk access will be needed for each of the records in the search result because the record itself must be read from the disk. Therefore, the total number of accesses needed to read all records for 'Smith', N_A, is given as follows:

(33)

$$N_A = \text{Total no. of records in search result}$$
$$+ \text{ Number of levels in index}$$
$$+ e$$

where e = A small integer with a value close to 1

Because the number of levels in an index is usually fairly small, from (33) we see that the total number of disk accesses is approximately equal to the number of records in the search result, plus a small number close to unity.

Table 5.2	Comparison of Required Disk Accesses for Indexed and Non-indexed Searches

Type of Search	Required Number of Accesses
Sequential	500
Indexed	20

A sequential search, by contrast, requires that every record in the file be read. If B_R records fit into a block, then the total number of disk accesses is given by

$$N_{AS} = N_R/B_R$$
$$\text{where } N_R = \text{total number of records in the file}$$

To illustrate this point, table 5.2 compares the number of disk accesses needed with the two types of searches for a hypothetical file containing 1000 records. We assume that the search result contains 15 records. Also we assume a value of 2 for B_R. Clearly, the disk-access requirements for the indexed search are nearly negligible in comparison to the sequential search.

In general, the disk-access requirements of a search are significant because they affect overall system performance—a process that makes heavy use of the disk tends to degrade system performance, which relies heavily on disk availability.

Of more immediate interest to single-user systems, such as most microcomputer applications, is a comparison of the difference in **real time** (actual clock time) between indexed and non-indexed searches. The number of disk accesses may be of no practical interest to the user, but the amount of time spent waiting for the results of a particular search may be very important.

Table 5.3 shows a group of experimental results of real time needed for different searches under a variety of conditions. The table shows that in all cases, even including a file of nearly 10,000 records, the time to search an index was considerably less than 0.5 seconds. By contrast, the sequential search time increased linearly with the total number of records in the file, and the searching of a 9,600-record file required nearly one minute.

Multi-file searching. The discussions concerning file searching have been oriented around databases consisting of a single file. As we shall see in subsequent chapters, a database may consist of several related files. Many DBMS's have developed query languages capable of specifying a variety of complex searches involving many files. We shall investigate the nature of some of these languages in later chapters, after we have studied multiple-file databases.

Table 5.3	Real Time Required for Indexed and Sequential Searches			

No. of Records in File	Type of Disk	Approximate Search Times (sec)	
		Sequential Search	Indexed Search
200	Hard	1	<0.5
400	Hard	2	<0.5
800	Hard	5	<0.5
1600	Hard	10	<0.5
9600	Hard	56	<0.5
800	Floppy	7	<0.5
1600	Floppy	13	<0.5

All results were measured with an Apple II/e computer, a CORVUS 20 megabyte hard disk, a standard Apple floppy-disk unit, and a stopwatch. Records were 10 bytes in length.

Database Reporting

Reporting is the means by which a database management system communicates to the outside world something about its stored information. A report may be as simple as the display of a single record, or it may be a carefully prepared summary of a large number of records drawn from many different files. Different DBMS's offer varying amounts of flexibility in terms of how information may be reported. Some systems have only a few commands for the display of data. Others offer sophisticated built-in packages that allow the user to design a large variety of report types. Many DBMS's, particularly older ones, rely on user-written programs for the generation of reports.

In this section, we shall briefly examine some of the more common methods used for generating database reports. It should be emphasized that, as in the previous section, the examples used here are for the purpose of illustrating concepts. The intention is not to give complete coverage to all of the various reporting possibilities, but rather to indicate some of the more common reporting methods and styles.

Standard Output

Many DBMS's offer one or more simple command sequences for outputting a search result in a standard format chosen by the DBMS. Almost invariably, the command sequences include the following options:

1. The destination of the output. This is normally either a printer attached to the computer, or a display monitor
2. The fields to be output from the records in the search result

The standard output format used by a DBMS will be some type of reasonable arrangement of the specified fields.

To illustrate, consider the following simple dBASE III command sequence, which outputs the NAME, CITY, and BALANCE fields for a particular subset of records in the CUSTOMERS file shown in figure 5.2:

(34)

```
USE        CUSTOMERS
DISPLAY    FIELDS NAME, CITY, BALANCE;
           FOR CITY = 'Oakland'
```

This sequence is a slight variation on an example used earlier in this chapter. The DISPLAY command again serves multiple purposes, specifying the following items:

1. The search conditions (CITY = 'Oakland')
2. The fact that a standard output is to be generated
3. The fields to be included in the output

Figure 5.5 illustrates two styles of standard output formats in common use. Many other possibilities also exist.

Normally, the absence of a particular option results in a **default** choice being made by the DBMS. For example, if no field names are specified, a common default is that *all* fields are output.

A great many needs are satisfied by the "quick and dirty" type of reports generated by whatever standard output formats are available with a particular DBMS. For example, as a user is browsing through a file, (s)he may wish to issue a particular query and then take a quick look at the search result. For this purpose, any reasonable type of output that can be generated with a simple command will be adequate. On the other hand, many applications require report formats far beyond the capabilities of standard output commands. For these purposes, other approaches must be taken.

Figure 5.5
Two styles of report
formats: (a) columnar
output and
(b) noncolumnar output.

(a)

NAME	CITY	BALANCE
Harris, Peter	Oakland	155.75
Norman, Samuel	Oakland	0
Smith, Alfred	Oakland	0

(b)

```
NAME = Harris, Peter

CITY = Oakland

BALANCE = 155.75


NAME = Norman, Samuel

CITY = Oakland

BALANCE = 0


NAME = Smith, Alfred

CITY = Oakland

BALANCE = 0
```

Complex Report Generation

Many different methods exist for generating complicated reports but they can be grouped into two broad categories. One of these takes the form of a set of built-in programs, commonly referred to as a **report generator, report writer,** or other similar name. It generates a report based on a set of user-supplied specifications describing the details of the desired report format.

The second general procedure for the production of a report involves the use of a specially-written application program. This must be either in an ordinary language such as COBOL or BASIC, or in a language that is an inherent part of the DBMS being used.

The basic difference between the two methods of generating reports is as follows. When employing a report writer, a user enters a set of specifications, which describe to the report writer the manner in which the various parts of a particular report are to be laid out, much as one might describe to an architect the various features to be incorporated into the design of a house. A report writer may be thought of as a prewritten program containing several blank spaces which the user fills in.

On the other hand, the writing of an application program involves something quite different. Here, the user must construct a set of logically related instructions that directly process each of the records in the search result. This program must be concerned not only with many details connected with a particular report, but also with the logical connections between these details. Chapter 6 will discuss user-written programs for outputting reports. The remaining section of this chapter will focus on report writers.

Report Writers

The success of report writers is based on the fact that although there are many different types of reports, they share a large number of common characteristics. These common attributes are built into a report writer. The user supplies a set of specifications, as shown in figure 5.7, which are then used by the report writer to produce the report.

For example, a common feature of many types of reports is a **page header,** which is a title appearing at the top of each page. Consequently, many report writers give the user the option of specifying a page header. The logic concerned with the generation of a page header (i.e., go to the top of the page, and center each header line) is contained in the report writer. The user need only supply a specification with a value for the page header. In figure 5.7, three headers have been specified.

Report attributes. The following paragraphs describe some of the specifications commonly supplied by a user to report writers. Naturally, not every report writer allows all of these. On the other hand, many report writers include many features not described here.

- **Titles and headings.** A report may include a variety of different titles and headings, including the following: an **opening title** at the beginning of a report; a **header** at the top of each page and a **footer** at the bottom; **column headings** at the top of each column, usually repeated at the top of each page; a **closing title** at the conclusion of the report; **subtotal titles,** if subtotals exist.
- **Record fields.** Frequently, reports do not include all record fields. Instead, a list of fields to be output is included as part of the specifications. Most report writers assume that the basic format for record output is columnar. Consequently, the exact column positions to be occupied by each field must also be specified.
- **Sorting options.** Frequently, it is necessary to output the records in a search result sorted by various fields. Therefore, a commonly included specification is the way in which output data is to be sorted in the report. This is an extremely powerful and desirable feature, especially if it allows for simultaneous sorting on several fields.
- **Control breaks and totals.** Suppose that a given search result is to be sorted by the CITY field, so that all of the records for Albany will be output first, followed by those for Berkeley, and so on. A **control break** on CITY is said to occur whenever the value of CITY changes from one record to the next. A control break is where subtotals are computed and output. For example, in the report shown in figure 5.9, a control break occurs after the record that begins 'Andersen, Jim'. Note that a control break on CITY makes sense *only* if the records are sorted in order by CITY.

Control breaks are important because it is often desirable to output subtotals of specific fields at each control break. For example, if the BALANCE field contains the outstanding balance of each customer, then it might be desirable to print the BALANCE subtotal for each city, as shown in figure 5.9. A technical way of stating this is that a subtotal on BALANCE is to be printed for each control break on CITY. It might also be useful to print the final total of the BALANCE field for all records output in the report. The ability to print totals and subtotals are common options with many report writers.

A Sample Report Writer

Many of the previously discussed ideas underlying the use of report writers are illustrated with the SAMPLE report shown in figure 5.6. We assume that the records displayed in this figure are the result of a query of a CUSTOMERS database. Figure 5.7 illustrates a hypothetical set of specifications that might have been used to generate this report. These specifications would be submitted to the report writer, which would then process the records, using these specifications to generate the report. Although the syntax used in this example is to some extent fictitious, the simplicity of each specification as shown is representative of that for many actual report writers.

Figure 5.6
Sample report on a
CUSTOMERS search
result.

```
Customers in California                                       Page 1

    CUSTOMER NAME          CITY                     BALANCE DUE

    Harris, Thomas         Albany                        750.00
    Jackson, Peter                                       647.68
    Rawson, Clarence                                     595.29
    Carson, Horatio                                     1255.73
                                      Subtotal:          3248.70
    Hegerman, Leroy        Berkeley                      919.87
    Ruben, Sonny                                         654.32
    Jones, Terence                                       932.43
                                      Subtotal:          2506.62
    Baker, Able            Oakland                       755.00
    Darkness, Emil                                      1500.00
    King, Prince                                         822.12
    Wasserman, Lew                                      1833.00
                                      Subtotal:          4010.12
                                   Final total:          9865.44
```

Figure 5.7
A set of specifications
for generating the
report in figure 5.6.

```
 1. HEADER1 = "        Customers in California      Page #
 2. HEADER2 = "                                            "
 3. HEADER3 = " CUSTOMER NAME        CITY        BALANCE DUE"
 4. FIELD = NAME(5,25)
 5. FIELD = CITY(30,25)
 6. FIELD = BALANCE(60,10)
 7. SORT ON CITY
 8. BREAK ON CITY
 9. SUBTOTAL ON BALANCE
10. TOTAL ON BALANCE
```

This example illustrates a significant principle—a relatively complicated and sophisticated report can be generated with very little effort on the part of the user, who has only to write down a set of specifications. Notice in figure 5.7 that there is no logic connecting the specifications, which in fact may usually be written down in any order. Rather, each specification describes a separate quality of the report to be written. All of the necessary logic is contained in the report writer, which generates the report based on the supplied specifications.

Figure 5.8
Report generation
dialog between dBASE
II and user. Shaded
areas are user input.

```
1.   ENTER REPORT FORM NAME:              Report.std
2.   ENTER OPTIONS, M=LEFT MARGIN,
3.                   L=LINES/PAGE,
4.                   W=PAGE WIDTH:        M=10, L=60, W=70
5.   PAGE HEADING? (Y/N)                  Y
6.   ENTER PAGE HEADING:         Monthly CUSTOMERS report
7.   DOUBLE SPACE REPORT?                 N
8.   ARE TOTALS REQUIRED? (Y/N)           Y
9.   SUBTOTALS IN REPORT? (Y/N)           Y
10.  ENTER SUBTOTALS FIELD:               City
11.  SUMMARY REPORT ONLY? (Y/N)           N
12.  EJECT PAGE AFTER SUBTOTALS? (Y/N)    N
13.  COL    WIDTH,  CONTENTS
14.  001    25,      Name
15.  ENTER HEADING: Customer name
16.  002    10,    Balance
17.  ENTER HEADING: Balance due
18.  ARE TOTALS REQUIRED? (Y/N)           Y
19.  003    10,    Credit
20.  ENTER HEADING: Credit limit
21.  ARE TOTALS REQUIRED? (Y/N)           Y
```

Let us briefly examine the particular specifications in figure 5.7 (also compare them with the report shown in figure 5.6). Lines 1–3 describe information to appear in the header of each page. The first two header lines specify the page title, whereas the third furnishes column headings. Lines 4–6 each specify a particular field to be included in the report, along with specifications of the starting position and column width. Line 7 specifies that the records are to be sorted on the CITY field. Line 8 indicates that a control break is to occur with respect to the CITY field; and line 9 indicates that a subtotal on the BALANCE field is to be printed at each control break. Finally, line 10 indicates that a final total is desired on the BALANCE field at the conclusion of the report.

Notice that a great deal of detail concerning the report format is left up to the report writer. For example, the placement of the words SUBTOTAL and TOTAL is not specified by the user. A scrutiny of the report will reveal other examples. This is natural, since the reason for using a report writer is to simplify the task of generating a report as much as possible. There is no free lunch however, and the price of simplicity is conformity.

The specifications shown in this example are by no means the only ones allowed in report writers, many of which provide the user with a great deal of latitude in the control over the details of the report structure.

Figure 5.9
A report generated by
dBASE II.

```
Page No. 00001
                                    Monthly CUSTOMERS report
                                Balance                 Credit
         Customer name          due                      limit


         *   Albany
         Drue, Ellen            3527.98              10000.00
         Andersen, Tim           327.13               5000.00
         **  Subtotal  **       3855.11              15000.00


         *   Berkeley
         Smith, Jennifer            0.00               5000.00
         LaRue, Elaine            955.00               1000.00
         Gregory, Robert         1857.32               5000.00
         Baker, James             125.15              10000.00
         **  Subtotal  **        2937.47              21000.00


         *   Newark
         James, Jesse             532.87               5000.00
         **  Subtotal  **         532.87               5000.00


         *   Oakland
         Harris, Peter            155.75               1000.00
         Norman, Samuel             0.00                  0.00
         Smith, Alfred              0.00               1000.00
         **  Subtotal  **         155.75               2000.00


         *   Pittsburg
         Clark, Kent              395.15               1000.00
         **  Subtotal  **         395.15               1000.00


         **  Total  **           7876.35              44000.00
```

The dBASE II Report Writer

Another type of built-in report writer is illustrated by the dBASE II® system,[1] in which the user is prompted with a series of questions concerning the details of the report to be generated. Figure 5.8 illustrates a typical dialog. The bold-faced text shows the dBASE II prompts; and the other text represents user responses. Figure 5.9 shows the results of the report generation, applied to the contents of the CUSTOMERS file shown in figure 5.2. (Note that the records have been presorted by another dBASE command, which is not shown.)

®dBASE II is a registered trademark of ASHTON-TATE.

[1]Although dBASE II is an older system, its report writer is useful as an example because of its extreme simplicity. Details on using the dBASE III report writer are given in the workbook accompanying this text.

A few entries in figure 5.8, require some explanation. In line 1, the user enters the name of the file where the report specifications are to be stored: RE-PORT.STD. This allows the same report format to be reused without having to re-enter the details. In lines 9 and 10, the user specifies that a control break is to occur on the CITY field. That is, each time a new value of CITY appears, subtotals will be printed for whatever fields the user specifies (lines 18 and 21). The result of this is that subtotals are printed for the BALANCE and CREDIT fields: the subtotals represent totals for each city.

In lines 13–21, the user enters the names of the fields to be output, including column widths and headings for each field. Note that the system asks the user whether subtotals are to appear only for numeric fields.

Once familiarity has been gained with this type of report generator, it may be easily used to produce reasonably well-formatted output. The price to pay for this simplicity is restrictiveness—the user does not have a lot of choice in the output format, because most of it is automatically supplied by the system. Because of these limitations, many users prefer to write programs so that they may specify every detail of a report.

Summary

Searching and reporting are two outstanding features of database management systems. These processes go hand-in-hand—a database search must be followed by a report if the user is ever to see the results. Searching and reporting may be done either interactively or in batch mode. Interactive use is convenient for ad hoc queries, especially in situations in which the user is simply browsing through a database. Batch operations are useful in situations where either the same types of queries are done on a routine basis, or where a large amount of data must be processed.

The process of searching begins by specifying the file to be searched, as well as the particular set of search conditions to be satisfied by each record included in the search result. Search conditions may, in general, be quite complex, with each DBMS having its own rules concerning the allowed degree of complexity. The product of a search is a search result, from which a report is generated.

Searching may be done sequentially, or with the aid of an index. The creation of an index involves a trade-off: reduced search time against required disk storage for the index. When it is anticipated that a large file will be searched frequently in the same way, the use of an index may be indispensable. Some simple computations may often be of value in deciding whether the creation of an index would be useful. Many DBMS's allow the ad hoc creation and deletion of indexes; whereas other systems permit index creation only at the time the file itself is created.

Some DBMS's use the same search-command syntax for both indexed and sequential searching. The user specifies the desired result by using a set of search commands, and the DBMS automatically makes use of any existing indexes. Most database systems require different sets of commands for the two types of searches.

Indexes may also be used to generate ordered lists of records, and an index may often be based on the values of several fields.

Reports may take many different forms, ranging from simple screen displays in crude form to elegant formats requiring a good deal of manipulation of search results. Many systems have built-in program packages for the easy generation of reports in a variety of formats. These packages come in various styles, but their common feature is that they take on the burden of dealing with the programming logic involved with a report generation. The user must simply supply a few details concerning report content.

For situations in which the user wishes to exercise more control over report format than is allowed by a built-in package, application programs must be written. Although this is tremendously more time-consuming than using a built-in report writer, the end-result is a report in precisely the desired format.

Chapter Review

Terminology

Boolean operator
control break
database search
default
footer
formatting
header
indexed search
query

real time
relational operator
report
report writer
search conditions
search range
search result
sequential search

Review Questions

1. What information must be contained in a query command for performing a search?
2. Under what conditions is the use of interactive queries valuable?
3. Can you give an example of a situation in which it would be useful to use a batch program for generating database queries?
4. When would you choose to use a sequential search of a file in preference to creating an index for performing the same search? Does your answer depend at all on the size of the file being searched? Does your answer depend on whether you have a 40 megabyte hard disk as opposed to a dual drive floppy-disk system?
5. We have a tendency in common speech to use the words *and* and *or* interchangeably. For example, the phrase "My friends who live in Berkeley *and* Oakland. . . ." really refers to people living in *either* city, but not both. The word *or* should be substituted for *and* in order for the

phrase to be semantically correct. Review the section on Boolean operators and think about whether you have any speech habits that might tend to interfere with your ability to write search commands accurately.

6. If you have a computer, measure the time needed to perform sequential searches on different size files, say 100, 200, or 500 records. Is the total search time close to being proportional to the file size?

7. Create an index on each of the files discussed in question 6. How does the index creation time vary with the size of the file? Using the indexes, perform the same searches for each file as you did for question 6. What differences do you measure in the search times, compared to the results in question 6?

8. What standard commands does your database system have for listing on the display monitor the contents of a search result? Do these commands give you any control over the format of the output?

9. If your DBMS has a built-in report generator, familiarize yourself with it. How many report details can you specify with it? How many can you not specify that you would like to be able to?

10. The report shown in figure 5.9 of the text is adequate, but it leaves something to be desired. Can you find any faults with the format?

Problems

Problems 1–7 refer to a CUSTOMERS file consisting of the following fields (numbers in parentheses are field lengths):

NAME (25)	ZIP (5)
STREET (25)	PHONE (13)
CITY (15)	CREDIT (8)
STATE (2)	BALANCE (8)

The file contains 1700 records.

1. Using dBASE III syntax, write search queries to find records for each of the following groups of customers:
   - Those living in Kalamazoo
   - Those who live in Pittsburgh, CA
   - Those for whom a phone number is unknown
   - Those whose balance exceeds their credit limit
   - All of the branches of "Peter's Chocolates," except the ones in Oakland

2. Write a search command for "Those whose balance exceeds their credit limit." This should be different from your solution in the previous problem.

3.   a. Write a search command to find all of the customers who live either in Oakland or Boston, and whose credit limit is greater than $1000.

      b. Write a search command to find all customers other than those specified in (3a).

4. A report is to be generated, listing every customer in the file in increasing order of balance due.
   a. Design an index that could help to generate the report.
   b. Estimate the amount of disk space required for the index.
5. A report is to be generated with the records sequenced by city. Within each city, the records are to be sequenced by customer name.
   a. Design an index that could be used to help generate the report.
   b. Estimate the amount of disk space required for the index.
   c. Both the CUSTOMERS file and the index are to reside on a floppy disk with a total data-storage capacity of 360,000 bytes. Estimate how much storage space will remain after the index is placed on the disk. Also, estimate how many additional CUSTOMERS records will fit on the disk. When performing this calculation, remember that the index will also grow as new records are added to the file.
6. Suppose that an index has been created on the ZIP field. Write a set of search commands to utilize the index to find all of the records whose ZIP lies between 12345 and 12990. (*Hint:* use the FIND and DISPLAY . . . WHILE commands similar to those shown in (29) of this chapter.)
7. Using the syntax shown in figure 5.7, design a report for the CUSTOMERS file outputting the name, address and balance due for each customer represented in the file. The output should be sorted by STATE, with control breaks occurring on that field. Subtotals should be included for each state, showing the total balance due.
8. The following experimental data has been compiled for a file, using different totals for records in the file:

Number of Records in File	Time to Sequentially Read the Entire File (seconds)	Time to Create an Index on Field F (seconds)
100	10	30
200	21	65
400	41	140
2000	215	900
4000	425	1820

   a. Suppose that a number of searches are to be done on field F for a file containing 5000 records. Using the above data, estimate how many searches would have to be done in order to justify the time required for building an index on field F to assist in the searching.
   b. Estimate the difference in required time for a sequential and indexed search of the 5000 record file.

Chapter Six

Programming in the Database Environment

Introduction

In previous chapters, we have shown some of the built-in powerful features that can be expected from many database management systems. Standard characteristics of these systems invariably include functions such as database searching and reporting, and the capability for addition and modification of records. For many purposes, these and other built-in functions are sufficient to provide the user with all of the power necessary for using a database. Frequently, however, the user encounters requirements for which the standard DBMS commands are inadequate. For example, a very specialized type of report might be needed with a format that is beyond the capability of the built-in report generator.

When situations such as these occur, the user has one of several choices. First, and least attractive, the requirement can be put aside entirely. Alternatively, it might be simplified to the point that the DBMS can deal with it. Finally, and most desirable, a program could be written by the user. This program would be used in conjunction with the DBMS to handle the needs of the application.

Application programs are used throughout the field of database management, and in this chapter we shall survey some of the ways in which they may enhance the performance of database systems.

For simplicity, we shall refer to any user-written program simply as a *program.* These are to be distinguished from built-in programs, such as report writers, which are an integral part of a DBMS.

One significant way to categorize database systems is whether they have the ability to interface with programs. Those that cannot have definite limitations dictated by the available repertoire of built-in database commands. Many of the currently available DBMS's are able to interface with programs, because programs can be written to accomplish a very wide range of tasks. The result is a tool vastly more powerful than the DBMS by itself.

Nearly all large-computer DBMS's have program-interfacing capabilities, whereas only a fraction of the micro-based systems do. File managers, for example, are designed for use by individuals with little or no computing background, and the very concept of user-generated programs is contrary to the spirit of these systems. Even some of the more widely-touted and popular DBMS's that lay claim to being highly flexible do not have programming capability. If the available commands for a particular DBMS are inadequate to meet a user's particular needs (s)he must choose between modifying the requirements or acquiring another DBMS.

Common Programming Applications

User-written programs cover a wide spectrum of applications. Some of the more common ones follow:

Frequently used command groups. Often, a lengthy set of DBMS commands needs to be repeated on a regular basis. For example, suppose that we wish to issue a monthly report on a CUSTOMERS file, listing the names and addresses of customers whose BALANCE_DUE exceeds $1000. This report would involve (1) one or more commands to perform a search of the file; and (2) one or more commands for the generation of the report. Rather than re-entering all of the commands each time a report is to be issued, a program may be built that contains all of these commands. This program may be used whenever necessary, and each time it is run, all of the search and report commands will be executed.

Some DBMS's have a facility for defining a **macro,** which is a very restricted type of program. A macro is a file which stores a group of DBMS commands. These commands may be executed in sequence by running the macro. This usually involves simply typing in the macro name as though it were an ordinary DBMS command. The DBMS then executes each instruction in the macro file. Macros are a simple subset of true programs, in that each macro can *only* store and execute a group of DBMS commands. It has none of the other features of full programming languages.

As a simple example, figure 6.1 illustrates the contents of a simple dBASE III program for displaying a particular subset of CUSTOMERS records. In this example, a temporary index is created, so that the customers are listed alphabetically.

Working with multi-file databases. Many databases contain more than one file. When working with these databases, it is often necessary to access more than one file simultaneously. For example, a particular type of query might require that information from several files be compared, collated, then output. Often, the logic involved with this type of multi-file access may be sufficiently complicated to require the use of one or more programs.

Report generation. In many ways, the value of database information is limited by the way in which it is presented to the external world. Many database systems have built-in facilities for producing reports, often in a wide variety of styles and formats, including tabular reports, bar graphs, pie charts, and so on. A variation on Murphy's most popular law is that no matter how much flexibility a DBMS

Figure 6.1

A simple dBASE III
command file. This
command file outputs a
list of customers whose
balance is outstanding.

```
1.   USE CUSTOMERS
2.   INDEX ON NAME TO TEMPINDX
3.   SET INDEX TO TEMPINDX
4.   DISPLAY FIELDS NAME, ADDRESS, CITY, STATE, ZIP;
           FOR BALANCE > 1000
5.   DELETE FILE TEMPINDX
```

possesses in a given area, a user will sooner or later want more. The generation of reports is no exception in this respect, and frequently it is necessary to utilize a specially-written program to produce a report with the required format.

User-friendly environments. Databases are often accessed *interactively* by users who do not wish to become involved with learning the complex syntax of the system. For these situations, a user-friendly environment may be created by a program that guides a user through the entire interaction with the database. At each step, the user is asked a question by the program. The user's response then points the way for the program to go on to the next step. Menu-driven programs are examples of this type of application, and in later sections of this chapter we shall give examples of these.

Specialized database manipulations. Often, specific database applications require the use of logical operations in addition to the normal database commands. For example, one might wish to produce a report in which the presence or absence of specific record fields depended on the values of other fields. This type of logic often requires the assistance of a specialized program.

Data checking. Many types of data errors can be detected by performing various types of tests on input data. Programs may be used to provide a friendly environment for data entry. In addition, these programs can also *interactively* inform the data-entry clerk whenever an error occurs, even stating the nature of the error. An example of an error that can be easily detected is a **range error.** To illustrate this, suppose that the field AGE contains values of people's ages. A data entry program can check each value input for AGE. If a number is entered that is outside a specified range of values (say 15–95), the program rejects it with an informative message to the user.

The types of data errors that can be detected by on-line programs are virtually endless, often limited only by the ingenuity of the database designers and programmers.

Database security. In many situations, it is important that computerized information be accessible only to authorized personnel, for reasons of personal privacy, company security, and so on. One way to enforce security is to limit database access by means of **password protection.** A program that interfaces between the users and a database is a natural place to put password-checking mechanisms. Thus, a user would have to furnish a valid password to a program before any type of database access would be permitted.

Obviously, this type of protection is useful only when users are required to interact with a database by means of a specific program. Usually, this is most effective when users are unfamiliar with the details of how to interact directly with a DBMS.

Programming Languages

Many different programming languages are used in conjunction with various DBMS's, but the fundamental objective behind their use is the same: to combine the power of a DBMS with the logic and flexibility inherent with a programming language. A great many different programming languages are used in conjunction with database systems, but they all may be grouped into two categories: standard or built-in.

Standard Languages

The category of standard languages encompasses many of the common programming languages in use today. The first language used in connection with DBMS's was COBOL, but the list has since been extended to include FORTRAN, Pascal, BASIC, PL/I, RPG, and others of less popularity.

In order for programs written in a standard language to be able to interact with a database system, the system must have a specialized set of software built into it. This **host language interface** allows communication between the DBMS and the programs. The interface is language-specific, which means that each programming language requires a different host language interface. Some DBMS's incorporate many interfaces, while others have only one.

Standard languages may interact with a DBMS using either embedded commands or subroutine calls.

Embedded Commands

An embedded command is a standard DBMS command, but it appears just as though it were an ordinary part of the program. When one of these commands is encountered during program execution, it is sent to the DBMS, which treats the command just as though it had been entered interactively at a keyboard. In order for this approach to work, the language compiler must be extended to accommodate every DBMS command that might appear in a program.

Figure 6.2 illustrates a short Pascal program segment in which a pair of DBMS commands are embedded.

Figure 6.2
A Pascal program
segment containing
embedded DBMS
commands. This
segment outputs the
first N records in the
CUSTOMERS file. The
DBMS commands have
been capitalized for
ease in reading.

```
Program test (Input, Output)
               .
               .
Var            .
    I,N: Integer
               .
               .
Begin
    Readln (N);
    USE CUSTOMERS;
    For I = 1 to N do begin
        DISPLAY NEXT
    End;
               .
               .
               .
```

Subroutine Calls

In this method of DBMS interaction, a program issues a separate subroutine call for each action that is required of the DBMS. In this case, the host language interface of the DBMS consists of a set of subroutines, each of which performs a particular DBMS task.

Figure 6.3 illustrates the same program shown in figure 6.2, but with calls to DBMS subroutines substituted for ordinary DBMS commands.

When subroutine calls are used for program-DBMS communication, the language compiler may not need to be modified. On the other hand, subroutine calls are not quite as elegant as simple DBMS commands.

Built-in Languages

Many of the newer DBMS's include a built-in programming language as an integral feature. Because this type of language is integrated with the database system, program-DBMS communication is simplified, and the user often may use the full range of DBMS commands that are available in the interactive mode.

In the following discussions, we shall differentiate between standard and built-in programming languages.

Trends in DBMS Programming

In the early days of database management, the only programming languages available for interfacing with DBMS's were the standard ones, in particular COBOL and FORTRAN. In recent years, there has been a growing tendency for database systems to develop their own built-in languages, particularly in the case of microcomputer-based DBMS's. The primary reason for this trend is that

Figure 6.3
A program similar to
that shown in figure 6.2,
but with DBMS
subroutine calls
substituted for DBMS
commands.

```
Program test (Input, Output)
            .
            .
Var
            .
    I,N: Integer
            .
            .
Begin
    Readln (N);
    OPENFILE (CUSTOMERS);
    For I = 1 to N do begin
        DISPLAY_NEXT_RECORD (CUSTOMERS)
End;
            .
            .
            .
```

a built-in language is designed as part of a DBMS package, and as such it can be built very compactly to include only those elements that are useful for database applications.

By contrast, the standard languages are all generalized to some extent in order to cover a wide variety of applications. Using any of these for a database application often means carrying along a good deal of unnecessary "excess baggage." This can be a significant factor, particularly in the case of micro-based systems, which have both memory and speed limitations. Furthermore, building a host language interface for a standard language may involve compromises in terms of choosing which features of the DBMS should be accommodated.

Unlike modern database systems, older DBMS's were designed from their inception to be called from batch applications programs written in COBOL or PL/I, and for these systems, a standard language is required. These DBMS's have had significant impact on large-computer database management, which still relies heavily on this style of DBMS-program interaction. Table 6.1 summarizes the general trends with respect to the types of languages used with various classes of database systems.

The DBMS—Program Interface

The general interaction between a DBMS and a program is summarized in figure 6.4. It is assumed that the program is concerned in some manner with information from a particular database. As with all DBMS interactions, *the database itself is directly accessible only to the DBMS*. The program communicates directly with the DBMS, not the database. If the program is interactive, it also communicates with a user.

Table 6.1

General Trends in Database-oriented Programming Languages

Type of Computer on Which Database System Runs	Type of Programming Language
Microcomputers	For most DBMS's, no programming language is available; user is limited to whatever built-in facilities are available with the DBMS.
	For a few DBMS's, a built-in programming language is available. The language typically contains features for (1) constructs such as IF_THEN_ELSE, etc; (2) input/output; (3) all normal DBMS commands.
	One or two database systems interface with standard languages.
Larger machines (mainframes & minis)	Nearly all DBMS's support standard languages. A very few support a built-in language.

The standard programming languages most commonly used with database management systems are: FORTRAN, COBOL, PL/I, Pascal, BASIC, C, RPG.

Figure 6.4
The DBMS–program interface.

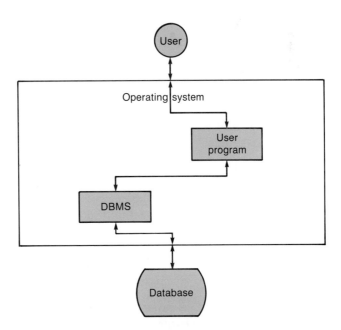

The interaction between a DBMS, a user, and a program usually has the following characteristics. Communication between the program and the user is conversational, with the user entering simple responses to different instructions presented by the program. In contrast, communication between the program and the DBMS is exclusively in terms of (1) database information and DBMS commands that the program sends to the DBMS; and (2) database information sent to the program by the DBMS in response to program-generated commands. This information is in turn passed on to the user.

Each programming language possesses its own particular set of features, and the strengths of one language may be the weaknesses of another. This is because each language has been designed with specific goals and purposes in mind. For example, COBOL was conceived to serve the needs of the business community. As a result, it is strong in the area of input/output but quite weak in the area of computation. FORTRAN, on the other hand, was designed as a computational tool for scientific purposes, so it is very powerful in numerical areas and fairly weak in handling input/output.

In spite of the many differences among the popular standard languages, most of them possess features that make them suitable for interaction with database systems. Naturally, the strengths and weaknesses of a language will be reflected in how well it deals with different types of database applications.

Each built-in programming language has its own particular limitations, often lacking features that are normal parts of standard languages, such as flexible control structures or multi-dimensional arrays.

Every language used with a DBMS must contain certain minimal characteristics. This is true both for built-in and standard languages. These characteristics are listed below.

Access to Database Records and Fields

The fundamental requirement for any language is that it provide a means for accessing the data in DBMS-maintained files, for the purposes of outputting or modification. Moreover, the language must provide mechanisms for storing new records in a file. In addition, access to records must be at the field level. That is, each field within a record must be directly addressable by a program. The flexibility with which records may be stored and retrieved by a program is determined by how much access the language has to the full power of the DBMS.

Availability of DBMS Commands

Modern database systems are designed to run interactively, with users having access to a wide range of system commands. Ideally, a programming language should have access to all of the DBMS commands available in the interactive mode so that the full power of the DBMS may be utilized. Unfortunately, this is often not the case, particularly with standard languages. Rather, a subset of the DBMS commands are available to the language, sometimes in the form of a set of DBMS subroutines, as discussed earlier.

For built-in languages, the general rule is that most or all of the DBMS commands are available. This is to be expected, since the language is designed as an integral part of the DBMS. Thus, this type of language usually has the full power of the DBMS available to it.

This discussion is not applicable to older DBMS's, for which the basic design centers around operation in the batch program environment, rather than the interactive mode (when the first DBMS's were designed, there was no such thing as an interactive mode). For these older systems, the full DBMS power is by definition available through application programs; and the interactive mode of operation (if any at all exists) has come much later in the life cycle of the system, usually as an add-on set of packages.

Input/Output

A program must be able to issue commands for outputting selected parts of files, records, and fields in a flexible manner. In addition, it must be possible to input data for the construction of new records and the modification of existing ones. Input and output is a strong feature with standard languages, usually including a great many flexible options. With built-in languages, a special set of input and output statements are usually included so that data may be transferred between the outside world and a database.

Structured Aspects

One of the great strengths of a language lies in the various types of control structures that are available. These structures give the language flexibility for dealing with various types of logical situations that are part of complex database programming applications. The most common types of structures are looping, path control, and modularization. The simple types of macro definition available with some database systems do not have any structured aspects, and for this reason they have limited programming value.

Looping

Looping is the ability to perform a set of operations repetitively. The beginning and ending of a loop is controlled by a specified set of conditions. Loops may be **unconditional** or **conditional.** An unconditional loop is performed a specific number of times, whereas a conditional loop continues until a particular condition becomes true (or false).

Looping is available with all standard languages, such as the DO loop of FORTRAN, the DO-WHILE of Pascal, and the FOR-NEXT of BASIC. A built-in language must contain a looping facility of some type, or it is nothing more than a macro-defining facility in disguise. Most built-in languages contain both conditional and unconditional looping capabilities.

Conditional and Unconditional Path Control

Path-control, or **branching** structures are a vital part of all programming languages. Conditional path control most frequently takes the form of logical testing in an IF-THEN-ELSE type of statement; unconditional control usually is some type of GO TO. All standard languages have this type of statement in some form. In early BASIC and FORTRAN dialects, the IF-type statements are quite primitive but nevertheless functional. Built-in languages invariably contain a full IF-THEN-ELSE structure.

Another type of conditional path control appears in the CASE statement, which is an extension of the IF-THEN-ELSE. The latter is a two-branch control statement, whereas CASE is a multi-branch type of statement. Pascal and its successors contain a CASE control structure, as do some of the built-in languages such as dBASE II and dBASE III.

Modularization

The ability to build a complex program in separate reasonably sized pieces, or modules, is a powerful feature, and experience has shown that it is almost a necessity for large applications. This process of **modularization** is at the heart of modern thinking about program design: it greatly simplifies the processes of writing, reading, and debugging programs. It is available in some form with all of the standard languages, although with early BASIC it is particularly primitive. Many built-in languages contain modularization capabilities.

Variables and Arrays

Another important feature, universal to nearly all languages, is the ability to define variables of different types, such as REAL, LOGICAL, and so on. The ability to create arrays of these various types enhances this vital programming feature. There is a great variation in the extent to which different languages contain these features.

To be useful, a language must also be able to handle all of the data types that can be stored by the DBMS. This is usually not a problem with standard or built-in languages.

Table 6.2	## Summary of Important Programming-language Features

Database-oriented Features

Access to database files, records and fields

Access to DBMS features, either through direct DBMS commands, or via subroutine calls

Programming-oriented Features

Adequate input/output for manipulating database information

Control structures: Looping (conditional/unconditional)
Unconditional branching, such as GO TO
Conditional branching, such as IF-THEN-ELSE

Modularization

Definition of variables and arrays

Other Features

The features that have been discussed are summarized in table 6.2. They form the backbone of any language that functions reasonably well in a DBMS environment. However, this list is by no means inclusive. Different languages contain many additional features and qualities, and a great many pages could be devoted to a discussion of them. Since the variation from language to language is large, however, such a discussion is not appropriate here.

A Survey of Programming Applications

In this section, several examples of programs written in the context of a database environment are given. These examples are not intended to cover the full range of possible programming applications, but they do illustrate some of the types of techniques and applications that are possible.

Some of the examples are given in the context of the dBASE III programming language; others are written in the context of standard languages.

In studying the various program examples, it is important to keep the following points in mind:

1. The *function* of each program; that is, the specific task that is to be carried out, and whether it could be done without a program
2. The *context* of each program; that is, the way in which it interacts with a user and the DBMS

Figure 6.5
Program to generate a
set of mailing labels
from the CUSTOMERS
database. The
language used is
dBASE III (built-in).

```
***********************************************
*                                              *
*   This program generates a set of mailing    *
*   labels for the CUSTOMERS database.          *
*                                              *
*   COMMENT lines are begun with triple         *
*   asterisks (***)                             *
*                                              *
*   The program is written in dBASE III         *
*   syntax                                      *
*                                              *
***********************************************

11.   SET PRINT ON
12.   USE CUSTOMERS
13.
14.   *** Loop through the file, one record at a time
15.   *** Exit the loop when the END_OF_FILE is
16.   *** reached
17.
18.   DO WHILE .NOT. EOF()
19.
20.      *** Print the label for the current record
21.      *** Each statement beginning with a "?"
22.      *** prints a new line
23.      ?
24.      ? NAME
25.      ? STREET
26.      ? CITY, "," , STATE, " " , ZIP
27.      ?
28.
29.      *** Go to next record in the file
30.
31.      SKIP
32.   ENDDO
33.   RETURN
```

Example 1: A Mailing Label Program

In this first example, we illustrate a program for generating mailing labels from the CUSTOMERS file shown in figure 2.7. A label is to be printed for each record in the file, with the customer's name and address taken from appropriate fields.

This example illustrates two things: the use of a built-in programming language (dBASE III); and the use of a batch program, that is, one that executes without any user intervention or interaction.

Figure 6.5 shows the program, and the following paragraphs discuss the meanings of various program statements. The line numbers shown in the figure are for discussion purposes only—they are not part of the actual language.

The USE CUSTOMERS command in line 12 gives the DBMS the name of the file to be accessed; it also positions the file to the first record so that whatever file-access commands are used will reference the first record in the file. Note that this command does not itself return any records to the program. It simply makes the file accessible for other commands.

Line 11 specifies the output destination to be the line printer. Lines 18–33 form the overall loop; each time through this loop, a single record in the file is processed. Lines 24–28 do the actual outputting to the printer, which presumably contains a continuous string of labels. Line 32, the last statement in the loop, positions the file to the next record. When the end-of-file is reached, the program exits from the loop, as dictated by the DO WHILE .NOT. EOF( ) statement in line 18.

Points to Ponder

- **Direct data-access.** A particularly important point to note about this program is contained in lines 25–27, in which the program directly accesses individual fields of the current record. This type of direct database access greatly simplifies the programming effort, particularly with complicated programs in which a great deal of data manipulation is involved.
- **Command/statement mixing.** This program is also an interesting example of the natural way in which DBMS commands (lines 11, 12, and 24–28) are interspersed with program-control statements (lines 18, 33, and 34). Of particular interest is the fact that DBMS commands are contained within a program-language loop structure, namely the DO—ENDDO. This natural blending of DBMS commands and program-language statements is a result of the fact that the language is an integral part of the database system.

Example 2: Another Mailing Label Program

This example, shown in figure 6.6, is similar to the previous one, in that a set of labels is to be generated from the CUSTOMERS file. In this case, however, we illustrate a method by which a standard language interfaces with a database system. The language chosen for this example is an extended version of BASIC.

In this program, several subroutine calls are made. Each subroutine, which is part of the host language interface contained within the DBMS, has a specific function, as outlined below.

DBUSE (*filename*): Opens the file named *filename* and positions it at the first record.

DBGET (*fieldname*, *var*): Retrieves the value of the field *fieldname* from the current record and stores it in variable *var*.

Figure 6.6
This program illustrates
the interfacing of a
standard language to a
database system via a
host language
interface, which
consists of a set of
callable subroutines.
The language used in
this example is a
dialect of extended
BASIC.

```
    REM
    REM        This program generates a set of mailing
    REM        labels
    REM
    REM        Language used: Extended BASIC
    REM
    REM        Temporary variables are indicated by a
    REM            terminating $
    REM
    REM
    REM     Inform the DBMS which file is to be accessed
10. CALL DBUSE (CUSTOMERS)

    REM    Retrieve the necessary fields from the
    REM    current record, and store them in
    REM    temporary variables

15. CALL DBGET (NAME , NAME$    )
16. CALL DBGET (STREET, STREET$)
17. CALL DBGET (CITY , CITY$    )
18. CALL DBGET (STATE , STATE$ )
19. CALL DBGET (ZIP , ZIP$     )

    REM    Print the label for this record

20. PRINT ' '
21. PRINT NAME$
22. PRINT STREET$
23. PRINT ( CITY$ + ',' + STATE$ + ' ' + ZIP$ )
24. PRINT ' '
    REM    Read the next record from the CUSTOMERS
    REM    file: EXIT on an END_OF_FILE condition
    REM    Otherwise, loop back to print the next
    REM    label

25. CALL DBNEXTREC (CUSTOMERS)
26. CALL DBENDFILE (CUSTOMERS, EOF$)
30. IF NOT (EOF$) THEN 15

    REM    END_OF_FILE reached.
31. STOP
```

DBNEXTREC (*filename*): Advances to the next record in *filename*.

DBENDFILE (*filename, var*): Sets the variable *var* to the value TRUE if an end-of-file condition is detected in *filename;* otherwise, *var* is set to the value FALSE.

The program begins by gaining access to the CUSTOMERS file, by a call to DBUSE in line 10. In lines 15–19, values for the name and address of the current record are accessed from the appropriate fields and stored in the temporary variables NAME$, and so on. In lines 21–23, the values in these variables are used to print the label. Line 25 sets up the next record in the file for access; and the following two statements test for an end-of-file condition. If the condition exists, the program ends; if not, a jump is made to line 15, and the next label is printed.

Notice that the program in this example is somewhat more complicated than example 1. Here, the BASIC program accesses the data contained in the various records by making subroutine calls and storing values from the various fields in temporary program variables. A line-by-line comparison of the programs in figures 6.5 and 6.6 would be instructive in showing the differences between the two types of programs, particularly with regard to the accessing of database information.

Example 3: Updating Database Information

The purpose of this example is to illustrate the use of an interactive program for assisting a user in performing a fairly lengthy database operation. Programs of this general type are quite common, and the example gives a hint of the power at the fingertips of the creative programmer.

Suppose that we wish to review the credit limits of all records in the CUSTOMERS file and possibly update some of these limits. We could do this *manually* by issuing DBMS commands for each of the following steps:

1. Access the CUSTOMERS file
2. Display the contents of the current record
3. If we wish to change the value of the credit limit (the LIMIT field), enter the new value, replacing the current value
4. Go to the next record in the file
5. Check to see if the end-of-file has been reached; if it has not, go back and repeat steps 2 through 5

This would be a slow, tedious, and error-prone process because of the large amount of thinking and keystroking required.

A much better way to accomplish the same objective would be to write an interactive program to cycle through the file automatically, essentially performing steps 1–5. This is the purpose of the program shown in figure 6.7.

This program cycles through the entire CUSTOMERS file. Each time through the overall loop (lines 3–19), the next record in the file is processed. For each record, information relating to the customer's name, address, and financial status

Figure 6.7
An interactive dBASE III
program. A user is
given the option to
update credit limit data
for each record in the
CUSTOMERS file.

```
A dBASE III Program to change credit limits for
customers

This program cycles through the CUSTOMERS file.
Each record is displayed, and the user is given
the option of changing the credit limit by
entering a new value.

COMMENT lines are begun with a triple asterisk
(***)
```

```
 1.  SET DEVICE TO SCREEN
 2.  USE CUSTOMERS

     *** Cycle through the entire file; terminate when
     *** the END_OF_FILE is reached.

 3.  DO WHILE .NOT.(EOF)

         *** Display name, address, and financial
         *** information for the current record.

 4.      CLEAR
 5.      ?   NAME
 6.      ?   STREET
 7.      ?   CITY, ", " , STATE
 8.      ?
 9.      ?   " Outstanding balance: " , BALANCE
10.      ?   " Credit limit: " , LIMIT

         *** Ask the user if the credit limit is to be
         *** changed. If the answer is 'yes', get the
         *** new value from the user and replace the
         *** existing value with the new one.

11.      ?   "Do you wish to change the credit limit
             (Y_N)? "
12.      Accept to ANSWER

13.      IF ANSWER = "Y"
14.          ? "Please enter new limit:"
15.          INPUT to NEWLIMIT
16.          Replace LIMIT with NEWLIMIT
17.      ENDIF

18.      SKIP
19.  ENDDO

     *** Exist on END_OF_FILE

20.  RETURN
```

is displayed (lines 5–10). In lines 11–17, the user is given the opportunity to enter a new value for the credit limit. If a new value is entered, it replaces the old value (line 16). As in prior examples, the loop is exited and the program terminated when the end-of-file is reached.

Points to Ponder

- **User-friendliness.** Note that this program is designed so that the user need not know any database syntax. Instead, the program itself generates all of the necessary DBMS commands. At each step where a decision must be made, the user is prompted by the program for information. Thus, in line 11 the user is instructed to enter a value of either **Y** or **N** in response to a question. Similarly, line 14 prompts the user to enter a value for the new credit limit.
- **Types of database users.** The issue of user-friendliness brings up another important point concerning database usage—the fact that there may be two quite different types of database users. There are: (1) those who wish to access a database with as little understanding as possible of the inner workings of the database system; and (2) technically-oriented persons who may wish to use a DBMS for their own purposes, or whose job is to make the DBMS accessible and palatable for the first kind of user.
- **Repetition.** The repetitive tasks associated with cycling through the file are all handled by the program, freeing the user to concentrate on the important decision: whether or not to update the data for each record.
- **Program variables.** The program makes use of two variables for temporarily storing information. For example, in line 12, user input is stored in the variable ANSWER. As mentioned earlier, variables are essential for any but the most trivial programs.
- **Complex control structures.** This program illustrates the power that is derived by having various types of control structures available. The main body of the program is contained within a DO WHILE/ENDDO loop. Moreover, contained within this loop is a conditional-transfer control structure (lines 13–17), lending power and flexibility to the program.

Example 4: A Set of Menu-driven Programs

In this example, we outline a complete package of programs for adding, deleting, and modifying records in the CUSTOMERS file. As with the last example, these programs are designed to be quite user-friendly. The name of each program, along with its function, is listed in table 6.3. Two programs from the complete set are shown in figures 6.8 and 6.9: MASTER_MENU and DELETE_REC.

Table 6.3	List of Programs Used for Updating the CUSTOMERS File

Program Name	Function
MASTER_MENU	Prompts the user to choose the function to be executed (add a record, delete a record, etc.). In response to the user input, the appropriate program (one of those listed below) is called into execution .
ADD_REC	Adds a new record to the CUSTOMERS file. The user is prompted for the data to be entered for each field.
DELETE_REC	Deletes a record. The user enters the customer name corresponding to the record to be deleted. Customer names are assumed to be unique.
MODIFY_REC	Modifies a record. The user enters the customer name corresponding to the record to be modified. A dialog is then established between the user and the program for modifying the record fields, similar to that contained in the program in figure 6.9.

The MASTER_MENU program, which is directed by user inputs, controls which of the other programs is to be executed, and its logic is quite straightforward. After the CUSTOMERS file has been accessed (line 1), the menu of possible choices is displayed (lines 2–11). A prompt is then written to the screen, and the program waits for the user to enter his or her choice (lines 12 and 13).

On the basis of the user's choice, the appropriate program is called into execution (lines 14–22). When this program has terminated, it returns control to MASTER_MENU, which then continues to wait for additional user input. If an incorrect option is entered by the user, it is ignored by the program. An input value of 4 terminates MASTER_MENU.

If the user wishes to delete a record, option 2 is chosen, and the DELETE_REC program is called into execution by the statement in line 18. When this program is entered (see figure 6.9), it prompts the user for the name of the customer whose record is to be deleted (lines 3 and 4). After a customer name has been entered (line 5), the program initiates an indexed search of the CUSTOMERS file for a matching record (line 6). If no record is found, a message to that effect is displayed, and the program returns to the MAIN_MENU program. If a corresponding record is found, it is deleted from the file (line 12), and the program then returns.

Figure 6.8

Menu program for
driving a set of
programs to modify the
CUSTOMERS file.

```
                    MASTER MENU PROGRAM
                    _____

This program controls what action is taken with
respect to the CUSTOMERS file. The user is given
the choice to do one of following:

              1. Add a new record
              2. Delete an existing record
              3. Modify an existing record
              4. Terminate the program

The program will continue cycling until option 4
is chosen.

The program is written in dBASE III syntax.
```

```
 1. USE CUSTOMERS

     *** Mainloop

 2. DO WHILE CHOICE <> 4

           *** Display the menu

 3.       CLEAR
 4.       ?      "       1. Add a new record "
 5.       ?      "
 6.       ?      "       2. Delete a record "
 7.       ?      "
 8.       ?      "       3. Modify a record "
 9.       ?      "
10.       ?      "       4. Terminate session"
11.       ?      "
12.       ?      "    Please enter your choice (1-4) : "

           *** Get user's choice

13.       ACCEPT TO CHOICE

           *** Call the selected program

14.       IF CHOICE=1
15.              DO ADD_REC
16.       ENDIF

17.       IF CHOICE=2
18.              DO DELETE_REC
19.       ENDIF

20.       IF CHOICE=3
21.              DO MODIFY_REC
22.   ENDIF
23.   ENDDO

       *** Terminate on user option. . .

24.   RETURN
```

Figure 6.9

Program for deleting a
CUSTOMERS record.
The user specifies the
customer name of the
record to be deleted.

```
                    DELETE__REC PROGRAM

This program deletes a particular record in the
CUSTOMERS file. The user specifies the exact
record by supplying the value of the NAME, an
indexed field. If a corresponding record exists,
it is deleted. If not, a message to that effect
is displayed for the user. Finally, control
returns to the calling program (MENU).


 1.  USE CUSTOMERS INDEX NAMEINDX
 2.  CLEAR
 3.  ?   " Please enter the NAME of the customer whose
           record "
 4.  ?   "      is to be deleted: "

     *** User enters name

 5.  ACCEPT TO KEY

     *** Search for the corresponding record, using an
     *** indexed search. An END__OF__FILE condition
     *** indicates that no record was found.

 6.  SEEK KEY

 7.  IF EOF
 8.       ?   "There is no record with that key
               value...."
 9.       ?   "Program terminated."
10.       RETURN
11.  ENDIF

     *** The record was found; delete it.

12.  DELETE
13.  RETURN
```

Points to Ponder

- **Program control.** The MAIN_MENU program controls the major logic
  paths taken, in response to user inputs. That is, each of the other
  programs may be called only from MAIN_MENU program. Therefore,
  by illustrating only two of the programs (MAIN_MENU and DELETE_
  REC) we can understand the total concept of the design.

- **Modularization.** The programs MAIN_MENU, DELETE_REC, ADD_
  REC, and MODIFY_REC form a complete package for modifying data
  in the CUSTOMERS file. Each distinct function, such as record addition,
  has been built into a separate program. As we mentioned earlier, the

ability to modularize is an important feature of any programming language that is to be used to build large programs for database applications.

- **User-friendliness.** As in prior examples, the programs are designed to be quite user-friendly, requiring no user knowledge of DBMS commands— the user simply responds to prompts generated by the programs. The programs are also designed to be bulletproof, meaning that the user cannot inadvertently issue a command that could result in the loss of data because all DBMS commands are built into the programs. Of course, there is nothing to prevent a user from accidentally deleting the wrong record by entering an incorrect name. Database backups are essential for recovering from such inevitable errors.

- **Unique customer names.** The reader may have noted that the success of DELETE_REC is based on the assumption that customer names are unique. If this assumption is not valid, additional programming would be needed.

Other Applications

The preceding examples are only a small drop in a very large bucket of database programming applications. These examples were all based on a special circumstance—databases consisting of a single file. In later chapters, we shall see how multiple-file databases offer many opportunities for highly complex programming applications.

Summary

This chapter has been a very brief introduction to the rich subject of programs written for the database environment. This type of program can enormously enhance the flexibility with which databases may be utilized in the batch and interactive modes.

Interactive programs have a wide range of applications. Various activities, such as database querying and data entry and modification are often most conveniently performed in this mode. Interactive programs also serve to protect both users and databases: users are freed from the tedium of repeatedly entering the same groups of commands; and data may be protected from accidental damage by incorrect command sequences. This type of program may serve to form a friendly and flexible interface between the outside world and a database, relieving users of the need for familiarity with DBMS commands. Finally, the programs may perform data checking, user password validation, and complex manipulations involving several database files.

A program may be written in the batch mode usually to carry out a standard set of DBMS procedures, often involving large amounts of data processing. This could be the generation of a standard report, the processing of a set of previously prepared input data, or some other type of complicated data manipulation.

Many database management systems do not offer the means for generating user-written programs. For these, users are limited to whatever flexibility is built into the DBMS, and this may often be sufficient for many database applications.

For complex database applications, programs are often a necessity, and the most flexible database systems are those that offer programming capability.

Chapter Review

Terminology

built-in programming language
control structure
embedded command
host language interface
interactive program

interface
macro
menu-driven
modularization
standard programming language

Review Questions

1. Why may a macro be considered as a program? In what ways might a macro-definition capability be inferior to a programming capability?
2. List several general categories for which programs may be beneficial in a business environment.
3. List advantages for both built-in and standard programming languages.
4. Compare the two program segments in figures 6.2 and 6.3. Discuss the pros and cons of each style. Which do you prefer?
5. What special requirements must be met by a language used for database applications?
6. Can you think of any ordinary language characteristics that might be considered "excess baggage," that is, superfluous for database applications?
7. What are the advantages of having a DBMS interface between a program and the data, as opposed to having a program directly read and/or write data files?
8. Many file-managers perform the functions equivalent to the MASTER_ MENU program in figure 6.8, *without* any user-written programs. How do you suppose this is done? If this is so, why would there ever be a need to write a set of programs similar in style to MASTER_MENU and those that it calls?

Problems

1. Outline a separate program that allows user access to the MASTER_MENU program (figure 6.8) *only* upon entry of a valid password. Notice how this technique separates (modularizes) the process of password checking from any other database-accessing programs. For this problem, use any language with which you are familiar, or simply sketch your answer in commonly-used English terms.

2. Indicate how the CREDIT_LIMIT program in figure 6.7 could be modified to check that the new credit limit is in the range 0–5000. If it is not, the program would inform the user, requesting that another value be entered.

3. Outline the structure of the ADD_REC program called by MASTER_MENU. (*Hint:* List the main functions that should be included in the program; then go back and expand on each of these.)

4. Suppose that we wish to add a new function to the group of programs controlled by MASTER_MENU: the ability to display a specific record on the screen. Assuming that this new function would be incorporated into a program called DISPLAY_REC, outline the necessary changes to the MASTER_MENU program.

5. Outline the program DISPLAY_REC described in problem 4.

6. Suppose that the DBMS managing the CUSTOMERS file has no built-in report writer. Using a programming language with which you are familiar, write a program to generate a report consisting of the names and balance due for all records in the CUSTOMERS file. The output should be in columnar format. In writing your program, use the group of subroutine names used by the program in figure 6.6.

Chapter Seven

A Two-file Database

Introduction

In the previous chapters we have explored some of the basic ways in which databases are used, including the processes of defining a database, information modification, searching and reporting, and others. Because these discussions were of an introductory nature, they were limited to single-file databases.

Many situations are well-represented by single-file databases. These normally consist of simple applications in which the real-life objects to be represented are of the same type. For example, in the case of the CUSTOMERS database, the objects of interest are all persons who buy from Jellybeans, Inc. Furthermore, these real-life objects form a closed universe, in the sense that database information about them is useful without reference to different types of objects. Some examples for which single-file databases are adequate are the following:

Recipe list. Each record contains the list of ingredients for a particular recipe
Personal datebook. Each day of the year is represented by a separate record, which contains a summary of daily commitments
Literature citations. Each record contains information necessary to locate a particular reference, plus a short summary of the reference contents.

In each of these examples, the information in a single record forms a complete package, in that no other relevant data is required or available from the database. For example, a record describing a particular recipe would be complete by itself—no other related information exists within the database.

Quite frequently, real-world information is not simple enough for a one-file database description to be adequate. Data is frequently very complicated; and it often must be conceptualized into many different types of simple data objects, each of which can then be described by a record-type. In fact, a large fraction of database applications, particularly those related to businesses, are sufficiently complicated to require databases consisting of multiple files.

177

In entering into the realm of multiple-file databases, we begin to understand more completely the meaning of the term *database,* which is a collection of organized data that represents a particular real-world situation. We shall see that in this more complex type of environment, the demands on a DBMS become much more rigorous—not only must many different files be maintained within a particular database, but also relationships among the records belonging to these files must be maintained as well. This is because a multiple-file database consists of a set of *organized* data. Thus, even though different types of data exist in different files, strong connections will exist among various pieces of data. If a database is to be useful to the fullest possible degree, these connections must be available to the database user.

In chapter 8, we shall examine the general concepts of designing multiple-file databases. However, in order to introduce this subject, the present chapter is devoted to the exploration of a two-file database. This example represents many of the features of multiple-file databases, but at the same time limits the degree of complexity that might otherwise overwhelm the student. The power to be gained from the use of multiple-file databases will be clearly demonstrated; and some of the design problems and technical issues associated with multiple-file databases will be brought into focus. This will set the stage for a more complete study of the subject in the next chapter.

The example used in this chapter is an extension of the single-file Jellybeans, Inc. database used earlier. Once again, this particular example is chosen for illustrative purposes only. A general method for expanding the Jellybeans, Inc. database into a more comprehensive design will be the subject of the following chapter.

Extending the CUSTOMERS Database: The ORDERS File

General Considerations

Assume that the use of the CUSTOMERS database has proven to be of great value to Jellybeans, Inc. A decision has therefore been made to extend the database to include information related to jellybean orders placed by various customers of Jellybeans, Inc. The justification for this particular choice is the following. For each customer, there exist many different orders, and the information associated with all of these orders represents the single greatest source of data that could benefit from computerization. Also, as a next step in automation, it seems natural to include data that is directly related to the existing CUSTOMERS database.

Designing the File

The objective is to design a file that contains relevant information concerning customer orders, so as to best serve the needs of Jellybeans, Inc. In pursuing this, many of the design methods used in chapter 2 will be useful, and it might be helpful to review that material at this point.

Figure 7.1
The Jellybeans, Inc.
two-file database.

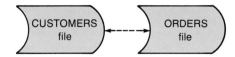

Studying the Nature of Orders

To begin the design work, we must first study the physical processes associated with the ordering of jellybeans. An order from a customer consists of a piece of paper that contains a request for shipment of a given number of jellybeans of a particular flavor. In addition, each order contains the name and address of the customer, as well as the date of order. Finally, over an extended period of time, a given customer may submit many orders.

Since each order exists as a separate entity, it seems natural, at least as a first design attempt, to associate one order with a single record. One more step in logic leads us to the conclusion that *a new file should be designed that will contain all of the records representing customer orders.* This is a bold step, and we make it tentatively, being prepared to modify it as required by subsequent considerations. For convenience, we give this new file the name ORDERS. Figure 7.1 shows the overall picture of the new database design. The arrows indicate that the two files will be related, in ways as yet to be established.

The decision concerning orders embodies an important database design principle:

Design Principle #1

Each real-world object or entity may be represented by a single database record. The set of records that represents a group of similar real-world entities may form a separate file.

Having decided on the overall structure into which the information about orders will be molded, we can proceed to the next level of detail, which is to choose the particular data to be contained in each ORDERS record. To do so, the following factors must be considered.

User Requirements

An important issue to be addressed is that of **user requirements,** which are the various ways in which the company personnel need to make use of orders information. Again, this can be answered only by studying the operation of the company, and in particular, by interviewing those personnel dealing with orders.

Some of the user requirements will be easy to identify, such as the following:

- **Reports required on a regular basis.** Examples might be: (1) a monthly list of all unfilled orders; and (2) a list of orders received in the current month. Many such reports may exist, and it is crucial that the design of the ORDERS file accommodate all of these.
- **The type of information that users need on an ad hoc basis.** These might include: (1) the name of the customer associated with a particular order; (2) the flavor of jellybeans for a particular order; (3) the list of orders received during the last week from a particular customer.

Although current user requirements may be easy to identify, future ones may be quite unpredictable. The way in which a database can be used depends on its actual design, so that in a very real sense a chicken-and-egg dilemma exists during the design process. The best that a designer can do is to base the design on current user requirements, drawing on past experience to incorporate as much flexibility as possible for dealing with future user needs.

Design as an iterative process. One of the major difficulties associated with database design is that many of the design factors are strongly interrelated, so that the solution to one problem depends to some extent on how the other problems are handled. For example, a user shown a preliminary design might respond, "This looks fine but how can I generate a report that contains data items x, y, and z?" The answer might lie in a modification to the design.

Thus, the database design process becomes an iterative one. A tentative solution is proposed, and subsequent considerations may reveal weaknesses or inconsistencies that cause this solution to be modified, perhaps many times.

Choice of Fields

As in the case of the CUSTOMERS file, each ORDERS record will consist of a set of fields, each of which represents a particular item, or attribute, that is part of an order. In deciding which fields are to be included in the ORDERS records, a compromise must be struck between two opposite requirements. On the one hand, we wish to include as much pertinent information as possible relating to an individual order. On the other hand, we do not wish to go overboard by introducing excessive detail into each record. Too much detail will place an unnecessary burden both on the available file-storage resources and on the ability of the user to easily manage the data.

In deciding whether or not to include a particular piece of information as a field, we will use the following principle:

Using this principle, along with a study of user requirements, we arrive at the following *tentative* list of items to be represented by fields in the ORDERS file:

1. Order number
2. Name and address of the customer
3. Date of order
4. Name of employee at Jellybeans, Inc. who received the order
5. Flavor of jellybeans ordered
6. Quantity of jellybeans ordered
7. Total price of the order
8. Desired delivery date

Upon reviewing these items and taking into account the aforementioned design criteria, we discover that there is no current or expected need for the name of the person who actually receives an order from a customer. Consequently, we delete item (4) from the list.

As a first design attempt, the preceding items, excluding (4), are translated into a list of fields, as shown in table 7.1. Along with each field, a choice of field type and field length has been made. The field lengths have been chosen on the basis of expected largest values. The fields AMOUNT and PRICE have been chosen to contain numeric quantities, because arithmetic will most certainly be performed on values in these fields.

Experience may require changes in some of these field parameters at a later date. For example, the choice of 7 for the length of the PRICE field limits the maximum price to $999.99. If Jellybeans, Inc. acquires a very large customer, the value of orders might begin to exceed this upper limit, forcing an increase in the length of PRICE.

Table 7.1

First Attempt at Choice of Fields for the ORDERS File

Field Name	Contents	Type of Field	Field Length
ORDER_NO	Order number	Alpha	6
NAME	Customer name	Alpha	25
STREET	Customer address	Alpha	25
CITY	Customer address	Alpha	15
STATE	Customer address	Alpha	2
ZIP	Customer address	Alpha	5
ORD_DATE	Date of order	Alpha	8
FLAVOR	Flavor to be shipped	Alpha	10
AMOUNT	Quantity to be shipped (lbs)	Numeric	3
PRICE	Total price of order	Numeric	7
DATE_NEEDED	Desired delivery date	Alpha	8

Relationships

An important aspect of database design involves a determination of the relationships that may exist between records in different database files—in this case CUSTOMERS and ORDERS. This is actually an examination of the relationship between real-life customers and orders, since the relationships among records should be a reflection of those among the actual entities.

The one-to-many relationship. As mentioned earlier, each customer may submit many orders to Jellybeans, Inc. Therefore, the following conditions will hold within the database:

- For each record in the CUSTOMERS file, there may be zero or more records in the ORDERS file
- For each record in the ORDERS file, there should be exactly one record in the CUSTOMERS file

These two conditions define what is known as a **one-to-many relationship,** which is represented in the diagram shown in figure 7.2. This type of diagram, which shows relationships between two or more record-types, is known either as a **Bachman diagram,** or a **structure diagram.** The arrows in this figure indicate the

Figure 7.2
A structure diagram for
the Jellybeans, Inc.
database.

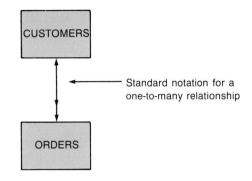

Standard notation for a
one-to-many relationship

Figure 7.3
A particular occurrence
of the CUSTOMERS-
ORDERS relationship.

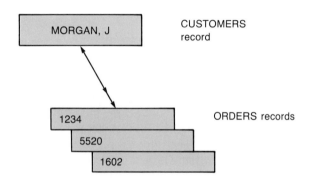

nature of the relationship. A single arrow (→) indicates exactly one record; and
a double arrow (→→) indicates zero, one, or several records. We shall use structure diagrams extensively when discussing multiple-file databases.

Occurrence of a relationship. An **occurrence** is defined simply as a group of
related entities. A particular occurrence of the CUSTOMERS/ORDERS relationship is shown in figure 7.3. Several ORDERS records are shown corresponding to the customer record of MORGAN, J.

This figure uses a common technique for representing particular records,
namely by values of a unique field. Thus, each ORDERS record is represented
by its ORDER_NO value.

The relationship between CUSTOMERS and ORDERS records is indicative
of the ways in which we may wish to use the ORDERS file in conjunction with
the CUSTOMERS file. For example, the following types of queries are likely to
be made of the database:

- Find all of the ORDERS records corresponding to a particular customer
- Find the CUSTOMERS record that corresponds to a particular order

These two types of queries suggest one of the most important aspects of a database design:

An occurrence of a relationship must be easily accessible *as a group*. In other words, every member of a group of related records must have contained within it information that gives easy access to all of the other members.

Redundancy Considerations

If we compare the list of fields for the ORDERS file with those for the CUSTOMERS file, shown in tables 7.1 and 7.2 respectively, we see that there is a considerable overlap, in that five fields are common to both files. The consequences of this fact are the following. Suppose that a particular CUSTOMERS record exists, and that furthermore a single ORDERS record also exists for this customer. The information contained in the fields NAME, STREET, CITY, STATE, and ZIP will be contained *twice* in the overall database—once each in the CUSTOMERS and ORDERS files. In this example the extra disk space amounts to a total of 72 bytes.

This situation is known technically as **data redundancy,** which has several negative side effects, in addition to the required extra disk storage. These include the extra effort needed for the data entry, as well as the possibility of inconsistencies within the database. For example, a customer name might be misspelled in one or more of the records, perhaps making it difficult to associate that record with any other database information.

To illustrate, consider a situation in which *several* ORDERS records correspond to a single CUSTOMERS record, such as shown in figure 7.3. In this case, there will be 72 redundant bytes of storage needed for each of these ORDERS records. To get an idea of the total cost of this redundancy, suppose that there are 200 records in the CUSTOMERS file; and that on the average there are 10 ORDERS records associated with each CUSTOMERS record. There will then be a total of 144,000 bytes of redundant disk storage! Even on a mainframe machine, this is not a trivial amount of storage, and on a small microcomputer-oriented DBMS, this could represent a significant portion of the available disk storage.

Table 7.2

Initial Design for the CUSTOMERS File

Data Item	Field Name	Type	Length
Customer name	NAME	Alpha	25
Address	STREET	Alpha	25
	CITY	Alpha	15
	STATE	Alpha	2
	ZIP	Alpha	5
Telephone number	PHONE	Alpha	13
Credit limit	CREDIT	Numeric	8
Outstanding balance	BALANCE	Numeric	8

Based on these considerations, we strive to achieve a design satisfying the following:

Design Principle #4

A database design should minimize, as much as possible, the amount of contained redundancy, while at the same time not sacrificing information content.

We therefore seek ways of eliminating the redundancy associated with the initial design of the ORDERS file as much as possible, while at the same time not losing any information.

Finding a Common Key Field

One common technique for minimizing redundancy within two related files is the following:

- Establish a *unique* key field within the CUSTOMERS file (one for which no two records may have the same value).
- Establish the same field as a *nonunique* field within the ORDERS file.

Figure 7.4
Using a common KEY
field to link ORDERS
and CUSTOMERS
records. Related
records have the same
key value.

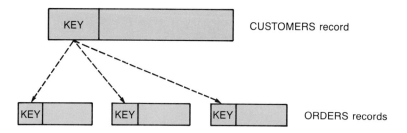

This common field, or key, serves to link together related records, as suggested by figure 7.4. The arrows indicate that the key value in any particular CUSTOMERS record may be used as a means of accessing the corresponding ORDERS records, and vice versa. The exact techniques for doing this are quite straightforward and will be discussed later in this chapter.

Because a common key furnishes a direct path between related records, redundant information in the ORDERS records becomes unnecessary and can be eliminated.

The problem, therefore, is to establish a field that is common to both files, and whose values are unique for the CUSTOMERS records. By considering the list of fields in table 7.1, we see that one likely possibility is the NAME field, since it exists in both the ORDERS and CUSTOMERS files. This is not necessarily a good choice, primarily because it may not be possible to guarantee uniqueness of customer names. For example, suppose that there were two CUSTOMERS records with the entry, "SMITH,J." If an ORDERS record contained the value "SMITH,J" in the NAME field, there would be no way to distinguish which of the two CUSTOMERS records contained the corresponding customer data.

Fields containing personal names are not the best choice for unique keys for another reason—the difficulties involved with spelling names consistently. For example, consider the following two spellings: (1) Holtenstein, Anton Grubernitz and (2) Holtenstein, Anton Grubernitz. They are not the same, and only a careful inspection will reveal the difference (can you spot it?). To a computer, however, the difference would be significant. The point to be made here is that it is very easy to misspell a name in a variety of ways. Personal name fields may be used as unique keys, but only if strict guidelines relating to spellings are followed.

The reasons for not using personal name fields apply equally well to address fields. In fact, an inspection of tables 7.1 and 7.2 reveal that there is no suitable field that can be used as a common key.

Another possibility exists, namely to create a new field that is common to both files and has values in the CUSTOMERS records that are unique. An arbitrary field could be concocted out of thin air, but this would be somewhat unsatisfying and difficult to use. A field that has some real-life significance is easier to use than one that does not. We can overcome this difficulty by adopting a solution that is in fact common practice: each customer is assigned a unique identification

Table 7.3	Modified CUSTOMERS Field List			
Field Name	**Contents**	**Type of Field**	**Field Length**
NAME	Customer name	Alpha	25
CUSTOMER_ID	Customer identification	Alpha	5
STREET	Customer address	Alpha	25
CITY	Customer address	Alpha	15
STATE	Customer address	Alpha	2
ZIP	Customer address	Alpha	5
CREDIT	Credit limit	Numeric	8
BALANCE	Balance due	Numeric	8

number. The responsibility for assigning these numbers will naturally rest with Jellybeans, Inc., although a programmer might at some point devise a way to have the numbers computer-generated.

To summarize the proposed steps to be taken:

- Each customer of Jellybeans, Inc. will be assigned a unique identification number
- This value will be placed in a new field, CUSTOMER_ID, which will be added both to the CUSTOMERS and ORDERS files. This field should be alphanumeric, in order to allow the possibility of using characters as part of the identification-number code.
- The following fields will be deleted from the tentative list for the ORDERS file: NAME, STREET, CITY, STATE, and ZIP.

Tables 7.3 and 7.4 list the modified field lists for the CUSTOMERS and ORDERS files.

There are two points worth reviewing with regard to the database design up to this stage. First, the term *database* now refers to both the CUSTOMERS and ORDERS files, considered as a total entity.

Secondly, data redundancy has been removed by the deletion of the NAME, STREET, CITY, STATE, and ZIP fields from the ORDERS file. However, the addition of the CUSTOMER_ID field to the two files creates its own data duplication, amounting to 5 bytes per ORDERS record. This duplication is necessary in order to create a common link among related records, and it is the *minimum* amount of duplication possible.

Table 7.4	**Second Design for the ORDERS File**			
Field Name	**Contents**	**Type of Field**	**Field Length**	
ORDER_NO	Order number	Alpha	6	
CUSTOMER_ID	Customer identification	Alpha	5	
ORD_DATE	Date of order	Alpha	8	
FLAVOR	Flavor to be shipped	Alpha	10	
AMOUNT	Quantity to be shipped (lbs)	Numeric	3	
PRICE	Total price of order	Numeric	7	
DATE_NEEDED	When jellybeans must arrive	Alpha	8	

Working with the Two-file Database

Having established a preliminary version of the ORDERS file, as well as a modified version of the CUSTOMERS file, we are ready to explore the separate processes of data retrieval, entry, and modification with the two-file database. As we look at each of the different types of data manipulation, keep in mind that the database design is still very much a tentative one. If it does not allow for a particular type of data handling that is felt to be important, then consideration must be given to the possibility of modifying the design.

As each type of data manipulation is examined, we shall see that the existence of more than one file in the database introduces many interesting complications, basically because of *relationships* that exist among the records in the different files. This leads to a new set of interesting and challenging problems to be addressed.

Data Retrieval

Inasmuch as information retrieval is, in a sense, the end product of a database, we begin by studying the different ways we may wish to obtain data from the Jellybeans, Inc. database. To begin, we shall construct a list of the types of queries that are of interest to users. We will then determine whether or not these queries can be satisfied by the current design.

In constructing this "wish list" we must recognize that there are two types of data retrieval: (1) those that come exclusively from a single file; and (2) those that require data from both files. We shall only briefly touch on the first type, since that subject has already been covered in the chapter on searching and reporting.

Single-file Queries

Many queries may be satisfied by searching only one file of a multi-file database. We have seen several query examples relating to the CUSTOMERS file in previous chapters. For the ORDERS file, some of the potential types of queries are:

- A list of all orders in the file
- A list of all orders received on a particular date
- The total number of orders received since a particular date
- A list of all orders for jellybeans of a particular flavor
- A list of all orders totaling more than a particular dollar amount

This list is not intended to be complete. It is merely a sample of the type of information that can be obtained exclusively from the ORDERS file. All of the searching and reporting techniques discussed in chapter 5 may be used to satisfy these as well as other queries.

Two-file Queries

This section deals with situations in which desired information involves data from both files. Many of the techniques for single-file searching and reporting will not be directly applicable to the two-file situation so new methods will need to be developed. We begin by listing two fundamental types of two-file queries that may be made:

- For a particular order, find the relevant database information pertaining to that order and also to the associated customer
- For a particular customer, (1) find the database information pertinent to that customer; *and* (2) find the database information concerning all orders for that customer

Figure 7.3 suggests the ways in which these queries may be satisfied. The first of the two queries involves the process of going from a particular ORDERS record to a particular CUSTOMERS record, represented by the direction of the single arrow. The second query type represents the process of finding first a particular CUSTOMERS record, and then locating the associated ORDERS records, as represented by the double arrow.

We shall study each of these two types of queries using the sample CUSTOMERS and ORDERS files shown in figures 7.5 and 7.6. In presenting examples, we shall assume that we are using the *interactive* query mode.

Example #1: from ORDERS to CUSTOMERS. Suppose that we are browsing through the ORDERS file and come upon a particular record that catches our attention for some reason. Perhaps the amount of the order seems high, and we would like to verify it with the customer. To do so, we need to find the identity of the customer, but this information is not directly available from the ORDERS record. However, what is available from the record is the value of the customer's

Figure 7.5
The modified
CUSTOMERS file with
sample records. The
ADDRESS fields are not
shown, for the sake of
brevity.

NAME	CUSTOMER_ID	CREDIT	BALANCE
Smith, Jennifer	12100	5000	0.00
Harris, Peter	15125	1000	155.75
James, Jesse	14511	5000	532.87
Norman, Samuel	15166	0	0.00
LaRue, Elaine	12125	1000	955.00
Clark, Kent	11300	1000	395.15
Gregory, Robert	11255	5000	1857.32
Drue, Ellen	12501	10000	3527.98
Smith, Alfred	14587	1000	0.00
Andersen, Tim	19873	5000	327.13
Baker, James	12560	10000	125.15

Figure 7.6
The modified ORDERS
file with sample
records.

ORDER_NO	CUSTOMER_ID	ORD_DATE	FLAVOR	AMOUNT	PRICE	DATE-NEEDED
225110	12560	04/13/84	Chocolate	50	25.00	05/15/84
214987	12125	03/25/84	Vanilla	150	75.00	--
225125	12560	05/18/84	Cranberry	80	48.00	06/01/84
215301	11255	03/29/84	Chocolate	130	65.00	05/01/84
229881	12560	06/22/84	Marshmallo	30	15.00	--
227540	19873	04/05/84	Vanilla	200	100.00	05/01/84
215000	12125	06/30/84	Mint	40	20.00	07/01/84
234125	12100	05/22/84	Chocolate	150	75.00	06/15/84
225211	12560	04/25/84	Vanilla	100	50.00	06/01/84
216789	12125	05/15/84	Strawberry	150	90.00	07/01/84
251834	14511	02/18/84	Mint	60	30.00	04/01/84
227615	19873	02/25/84	Cranberry	50	30.00	03/01/84
235100	12125	07/05/84	Mint	1000	500.00	08/01/84

identification number (assume that it is 12125). By itself, this number is not particularly useful, unless we happen to remember the name and address of the corresponding customer. (If our memory were that good, we wouldn't need a computer.) However, the number can point to the customer information that we need. Recall that the database design specifically put the CUSTOMER_ID field in both the CUSTOMERS and ORDERS files. Therefore, given a particular ORDERS record, we may use the CUSTOMER_ID value of this record as a search item for the CUSTOMERS file. In other words, we may search the CUSTOMERS file for a record whose CUSTOMER_ID field contains the value 12125.

The entire search process is summarized in table 7.5.

Table 7.5

Steps Involved in a Search of the Jellybeans, Inc. Database

1. Access the ORDERS file for browsing

2. Browse through the file, using whatever commands are convenient

3. Locate a particular record of interest

4. Note the value of the CUSTOMER_ID field (12125)

5. Access the CUSTOMERS file for searching

6. Find the record corresponding to a CUSTOMER_ID value of 12125 (this may be either an indexed or sequential search)

7. Extract the desired information from the CUSTOMERS record.

This process involves several steps, including the transfer of searching activity from one file to the other. Often, with procedures like this that involve several files, much of the manual effort can be eliminated by the use of cleverly written programs.

The common field CUSTOMER_ID is crucial to the success of the process. It is the vehicle by which a connection is made between the ORDERS record and the corresponding CUSTOMERS record. Also, note that the precise reasons or criteria by which the particular ORDERS record is isolated is unimportant. In fact, no matter how a particular ORDERS record is chosen, the steps outlined above may be used to find the corresponding CUSTOMERS record.

Example #2: from CUSTOMERS to ORDERS. In this example, we illustrate the second of the two types of two-file queries. To restate: Find all of the information in the database that pertains to a particular customer. This includes (1) personal information, which happens to be located in the CUSTOMERS file; and (2) data concerning orders for that customer, which are stored in the ORDERS file.

The steps to be carried out are summarized as:

1. Find the corresponding CUSTOMERS record
2. Find all corresponding ORDERS records

Locating the CUSTOMERS record from available data. In general, the information most likely to be available is a customer name. For example, we are much more likely to encounter the question "What is Joe Blow's address?", than "Who lives at 3 Park Place in Boston?" or "What is the address of the customer whose identification number is 12345?" Consequently, the most common type of on-line search of the CUSTOMERS file for a particular record will be based on a personal name.

| Table 7.6 | Steps in Performing a Search of the Jellybeans, Inc. Database |

1. Select the CUSTOMERS file for searching

2. Locate the particular record of interest, using whatever information is available

3. When the correct record has been found, note the CUSTOMER_ID value, as well as any other desired information

4. Select the ORDERS file for searching

5. Search the file, using the CUSTOMER_ID value as a search key

6. Output the results of the search in whatever format desired.

On the other hand, we might know only a customer ID number. Regardless of whether the search is based on the customer name, the identification number, or other fragments of information, the objective is to locate a particular CUSTOMERS record. Once this record has been located, it can furnish whatever customer data is of interest. In addition, it will supply the value of CUSTOMER_ID, which aids in finding the related ORDERS records.

Locating the ORDERS records. Let us suppose that a search of the CUSTOMERS file has produced the desired record, which for the sake of discussion we assume to be the fifth record in figure 7.5. The CUSTOMER_ID value for this record is 12125, and this may be used as the key value for searching the ORDERS file. This search would most likely be done with an index on the CUSTOMER_ID field for the ORDERS file.

The steps involved in this search process are outlined in table 7.6 and are illustrated in figure 7.7. The complete set of data located by this search is shown in figure 7.8. Notice that this is a particular occurrence of the one-to-many relationship that exists between CUSTOMERS and ORDERS.

The preceding examples have strong similarities: in each case, both files must be accessed, with separate queries being made against each one. Also, the success of each example rests on the existence of the CUSTOMER_ID field, which is common to both files.

It is not necessary that the fields in both files have the same name. For example, we could have named the CUSTOMERS field CUST_NO, and the ORDERS field CUST_ID. The crucial factors are that: (1) related records have the *same value* in these fields; and (2) the user be aware that CUST_NO and CUST_ID refer to the same logical quantity, namely the customer identification number.

Figure 7.7
A two-file search. The
search result generated
in step 1 is used as the
basis for the search in
step 2.

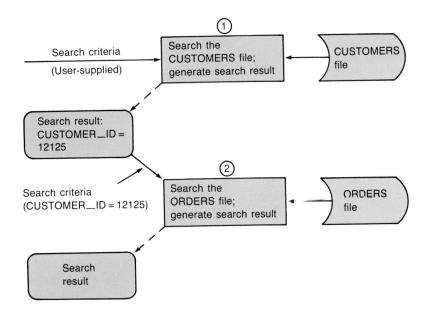

Data Entry and Consistency

In many ways, the process of data entry is similar for a two-file and single-file database: a file may be selected, and records added. However, in some respects the use of a two-file database introduces a new set of problems—one of the most significant of these concerns **data consistency.**

In the context of the two-file Jellybeans, Inc. database, the problem of data consistency develops because of the existence of *relationships* among the different records in the database. For each CUSTOMERS record, there may be several related ORDERS records, and for each ORDERS record, there must be one related CUSTOMERS record. Each of these facts raises a question of data consistency.

Consider the set of data shown in figure 7.8. The CUSTOMERS record, which corresponds to a CUSTOMER_ID of 12125, has associated with it four ORDERS records. Each of the ORDERS records also contain the value of 12125 for CUSTOMER_ID. The principle of data consistency requires that those records that are related *in principle* should also be related *in fact*. Suppose, for example, that one of the ORDERS records shown in figure 7.8 is entered with an incorrect value for CUSTOMER_ID, 12124 for instance. In this case, figure 7.8 represents the situation in principle but it does not represent the situation that actually exists within the database.

Once the record with value 12124 has been entered, it may be very difficult to detect the error at a later time. It might be noticed if the erroneous record were encountered during a perusal of the ORDERS file, and if a search were then made for the related CUSTOMERS record and no corresponding CUSTOMERS record were found.

Figure 7.8
A specific set of related
records. The
relationship exists by
virtue of the common
key value.

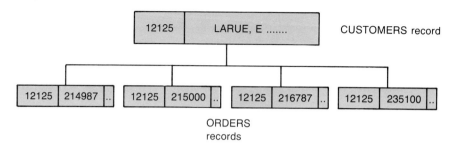

If there happened to be a CUSTOMERS record with a CUSTOMER_ID of 12124, however, the erroneous ORDERS record would only be uncovered if that customer were billed for the corresponding order! Or, if undetected, Elaine Larue would get a shipment for which she was never billed.

The point here is that a data-entry error in the CUSTOMER_ID value for an ORDERS record is very serious, and as much effort as possible must be made to guard against this type of error. One way of doing so is to check the CUS-TOMERS file as each ORDERS record is added, to make sure that a corresponding record actually exists. If there were such a record, the ORDERS record would be added. Otherwise, the following steps would need to be taken, in order to locate the source of the inconsistency:

1. Determine whether the CUSTOMER_ID value for the order is correct; if it is not, correct and reenter the record. Otherwise:
2. Determine why there is no corresponding CUSTOMERS record in the file. If the customer is new to Jellybeans, Inc., then add the appropriate record to the file. Otherwise:
3. Determine whether the record ever existed in the CUSTOMERS file, and if so, how it managed to disappear.

As a further check on the validity of the CUSTOMER_ID value for each order, the NAME of the corresponding CUSTOMERS record could be checked against the name on the physical order. This would guard against the possibility of accidentally entering an incorrect CUSTOMER_ID value that happened to coincide with another customer's identification number. To do this kind of data validation manually would be inordinately time-consuming. However, a user-written program could automate almost all of this procedure.

Referential integrity. In this discussion, we have implicitly assumed that each ORDERS record must have an associated CUSTOMERS record. We could raise the question of whether or not it makes sense to have an ORDERS record in the database for which there is no corresponding CUSTOMERS record. In terms of data consistency, it definitely does not make sense. This is the database principle of **referential integrity:** the existence of an ORDERS record implies the existence of a corresponding CUSTOMERS record.

Data Updating

The term **updating** includes any process that alters the contents of a database, such as deleting or modifying existing records. As in the case of data entry, the fact that a database consists of two interrelated files introduces several new problems related to updating.

Record Deletion

Consider the implications of removing each type of record from the set of CUSTOMERS and ORDERS records shown in figure 7.8. The crucial question to be answered is whether a deletion makes sense—not so much from a database standpoint but from a real-world point of view. Considering first ORDERS, under what circumstances would it make sense to remove one of these records? Some possibilities are:

- An order is cancelled
- It is discovered that a record was incorrectly entered into the database and must therefore be deleted.

Now consider the implications of removing a CUSTOMERS record. In this case, there might also be valid reasons for doing so, such as the fact that the customer has moved away, or for other reasons has stopped being an active customer of Jellybeans, Inc. Suppose, in fact, that a particular customer stops eating jellybeans, and the appropriate CUSTOMERS record is deleted. What happens to all of the related ORDERS records? The answer is that they are left "dangling" without any corresponding CUSTOMERS record—the principle of referential integrity has been violated. The real-life implication is that a group of orders exists for which there is no corresponding customer. The obvious solution to this situation is that the ORDERS records must also be deleted, preferably at the same time as the CUSTOMERS record.

This is another example of the need for data consistency, in that the data must be an accurate reflection of the world that it is attempting to represent. In the case of the removal of CUSTOMERS records, consistency could perhaps best be maintained by not allowing the casual removal of CUSTOMERS records. Instead, some sort of automated procedure might be used to guarantee that if a CUSTOMERS record were removed, all of the related ORDERS records were also removed or flagged to indicate that they were "dangling".

Data Modification

Data modification requires the same type of considerations that are involved in adding or deleting records. That is, care must be taken so that when any record modification is made, it does not destroy data consistency. For example, consider the implications of modifying one of the ORDERS records in figure 7.8. In particular, if the value of the CUSTOMER_ID field were altered, then that record would no longer be related to the same CUSTOMERS record. This could be a valid change—for example if the original CUSTOMER_ID value had been entered incorrectly. On the other hand, if this value were accidentally modified, data consistency would be violated, and the modified ORDERS record would then either be incorrectly related to some other CUSTOMERS record or it would be left dangling.

Notice that the incorrect modification of any other field in the ORDERS record is not as serious an error. A particular data value for a record could become incorrect, but the record itself would still be related to the correct CUSTOMERS record.

The same considerations apply to modifications of the CUSTOMERS record. If the CUSTOMER_ID field were to be incorrectly changed, then that record would become dissociated from all of its ORDERS records, with one of the possible results being that Elaine Larue might get a great deal of free jellybeans.

Tools for Complex Database Manipulation

We have seen that the various processes of data entry, retrieval, and updating in a two-file database environment may involve complexities that do not exist for a single-file database. These complications arise not only from the need to access both files for various processes, but also from the need to maintain information consistency.

Therefore, it is natural to expect that the complications for multiple-file databases may become even more involved as relationships among records become increasingly tangled. In order to make effective use of these databases, techniques must be implemented that help to simplify the complex tasks of data manipulation. This is true for technically-oriented users as well as laypersons.

The latter type of user, whose primary goal is to obtain information from a database, may not wish to become intimately familiar with the technical details of files, fields, and complicated relationships. The primary focus for these users is on *simple* methods for effectively accessing the body of information lying within a database. For technically-oriented database users however, the employment of sophisticated techniques for accessing and manipulating data may be enormously beneficial in terms of making more efficient use of database resources.

Programming for Connections

Many of the complexities associated with multiple-file databases lend themselves to the automation afforded by custom-tailored programs. For example, many data retrieval tasks use a database in a repetitive manner, in that the same *kind* of query is made on a regular basis, with only the details of each query changing. In these circumstances, a program can automate most of the repetition, thus minimizing both the time required for the process and the chance for making errors. In this section, the use of programs for streamlining interactions with the two-file Jellybeans, Inc. database will be demonstrated.

Example: a data-retrieval program. Suppose that Jellybeans, Inc. has a standard procedure requiring the periodic retrieval of information relating to various customers and their orders. The steps involved in this process were discussed earlier and shown in table 7.6.

An equivalent program for performing these steps is shown in figure 7.9. This program prompts the user for a value of CUSTOMER_ID. It then automatically carries out the steps shown in table 7.6 and displays the desired information in a convenient format.

In the following program description, numbers in parentheses refer to line numbers. The main body of the program is contained in a DO WHILE loop (2–32), which loops repeatedly until the user signals that execution is to stop. The loop begins by prompting the user for a customer identification number (3–5). A negative number is a signal to terminate program execution (6–8). If the number is positive, the CUSTOMERS file is accessed (10) and the CUSTOMER ID index is attached. We assume that this index, stored in CUSTINDX, has been previously built. An indexed search is then made for a record with the specified ID number (11). If no record is found, the program skips to the bottom of the DO WHILE loop (12–15). Otherwise, selected fields from the CUSTOMERS record are displayed (17–18).

The ORDERS file is then accessed (19) and the CUSTOMER_ID index is attached. Again, we assume that this index has been previously created. A search is made for the first ORDERS records corresponding to the specified ID number (20). If no record is found, the program skips to the end of the overall DO WHILE loop (21–22). Otherwise, selected fields are output for all corresponding ORDERS records (23–29). The program then cycles back to the start of the DO WHILE loop, again prompting the user for input.

One significant fact about this program should be noted: *a user of the program does not need to know anything about the internal structure of the database.* As a matter of fact, a user would only have to know how to enter a number at the keyboard and how to read information from the monitor. The program has taken on the burden of dealing with the complexities of the database structure, allowing the user to be concerned only with pertinent information about the customers.

This program again illustrates two distinct types of DBMS users:

- The technically-oriented user, who writes programs like the one shown in figure 7.9. This type of user, who may possibly have a background in professional programming, must have a detailed knowledge of the database structure and also of the workings of the DBMS.
- The end-user, whose primary interest is the *information* that may be obtained from the database. These are the people for whom the database primarily exists. It is important that information be made available to them in whatever ways are convenient to them. Programs are often written for the convenience of end-users.

Figure 7.9
Program for automating
the search of the
Jellybeans, Inc.
database.

```
************************************************************
* Sample dBASE-III program to demonstrate automatic *
*       searching of the Jellybeans, Inc. two-file *
*       database.                                   *
* The program prompts the user for a CUSTOMER_ID   *
* value. It then searches the database for the     *
* following:                                        *
*                                                   *
*              1. Descriptive customer data from the *
*                 CUSTOMERS file                     *
*              2. Orders related to the given        *
*                 customer, from the ORDERS file     *
*                                                   *
* The program cycles until a negative CUSTOMER_ID  *
* value is entered                                 *
*                                                   *
* COMMENTS are indicated by multiple               *
* asterisks: ****                                   *
************************************************************
  1. STORE 9999 TO IDENT
  2. DO WHILE IDENT >= 0

         ***** Get the value of the customer ID  *****
         ***** from the user.                    *****

  3.     ?   "Please enter the customer
                 identification; number..."
  4.     ?   " (Enter negative no. to terminate)"
  5.     ACCEPT TO IDENT
  6.     IF ( IDENT < 0 )
  7.        ? "Terminating program..."
  8.        RETURN
  9.     ENDIF

         ***** Find the appropriate record in the*****
         ***** CUSTOMERS file                    *****
         ***** If no record found, skip to bottom*****
         ***** of "DO WHILE" loop,               *****
         *****   using the LOOP command          *****

 10.     USE CUSTOMERS INDEX CUSTINDX
 11.     SEEK IDENT
 12.     IF (EOF)
 14.        ? "Sorry, no such record; try another;
                 number."
 15.        LOOP
 16.     ENDIF

         ***** Display selected parts of         *****
         ***** CUSTOMERS record.                 *****

 17.     ? NAME
```

Figure 7.9 [*Continued*]

```
18.        ? STREET, CITY, STATE, ZIP

           ***** Find any corresponding orders in  *****
           ***** the ORDERS file                   *****
           ***** If any records are found, display *****
           ***** selected fields                   *****

19.        USE ORDERS INDEX ORDINDX
20.        SEEK IDENT
21.        IF EOF
22.            ? No orders for this customer...
23.        ELSE
24.            ? "ORDER-NUMBER ORDER-DATE FLAVOR
                 AMOUNT(LBS) PRICE"
25.            ? "-------------------------------"
26.            ?
27.            DO WHILE CUSTOMER-ID = IDENT
28.                ? ORDER-NO,ORD-DATE,FLAVOR,;
                     AMOUNT, PRICE
29.                SKIP
30.            ENDDO
31.        ENDIF

32. ENDDO *** End of major DO_WHILE loop

    RETURN
```

It frequently happens that an end-user becomes highly involved with the technical end of DBMS manipulations. This may be for reasons of interest, or lack of funds to pay for professional assistance. It often happens that people in one profession find themselves becoming amateur professionals of database management as well as other types of computer applications.

Example: a data-entry program. As described earlier, the process of entering data must be done carefully in order to minimize the chance of making errors. This is particularly true in the CUSTOMER_ID fields that link the two different record-types together. In this example, a program for entering ORDERS records into the database is outlined. We assume that for each record, there *must* be a corresponding CUSTOMERS record. Therefore, as each record is entered, the program checks to see if a corresponding CUSTOMERS record exists. If such a record is found, the program displays the customer name from this record, allowing the data-entry person to make a visual check with the name on the order. This is to ensure that the customer record that has been found actually corresponds to the order for which data is being entered. The flowchart for this program is shown in figure 7.10, and the program is shown in figure 7.11.

Figure 7.10
Flowchart of data-entry
program.

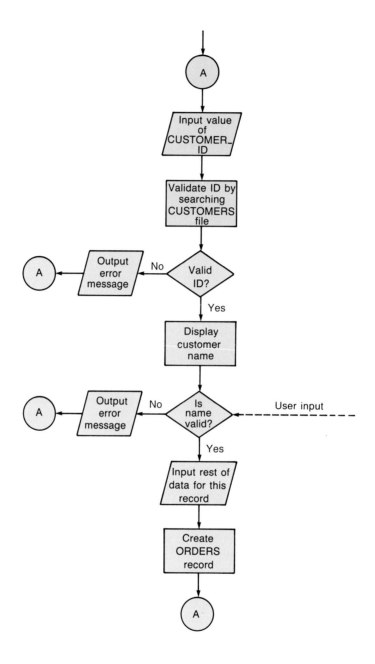

Figure 7.11
Data-entry program for
the ORDERS file.

```
Data-entry program for the ORDERS file of the
Jellybeans, Inc. database.

This program accepts input data interactively
from a user, one record at a time. The CUSTOMER_
ID is validated by checking for a corresponding
CUSTOMERS record. If no such record exists, the
user is informed. If a corresponding record does
exist, the customer name is displayed to the
user, so that a comparison can be made with the
name on the order currently being input.
```

```
       STORE TRUE TO MORE
 1.  DO_WHILE MORE

           ***** Begin inputting data for the next *****
           ***** record                            *****
           ***** First, input the CUSTOMER_ID value*****

 2.        ? " Please enter the customer ID number: "
 3.        ACCEPT TO IDENT

           ***** Exit on a negative input number   *****

 4.        IF IDENT < 0
 6.           RETURN
 7.        ENDIF

           ***** Check to see if there is a        *****
           ***** corresponding CUSTOMERS record    *****
           ***** If none exists, jump to the end    *****
           ***** of DO_WHILE loop                  *****

 8.        USE CUSTOMERS INDEX CUSTINDX
 9.        SEEK IDENT
10.        IF EOF
11.           OUTPUT "No CUSTOMERS record exists for
              this ID; try again..."
              LOOP
           ENDIF
```

Figure 7.11 [*Continued*]

```
                   ***** Display NAME of the CUSTOMERS    *****
                   ***** record that was found            *****
                   ***** User has option to abort input for*****
                   ***** this record if the displayed name *****
                   ***** does not match that on current    *****
                   ***** order                             *****

12.                ? " ####### PLEASE CHECK: Is this the correct
                     name (Y/N)? "
13.                ? NAME
14.                ACCEPT TO ANSWER
15.                IF ANSWER = "N"
17.                    ? "Aborting data input for this;
                        record..."
18.                    LOOP
19.                ENDIF

                   ***** Input the rest of data for this   *****
                   ***** record                            *****

20.                ACCEPT "Order Number :" TO ORDER_HOLD
21.                ACCEPT "Order Date :" TO DATE_HOLD
22.                ACCEPT "Flavor :" TO FLAVOR_HOLD
23.                ACCEPT "Amount :" TO AMOUNT_HOLD
24.                ACCEPT "Price :" TO PRICE_HOLD
25.                ACCEPT "Date needed :" TO NEEDED_HOLD

                   ***** Create the new ORDERS record,     *****
                   ***** using the values stored in the    *****
                   ***** temporary variables (XXXXX_HOLD)  *****

26.                USE ORDERS
27.                APPEND BLANK
28.                REPLACE ORDER_NO WITH ORDER_HOLD
29.                REPLACE ORD_DATE WITH DATE_HOLD
30.                REPLACE FLAVOR WITH FLAVOR_HOLD
31.                REPLACE AMOUNT WITH AMOUNT_HOLD
32.                REPLACE PRICE WITH PRICE_HOLD
33.                REPLACE DATE_NEEDED WITH NEEDED_HOLD
34.                REPLACE CUSTOMER_ID WITH IDENT

35. ENDDO
```

General Remarks about Programming

The preceding programs are samples of the type of automation that may be utilized with two-file or multi-file databases. Virtually any type of standard database procedure (one that is performed on a regular basis) can be automated by the use of a carefully written set of programs. The benefits to be gained from such user-written programs multiplies as the number of files contained in a database increases. Multiple-file databases, although enormously useful, can be very complicated to utilize effectively. Judiciously written programs can be of great help in this respect.

The importance of user-generated programs in the database environment cannot be overemphasized. Their use is essential to the successful utilization of many large, complex databases.

Advertisements by many authors of database systems would have one believe that many of these systems can be used by nontechnical people for every conceivable application, with no programming required. In fact, database systems that preclude the use of programming are always limited in what they can accomplish. It is true that a clever and innovative design may produce DBMS's that are capable of accomplishing a great many tasks automatically (without programming). Nevertheless, no DBMS can possibly include built-in features that cover all of the options and possibilities that may exist in the great variety of database applications.

More Sophisticated Query Languages

One of the most powerful techniques for data manipulation involves the use of advanced types of query languages. With these, single queries are capable of accessing several files simultaneously, manipulating related information in many complex ways. In chapter 11 we shall explore this type of language in some detail, but it is appropriate at this point to demonstrate their flavor with an example relating to the two-file database for Jellybeans, Inc.

Suppose that we wish to display information from the database about all of the orders for the customer Elaine Larue. The following *single* query accomplishes this:

```
SELECT  CUSTOMER_ID, ORDER_NO, ORDER_DATE,
        FLAVOR, AMOUNT, PRICE
FROM ORDERS
WHERE ORDERS.CUSTOMER_ID IN
        SELECT CUSTOMERS.CUSTOMER_ID
        FROM CUSTOMERS
        WHERE NAME = "Larue, Elaine"
```

This query is written in Structured Query Language (SQL), which is rapidly becoming a standard in the database industry. At this point, an understanding of all of the details of the query is not expected, but the following explanation may be of some assistance.

If the query is read in two parts, starting with the second (indented) part, it is possible to make some sense out of it. The indented part selects for the search result all CUSTOMERS records for which the NAME field contain the value Larue, Elaine. Since the search result should produce only one record, the final outcome of this part of the command is the single value 12125, which is the CUSTOMER_ID value for the record that corresponds to Elaine Larue.

The first part of the command selects those ORDERS records that satisfy the first WHERE clause, namely that the CUSTOMER_ID values are in the previously obtained search result, which is the single value 12125. Notice the use of the syntax "ORDERS.CUSTOMER_ID" to specify the CUSTOMER_ID field in the ORDERS file, as opposed to the field of the same name in the CUSTOMERS file.

If this explanation for the query example is not clear, let it be sufficient for now to say that this query is fundamentally equivalent to the modest size program shown in figure 7.9. Both approaches are aimed at finding a group of records corresponding to a particular customer. The difference lies in the fact that the preceding query automatically *generates* a program to do the file searching. Clearly, this approach is considerably more compact than that of the figure 7.9 approach. As mentioned, a detailed exposition of higher level query languages will be given in chapter 11.

Automatic Connections with Linked Lists

Various methods have been presented for dealing with the problem of data manipulation in the Jellybeans, Inc. database. All of these methods have one common feature: for any particular query, files must be searched for specific records. In the first method, as illustrated in tables 7.5 and 7.6, commands are *manually* entered by a user. The second method involves the use of user-generated programs, and the last involves higher level query languages that automatically generate database searching programs.

Another technique exists for manipulating data in a multiple-file database environment. This method involves the use of **linked lists,** which will be briefly outlined here, deferring a detailed discussion to chapter 13.

We will consider the particular set of records shown in figure 7.8, and describe how these records would exist in a DBMS environment in which linked lists were used. Figure 7.12 shows the single CUSTOMERS record and the four associated ORDERS records. We see that a new field has been added to each of these records. This is a special field that is supplied and maintained by the DBMS. Each of these fields contains a **pointer,** so named because it contains the address of another record to which it "points."

Figure 7.12
A set of related records
in a linked-list
environment. Heavy
arrows indicate links
between records.

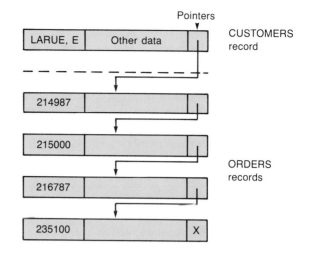

Figure 7.13
An example of using a
pointer.

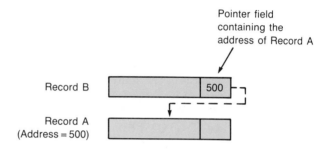

For example, suppose that record A were stored in disk address 500. If record B were to point to record A, then its pointer would contain the value 500, as shown in figure 7.13.

Suppose that we wish to find all of the orders for Elaine Larue. As before, the CUSTOMERS file is searched for the appropriate record, which is shown at the top of figure 7.12. The pointer in this record contains the address of one of the related ORDERS records (number 214987 in the figure), which can therefore be directly accessed. This is accomplished by a built-in DBMS program that first reads the address in the pointer field and then accesses the record at that address. In a similar manner, the pointer in record 214987 contains the address of another ORDERS record, which can in turn be directly accessed. Every ORDERS record that is related to Elaine Larue can be accessed in turn by following the set of pointers. This set of records is called a linked list.

The programs for establishing and maintaining linked lists are built-in parts of the DBMS. However, user-written programs are also needed in order to direct the DBMS in accessing various parts of a database via the pointers.

A little analysis will reveal that hardly any computing time is needed to find all of the records in a particular linked list, because virtually no file searching is involved. Each record in a list points *directly* to the next, so that only a single disk access is needed in order to find a record in the list. The price to be paid for this speed lies in the fact that a good deal of computer time is spent in maintaining the linked list as each record is added or deleted from the files. In addition, extra disk storage is needed to contain the pointer fields in each record.

The linked-list approach is widespread among DBMS's, particularly many of the older, mainframe-oriented systems. It is a powerful tool, and it will be investigated in more detail in chapter 13.

Summary

While many real-life situations may be represented by single-file databases, others cannot. This chapter has presented concepts related to the design and utilization of a two-file database. These concepts may be extended to multiple-file databases.

The redesign of the Jellybeans, Inc. database began by studying the nature of the company's operation and associated user requirements for those areas related to customers and orders data. User requirements include both current and projected needs, the latter being somewhat speculative.

On the basis of the study, an ORDERS file was designed, with fields chosen to include data items useful in satisfying user requirements. Part of the design was influenced by the fact that a one-to-many relationship exists between ORDERS and CUSTOMERS records, and groups of related records must be easily accessible. This latter requirement was implemented by the introduction of CUSTOMER_ID as a common field to both record-types. Data redundancy considerations also cast a strong influence on the design, requiring duplicated information to be kept to an absolute minimum.

Several techniques have been discussed for working with the new two-file database. Many types of database operations involve accessing data from both files. These are often facilitated by customized user-written programs, which serve several important purposes. They relieve the user of the burden not only of entering repetitive groups of commands, but also of needing to be intimately familiar with the details of the database structure. Programs also serve to protect the database from operations that could result in data inconsistencies.

Almost any type of standard procedure involving a database may be automated to some extent by the use of customized programs, and the advantages of using programs are increased many-fold when a database consists of multiple files.

Other techniques exist for interacting with complex databases. These include the use of sophisticated query languages capable of accessing several files simultaneously in a variety of complex ways, and linked lists that use pointers to find records.

Terminology

data consistency   referential integrity
data redundancy   relationship occurrence
linked list   structure diagram
one-to-many relationship   user requirements

Review Questions

1. What types of real-world situations may be adequately represented by a single-file database?
2. What are the most significant differences between using single-file and multiple-file databases?
3. List the most important factors to be considered when designing the ORDERS file.
4. Review each of the four design principles outlined in this chapter. Were they successfully applied in the design of the ORDERS file?
5. What are the two major types of queries that may be made of the Jellybeans, Inc. database?
6. Review the section that deals with referential integrity. Suggest alternate interpretations for the ORDERS records in which it would make sense for a record to exist without a corresponding CUSTOMERS record.
7. Why is a data-entry error for the CUSTOMER_ID fields much more serious than an error on any other type of field?
8. Review the various methods outlined in the chapter for searching the two-file database.

Problems

1. Suppose that the Jellybeans, Inc. database contains data for 100 customers, and that on the average, there are ten orders in the database for each customer.
    a. Calculate the amount of storage space required for the database.
    b. Suppose that indexes are created on the CUSTOMER_ID field for *both* files. How much additional storage space is required?
2. In many situations, a personal-name field is preferred as the link between different record-types within a database, instead of some type of identification number. Design a set of syntax rules for writing personal names. The purpose of these rules is to minimize the possibility of data inconsistencies due to misspelling when names are added to the database.
3. Suppose, for the sake of argument, that the STREET field is unique for the CUSTOMERS file. That is, it is known that each customer has a unique value for this field. Can you think of a reason why you would still

choose CUSTOMER_ID, rather than STREET, as the common field between CUSTOMERS and ORDERS? The answer to this question hints at an important design principle concerning common fields and entities. Can you deduce what it might be?

4. Make as complete a list as possible of the types of reports that might be required of the Jellybeans, Inc. database.

5. The design for the ORDERS file may not be perfect. Can you think of any other fields that might be added to improve the design? Justify any additions that you suggest.

6. Suggest two real-world situations that could each be described by a one-to-many relationship.

7. Design the outline of a program to find and output the names of those customers who submitted an order on a specific date.

8. Design the outline of a program to find and output the names of customers whose total number of orders exceeds 25.

9. Suppose that each customer order could contain an unlimited number of jellybean flavors. For each flavor the order would include flavor, quantity, etc. Would the current design for ORDERS be adequate? If not, how would the database design have to be modified?

10. The program in figure 7.9 uses CUSTOMER_ID as the search key. Suppose that the program were modified so that the user input was the customer NAME instead of CUSTOMER_ID. How would the program have to be modified, taking into account the fact that names may not be unique?

11. A particular college has several departments, and many students are registered in each. Design a two-file database in which the major entities represented are DEPARTMENTS and STUDENTS. Justify each field that you include in your design. Be particularly careful in choosing the common key field.

Chapter Eight

Conceptual Database Design

Introduction

Database design is a process of representation, whereby real-world systems are simulated by computer objects. The design process is creative, and requires a good deal of imagination and experience. It can also be extremely rewarding. Like any other creative process, database design is a skill that is acquired by much training, practice, and the ability to use past experiences to synthesize results in new situations.

A database is a model of a system, and the purpose of the model is to furnish information about that system to users. Since most things in the world change with time, databases must also be capable of modification. In fact, a database may be thought of as analogous to a process of time-lapse photography of an object, such as a growing flower: as the object slowly changes with time, a photograph of it is periodically taken. Each photograph represents the state of the flower at that particular moment in time.

Just as a photograph of a flower is only a representation of the actual flower, a database contains only an approximation of a system. A photographer may choose the way in which the flower is represented by varying parameters such as type of film, the orientation between flower and camera, exposure settings, and so on. The final photograph will thus be the particular representation of the flower that is desired by the photographer.

In a similar manner, a database designer chooses the particular representation of an object that best fills the needs of the potential database users. If the object to be represented is relatively simple, then not many options will be possible, and the database design will be straightforward. On the other hand, if a system is complex with a vast number of possibilities available for its representation, the design to represent the system will be quite complex and lengthy.

Steps in the Database Design Process

The design of a database is a step-by-step procedure, and for the purposes of this discussion the process is divided into the following separate stages, which are illustrated in figure 8.1.

Figure 8.1

The stages of database development.

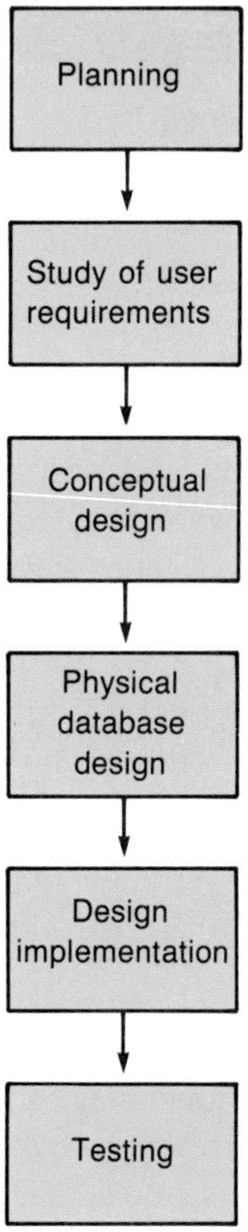

- **Planning.** The overall scope of the database design is laid out. That is, the precise limits of the system to be represented by the database are defined.
- **Study of user requirements.** The designer interacts with the potential database users in order to determine their current and projected needs.
- **Conceptual design.** An idealization of the proposed database is developed. This is called the **conceptual model** or **conceptual design.** It is a simplification of the real-world system, stated in terms of elementary concepts that can eventually be translated into an actual database design. A conceptual design is independent of any particular DBMS—its purpose is to bridge the gap between the actual system (very general) and the final database design (extremely specific).

As an analogy to this phase, consider the steps in writing a computer program. Once the problem has been defined, the program may be outlined using the tools of flowcharting. The flowchart is equivalent to the conceptual design in that it represents what the program is to do, but it is independent of any particular programming language.

- **Physical database design.** During this stage, the conceptual model is transformed into a **physical database model.** This is a design that is consistent with the actual database management system to be used. Using the preceding analogy, this phase is equivalent to translating the flowchart into a particular language, such as Pascal or BASIC.
- **Design implementation.** The physical database model is entered into the DBMS being used. This would be the equivalent of entering a Pascal program into the computer, using the particular dialect of Pascal understood by the machine.
- **Testing.** The implemented design is tested to ensure that the DBMS behaves in the expected manner.

In the following paragraphs, we shall briefly discuss the first two of these stages. The remainder of the chapter will be devoted to the topic of conceptual design. Later chapters will address the issue of transforming conceptual into physical designs.

Database Planning

Scope of the design. A major consideration of a designer should be the extent of the real world that is to be represented by a proposed database. This usually involves two steps, the first of which is to define the general system of particular interest (see figure 8.2). In the second stage, the scope is narrowed even more to include only specific portions of the general system. For a simple situation, such

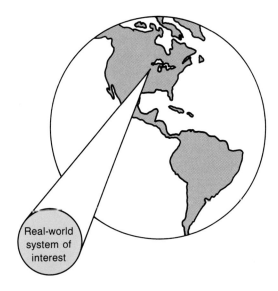

Figure 8.2
Selecting a system to
be the basis of a
database design.

Real-world
system of
interest

as a database to contain information concerning all of one's friends, the choice of scope is straightforward. On the other hand, if the system is a large and complex organization, the choice of scope may be very difficult. For example, experience has shown that it is impractical to attempt to design a single database to represent all aspects of a very large, complex system. Many failures are the result of overly ambitious attempts at database design, and these failures occur for a variety of reasons. The significant causes can be summarized as follows: (1) the existence of too many different types of data with too many complex interrelations; (2) the presence of too many people with diverse and conflicting interests; and (3) unexpected costs in design time, partially due to the latter two factors.

The approach that has been found to be workable for such complex situations is to modularize the overall system into several smaller, well-defined parts, each of which is then represented by a separate database. These might be maintained on the same computer, or on separate machines. The latter approach is commonly known as distributed database processing.

Regardless of the size of the proposed database project, it is vital that the scope of the planned database be carefully and clearly planned, so that there will be a minimum number of surprises for the users when the database becomes operational.

Design constraints. Many types of constraints affect the choice of scope for a database design. These restrictions may be related to direct financial considerations, or to limitations on hardware, software, or personnel. It is not unusual for a final database design to be a compromise between users' needs and the limitations imposed by various considerations. For example, if financial limitations require that a proposed database run on existing computer hardware and software with existing personnel, then the scope of the design is automatically restricted to the capabilities of the available system and employees.

The design and implementation of a database may include many people involved with planning, design, personnel education, programming, and other related areas. The associated costs must be carefully assessed during the planning stage to ensure that they fall within available financial and personnel resources.

Whatever restrictions exist, they must be taken into account during the planning stage of the database, so that the overall scope of the database design and implementation will be consistent with the available resources.

Planning for change. During the planning phase, the database designer must be concerned with various aspects of change. These changes involve the system to be represented by the database, the database itself, and the users of the database.

During the life cycle of a database, there can be little doubt that the system represented by the database will evolve. Furthermore, users' requirements will change, partially because the system itself evolves, and also because a flexible DBMS gives users the opportunity to shift their perspectives.

From a design point of view, one of the most difficult issues to deal with relates to the changing needs of users. As users gain familiarity with the power of databases, they invariably expand their horizons in terms of expectations from a database. The designer must try as much as possible to plan for this type of variation, in part by suitable choice of hardware and software, and also by building flexibility into the original design.

Finally, as the system evolves over the course of time, the relevant changes must be reflected in the database. These database changes may take one or more of three forms:

- **Alterations to existing data.** It is inevitable that the information within a database will undergo constant change. This presents little problem for the designer, since every DBMS has built into it facilities for data modification.

- **Growth of information.** Most databases tend to grow during their life cycle. This may be due to natural growth of the system represented by the database, or from unforeseen expansion of database usage. In either case, the growth potential must be taken into account during the planning stage, in terms of both software and hardware limitations. Many serious problems have occurred as a result of databases "outgrowing their clothes," so to speak. Designers must plan ahead in terms of the maximum expected growth of a database over some reasonable period of time, and both software and hardware must be chosen carefully to accommodate this potential growth.

- **Changes to the database design.** Few database designs are so universal that they can remain totally unchanged for their entire life cycle. If a design has a high probability of undergoing significant changes, the software and hardware must be chosen with care to accommodate the potential changes.

| Table 8.1 |

Factors Involved in Database Planning

Choosing an appropriate scope to be covered by the database

Constraints affecting the proposed design:
    Finances
    Equipment
    Software
    Personnel

Planning for change:
    Data modifications
    Growth of database contents
    Design alterations

Table 8.1 summarizes the major factors to be addressed during the database planning stage.

Studying User Requirements

Before a database design can proceed, an assessment must be made of the requirements of the various types of users who will be accessing the database. Each user will have his or her own particular needs, and each will have a different concept, or view, of the database. Moreover, a particular person might need to access a database in a variety of ways.

For some users, the primary interest may be a very broad picture of the system represented by the database; whereas for others the primary focus may be detailed information concerning a particular aspect of the system. Thus, the president of an organization would be interested in information such as the total amount of Cash-On-Hand, or the total amount of Accounts Receivable. On the other hand, a chief accountant would wish to access details of who owed how much to the company.

The conglomeration of all user requirements is one of the main sources of information upon which the conceptual database design is built, and the database designer must gain a thorough understanding of all of these different requirements before the design can be developed. This process can involve a great deal of interaction with the various potential users, and it can often be difficult, because the potential users may have had no prior experience with databases or computers. When first confronted with a question such as "What information would you wish to get from your database?" a user may be at a total loss for an answer.

In these situations, the users must be educated with respect to computers and databases, so that they may contribute meaningfully to the database design. The database designer may have to assume the responsibility of furnishing this education. For example, a user may have no concept of files, records, or fields. Once users are taught to understand these concepts, they may in turn be of assistance to the designer in terms of defining their needs.

From the study of users' requirements comes a great deal of information vital to the database designer. This information may be classified in several ways, such as:

- A list of all reports needed by various users. This would include reports currently being issued on a regular basis, as well as other useful reports that will be convenient to produce from the database.
- A list of various types of database queries that might be of interest to users. This list in particular requires a thorough understanding of the system by the designer, in order to be able to imagine the types of queries that will be meaningful and useful.
- A list of data items that are meaningful to users. Different users might have different names for the same data items, and each user will want to use the database with terminology that is familiar to him or her.

The process of learning about the different user requirements entails careful and detailed study so that the designer may gain a full understanding of the system. If the system is narrow in scope, such as a list of all one's personal acquaintances, then the process of familiarization will be straightforward and rapid. On the other hand, if the system is a large business, the familiarization process may occupy a good deal of time.

The importance of this latter point cannot be overemphasized. Too often, a designer will make a quick survey of a system and then hastily proceed to the design phase. Inevitably, the haste comes back to haunt the designer, with questions such as "Why can't I get such-and-such from the database?" A good design requires a *complete* understanding of all significant aspects of the operation of the system and the various user requirements.

Conceptual Design

After identifying the scope of the real-world system of interest to be represented by the proposed database, and studying the various user requirements, the next step is to develop a conceptual model for the database. This section deals with that development.

Many real-world systems are highly complex—much too complex, in fact, to be *completely and accurately* represented by a database. The purpose of designing a conceptual model is to simplify the system to the point that it may then be represented by some type of database. This simplification process involves extracting the important elements or qualities from the system. The conceptual model, then, is a tool that is used to identify and quantify the important features of the system.

A conceptual model is an abstract construct, which is represented as a set of tables and figures. This model stands midway between two tangible "things" with which one may identify: (1) the real-world system itself, such as a particular company or a group of recipes; and (2) the database that will represent the system. This database may be visualized in terms of records, files, and other familiar items associated with data processing.

A conceptual design is fundamentally independent of any particular DBMS. In contrast, the physical database design, which is *directly derived from the conceptual design,* is shaped to fit the mold of the particular DBMS being used. Thus, the conceptual design serves as a vital link between the real world and the limitations of any particular DBMS. (For brevity we shall henceforth refer to the real-world system of interest as simply the *system.*)

Tools of the Trade

The tools available for the design of a conceptual model basically consist of a few simple abstract constructs that help to organize the ideas of the designer. These consist of the following:

Entity-types: Represent real-world objects

Attributes: Describe the characteristics of real-world objects

Relationships: Describe associations among real-world objects

Constraints: Impose restrictions or conditions on a conceptual model, based on limitations imposed by the real-world system of interest

Diagrams and tables: An important means of expressing ideas; in conceptual design, simple types of visuals are frequently helpful

Each of these tools is described in depth in the following sections.

Entity-types

One of the fundamental problems facing the database designer is the task of representing a system by a set of entity-types. Each entity-type represents a group of similar objects or events. For example, suppose that we wish to design a simple database to hold information about all of our acquaintances. We would first design a simple conceptual model in which all of the acquaintances were represented by a particular entity-type, which we could arbitrarily call ACQUAINTANCES. Within this simple model, each particular acquaintance would be represented by an **instance** of the ACQUAINTANCES entity-type.

Note that there is a strong similarity between the idea of an entity-type and an ordinary file of records. Often (but not always), an entity-type is eventually implemented as a simple file, and each instance of an entity-type becomes a database record.

Entity-types may be used to represent different kinds of aspects of reality. In the simplest case, an entity-type may represent a group of physical things such as acquaintances. An entity-type could also represent a group of events, such as a series of concerts performed at a particular place over a period of time. For simplicity, we shall refer to any represented group of real-world things or events as *objects*. Some examples of possible entity-types are:

STUDENTS: All students at a particular school

CLASSES: All classes currently being held at a school. Alternatively, CLASSES might represent all classes that were *ever* held at the school

RECIPES: All of the recipes in which a chef is interested

INGREDIENTS: A list of all ingredients used by a chef in his or her cooking

CUSTOMERS: All of the customers of a company

ORDERS: All of the orders placed with a company

It is important to distinguish between a set of objects, such as a group of acquaintances, and their *representation* by an entity-type, such as the type named ACQUAINTANCES. For example, an acquaintance is a highly complex being, incapable of being completely and accurately described. On the other hand, a representation of an acquaintance must be limited to a set of simple characteristics: (1) that can be represented internally by a computer; and (2) that are meaningful to database users.

Attributes

An entity-type represents a group of objects in terms of the characteristics of those objects that are of interest: *within a conceptual design, each characteristic of interest is represented by an **attribute** of that particular entity-type.*

For example, suppose that the ACQUAINTANCES entity-type represents a group of people. Some characteristics of this group that might be useful to represent would be the following:

- Personal name
- Street address
- City
- State
- Telephone number
- Amount of money owed to you by the person
- Amount of money you owe to the person
- Degree of trustworthiness (rated on a scale of 0–10)

Each of these characteristics would be represented by a corresponding attribute of ACQUAINTANCES. Examples of characteristics that would probably *not* be of interest might be the name of an acquaintance's tailor, or what type of car (s)he drives.

Some attributes are more accurate representations than others. Thus, a personal name can be represented exactly, whereas the trustworthiness of a person can be only crudely approximated.

The easiest characteristics to represent are those that can be described by simple numeric or string values, because these are the types of quantities most easily handled by computers. Thus, the name and address of an acquaintance can be stored as a set of distinct character values. On the other hand, it would be extremely difficult to represent the effect that the personality of a particular friend has on your state of mind.

We shall adopt the following notation for describing entity-types and their attributes:

(1)

ACQUAINTANCES [NAME, ADDRESS, PHONE]

Qualities of Attributes

Attributes of an entity-type have certain properties of their own, and when an attribute is defined, values must be assigned to each of its properties. Each of these properties are discussed in this section.

NAME.   Each attribute must be assigned a unique name, usually chosen to indicate the characteristic of the set of objects represented by the entity-type. Most DBMS's allow a sufficient number of characters for an attribute name so that it is reasonably self-explanatory. In addition, some DBMS's allow multiple names, or **synonyms,** to be assigned to an attribute. Synonyms are often used to represent the different meanings associated by different users to a particular attribute. Synonyms are particularly useful when a database is used by more than one person, each of whom has his or her favorite name for an attribute.

TYPE.   Although many different kinds of characteristics can be represented by attributes, only a small number of attribute types, such as numeric and string, are possible because of DBMS limitations. Each particular DBMS has its own built-in selection of legal types. These limitations should be observed during the conceptual design process, provided the designer knows which DBMS will be used for the actual implementation. This is an example of how a conceptual design is influenced by the choice of DBMS to be used for implementation.

Figure 8.3 lists a few of the more commonly used attribute types, along with a brief description of each. Almost without exception, DBMS's permit *at least* the two basic types, numeric and string. In addition, various DBMS's permit many other types.

Required and optional attributes.   Often, logic dictates that values for particular attributes *must* be specified for each instance of an entity-type. As an example, consider the following entity-type:

(2)

STUDENTS [ID_NUMBER, NAME, Address, Phone]

Attribute type	Comments
Alphanumeric	Contains textual data. Allowable characters include most of those found on keyboards.
Numeric: integer	Many DBMS's do not distinguish between INTEGER and DECIMAL (containing a decimal point) numbers.
Numeric: decimal	Others offer a large variety of numeric attribute-types.
Numeric: floating-point	
Numeric: fixed-point	
Date	Usually in a form similar to MM-DD-YY
Logical or boolean	Limited to values of TRUE and FALSE

The ID_NUMBER must be given a value for each student so that each record is adequately defined. The same is probably true for NAME. On the other hand, it is not crucial that values be supplied for the other attributes. We say that ID_NUMBER and NAME are **required** attributes, whereas the remaining ones are **optional.**

Often, it is useful to specify that a particular attribute be required, but that a default value be assigned to that attribute in the event that an input value is not supplied.

Extension to notation for entity-types. As indicated in (1), we shall adopt the following notation:

- A required attribute is indicated by writing its name in all upper case
- An optional attribute is indicated by capitalizing only the first letter of its name

The required/optional specification for each attribute may be an important component of a conceptual design. Like many other features, the precise manner in which these specifications will be implemented is not relevant to the conceptual design. If one or more attributes are specified to be required by the design, then it is assumed that during the database implementation phase, these specifications will somehow be carried out.

In point of fact, many DBMS's allow attributes to be specified as either required or optional. For this type of DBMS, data for each required attribute *must* be entered for each record. Otherwise, the DBMS will either reject the record or assign a default value (specified by the user) to each missing required value.

If this type of automatic capability is not a feature of the DBMS being used, it may be desirable, or perhaps even necessary, to enforce required specifications with application programs.

Multiply-occurring attributes. To illustrate the concept of attribute **occurrences,** we consider the following entity-type definition for a group of customers:

(3)

> CUSTOMERS [ID_NUMBER, NAME, Address, Phone]

Within the framework of this design, each customer is represented by an identification number, name, address, and telephone number. A potential problem exists with this design, in that it does not allow for the possibility of more than one telephone number per customer. If this is an important consideration, a modification to the design can be made, as follows:

(4)

> CUSTOMERS [ID_NUMBER, NAME, Address, Phone1,
> Phone2, Phone3]

The attributes Phone1, Phone2, and Phone3 each represent a different phone number, so each customer could have up to three numbers recorded in the database.

There are several problems with the design in (4), one of which is the fact that most customers probably do not have three different telephone numbers. This design results in a good deal of wasted storage, because even though Phone2 and Phone3 are empty for a particular database record, the space still exists within that record. This is a consequence of the fact that most DBMS's work only with fixed-length records. Another difficulty has to do with the fact that some customers may have more than three telephone numbers; for these customers, the design shown in (4) is inadequate. In fact, it is never possible to guarantee that *any* number of Phone attributes will always be sufficient.

A much better solution to the problem is to state that the Phone attribute in (3) may have **multiple occurrences.** That is, the design of CUSTOMERS allows for a variable number of occurrences for Phone, so that any particular CUSTOMERS record might have zero, one, or several occurrences of this attribute.

An attribute that is specified to be multiply-occurring is normally referred to as a **repeating group,** a term that we shall use frequently in this text. If an attribute is not a repeating group, it is said to be **singly-occurring.** We shall adopt the following convention: A multiply-occurring attribute is indicated by enclosing its name in parentheses. Thus, the design for CUSTOMERS is represented as follows:

(5)

> CUSTOMERS [ID_NUMBER, NAME, ADDRESS, (Phone)]

Splitting of repeating groups. Although repeating groups are an important element of conceptual design, most DBMS's cannot deal directly with them. By definition, a record that contains a repeating group must be variable in length; as mentioned earlier, most DBMS's cannot work with such records.

This inconsistency between the requirements of conceptual design and the limitations of DBMS's systems is often dealt with during the conceptual design in the following way. If an entity-type contains a repeating group, it can be **split** into two new entity-types, neither of which has the repeating group.

As an example of this splitting process, consider the CUSTOMERS entity-type shown in (5), which contains the repeating group "Phone." We replace CUSTOMERS by the following pair of entity-types:

(6a)   CUSTOMERS [ID_NUMBER, NAME, ADDRESS]

(6b)   PHONE_NUMBERS [CUSTOMER_ID, PHONE]

This process of splitting entity-types is part of a more general process called **normalization,** which refers to the optimization of entity-type design. Normalization is discussed in detail in chapter 10. It is not absolutely necessary that all entity-types containing repeating groups be split during the conceptual design of a database. Whether such splitting is done is a matter of personal preference on the part of the designer. However, unless the chosen DBMS directly supports variable length records and repeating groups, splitting will be necessary at some point before the design is implemented.

Within the context of the new design shown in (6a) and (6b), each customer is represented by: (1) a single occurrence of CUSTOMERS; and (2) one occurrence of PHONE_NUMBERS for each telephone number belonging to the customer. Any number of phone numbers may be accommodated for a given customer, but at the same time all database records are fixed-length. In addition, although PHONE is an optional attribute in the original definition of CUSTOMERS shown in (5), it is a required attribute in the definition of PHONE_NUMBERS.

Common attributes. The link among the CUSTOMERS and PHONE_NUMBERS records that refer to a particular customer is established by the common attribute ID_NUMBER, which is given the alternate name CUSTOMER_ID in PHONE_NUMBERS. The attributes ID_NUMBER and CUSTOMER_ID are synonyms because they refer to the same set of values. A particular instance of CUSTOMERS and PHONE_NUMBERS is shown in figure 8.4.

Figure 8.4
CUSTOMERS and
PHONE_NUMBERS
entity-types.

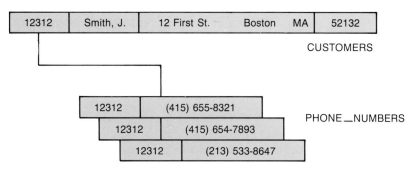

Table 8.2	Qualities of Entity-type Attributes	

Quality	Meaning
Name	Chosen to indicate which characteristic of the corresponding objects is represented by the attribute
Type	The kind of information contained in the attribute, such as numerical, alphabetic, etc.
Required/Optional	Specifies whether or not values *must* be supplied for the attribute
Singly/Multiply-occurring	Specifies whether the attribute is single-valued, or whether it may contain multiple values

To summarize the preceding discussion, table 8.2 lists the various qualities that must be specified for each attribute of an entity-type.

Choosing Entity-types and Attributes

Designing a set of entity-types to represent a large system can be a complex process, and the following guidelines are often useful:

- The system must be represented by a sufficient number of entity-types and corresponding attributes so that an adequate amount of information concerning the system can be stored and retrieved from its database representation
- The principle of the golden mean applies: a design that contains either too few or too many entity-types will adversely affect the usefulness of the database

Example 1. To illustrate these points, we will consider two different examples of database models, each of which is an attempt to represent the Jellybeans, Inc. enterprise.

As an extreme first example, we will represent the entire operation of Jellybeans, Inc. by a *single* entity-type. Each instance of this entity-type then represents the total state of the company at any particular moment in time. The actual database implementation would consist of a set of records, all of the same type, and each of which represents the entire state of the organization at any given moment. A possible set of attributes that might be used for this representation is shown in table 8.3.

Although the list in table 8.3 is by no means complete, a little study will reveal that this database design would have limited usefulness because it does not allow for the storage of sufficiently detailed information. That is, not enough data can be stored to be meaningful and useful to the various employees of the company.

Table 8.3	A Simple Record Design for a Jellybeans, Inc. Database

Total cash on hand

Total value of Accounts Receivable

Total value of Accounts Payable

Number of active customers

Total amount of jellybeans on hand

Total amount of jellybeans on order from suppliers

Total amount of jellybeans ordered by customers but not yet shipped

Number of cities served by Jellybeans, Inc.

For example, consider the attribute TOTAL_VALUE_OF_ACCOUNTS_RE-CEIVABLE. Its value might be of interest to the president of the company, but it would be of no use to the person in charge of sending out monthly bills.

Example 2. As another example of the importance of the proper choice of entity-types, we examine the problem of how best to represent the stock of jellybeans on hand at any moment. The problem may be stated as follows: what choice of entity-type(s) should be used to represent the stock on hand (jellybeans of various types), so that the database contains enough information to serve the needs of the employees? There are several alternatives from which to choose, and the most likely ones are listed in table 8.4.

Notice that as one reads down the table, the entries represent an increasing degree of complexity for the representation of the stock on hand. In arriving at the best choice of entity-type from the alternatives, the designer has two principal criteria to follow: (1) the degree of information detail that would be most useful; and (2) data storage limitations imposed by the software and/or hardware.

With respect to the first issue, the following types of question must be addressed. Is it important to know about each individual jellybean on hand, or is it sufficient merely to have data concerning the total number of pounds of jellybeans on hand? Is some other representation more desirable?

Balanced against questions of this type are the realities of data-storage limitations. Each choice of entity-type shown in table 8.4 has associated with it certain data-storage requirements. These can be calculated, so that the relative requirements of each entity-type can be compared, both against each other and with the amount of available storage.

To illustrate these considerations, table 8.4 contains a possible set of attributes for each choice of entity-type. It also contains estimates for the data-storage requirements for 10,000 lbs. of jellybeans. By studying the various entries in the table, we see that the requirements will depend very much on the particular entity-type that is chosen.

Table 8.4

A List of Possibilities for Representing the Stock on Hand of Jellybeans, Inc.

Possible Entity-types to Represent Stock on Hand	Typical Attributes	Estimated Required Data Storage for 10,000 lbs of Jellybeans (Bytes)
The total number of lbs. of jellybeans on hand	Total amount (lbs.)	5
The total number of lbs. of each type of jellybean on hand	a. Type of jellybean b. Amount (lbs.)	175
The total number of jellybeans of each type on hand	a. Type of jellybean b. Number of jellybeans	250
Individual jellybeans	a. Type of jellybean b. Jellybean ID Number	100,000,000

Figures in the last column are based on the following assumptions: (1) maximum stock on hand = 10,000 lbs.; (2) 1000 jellybeans = 1 lb.

For example, the first item in the table would require storage for only a single record. For this choice, the issue is not whether sufficient storage would be available, but whether enough information concerning the stock on hand could be stored to be useful (reminiscent of our attempt to represent Jellybeans, Inc. by a single record). The last entry in the table represents the other extreme: this choice of entity-type would require a separate record for each jellybean in stock. Using this particular model would produce several obvious problems, not the least of which would be the fact that each jellybean would have to have its own identification number (a state of affairs too horrible to contemplate). Additionally, the data-storage requirements for this model would be enormous, and it is questionable whether the amount of data stored would be useful.

If the first and last entries in table 8.4 are eliminated on the basis of the preceding discussion, only the middle two possibilities remain. The various entries in the table show that neither of these choices would involve an unreasonable amount of data storage. Consequently, the final decision would depend on which type of information would be more useful: number of jellybeans or number of pounds of jellybeans. Jellybeans are rather small objects, and the second entry in table 8.4 would probably be the best choice for the representation of the stock on hand.

By generalizing the lessons illustrated by the previous examples we see that the choice of entity-types to be used in constructing a conceptual database model must be based on considerations of: (1) the type of information that is needed and how it will be used; and (2) data-storage requirements and limitations. It is possible that a compromise may have to be made between what is optimally desired in terms of available information, and what is possible in terms of available data-storage facilities.

Relationships

Relationships are an important aspect of database design. Many different kinds of relationships may exist between objects, some of which are important from an informational point of view. A database model must reflect these by establishing corresponding relationships between entities. These relationships are as much a part of a conceptual database model as are the entity-types themselves.

As an introductory example of a relationship, we shall review the two-file CUSTOMERS/ORDERS database that was described in chapter 7. The conceptual design definitions for the two entity-types that make up the database are as follows:

(7a)   CUSTOMERS [ID_NUMBER, NAME, STREET, CITY,
                             STATE, PHONE, ZIP, CREDIT, BALANCE]

(7b)   ORDERS   [ORDER_NO, CUSTOMER_ID, ORD_DATE,
                             FLAVOR, AMOUNT, PRICE, Date_needed]

As noted in chapter 7, a particular type of relationship exists between the CUSTOMERS and ORDERS entity-types, namely the fact that several orders may be related to a particular customer. This relationship is reflected in the actual database itself—several ORDERS records may correspond to a single CUSTOMERS record.

The CUSTOMERS/ORDERS database is useful not only because it contains data on various customers and orders, but also because it represents relationships between particular CUSTOMERS and ORDERS records. (At this point, a review of the chapter 7 material pertaining to relationships would be helpful.)

The Usefulness of Relationships

Relationships are important in regard to many different aspects of database usage, including the maintaining of data consistency and data retrieval.

Data consistency. Often, the presence of a particular record in a database requires the presence of one or more other records. For example, in the case of the CUSTOMERS/ORDERS database it does not make sense to allow an ORDERS record to exist unless there also exists a corresponding CUSTOMERS record. Similarly, if a particular CUSTOMERS record is to be deleted, the principle of data consistency requires that all related ORDERS records also be deleted. The presence of a relationship between the ORDERS and CUSTOMERS records is of great assistance in maintaining such data consistency.

Data retrieval. Another important aspect of maintaining record relationships has to do with the ability to access database information. Often, a database query necessitates the simultaneous retrieval of records from several different files. The maintaining of record relationships is of enormous assistance in yielding this desired information quickly and efficiently.

The Nature of Relationships

The fact that a particular relationship is specified to exist as part of a conceptual database design implies that when the design is implemented, the relationship must be maintained by the DBMS. However, the precise way in which the relationship is to be maintained is not specified by the conceptual design because the design may well be done *before* a DBMS is chosen. For example, figure 8.4 implies that a relationship exists between CUSTOMERS and PHONE_NUMBERS records, but it does not indicate anything about the manner in which the relationship is to be implemented.

One of the major differences between DBMS's concerns the method by which relationships are maintained. In fact, DBMS's are often categorized according to this characteristic. In chapter 7, one such method involved user-written programs. In later chapters, other widely-used techniques for maintaining record relationships will be described.

Types of Relationships

It is possible to imagine many different types of relationships existing among objects and conceptual entity-types. In practice, however, only a small number of different types of relationships are used in the design of conceptual models. There are two reasons for this. First, experience has shown that a large percentage of the significant types of relationships that exist among objects can be represented quite well by only a small number of relationship-types. The second reason has to do with the limited capabilities of computing machines. In practice, only a small number of techniques for representing relationships have been found to be practical.

In spite of these apparent limitations, those relationship-types that can be easily used have been found to be adequate for a large number of different situations. In this section, we shall describe these types of relationships. The reader should keep in mind the following: relationships described are those that exist among entity-types; they are *models* of those relationships that exist among objects.

Figure 8.5

A one-to-many
relationship between
entity-types A and B.

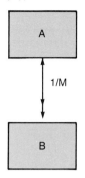

The one-to-many relationship. One of the most common types of relation-ships to exist between two entity-types is the **one-to-many.** This type of relation-ship was discussed in chapter 7 but will be expanded upon in this section. The nature of this type of relationship is the following: for each existing entity of type A, there may exist zero, one, or many related entities of type B. On the other hand, for each existing entity of type B, there exists exactly one entity of type A.

Figure 8.5 illustrates this type of relationship, using a common graphical format, the **data-structure diagram.** In this type of diagram, entity-types are rep-resented by a simple shape, usually a rectangle or oval. Relationships between entity-types are represented by straight lines, and the nature of a particular re-lationship is illustrated by the number of arrows at the ends of the line. For ex-ample, a one-to-many relationship is illustrated by one single arrow and one double arrow, as shown in figure 8.5. An alternative way of illustrating a one-to-many relationship is by affixing the notation *1/M* to the diagram (also shown in figure 8.5).

The world abounds with one-to-many relationships, or more precisely, with situations that can be *represented* by the one-to-many type of relationship. Some examples follow.

Instructors-Classes. Consider the example of an educational institution. Al-though this type of institution is highly complex when considered as a whole, in this example we shall focus attention on the relationship between two particular subsets of objects, namely instructors and students. Each of these could be mod-eled by entity-types as follows:

INSTRUCTORS [NAME, INSTRUCTOR_ID, OFFICE]

CLASSES [CLASS_ID, TIME, ROOM, INSTRUCTOR_ID]

Typically, each instructor will conduct several classes, whereas each class will have a single instructor in charge. Thus, there exists a one-to-many relationship between the two entity-types. Figure 8.6(a) shows the data-structure diagram for INSTRUCTORS and CLASSES, and figure 8.6(b) illustrates a particular occurrence of this relationship. For example, figure 8.6(b) shows a single IN-STRUCTORS entity and several related CLASSES entities. Together they con-sist of a single occurrence of the relationship defined between INSTRUCTORS and CLASSES.

It should be pointed out that each large rectangular box in figure 8.6(b) rep-resents an instance of a particular entity-type. Alternatively, you might find it helpful to think of each box as a record in a database.

The INSTRUCTOR_ID attribute is common to both INSTRUCTORS and CLASSES. Therefore, it can be thought of as a conceptual link between a par-ticular INSTRUCTOR entity and all of the associated CLASSES entities. Figure 8.6(b) illustrates this conceptual association, or relationship, through the use of heavy lines.

Figure 8.6
The INSTRUCTORS_
CLASSES one-to-many
relationship:
(a) structure diagram;
(b) a specific instance
of the structure.

(a)

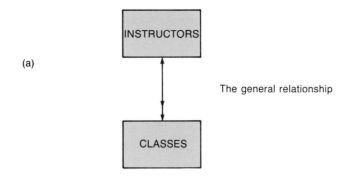

The general relationship

(b)

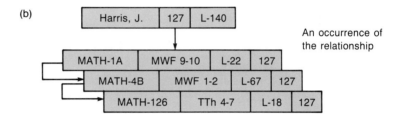

An occurrence of
the relationship

Keys. Keys play a significant role in maintaining relationships among entities. By recalling the definition of primary and secondary keys, we can see that the attribute INSTRUCTOR_ID can be thought of as a primary key for the IN-STRUCTORS entity-type, and a secondary key for CLASSES. In other words, a particular value of INSTRUCTOR_ID uniquely specifies a particular IN-STRUCTORS entity. On the other hand, several CLASSES entities could have the same value for INSTRUCTOR_ID.

It is typical that in a one-to-many relationship, the primary key of one of the entity-types plays a role in the relationship. Keys often play similar roles in other types of relationships as well.

Fathers-Children. As another example of a one-to-many relationship, we consider the association between fathers and their children. A father may have zero, one, or several children but each child has exactly one father. This is precisely the definition of a one-to-many relationship. Typical representative entity-types for fathers and children would be:

(9a)   FATHERS [NAME, ADDRESS, AGE]

(9b)   CHILDREN [NAME, ADDRESS, FATHER_NAME]

Figure 8.7
One-to-one
relationships.

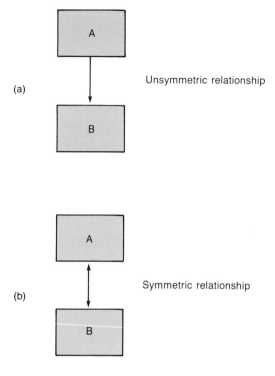

(a)

Unsymmetric relationship

(b)

Symmetric relationship

The attributes NAME and FATHER_NAME represent common information. They form the conceptual link between related FATHERS and CHILDREN entities (or records), in that related entities have the same values for these attributes. Note that NAME could be the primary key for FATHERS, and FATHER_NAME a secondary key for CHILDREN.

The one-to-one relationship. A special case of the one-to-many relationship is the **one-to-one,** which has the following definition. For each existing entity of type A, there exists exactly one related entity of type B. On the other hand, for each existing entity of type B, there may or may not exist a corresponding single entity of type A. This type of relationship is illustrated in figure 8.7(a). A variation of this relationship is one that is completely symmetric: what is true for A is also true for B. That is, if an entity of type B exists, then exactly one corresponding entity of type A exists. This type of one-to-one relationship is illustrated in figure 8.7(b).

The many-to-many relationship. Another common connection that exists among entities is the **many-to-many.** This type of relationship also involves two entity-types, and has the following characteristics. For each existing entity of type A, there may exist zero, one, or many related entities of type B. The relationship is also symmetric—for each existing entity of type B, there may exist zero, one, or many related entities of type A.

Figure 8.8
The STUDENTS_
CLASSES many-to-
many relationship.

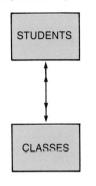

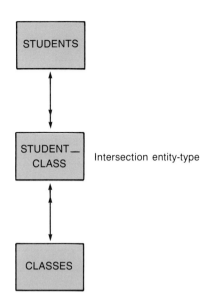

Intersection entity-type

Figure 8.9 The representation of the STUDENTS_CLASSES relationship by the introduction of the STUDENT_CLASS intersection entity-type. The result is two one-to-many relationships.

As an example of this type of relationship, we consider the situation of a group of students and their classes in a particular school. Definitions for the corresponding entity-types would be the following:

(10a)　　　　　STUDENTS [STUDENT_ID, NAME, Address, Phone, GPA]

(10b)　　　　　CLASSES [CLASS_ID, INSTRUCTOR, TIME, ROOM]

Each student may be enrolled in none, one, or several classes. Similarly, each class may have any number of students in attendance. Thus, a many-to-many relationship exists between STUDENTS and CLASSES. Figure 8.8 shows the data-structure diagram for STUDENTS and CLASSES. In this figure, the two sets of double arrows indicate that the relationship is a many-to-many, and often, the symbol M/N is placed in the diagram to reinforce this fact.

In practice, DBMS's usually cannot directly implement a many-to-many relationship. Instead, such a relationship must be **decomposed** into two one-to-many relationships by the introduction of another entity-type, usually known as an **intersection entity-type.** We illustrate this technique by using STUDENTS/ CLASSES as an example. The intersection entity-type that is introduced is called STUDENT_CLASS, defined as follows:

(11)　　　　　STUDENT_CLASS [STUDENT_ID, CLASS_ID, GRADE]

Figure 8.9 illustrates the two one-to-many relationships that exist between STUDENTS, CLASSES, and STUDENT_CLASS as a result of the decomposition. Note that each instance of the STUDENT_CLASS entity-type represents a particular student taking a particular class.

229　Conceptual Database Design

Figure 8.10
Occurrences of the
STUDENTS and
CLASSES relationship.
Only a few of the
attributes are shown.
The one-to-many
relationships are
indicated by dotted and
dashed lines.

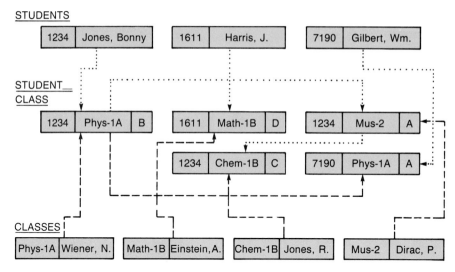

The STUDENT_CLASS entity-type contains the attribute STUDENT_ID, which is also an attribute of STUDENTS. Thus, STUDENT_ID can be thought of as the link in the one-to-many relationship between STUDENT_CLASS and STUDENTS. By the same token, the CLASS_ID attribute is the link between STUDENT_CLASS and CLASSES.

STUDENT_CLASS also contains the attribute GRADE. Values for this attribute are known as **intersection data,** because a particular grade is not specific to a given student or to a given class, but rather to a combination of a particular student and class.

Figure 8.10 illustrates a few occurrences of the two relationships existing between STUDENTS/STUDENT_CLASS and CLASSES/STUDENT_CLASS. Consider the STUDENT_ID value of 1234. This links Bonny Jones with the particular classes of Physics-1A, Music-2, and Chemistry-1B. Similarly, a CLASS ID value of Phys-1A links the class Physics-1A with Bonny Jones and William Gilbert. Finally, the particular intersection entity linking Bonny Jones with Physics-1A shows that she received a grade of B in that class.

Many real-life situations can be represented by the many-to-many type of relationship. Two examples follow.

Recipes–Ingredients. Consider the situation of a restaurant that prepares many different recipes for which a large number of ingredients are kept in stock. Each recipe calls for many different ingredients, and any particular ingredient may be used in many different recipes. Hence, the relationship between recipes and ingredients is many-to-many.

Doctors–Patients. In a particular city, there may be many different doctors, each of whom has a group of patients. Some of these patients may see more than one doctor, thus establishing a many-to-many relationship between doctors and patients.

Figure 8.11
A relationship within the
STUDENTS entity-type.

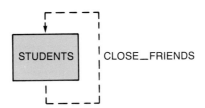

In summary, a many-to-many relationship can be broken into two one-to-many relationships by creating an intersection entity-type. The reason for the decomposition process is that most DBMS's can implement one-to-many relationships, but not many-to-many relationships. An intersection entity-type may consist of two kinds of attributes: those that are useful for establishing the one-to-many relationships, and those that contain intersection-type data.

In many situations, the intersection entity-type may contain no intersection-type data. For example, suppose that in the STUDENTS/CLASSES situation described previously, the data is for classes currently in progress. Grade information is therefore not applicable, and the GRADE attribute in STUDENT_CLASS would be unneccesary. Consequently, it is possible for an intersection entity-type to contain only pointers.

Other Types of Relationships

Each of the relationships that have been discussed so far involve two entity-types. Although these kinds of relationships are the ones most frequently encountered in database design, there are others.

Relationships within a single entity-type. Sometimes, relationships may exist within entities of the same type. Such relationships are called **recursive.** For example, consider the population of students at a particular school, represented by the entity-type STUDENTS:

(12)   STUDENTS [STUDENT_ID, ADDRESS, GPA]

Suppose that we wish to consider the relationship that describes *close friends.* For each student, there exists a group of classmates who are considered to be the friends of that student. An instance of this relationship consists of one particular member of STUDENTS (representing a specific student), plus several other members of STUDENTS (representing the friends of the former). Technically, STUDENTS is said to have a relationship with itself and is therefore recursive.

One way to pictorially represent the close friends relationship is shown in figure 8.11. Because the arrow by itself in the figure would have no meaning, the relationship is given the name CLOSE_FRIENDS.

Often, a recursive relationship is decomposed in a manner similar to that described for many-to-many relationships: an intersection entity-type is defined,

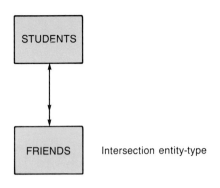

Figure 8.12
The decomposition of
the CLOSE_FRIENDS
relationship by the
introduction of the
FRIENDS intersection
entity-type. The
relationship between
the entity-types is one-
to-many.

Intersection entity-type

Figure 8.13
An occurrence of the
STUDENTS-CLOSE_
FRIENDS relationship
(indicated by the
broken lines).

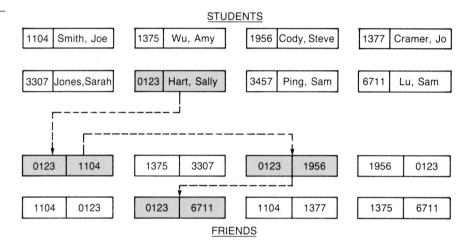

and it forms a one-to-many relationship with the original entity-type. For example, the CLOSE_FRIENDS relationship may be implemented by defining a new intersection entity-type as follows:

(13)

FRIENDS [STUDENT_ID, FRIEND_ID]

Figure 8.12 depicts the relationship between STUDENTS and FRIENDS, which is one-to-many.

An occurrence of the CLOSE_FRIENDS relationship is shown in figure 8.13 for Sally Hart and her friends. Notice that FRIENDS contains two attributes, one of which (STUDENT_ID) acts as a link to STUDENTS.

A frequently used example of a recursive relationship is the following. A particular manufacturer assembles various parts, each of which consists of other parts. Some parts are *fundamental,* in that they have no constituents, while other parts are *complex,* that is, built up from simpler parts (some of which themselves may be complex). We may represent all parts in stock by the following entity-type:

(14)

PARTS [PART_NO, DESCRIPTION, UNIT_COST]

We may say that a relationship exists among various instances of PARTS because some parts consist of others.

Although the PARTS entity-type may adequately represent the stock of parts, it does not represent the relationships among them. In order to do so, we introduce a second entity-type:

(15)

COMPONENTS [PART_NO, COMPONENT_NO]

To explain this entity-type, suppose that a particular part, represented by PART_NO in (15), consists of several components. Each component is represented by an instance of COMPONENTS. For example, if a particular part has five components, there will be five instances of COMPONENTS: each will have a different value for COMPONENT_NO but the same value for the attribute PART_NO.

Note that the relationship between PARTS and COMPONENTS is one-to-many, as shown in figure 8.14(a). Figure 8.14(b) illustrates an occurrence of the relationship.

Relationships among more than two entity-types. Many real-world situations exist in which there is a direct relationship among three or more distinct types of objects. As an example, consider the case of a company that manufactures many different types of gadgets, each of which is assembled from several different parts. Many different suppliers furnish a variety of parts to the company. Furthermore, each particular part may be provided by several different suppliers.

An additional complication is that a particular part may be used in the assembly of several different types of gadgets. However, for a particular part used in the assembly of a particular gadget, only specific companies are allowed to supply the part. The relationship among PARTS, GADGETS, and SUPPLIERS is illustrated in figure 8.15. We shall not discuss the details of how such a relationship would be implemented, but merely indicate that one method would involve decompositions similar to those already described.

Relationships may exist among several entity-types. These would be depicted in a manner similar to that shown in figure 8.15. Clearly, the complexities involved in representing such relationships would increase as the number of entity-types that are involved increase.

Figure 8.14
The relationship
between PARTS and
COMPONENTS. (a) The
general relationship and
(b) an occurrence of the
relationship.

(a)

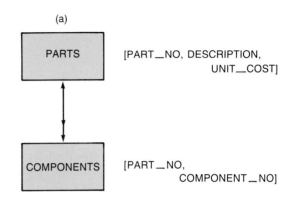

PARTS   [PART_NO, DESCRIPTION,
                 UNIT_COST]

COMPONENTS   [PART_NO,
                COMPONENT_NO]

(b)

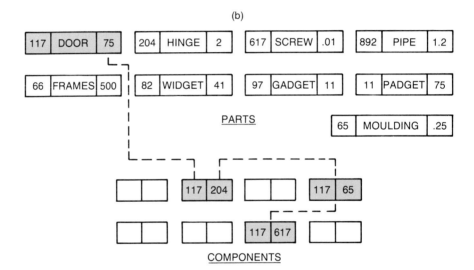

PARTS

COMPONENTS

Figure 8.15
The relationships
among PARTS,
SUPPLIERS, and
GADGETS. The
relationship of PARTS
and GADGETS is many-
to-many, while the
PARTS, GADGETS, and
SUPPLIERS relationship
is complex.

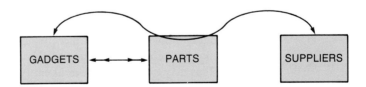

GADGETS   PARTS   SUPPLIERS

Special relationships. In the real world, many different kinds of relationships exist. Most of these can be represented by the idealized relationship types discussed previously. For those special types of relationships that cannot, implementation may depend on user-written programs.

Constraints

Just as entities may exist within the context of relationships, they may also be subject to various types of restrictions, or **constraints.** In general, these fall into three broad categories:

1. Constraints on values of particular attributes
2. Constraints involving two or more attributes of the same entity
3. Constraints involving attributes of two or more entities

Intra-entity Constraints

Within a single entity, constraints may apply to individual attributes or to combinations of two or more attributes. Examples of the first type would be the following:

- Restrictions placed on the allowable range of values for a numerical attribute. For example, the CREDIT_LIMIT attribute within a CUSTOMERS entity might have limits of 0 to 5,000.
- Restriction to a given set of specific values. For example, a MONTH attribute might be limited to the values (Jan, Feb, . . .).

The **type** of an attribute also implies a form of constraint. Thus, input data for numeric attributes is usually restricted to the character set consisting of digits, plus and minus signs, and the decimal point.

Constraints often apply to combinations of attributes within a single entity. For example, consider the following entity-type:

(16)   STUDENTS [ID_NUMBER, NAME, Street, City, State, Zip]

The only required attributes are ID_NUMBER and NAME; the remaining attributes are optional. However, if the Street attribute is given a value, then it makes sense that the City, State, and Zip attributes must also be given values.

Other types of intra-entity constraints could involve various types of allowed combinations of values among different attributes.

Derived Attributes

One particularly interesting constraint has to do with so-called **derived attributes.** This type of attribute obtains its value not directly from external data input, but rather from some type of automatic computation done internally. Consider the following sample entity-type definitions, relating to customers and orders submitted by those customers:

(17a)　　　　　CUSTOMERS [NAME, ID, ADDRESS, NUMBER_OF_ORDERS]

(17b)　　　　　ORDERS [CUST_ID, ITEM, UNIT_COST, ORDER_DATE]

The attribute NUMBER_OF_ORDERS is defined as the total number of orders submitted by a customer. It could be specified to be a derived attribute, in the sense that its value is obtained from other internal data, namely the number of corresponding ORDERS records.

Some DBMS's have built-in facilities for defining and maintaining derived attributes—the database definition includes the specification of each derived attribute, and the DBMS automatically maintains their values. In other cases, values for derived attributes must be maintained by application programs.

Inter-entity Constraints

Many types of restrictions may apply to attributes of two or more entities, or to two or more entities themselves. Frequently, these constraints are a natural consequence of the relationships that exist among entities. For example, consider the INSTRUCTORS/CLASSES entity-types described in (8) and figure 8.6. The nature of this set of entity-types imposes the following constraint: if a particular CLASSES entity exists, then a corresponding INSTRUCTORS entity must also exist. This constraint is a direct result of the nature of the relationship that exists between the INSTRUCTORS and CLASSES.

These examples are but a few of the many different types of constraints that may apply to different situations. Each situation will have its own particular set of restrictions, most of which will fall into the categories described. Constraints form an important part of conceptual database design. They are reflections of the system being modeled, and if a model is to be an accurate one, it must take into account any pertinent constraints.

A Complete Conceptual Design

A complete conceptual database design is the composite of the various factors considered in the previous sections: entity-types, attributes of entity-types, relationships among entity-types, and constraints imposed on relationships. Although these tools are few in number and simple, an entire design may nevertheless be highly complex.

The list of entity-types and their attributes may be described in tables, or any other suitable format. The qualities of each attribute must be completely and

Figure 8.16
Part of a conceptual
design for a single
entity-type.

```
                                    Name of entity-type: STUDENT
    Attribute                      Required/    No.
      name        Type   Length Optional Occurrences         Constraints


    NAME        Alpha    20        R       Single
    IDENT_NO    Alpha    11        R       Single    1. Key: Must be unique value
                                                     2. Must be in Social-Security format:
                                                        ZZZ-ZZ-ZZZZ (Z = digit)
    YEAR        Alpha    2         R       Single    Restricted to one of the following
                                                     values: ( FR, SO, JU, SN, GR)

    STREET      Alpha    25        O       Single

    CITY        Alpha    15        O       Single    Must be present if a value for STREET is
                                                     given
    STATE       Alpha    2         O       Single    Must be present if a value for CITY is
                                                     given
    ZIP         Numeric  5         O       Single    -------------------- " ----------------
    PHONE       Alpha    13        O       Multiple  Must have the format: (ZZZ)ZZZ-ZZZZ
    GPA         Numeric  4         R       Single    1. Must have the format: Z.ZZ
                                                     2. Value must be in the range 0.00 to
                                                        4.00
    NO_CLASSES  Numeric  1         R       Single    A derived attribute, its value in a
                                                     record must be equal to the number of
                                                     STUDENT_CLASSES records corresponding
                                                     to the particular student



    Other Constraints: None
```

unambiguously spelled out. This includes the type of the attribute; whether it is required or optional; default value, if any; whether it is singly or multiply occurring; all pertinent constraints related to the attribute; and a list of possible synonyms.

Constraints and relationships form a vital and integral part of a conceptual design; it is essential therefore that they be expressed *clearly* and *completely*. The complete list of constraints for a complex design may be extremely large, possibly dominating the entire design. In this context, recall that every defined relationship defines at least one constraint. Relationships among the various entity-types may be listed in tables or depicted with data-structure diagrams.

Basically, a conceptual design is a carefully organized set of ideas, and there are many ways in which this may be done. As a simple example, figure 8.16 illustrates how part of a design might be organized for the following entity-type:

(18)

STUDENT [NAME, IDENT_NO, YEAR, Street, City, State,
Zip, (Phone), GPA, NO_CLASSES]

Note that the STUDENT entity-type would be only part of an entire design. In the next chapter, we shall develop an example of a complete conceptual design, including many entity-types, relationships, constraints, and so on.

Specialized Approaches

Several specialized approaches have been developed for designing conceptual models. The purpose of each of these is to specify as precisely as possible the various elements of a design, such as entity-types, relationships, and so on. Two of the more widely-known of these are the **entity-relation model** developed by Chen (1) and expanded on by others (2); and the **semantic data model,** which has had many contributors.[1]

Automated Design

Because conceptual designs may become quite large and complex, several computer packages have been built for the purpose of helping in the design process. These packages furnish valuable assistance in various aspects of a design, including bookkeeping involved with a great many entity-types and relationships, report generation, and graphical aids.

One of these packages is GDOC, a comprehensive software tool developed in Italy (5). It is particularly interesting because it runs on CP/M-based microcomputers, and is oriented around dBASE II. GDOC allows a user to specify interactively a complete conceptual design, including entity-types, relationships, and constraints. It then generates the entire documentation for the design, including both text and figures. In addition, the system may be used to construct automatically the entire database structure within dBASE II, and more yet, also generates the relevant data entry, update, and delete programs for the database!

Another automated approach to database design is the ADL IRMA (Information Resource Management Aid) system, developed by Arthur D. Little, Inc. for IBM-PC compatible microcomputers (6). Like GDOC, this system generates figures and reports to assist in the conceptual design process.

Other Design Considerations

One of the most important aspects of a conceptual design is that it is fundamentally an iterative process. Periodically, the current design status must be checked both with users' perceptions and with the actual system to ensure that important features are being modeled accurately. As the design proceeds, it may be necessary frequently to backtrack and modify prior decisions as new considerations reveal flaws in the existing design.

---

[1]Students wishing to pursue the design of complex databases further may consult the references at the end of this chapter.

The creation of a conceptual database model is as much an art as a science. There is no specific formula that can be used for representing a system with a model. Experience, judgment, and common sense are the best teachers, and it is hoped that the examples in this text will furnish a student with a good starting point.

Summary

The development of a database design proceeds in several distinct steps: (1) planning; (2) study of user requirements; (3) design of a conceptual database model; (4) transformation of the conceptual model into a physical model; (5) design implementation; and (6) implementation and testing. The first two phases are concerned with general planning and strategy, in which decisions are made concerning the scope and content of the database. These decisions are made on the basis of available resources, constraints imposed by financial and other considerations, and present and projected users' needs.

The design of a conceptual database model is a process of simplification in which the real-world system of interest is represented by idealized elements. A conceptual model is used to bridge the gap between the complex real world and the very simplified world of a DBMS. The model is derived from a study of the system of interest, and it is the basis from which the actual database design is eventually implemented. Although a conceptual design is independent of any particular DBMS in principle, the scope of the design must be consistent with the expected capabilities and limitations of the DBMS to be used. For example, the basic approach taken towards designing a personal mailing list would differ considerably from that taken in designing an order-entry system for General Motors.

A conceptual model consists of various entity-types, attributes, relationships, and constraints. These elements are chosen so as to best represent the important aspects of the system. Each entity-type represents a particular set of similar objects or events, and the characteristics of these objects or events are represented by various attributes of the entity-type. A great deal of care and judgment must be exercised in developing entity-types so that enough detail will be incorporated into the eventual database to serve the needs of the users. By the same token, the amount of detail must be kept within limits that are acceptable from a data-storage point of view.

Relationships are an important part of conceptual design. Certain types of real-world relationships may be represented within a conceptual model. Interestingly enough, a large variety of complex situations can be represented by only a small number of relationship types. The most common of these are the one-to-many and the many-to-many, which are particularly useful because they may be easily represented by various database systems. The utility of these relationships becomes apparent during the actual use of a database, when they often furnish assistance in data retrieval and updating.

Conceptual design is best approached as an iterative process in which the designer constantly checks ideas with potential users, both for accuracy and completeness. In this way, the resultant database implementation will best serve the needs of the users.

Chapter Review

Terminology

attribute
attribute occurrence
attribute quality
attribute type
conceptual database model or design
constraint
database implementation
decomposition
default value
derived attribute
entity-type
entity-type instance
entity-type splitting

intersection data
intersection entity-type
many-to-many relationship
one-to-many relationship
optional attribute
physical database model
recursive relationship
relationship
relationship occurrence
repeating group
required attribute
synonym
user requirements

Review Questions

1. Discuss the significance and importance of each step in the database development process.
2. Consider two database extremes: (1) a relatively small mailing list for personal contacts; and (2) a database to incorporate the major activities of a medium-size business. With respect to question (1), how much *relative* effort would you expect to be devoted to each step for each of the two cases?
3. Would you agree or disagree with the following statement: "In the last analysis, *all* constraints on the scope of a database design arise from financial considerations"?
4. Discuss the various ways in which a database may be expected to change during its life cycle.
5. Discuss each of the fundamental tools used to develop a conceptual design.
6. What are the main factors that influence the choice of attributes for a given entity-type? If it were not clear whether or not a particular attribute should be included in a design, what factors would influence the decision regarding its inclusion?
7. In general terms, describe the kinds of relationships among real-world objects or events that may be modelled by relationships within the framework of a conceptual design. Give some examples of real-world relationships that *cannot* be modeled.

8. When is it necessary to split a design containing repeating groups? Can you see any conceptual advantage to *not* splitting an entity-type with a repeating group? You might use the designs in (5) and (6) of this chapter as a focus for your answer.

9. Can you see any advantage to *not* decomposing a many-to-many relationship into two one-to-many relationships during the conceptual-design stage? Use the designs in (10) and (11) of this chapter as a focus for your answer.

10. Summarize each of the types of relationships discussed in this chapter. Give an example of a real-world situation that could be modeled by each type.

11. Discuss each of the major types of constraints that may exist within a conceptual design.

12. Explain how the specifications of an attribute's type, number of occurrences, and required/optional choice are all different types of constraints.

Problems

1. A database for a small company is being designed and implemented on a small microcomputer. As an initial step, a single-file CUSTOMERS database is to be implemented, with the design of the file following that shown in table 7.3. It is planned that at a later time, the design will be expanded to incorporate other aspects of the company.

   It is expected that a maximum of 300 CUSTOMERS records will be stored in the database. In addition, a DBMS has been selected that fits entirely on one floppy disk. Tentatively, a pair of 191,000 floppy-disk devices have been chosen as the secondary storage devices to be used with the computer system. Do you agree or disagree with this latter decision? Justify your answer.

2. Consider the CUSTOMERS and ORDERS designs shown in tables 7.3 and 7.4.
   a. For each entity-type, which of the attributes would you choose to be required, and which optional? Justify your choices.
   b. Using your choices from (a), write down the designs for each entity-type, using the notation developed in this chapter.

3. Suppose that the ORDERS design shown in table 7.4 is to be modified so that many different flavors of jellybeans could be specified in each order. Develop a design for ORDERS to accomplish this. Use the entity-type notation used in this chapter to express your design.

4. a. Must the primary key of an entity-type always be required? Explain your answer.
   b. Suppose that a primary key consists of the concatenation of several attributes. Is it possible for one of the attributes to be optional while others are required?

5. Suppose that you are designing a database to contain information on the following groups:

Your friends
People you dislike
People to whom you owe money
People who owe you money

    a. Develop a design in which each category is represented by a separate entity-type.
    b. Develop a design incorporating only a single entity-type to accomplish this.
    c. Discuss the pros and cons of each design.
6. Develop designs for FATHERS and CHILDREN entity-types discussed in the text. Draw a data-structure diagram illustrating the relationship between the two entity-types. Also, draw an occurrence of the relationship.
7. Show how the FATHERS/CHILDREN design from problem (6) is actually a decomposition of the following entity-type, which has a recursive relationship:

PERSONS [NAME, AGE, SEX, ADDRESS]

Use a set of specific instances of PERSONS to assist in your explanation.
8. Consider the following two entity-type designs:

CUSTOMERS [NAME, ADDRESS, PHONE]
ACCOUNTS_RECEIVABLE [CUSTOMER_NAME, AMOUNT_OWED]

    a. What type of relationship exists between them?
    b. Show how the two designs could be incorporated into a single entity-type. Can you draw any general conclusions from this?
    c. Discuss the pros and cons of replacing the above two entity-types by a single one.
9.   a. Develop a design for the RECIPES_INGREDIENTS example discussed in the text. Clearly indicate both required and optional attributes, as well as any other types.
    b. Design an intersection entity-type for this example. What intersection data, if any, should be part of the design?
10.   a. Develop a design for the DOCTORS_PATIENTS example discussed in the text. Include an intersection entity-type as part of the design.
    b. Suppose that some doctors are patients of other doctors. How would the design be affected?

c. Show how the DOCTORS/PATIENTS design is actually an expression of the recursive relationship that exists within the following entity-type:

PERSONS [NAME, ADDRESS, PHONE, PROFESSION]

Use a set of instances of the PERSONS entity-type to assist in your explanation.

11. List as many constraints as possible that apply to the CUSTOMERS and ORDERS designs shown in tables 7.3 and 7.4. To keep things orderly, tabulate the attributes for each table, listing the relevant constraints for each individual attribute. Then list the inter-entity constraints.

References

1. P. P. S. Chen. "The Entity-Relationship Model—Toward a Unified View of Data." *Association for Computing Machinery Transactions on Database Systems,* V. 1, No. 1 (March, 1976).
2. P. P. S. Chen (ed). "Entity-Relationship Approach to Systems Analysis and Design." North-Holland (1980).
3. H. A. Schmid and J. R. Swenson. "On the Semantics of the Relational Data Model." *Proc. 1975 Association for Computing Machinery SIGMOD International Conference on Management of Data.*
4. M. Hammer and D. McLeod. "The Semantic Data Model: A Modelling Mechanism for Data Base Applications." *Proc. Association for Computing Machinery SIGMOD,* 1978 Conference, Austin, Texas.
5. F. Massimo and C. Batini. "GDOC: A Tool for Computerized Design and Documentation of Database Systems." *Data Base,* V. 15, No. 4 (1984).
6. R. M. Curtice. "IRMA: An Automated Logical Data Base Design and Structured Analysis Tool." *Database Engineering,* V. 7, No. 4 (December 1984).

Chapter Nine

A Conceptual Database Design for Jellybeans, Inc.

Introduction

In this chapter, we shall use the various tools and ideas discussed in chapter 8 to develop a **conceptual database design** for the Jellybeans, Inc. company. This model will not necessarily be unique because many different methods exist for designing conceptual models, and the final design depends to some extent on the method used.

There is no single best design method—each has its strengths and weaknesses, and all are to a great extent heuristic. The approach used in a particular situation depends on many factors such as the style, personal preferences, and intuition of the designer. The method used in this study is relatively straightforward, and it should furnish a variety of ideas and techniques that can be applied to many types of situations.

In developing the design for Jellybeans, Inc., we shall make several simplifying assumptions and ignore many details. These simplifications will not detract from the validity of the analysis that is used, but they will allow the attention to be focused on the important design issues rather than on a host of details.

The Planning Stage

During the planning stage, key decisions are made concerning the overall scope of the proposed database design. These decisions are based on many factors, including financial and personnel constraints. A brief overview of the important issues that are involved with the planning stage of a database design was given in chapter 8.

Table 9.1	**List to be Included in the Proposed Database of Major Areas**

Customers

Suppliers of jellybeans

Accounts receivable

Accounts payable

Principal financial transactions (bills paid, etc.)

Ordering and shipping

Stock on hand

For the purposes of this chapter, we shall assume that a preliminary study of Jellybeans, Inc. has been made, and that the following conclusions and decisions have been reached:

- A list has been compiled of those areas of the company's operation for which information should be contained in the proposed database. This list is the result of an extensive study of the company's activities, including lengthy discussions with company personnel. The final contents of this list were decided on jointly by the database designer and key personnel. The list is shown in table 9.1, and will be referred to many times in this chapter.
- The financial situation of the company is good, and sufficient funds will be made available to acquire the necessary hardware and software to implement whatever database is designed. Funds will also be available to support personnel who are assigned to design and implement the database.

A Study of User Requirements

Because the primary purpose of a database is to serve the users, it is vital that the designer has a full and clear understanding of users' needs. To accomplish this, a careful study of Jellybeans, Inc. must be made with the following questions addressed:

- What are the informational needs of the various individuals within the company with regard to the areas of interest shown in table 9.1?
- For each of these areas, what are the major data items of interest?

The answer to each of these questions will be quite complex, and will require lengthy and detailed interviews with various company personnel. Techniques for conducting such interviews generally come under the heading of **systems analysis,** a subject that will not be covered in this book.

Although we will bypass the details of studying user requirements, the underlying assumption throughout this chapter is that a thorough study has been made of the business activities of Jellybeans, Inc. This study is the basis for many of the important facts used and choices made in the database design.

Similarly, although the study of user requirements is omitted, most of the choices made in this chapter are consistent with the operation of an ordinary business—Jellybeans, Inc. has customers, it receives and ships orders, pays bills and receives payments from customers, and so on.

Development of the Conceptual Database Design

In this section, we shall go through the detailed steps necessary to generate a conceptual database design that encompasses the areas listed in table 9.1. Although this design is independent of any particular database management system, it will be the foundation on which a **physical database design** is generated. (Recall that the physical design must be consistent with the actual DBMS used for implementation of the database.)

Listing the Major Transactions

A **transaction** within a company is defined as a set of one or more *integrated* operations, occurrences, or steps that produces a significant or noticeable change in the state of the company. Only those operations that are part of the *normal* business pattern come under this definition. For example, one type of transaction is the payment of a bill by a customer. This qualifies as a valid transaction because: (1) it produces a significant change (in the amount of money owed to the company by the customer); and (2) it is a normal part of the business cycle of the company. On the other hand, the accidental smashing of a window would not be a transaction because it would not be a normal part of business activities. The expense of replacing the window, however, might come under a "miscellaneous expenses" type of transaction.

Transactions are important because experience has shown that any change that occurs in an organization as a result of a normal transaction must be reflected in a representative database. Therefore, one of the first steps in the database design process is to generate a list of the principal types of transactions that occur within the company. Attention will be confined to those areas that are listed in table 9.1.

Table 9.2 shows the list of transactions that are considered to be important with respect to the items in table 9.1. Again, it must be stressed that this list is the result of a careful analysis of the company's operation, and we shall see that this list of transactions plays a vital role in the database design process. It is important, therefore, to have a clear understanding of the meaning of each type of transaction in table 9.2.

Table 9.2

Transactions Associated with Jellybeans, Inc.

An order is received from a customer

A shipment is sent to a customer

A payment is received from a customer

An order is placed with a jellybean supplier

A shipment of jellybeans is received from a supplier

A bill is received from a creditor

A payment is made to a creditor

Table 9.3

Principal Report Types

Type of Report	Frequency
List of accounts receivable, including totals	Monthly
List of accounts payable, including totals	Monthly
List of current customers	Ad hoc
List of current suppliers	Ad hoc
List of customer orders not yet entirely filled, including the outstanding items for each order	Weekly
List of jellybean orders sent to suppliers which have not been completely received, including the outstanding items for each order	Weekly
List of flavors and corresponding amounts to be ordered	Weekly

Listing the Required Reports

Reporting is the fundamental way in which database information is communicated to the outside world. In general, a report may be defined as *any* type of output that is obtained from a database. In order to be complete, a conceptual database design must take into account the various types of reports that are likely to be required of the database. Admittedly, not all possible database uses can be foreseen during the conceptual design phase—as users' experience with a database grows, so will their demands and expectations of the database.

Table 9.3 shows a list of the more important types of reports that have been determined to be of interest to the various personnel of Jellybeans, Inc. Although this is only a preliminary list, it will be extremely useful in developing the conceptual design. Again, this list is a result of extensive studies of the company's operation and users' requirements.

Entity-types and Relationships

One of the chief objectives of a conceptual database design is the selection of a suitable set of entity-types and relationships. These become the foundation for building the entire design. To assist in the design process, three **design rules** that have been shown by experience to lead to workable conceptual designs are presented. These rules are similar to the design principles stated in chapter 7.

Entity-lypes

Drawing on discussions in the previous chapter, the following design rule can be used as a guide for choosing suitable entity-types:

Design Rule #1

An entity-type represents a set of real-world facts. An instance of an entity-type, which may be thought of as a conceptual entity, represents a particular fact from the set. All of the facts contained in the set are used in the same way within the real-world system of interest.

Facts.   The term **fact,** as used in the preceding context, refers to any of the following possibilities:

- A real-world object. In this case, the fact is the existence of the object. For example, the existence of a particular customer is by itself a fact.
- A particular event, such as the payment of a bill
- Any piece of information concerning one or more objects or events. For example, the reality that a customer owes a certain sum of money to a company is a fact

For the remainder of this chapter, the term *fact* will be used to refer to any single aspect of Jellybeans, Inc. that might be represented by a conceptual entity.

Attributes

As each entity-type is selected, its attributes must also be designed. To assist in the design, we shall apply the following design rule:

Design Rule #2

Attributes of an entity-type are chosen to represent characteristics of the set of facts represented by that entity-type. The selected characteristics are those considered to be important by potential users of the database.

With respect to a particular instance of an entity-type, an attribute represents a particular piece of information about the fact represented by the instance.

As the design proceeds, and as attributes are selected for each entity-type, it is important to keep in mind that the particular choice of attributes is *provisional*. The designer must always be prepared to alter part of a design as new information is acquired, or as the designer's view of the company expands and changes.

Relationships

As each type of transaction is studied, we shall also be looking for possible relationships of importance between different entity-types. Consequently, as each new entity-type is developed, an analysis must be made in order to determine if it has relationships to any of the previously defined entity-types.

In seeking out possible relationships, the following design rule will be used as a guide:

Design Rule #3

A relationship may be said to exist between two entity-types if there exist logical connections or associations among the facts represented by the entity-types.

Relationships will become an important part of the final conceptual design, and a list of them must be maintained as the design proceeds.

Constraints

In addition to relationships, various constraints must be applied to different entity-types. A discussion of the various types of constraints was presented in the previous chapter. For the sake of minimizing the complexity of the analysis, we shall defer to the end of this chapter a discussion of the way in which constraints are incorporated into this design.

A Design Strategy

The best source of clues for choosing a reasonable set of entity-types comes from the lists of transactions and reports shown in tables 9.2 and 9.3. For example, consider the first type of transaction listed in table 9.2: "An order is received from a customer." Each transaction of this type involves two basic facts: (1) a particular customer does business with Jellybeans, Inc.; and (2) an order is submitted by that customer. Since this transaction type is a common one, orders and customers will be encountered frequently within the business, and are therefore good candidates for entity-types, which could be called CUSTOMERS and ORDERS_IN.

To find another possible entity-type, consider the first report-type listed in table 9.3: "List of accounts receivable." Each item in this type of report would contain the following data: (1) a customer name or identifier; and (2) the amount owed by that customer to the company. Each report item represents a specific fact, namely that a particular customer owes a certain sum of money to Jellybeans, Inc. The entire group of such facts is a likely candidate for representation by an entity-type, called ACC_RECEIVABLE.

In the next section, we shall develop a preliminary set of entity-types by adopting the following strategy:

> Using Design Rule #1 as a guide, we shall analyze each of the transaction types shown in table 9.2, and search for groups of similar facts that can be represented by entity-types. After all transaction types have been analyzed, each of the report-types shown in table 9.3 will be studied to determine whether any additional entity-types should be defined in order to be able to produce all of the desired types of reports.

Analysis of Transactions

An Order Is Received from a Customer

Each transaction of this type involves two facts: (1) a customer, and (2) an order from that customer. Using Design Rules #1 and #2 as a guide for choosing sets of entity-types and attributes, we can begin our list of entity-types with the following:

(E–1) CUSTOMERS [NAME, IDENT, ADDRESS, Phone]

(E–2)
```
                  [ CUSTOMER_ID, CUSTOMER_NAME,             ]
                  [ ADDRESS, Phone,                         ]
ORDERS_IN  [ ORDER_ID, ORDER_DATE, ORDER_STATUS,     ]
                  [ (FLAVOR, AMOUNT, TOTAL_PRICE,           ]
                  [ ITEM_STATUS)                            ]
```

CUSTOMERS and ORDERS_IN attributes have been chosen to represent those characteristics considered to be important. Thus, for CUSTOMERS, individual attributes have been included for a customer's name, address, telephone number, and an identification number, the latter assigned by the Jellybeans, Inc. staff.

Optional and required attributes. Within the CUSTOMERS and ORDERS _IN definition, only the Phone attribute is optional; all of the others are required, in that they must be given values for each instance of the entity-type. Stated more precisely, when the database is eventually implemented, each CUSTOMERS record must be assigned values for IDENT, NAME, and ADDRESS.

Repeating group. An important design feature of ORDERS_IN is the repeating group (FLAVOR, AMOUNT, TOTAL_PRICE, ITEM_STATUS). The nature of this group is as follows: FLAVOR may occur several times within a particular instance of ORDERS_IN, but each time it occurs, AMOUNT, TOTAL _PRICE, and ITEM_STATUS must also occur. As was discussed in chapter 8, these required attributes are indicated by writing the names of each in all upper case letters. Also, the repeating group must appear at least once in each occurrence of ORDERS_IN, although this is not explicitly shown in the definition (E–2).

The ORDERS_IN entity-type contains two different attributes for status information. The first of these, ORDER_STATUS, is designed to indicate the overall condition of a particular order, such as "partly filled," "completely filled," and so on (there may be several possible values for this attribute). The other status attribute, ITEM_STATUS, is used to indicate the condition of a particular item within an order, such as "shipped," "awaiting shipment," or "awaiting delivery from supplier."

Figure 9.1

Data-structure diagram
illustrating the design in
the first stage.

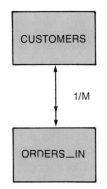

Synonyms. Another important characteristic of CUSTOMERS and OR-DERS_IN is that different names have been used in each definition for the attributes representing customer name and customer identification number. This is an example of how the choice of attribute names is a matter of syntactic clarity and/or convenience. Thus, referring to "CUSTOMER_NAME of CUS-TOMERS" seems redundant; whereas "NAME of CUSTOMERS" is more concise without any loss of clarity. The practice of using synonyms is common in database design, and it will be used to some extent in this study. In order to keep track of synonyms, a **synonym table** will be maintained as the design progresses. This table is shown in table 9.4, near the chapter end.

Relationships. We shall now investigate the possibility of a relationship existing between CUSTOMERS and ORDERS_IN. By studying the operation of the company, we note that each customer may make a large number of orders over the course of time. On the other hand, a particular order must be related to a particular customer. We are therefore led to the conclusion that there exists a one-to-many relationship between CUSTOMERS and ORDERS_IN. This relationship is an important part of the design, and it is the first of several that will be deduced during the course of the analysis.

As each relationship is uncovered, it will be noted in the following way:

(R–1)   CUSTOMERS/ORDERS_IN: 1/M

Data structure diagrams. We shall illustrate the design at various stages of development by using **data structure diagrams** to indicate the entity-types and relationships. The first of these is shown in figure 9.1.

It should be pointed out that in specifying the designs for CUSTOMERS and ORDERS_IN, no attempt has been made to optimize, in any sense, the choice of attributes for each entity-type. For this design, we are simply including all of the attributes that appear to be necessary for each entity-type, using Design Rule #2 as a guide. The advantage of this approach is that it is fundamentally intuitive and straightforward. However, note that it results in a design that produces a great deal of unnecessary redundancy in the final implemented database.

An example of this can be seen by inspecting the designs for CUSTOMERS and ORDERS_IN, in (E–1) and (E–2). The pair of attributes representing customer name and customer identification number appears in both designs. If left as is, this would result in a great deal of data duplication in the resulting database.

In chapter 10 we shall develop systematic methods for transforming preliminary designs, such as those being developed here, into a set of entity-types in which the distribution of attributes follows regular rules.

Also, in order to keep the discussion relatively simple at this stage, we are neglecting any reference to types of attribute or constraints. A section at the end of the chapter will be devoted to these subjects.

A Shipment Is Sent to a Customer

Each transaction of this type involves several different facts: (1) the customer to whom the shipment is sent; (2) the jellybeans included in the shipment; (3) the shipment itself; and (4) the bill incurred by the shipment. Since each of these facts is representative of a general type that is encountered frequently during the operation of the business, we shall design a separate entity-type to represent each one.

The design of the CUSTOMERS entity-type has been discussed and is shown in (E–1).

A shipment consists of quantities of one or more flavors of jellybeans that come from the company's stock on hand. The latter consists of various quantities of different flavors. As a shipment is made up, the amounts of particular flavors in stock are depleted. Thus, the stock on hand can be thought of as a set of facts, each of which is a particular quantity of jellybeans of a certain flavor. It can be represented by the following entity-type:

(E-3)   STOCK_ITEMS [FLAVOR, QUANTITY_ON_HAND, UNIT_PRICE]

This is a relatively straightforward definition, because there are no repeating groups and every attribute is required.

Each shipment represents a distinct fact, namely that a group of jellybeans is shipped to a particular customer. Because all shipments have similar qualities, and because they are all treated in more or less the same way, it seems reasonable to define an entity-type to represent the collection of all shipments:

	[SHIPMENT_ID, CUSTOMER_ID,	]
	[CUSTOMER_NAME	]
(E-4) SHIPMENTS_OUT	[ADDRESS, Phone, SHIPMENT_DATE,	]
	[(FLAVOR, AMOUNT, TOTAL_PRICE)	]

Although one might expect that the definition of SHIPMENTS_OUT would be the same as that for ORDERS_IN, it is in fact quite different. This is because a shipment to a particular customer may not correspond to any single order from that customer—a single shipment may fill many orders from a customer. On the other hand, only part of an order from a customer may be filled in a single shipment.

Another important feature of SHIPMENTS_OUT is the presence of the repeating group (FLAVOR, AMOUNT, TOTAL_PRICE). Each occurrence of this group represents a particular flavor of jellybean included in the shipment. Note that each attribute within the repeating group is required. In addition, there must be at least one occurrence of the repeating group within each instance of SHIPMENTS_OUT.

The attribute FLAVOR, which represents a particular type of jellybean, is common to both SHIPMENTS_OUT and STOCK_ITEMS. In this case, no synonyms have been used, since the term FLAVOR is suitable to both entity-type definitions.

The last significant fact connected with a shipment concerns customer billing. Presumably, a record must be kept of the amounts owed by each customer. When a shipment is sent to a customer, the total dollar value representing the sum of all occurrences of TOTAL_PRICE for that shipment must be added to the current outstanding balance for that customer. This necessitates the creation of an accounts receivable entity-type. A tentative definition for this entity-type is:

(E–5)

ACC_RECEIVABLE [CUSTOMER_ID, CUSTOMER_NAME,   ]
               [ADDRESS, Phone, BALANCE_DUE,   ]
               [LAST_BILLING_DATE, LAST_PAYMENT_DATE]

Relationships. We now wish to investigate whether any of the entity-types defined in (E–3) through (E–5) may be involved in relationships, either among themselves or with any previously defined entity-types. During the study of the company's operation, the following facts were noted:

1. Each customer may be the recipient of several shipments; whereas each shipment is associated with a single customer. Therefore a one-to-many relationship exists between CUSTOMERS and SHIPMENTS_OUT, which we note as follows:

(R–2)

CUSTOMERS/SHIPMENTS_OUT: 1/M

2. Each shipment may contain many stock items, and furthermore, each type of stock item may be part of many shipments. Therefore, a many-to-many relationship exists between SHIPMENTS_OUT and STOCK_ITEMS. At this point, we shall not decompose this relationship into two one-to-many relationships, as described in chapter 8. Instead, we shall leave the relationship as it is, deferring any decomposition to a later time.

(R–3)

SHIPMENTS_OUT/STOCK_ITEMS: M/N

3. For each customer, there is a single account receivable, and vice versa. Thus, a one-to-one relationship exists between CUSTOMERS and ACC_RECEIVABLE:

(R–4)

CUSTOMERS/ACC_RECEIVABLE: 1/1

Looking for possible relationships between the entity-types involved with shipments and any previously defined entity-types, we find that each customer order, represented by ORDERS_IN in (E–2), may contain many flavors, each of which represents a different stock item. This is indicated by the presence of the repeating group in ORDERS_IN. Furthermore, each stock item will undoubtedly be referenced by many different customer orders. Consequently, a many-to-many relationship exists between ORDERS_IN and STOCK_ITEMS:

(R–5)

ORDERS_IN/STOCK_ITEMS: M/N

Figure 9.2
Data-structure diagram.

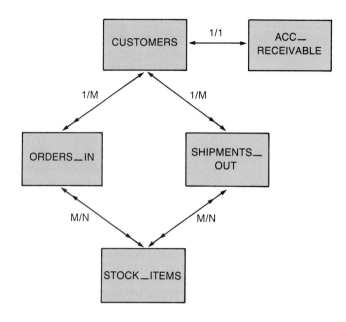

Figure 9.2 shows the current status of the design, including entity-types (E–1) through (E–5) and relationships (R–1) through (R–5).

A Payment Is Received from a Customer

Each transaction of this type involves the following facts: (1) the payment received; (2) the corresponding customer; and (3) the accounts receivable entry for that customer. Entity-types for the latter two have already been defined; a design for representing customer payments is as follows:

(E–6)   PAYMENTS [CUSTOMER_ID, CUSTOMER_NAME,   ]
                                  [AMOUNT, DATE_RECEIVED   ]

Over a period of time a customer may submit many payments; whereas a particular payment is always associated with a single customer. Thus, the following relationship exists:

(R–6)   CUSTOMERS/PAYMENTS: 1/M

An Order Is Placed with a Jellybean Supplier

This type of transaction introduces two new types of facts: (1) suppliers of jellybeans; and (2) orders placed by Jellybeans, Inc. to these suppliers. Before proceeding with designs for representative entity-types, note the following fact which was discovered during the study of the company's operations: not all jellybean suppliers deal in all jellybean flavors. That is, each supplier stocks only certain flavors, and the design must accommodate this information. Bearing this in mind, the following tentative designs are generated for suppliers of jellybeans and the orders they receive:

(E–7)

SUPPLIERS   [NAME, ID, ADDRESS, Phone,   ]
             [(FLAVOR_STOCKED, PRICE_PER_POUND)   ]

             [ORDER_ID, SUPPLIER_ID, SUPPLIER_NAME,   ]
(E–8)
ORDERS_OUT [ADDRESS, Phone, ORDER_DATE, ORDER_STATUS,   ]
             [(FLAVOR, AMOUNT, TOTAL_COST, ITEM_STATUS)]

The design for SUPPLIERS includes a repeating group that allows for the inclusion of a list of all flavors provided by each supplier. Also, in a manner similar to the design for ORDERS_IN, two status attributes are defined for ORDERS_OUT. ITEM_STATUS contains information concerning the status of a particular item on order from a supplier; and ORDER_STATUS relates to the status of the entire order, such as whether or not the entire order has been received from the supplier.

For syntactic simplicity, the definition of SUPPLIERS uses NAME and ID as attributes for supplier name and identification number. The corresponding synonyms in ORDERS_OUT are SUPPLIER_NAME and SUPPLIER_ID. These synonyms are included in the final synonym table, shown in table 9.4.

Reorder limits. Why would an order for jellybeans be placed? The answer is simply because the amount of that flavor in stock is running low. Since some stocked flavors move more quickly than others, what is considered low in stock for one flavor may not be so for another. It would be convenient to keep a value for each flavor, indicating when that particular flavor should be reordered. The most obvious place for this value would be within the database records themselves, so the design for STOCK_ITEMS must be modified to include this attribute.

It would also be convenient to know if a stock item that is running low has been reordered. This information could be contained in a *Boolean* attribute included as part of the STOCK_ITEMS definition. Recall that a Boolean attribute may contain only the values YES or NO.

The design of STOCK_ITEMS, modified to include these two additional attributes, is:

(E–3–A)

STOCK_ITEMS [FLAVOR, QUANTITY_ON_HAND, UNIT_PRICE]
             [REORDER_AMOUNT, REORDERED]

The attribute REORDERED would be assigned a value of YES only when an order for additional amounts of a particular flavor was pending.

Figure 9.3

Data-structure diagram
reflecting the current
state of the design.

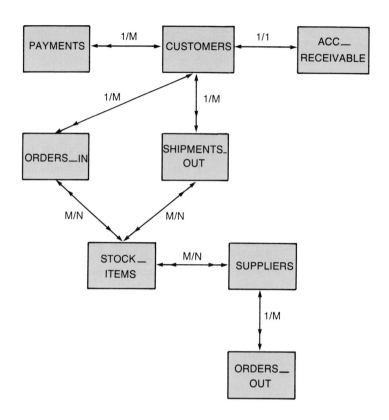

In searching for possible relationships, note that a supplier may be associated with many orders, whereas any particular order is associated with only one supplier. Another one-to-many relationship has thus been found:

(R–7)   SUPPLIERS/ORDERS_OUT: 1/M

An important relationship is implied by the repeating group in SUPPLIERS, namely the fact that each supplier may be the source of several jellybean flavors. Since many suppliers may stock a particular flavor, we conclude the following relationship:

(R–8)   SUPPLIERS/STOCK_ITEMS: M/N

A repeating group almost always implies the existence of some kind of relationship, possibly a one-to-many, or a many-to-many, depending on the situation. This becomes apparent when an entity-type definition containing a repeating group is decomposed into two entity-types in order to remove the repeating group (see the discussion in chapter 8).

Figure 9.3 shows the current state of the design, which is that shown in figure 9.2 with the addition of PAYMENTS, SUPPLIERS, ORDERS_OUT, and the relationships (R–6), (R–7), and (R–8).

A Shipment of Jellybeans Is Received from a Supplier

Each transaction of this type involves three different types of facts: (1) the shipment received; (2) the supplier from whom the shipment was sent; and (3) quantities of various flavors of jellybeans in the shipment. The last of these relates to the current stock on hand, because different stock items will be increased by the items included in the shipment. Designs for the entity-types STOCK_ITEMS and SUPPLIERS have already been given in (E–3–A) and (E–7) respectively. A tentative design for an entity-type to represent shipments from suppliers is the following:

(E–9)

```
                [ SHIPMENT_NO, SUPPLIER_ID,              ]
SHIPMENTS_IN [ SUPPLIER_NAME, ADDRESS, Phone,            ]
                [ SHIPMENT_DATE, (FLAVOR, AMOUNT,        ]
                [ TOTAL_COST )                           ]
```

The repeating group in (E–9) is to accommodate the fact that a shipment may contain more than one flavor. As in previous cases, each attribute within the repeating group is required.

With regard to possible relationships between SHIPMENTS_IN and other entity-types, note the following:

- Each supplier may send many shipments to Jellybeans, Inc. On the other hand, a particular shipment comes from a single supplier
- Each particular flavor may be part of many different shipments; furthermore each shipment obviously may consist of many flavors.

From these facts, we deduce the following relationships:

(R–9)   SUPPLIERS/SHIPMENTS_IN: 1/M
(R–10) SHIPMENTS_IN/STOCK_ITEMS: M/N

A Bill Is Received from a Creditor

This type of transaction involves one new type of fact: creditors of Jellybeans, Inc. The corresponding entity-type must contain standard data for each creditor such as name, address, and so on. In addition, it must contain the current amount owed to that creditor. The common term applied to groups of creditors is "accounts payable," and a suitable design for this entity-type is:

(E–10)

ACC_PAYABLE [CREDITOR_NAME, ADDRESS, Phone,
AMOUNT_OWED]

The AMOUNT_OWED attribute reflects the amount owed by Jellybeans, Inc. to creditors. A bill received from a particular creditor would result in an appropriate change to the AMOUNT_OWED attribute for the corresponding database record.

The only entity-type with which ACC_PAYABLE might possibly have a relationship is SUPPLIERS, since most suppliers will probably be creditors as well. However, the relationship is not clear because: (1) not all suppliers are necessarily creditors; and (2) not all creditors are suppliers (since Jellybeans, Inc. could owe money to groups or individuals other than jellybean suppliers). Therefore, it seems best to assume that ACC_PAYABLE has no relationships with any previously defined entity-types.

A more complete design might contain an additional entity-type to represent the individual bills received from creditors. Each bill would be represented by an instance of this entity-type (or an individual record in the implemented database). For the sake of design simplicity, however, we shall not include such an entity-type, preferring instead to assume that bills received are reflected indirectly in the AMOUNT_OWED attribute of ACC_PAYABLE.

A Payment Is Made to a Creditor

This is the last transaction-type to be analyzed, and it involves two types of facts: payments and creditors. The design for the latter is shown in (E–10) and a design for an entity-type to represent payments is as follows:

(E–11) PAYMENTS_OUT [NAME, ADDRESS, Phone, AMOUNT, PAYMENT_DATE]

In terms of possible relationships, note that each creditor may receive many payments from Jellybeans, Inc; whereas each payment is associated with only one creditor. Thus:

(R–11) ACC_PAYABLE/PAYMENTS_OUT: 1/M

Current State of the Design

We have now studied the major types of transactions for Jellybeans, Inc. and a number of entity-types have been produced that represent the important facts involved with these transactions. In addition, we have attempted to deduce the various relationships that exist among the entity-types from a study of the actual workings of the company. The design at this stage consists of the following items:

- A list of all entity-types definitions that have been developed. This list is shown in figure 9.4
- A list of all of the relationships that exist among the various entity-types. This is shown in figure 9.5
- A complete structure diagram, showing all of the entity-types and their various relationships. This is shown in figure 9.6
- A synonym table, shown in table 9.4, listing the various names used to describe the same attribute in different entity-types

```
CUSTOMERS          [ NAME, IDENT, ADDRESS, Phone              ] (E-1)


                   [ CUSTOMER_ID, CUSTOMER_NAME, ADDRESS, Phone,]
ORDERS_IN          [ ORDER_ID, ORDER_DATE, ORDER_STATUS,      ] (E-2)
                   [ (FLAVOR, AMOUNT, TOTAL_PRICE, ITEM_STATUS )]


                   [ FLAVOR, QUANTITY_ON_HAND, UNIT_PRICE     ]
STOCK_ITEMS                                                     (E-3-A)
                   [ REORDER_AMOUNT, REORDERED                ]


                   [ SHIPMENT_ID, CUSTOMER_ID, CUSTOMER_NAME, ]
SHIPMENTS_OUT      [ ADDRESS, Phone, SHIPMENT_DATE,           ] (E-4)
                   [ (FLAVOR, AMOUNT, TOTAL_PRICE)            ]


                   [ CUSTOMER_ID, CUSTOMER_NAME, ADDRESS,     ]
ACC_RECEIVABLE     [ Phone, BALANCE_DUE, LAST_BILLING_DATE,   ] (E-5)
                   [ LAST_PAYMENT_DATE                        ]


                   [ CUSTOMER_ID, CUSTOMER_NAME, AMOUNT,      ]
PAYMENTS                                                        (E-6)
                   [ DATE_RECEIVED                            ]


                   [ NAME, ID, ADDRESS, Phone                 ]
SUPPLIERS                                                       (E-7)
                   [ (FLAVORS_STOCKED, PRICE_PER_POUND)       ]


                   [ ORDER_ID, SUPPLIER_ID, SUPPLIER_NAME,    ]
                   [ ADDRESS, Phone, ORDER_DATE, ORDER_STATUS, ]
ORDERS_OUT                                                      (E-8)
                   [ (ORDER_ITEM, ITEM_AMOUNT, ITEM_COST,     ]
                   [ ITEM_STATUS)                             ]


                   [ SHIPMENT_NO, SUPPLIER_ID, SUPPLIER_NAME, ]
SHIPMENTS_IN       [ ADDRESS, Phone, SHIPMENT_DATE,           ] (E-9)
                   [ (FLAVOR, AMOUNT, TOTAL_COST)             ]


ACC_PAYABLE        [ CREDITOR_NAME, ADDRESS, Phone, AMOUNT_OWED ] (E-10)


PAYMENTS_OUT       [ NAME, ADDRESS, Phone, AMOUNT, PAYMENT_DATE ] (E-11)
```

Entity-types involved	Type of relationship	
CUSTOMERS/ORDERS_IN	1/M	(R-1)
CUSTOMERS/SHIPMENTS_OUT	1/M	(R-2)
SHIPMENTS/OUT/STOCK_ITEMS	M/N	(R-3)
CUSTOMERS/ACC_RECEIVABLE	1/1	(R-4)
ORDERS_IN/STOCK_ITEMS	M/N	(R-5)
CUSTOMERS/PAYMENTS	1/M	(R-6)
SUPPLIERS/ORDERS_OUT	1/M	(R-7)
SUPPLIERS/STOCK_ITEMS	M/N	(R-8)
SUPPLIERS/SHIPMENTS_IN	1/M	(R-9)
SHIPMENTS_IN/STOCK_ITEMS	M/N	(R-10)
ACC_PAYABLE/PAYMENTS	1/M	(R-11)

Figure 9.6
Final data-structure
diagram for the
Jellybeans, Inc., design.

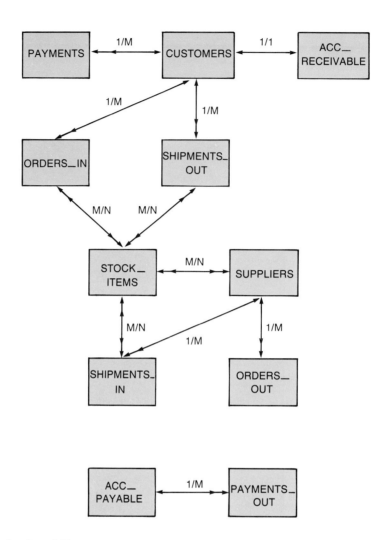

Analysis of Reports

Can the report types listed in table 9.3 be generated from the entity-types listed in figure 9.4? This question may be expanded into two parts:

1. Do adequate entity-types exist to generate the report?
2. If so, are their attributes adequate to impart the desired amount of detail to the report?

If the answer to either question is no, the design will have to be modified, either by the addition of suitable entity-types or by the modification of some of the attributes of one or more existing entity-types.

Table 9.4

Synonym Table for the Conceptual Design

Objects/Facts	Entity-type	Attribute Name
Customers of Jellybeans, Inc.	CUSTOMERS ORDERS_IN, SHIPMENTS_ OUT, ACC_RECEIVABLE, PAYMENTS	NAME CUSTOMER_NAME
Identification numbers of customers	CUSTOMERS ORDERS_IN, SHIPMENTS_ OUT, ACC_RECEIVABLE, PAYMENTS	IDENT CUSTOMER_ID
Names of jellybean suppliers	SUPPLIERS ORDERS_OUT, SHIPMENTS_IN	NAME SUPPLIER_NAME
Identification numbers of jellybean suppliers	SUPPLIERS ORDERS_OUT, SHIPMENTS_ID	ID SUPPLIER_ID

An examination of the items in table 9.3 reveals that the existing design is in fact adequate. For example, consider the first item: "List of accounts receivable, including totals." Clearly, the entity-type ACC_RECEIVABLE is ideally suited for this report-type, with the exception that a total of all accounts receivable must be calculated by a process external to any database record. This could be accomplished by an application program, or possibly by a report generator that is part of a DBMS.

Items 2 through 7 in table 9.3 each involve a single existing entity-type. Items 5, 6, and 7 are particularly interesting, because they each depend upon the values of particular attributes in specific entity-types. For example, the production of "A list of customer orders not yet entirely filled" depends on values for the ORDER_STATUS attribute of ORDERS_IN.

Thus, our preliminary design has been thorough enough so that no new entity-types or attributes need to be added at this stage. This is not too surprising, because most reports of interest are concerned with items related to the major transactions of the company and our design has been based on a study of these transactions.

No general conclusions should be drawn from this however, because it is always possible that at some point, either during the database design phase or during some later stage of the database life cycle, a report will be desired for which the current design is inadequate. As stated earlier, user requirements have a habit of changing and expanding with time.

Additional Design Considerations

Attributes and Constraints

The specifications encompassed in figures 9.4, 9.5, 9.6, and table 9.4 represent a good deal of the conceptual database design. However, more work is needed to complete the design, namely:

- Details about each attribute, including type and length, required/optional status, and so on
- Design constraints, including both inter-entity constraints and those that apply within a single entity. A full conceptual design may be dominated by the constraints specifications.

A complete discussion of attributes and constraints for the entire Jellybeans, Inc. design would be lengthy and repetitious. Instead, we shall confine our discussion to the entity-types related to the first type of transaction that was analyzed earlier—orders placed for jellybeans by customers. Recall that this type of transaction involves CUSTOMERS and ORDERS_IN entity-types.

Bear in mind that although the following discussion is in terms of entity-types and attributes, the relevance is actually to database records and record fields, or the equivalent. This may be of assistance in understanding the meanings of various constraints.

Inter-entity constraints. Almost invariably, if a constraint exists between two entity-types, the implication is that a relationship exists between them. To state it another way, if some type of relationship exists between entity-types A and B, then a constraint of some type also exists between them. As an example, by reviewing the relationship that was shown to exist between CUSTOMERS and ORDERS_IN, it is possible to deduce the existence of some type of corresponding constraint.

Logic dictates that a given customer may exist without there necessarily being any orders associated with that customer. For example, a customer may not have ordered any items over a long period of time, so that no current orders for the customer are on file. In terms of the database design, we can extend this fact to conclude that a CUSTOMERS entity may exist without there necessarily being an associated ORDERS_IN entity.

By contrast, the logic of the actual situation also dictates that an order for jellybeans may exist *only* if a corresponding customer also exists. (Otherwise, where would the order come from?) Similarly, a particular ORDERS_IN entity may exist only if there also exists a related CUSTOMERS entity. We may therefore define the following inter-entity constraint:

> An instance of ORDERS_IN may exist only if a corresponding instance of CUSTOMERS also exists.

Note that the correspondence between CUSTOMERS and ORDERS_IN entities is established by means of the attributes representing customer identification number. These are IDENT in CUSTOMERS, and CUSTOMER_ID in ORDERS_IN.

The preceding situation is characterized by saying that ORDERS_IN is **conditionally dependent** on CUSTOMERS. This type of constraint is usually found to exist between a pair of entity-types for which there is a one-to-many relationship. Thus, if the relationship between A and B is 1/M, it is likely that B is conditionally dependent on A. An examination of the various relationships in the Jellybeans, Inc. design will uncover many conditional dependencies.

Constraints within an Entity-type

In this section the various types of constraints within an entity-type are analyzed using the ORDERS_IN entity-type as an example.

Most constraints within an entity-type apply only to single attributes. For instance, the type and length of an attribute each imply definite restrictions on the set of legal values for that attribute. Thus, values for a numerical attribute would be restricted to those containing digits, plus and minus signs, decimal points, and perhaps one or two other special symbols. The values of some attributes may be restricted to a particular subset. For example, many numerical attributes are restricted to nonnegative values. Nonnumeric attributes, on the other hand, might be restricted to a certain small set of values. A MONTH attribute, for example, would be restricted to the values [JAN, FEB, etc.].

Figure 9.7 lists all of the ORDERS_IN attributes, as defined in (E–2). Accompanying each attribute is its detailed specifications:

- type
- length
- required or optional
- singly or multiply occurring
- any other constraints

In a sense, the constraints listed in figure 9.7 form a "wish list" for ORDERS_IN. Some of these constraints may be vital to implement, whereas others may not be so important. For example, it is crucial that each ORDERS database record have a value assigned for CUSTOMER_ID. The exact form of ORDER_DATE values, on the other hand, may be of secondary importance. Also, when the Jellybeans, Inc. database is implemented, the DBMS may be incapable of enforcing all of the constraints specified in the design. For example, many DBMS's do not distinguish between alphabetic and alphanumeric field-types. Therefore, even though the specifications distinguish between these two types, the implementation may not be able to do so.

Figure 9.7
A detailed set of
requirements for
ORDERS_IN.

Entity-type: ORDERS_IN

Attribute	Type	Length	Required/ Optional	Single/Mult. Occurrences	Constraints
CUSTOMER_ID	Alpha-N	6	R	S	1. A single letter followed by 5 digits
					2. Attribute key: must be unique
CUSTOMER_NAME	Alpha-N	30	R	S	None
ADDRESS	Alpha-N	50	R	S	None
Phone	Alpha-N	13	O	S	Must be of the form (ZZZ)ZZZ-ZZZZ
ORDER_ID	Alpha-N	9	R	S	None
ORDER_DATE	Alpha-N	8	R	S	Must be of the form MM/DD/YY
ORDER_STATUS	Alpha	1	R	S	Restricted to the following values:
					(a) "F" (filled)
					(b) "P" (partially filled)
					(c) "N" (not yet acted on)
FLAVOR	Alpha	15	R	M	Part of repeating group #1
AMOUNT	Numeric	3	R	M	1. Part of repeating group #1
					2. Must be >0
TOTAL_PRICE	Numeric	4	R	M	1. Part of repeating group #1
					2. Must be >0
ITEM_STATUS	Alpha	1	R	M	1. Part of repeating group #1
					2. Restricted to the following values:
					(a) "N" (not yet acted on)
					(b) "F" (filled)
					(c) "W" (stock not available)

Notes
1. Alpha: Restricted to the alphabetic characters
2. Alpha-N: May be any legal character
3. When an attribute name is written in all uppercase letters
   a value must be supplied

INTER-ENTITY CONSTRAINTS: Conditionally dependent on CUSTOMERS

Constraint Implementation

When a conceptual database design is implemented on a DBMS, the technical staff attempts to include as many as possible of the constraints specified in the conceptual design. Some constraints, such as attribute type and length, are usually enforced automatically. Others may be implemented only with great difficulty. In general, there are three ways in which constraints may work their way into a design implementation:

1. The DBMS may have a built-in capability for enforcing particular constraints. For example, many systems include a DATE field-type. Values for attributes of this type are automatically restricted to particular forms, such as mm/dd/yy. The DBMS will automatically reject any illegal values

2. An application program could be written to check input data for acceptable values

3. Data-entry personnel could be trained to be aware of the range of acceptable values for a particular data field, and to reject any input data that contain illegal values.

Of the three possibilities, the first is usually the most desirable because it requires the least amount of work on the part of those implementing the database. Unfortunately, it is also the least likely to be encountered in practice—only the more sophisticated DBMS's have any significant flexibility for enforcing constraint specifications.

User-written programs are the most common way of guaranteeing that data values conform to specific rules. It is not unusual to have data values input to an application program, rather than directly to the DBMS. The program validates any necessary data items, and sends on to the DBMS only those records for which all values are legal. If a particular value within a record is found to be illegal, a message is immediately displayed to the data-entry person so that the value may be reentered or the entire record disregarded.

If data is being entered in batch mode and an illegal value is noted by a data-checking program, the program rejects the record and sends an appropriate message to the output file.

The last possibility, training of data-entry staff, is of questionable value because it is nearly impossible for a data-entry person to check reliably for valid data values while at the same time entering data. Consequently, this approach is usually employed only as a last resort, that is when the DBMS cannot perform data validations, and when no programming facility exists with the DBMS.

A Complete Conceptual Design

The entire design for the Jellybeans, Inc. database would include a set of specifications for each entity-type similar to figure 9.7, in addition to the other design information such as data structure diagrams and so on. Specifications for the remaining entity-types will not be included here, since they would not contribute any further to an understanding of the conceptual design process.

Additional Decomposition of Entity-types

In developing the conceptual database design for Jellybeans, Inc., we have included many-to-many relationships as well as entity-types containing repeating groups. These logical structures are well-suited for representing various situations and are useful features of conceptual database designs. However, most database management systems cannot *directly* implement either of these types of structures, for various reasons that we shall not go into here. In order to implement either a repeating group or a many-to-many relationship, it must be decomposed into simpler conceptual structures that can then be directly implemented (decomposition processes were given in chapter 8).

Designer's choice. The designer of a conceptual model is faced with the choice of leaving these two types of structures as they are, or of decomposing them into the simpler ones that are more suitable for database implementation. Although there is much room for discussion as to which is the proper choice, the attitude adopted in this text is that the repeating group and many-to-many structures most clearly describe real-world situations, and for that reason are left as is in the Jellybeans, Inc. design.

To illustrate this issue of clarity, consider again the entity-type ORDERS_IN, which contains a repeating group representing the different jellybean flavors contained in an order:

(E–2)
```
            [ CUSTOMER_ID, CUSTOMER_NAME, ADDRESS,   ]
ORDERS_IN   [ Phone, ORDER_ID, ORDER_DATE, ORDER_STATUS ]
            [ (FLAVOR, AMOUNT, TOTAL_PRICE,           ]
            [ ITEM_STATUS)                             ]
```

The repeating group could be removed by decomposing ORDERS_IN into the following two entity-types:

(E–2–A)
```
            [ CUSTOMER_ID, CUSTOMER_NAME,            ]
ORDERS      [ ADDRESS, Phone, ORDER_ID, ORDER_DATE,  ]
            [ ORDER_STATUS                            ]


ORDER_ITEM  [ ORDER_ID, FLAVOR, AMOUNT, TOTAL_PRICE, ]
            [ ITEM_STATUS                             ]
```

However, the two new entity-types in (E–2–A) do not seem to enhance the clarity of the fundamental *meaning* of the design, namely that one order may contain several different flavors. Instead, more complexity is introduced into the design at all levels—there are two entity-types rather than one, and the data structure diagram must contain this information as well.

A similar situation exists with respect to a many-to-many relationship—the decomposition into two one-to-many relationships increases the complexity of the overall design without adding any clarity to its meaning.

An additional reason for not removing repeating groups or many-to-many relationships during the conceptual design phase is the fact that a conceptual design is supposed to be *independent of any particular DBMS*. Thus, even though most (but not all) DBMS's may not be able to implement particular structures, the issue of clarity should take precedence.

Summary

In this chapter, we have attempted to produce a conceptual design for the Jellybeans, Inc. database that reflects the important features of the company in a consistent manner. The first stages of the design involve a close scrutiny of the company in order to pinpoint the vital factors that should be represented in the database, and to identify any restrictions that may arise from financial or other considerations. After a list is compiled of those parts of the company's operation that are to be modeled, the employees of the company are interviewed extensively in order to gain a complete understanding of the company's operation.

During this study of users' requirements, lists are constructed, consisting of: (1) the significant types of transactions occurring within the company; and (2) the types of reports required by company personnel.

The design of the conceptual model then proceeds by selecting suitable entity-types to represent each of the important transaction types. At the same time, attributes are chosen for each entity-type, and relationships among them are established. In addition, lists of constraints are compiled to represent the real-life situation as closely as possible. Finally, data structure diagrams and lists of synonyms are built to become part of the design.

The final conceptual design, as developed in this chapter, is only provisional from two different points of view. First, whatever particular DBMS is chosen for the implementation will have its own particular limitations and restrictions, and the conceptual design will have to be adapted to these. In addition, users' experiences with the database will most likely result in changing requirements, necessitating design changes.

The techniques that have been employed here are applicable to a wide variety of situations, and the biggest challenge facing a designer is that of becoming adequately familiar with a new situation so that the design techniques may be utilized to best advantage.

Chapter Review

Terminology

conditional dependence	physical database design
data structure diagram	transaction
fact	

Review Questions

1. Review the material in chapter 8 relevant to the database design stages involving planning and studying user requirements. Briefly, discuss how the important features of each of these stages would apply to the Jellybeans, Inc. situation.

2. Review the list in table 9.1. Can you think of any other types of normal business activities that might be included in this list? Explain your choices.

3. Define the term *transaction,* and explain why a list of transactions, such as those shown in table 9.2 is a solid basis from which to develop a preliminary conceptual database design.

4. There exists a school of thought that adheres to the following idea: the basis for a conceptual database design should be the list of reports required by company personnel (as shown in table 9.3). Can you understand the basis for this point of view? Do you agree with it?

5. Review the basic tools used in developing a conceptual design. Make sure that you clearly understand the meaning and importance of each.

6. Review the connection between *transaction types* and *entity-types.* Be sure that you are clear on how one follows from the other.

7. In developing the design for the various entity-types, recall that the *details* concerning each of the entity-types attributes were not developed "in order to keep the discussion relatively simple." Do you agree with this approach, or do you think that attribute details should be developed at the time that the attributes are introduced?

8. The remarks made in the preceding question also apply to constraints. Do you think that it would be better to develop constraints during the design of each group of entity-types (as opposed to the approach used in the text)?

9. With respect to the design of CUSTOMERS in (E–1), can you explain why the "Phone" attribute is specified to be optional, whereas the remaining attributes are chosen to be required?

10. Referring to ORDERS_IN in (E–2), the text states that the repeating group *must* occur at least once for every occurrence of the entity-type (or for every ORDERS_IN record in a database). Can you justify this statement?

11. Explain the importance of synonyms in helping to clarify meanings within a conceptual database design.

Problems

1. Suppose that some customers have more than one telephone number. How would the Jellybeans, Inc. design be modified to accommodate this?
2. Suppose that for some of the customers of Jellybeans, Inc., orders are held up because of nonpayment of back bills. Devise a method for incorporating this information into the design, either by using existing entity-types and attributes, or by developing new ones if necessary.
3. Decompose the SHIPMENTS_OUT entity-type into two new ones, in order to remove the repeating group.
   a. What relationship, if any, exists between the two new entity-types?
   b. What relationships exist between each of the new entity-types and STOCK_ITEMS? Note that the original relationship between SHIPMENTS_OUT and STOCK_ITEMS was M/N. There is an important lesson to be learned here concerning the decomposition of a repeating group.
   c. Redraw the data structure diagram in figure 9.2, using the two new entity-types in place of SHIPMENTS_OUT.
4. With respect to STOCK_ITEMS shown in (E–3–A), develop a reasonable set of rules (or constraints) governing the relationships that must exist between the values of QUANTITY_ON_HAND, REORDER_AMOUNT, and REORDERED. (Hint: when would it not make sense for the value of REORDERED to be TRUE?)
5. As shown in (R–8), the relationship between SUPPLIERS and STOCK_ITEMS is many-to-many. Decompose this relationship into a set of one-to-many relationships. Introduce new entity-types if necessary. Redraw the data structure diagram in figure 9.3 to reflect your design changes. In your opinion, which design more clearly reflects the real-world situation—the original design or your modified one?
6. Suppose that Jellybeans, Inc. sends out bills on the first of each month. Modify the existing database design so that it includes billing information (a record of all bills sent out).
7. Modify the Jellybeans, Inc. database design to include bills received from creditors. List and explain each entity-type and attribute that you include in the modifications.
8. Suppose that the company has a discount scheme, whereby customers are given discounts for early payment of bills, according to the following schedule:

   - Payment within 30 days of *first* billing date: 3% discount from amount billed.
   - Payment within 60 days of first billing date: 1% discount from amount billed.

Alter the database design (including your modifications from problem 6) to allow customer billing information to include this discount schedule.

9. Make a list of the entity-types needed to generate each of the reports shown in table 9.3. Are there any entity-types shown in figure 9.4 that *do not* appear in your final list? If so, should they be deleted from the final design? Explain your answer.

10. Develop each of the entity-types SHIPMENTS_OUT and STOCK_ITEMS, using the style of figure 9.7 as a guide. Because each of these entity-types is involved in several relationships, you will need to pay particular attention to the specification of inter-entity constraints.

11. Make a list of all entity-types in the Jellybeans, Inc. design that are involved in conditional dependencies.

Chapter Ten

Relational Database Systems

Introduction

The previous two chapters were devoted to the ideas associated with conceptual database designs, which are fundamentally idealizations of real-world systems. The design of a conceptual database model is governed primarily by considerations of users' needs. That is, the objective during this phase of a database design is to produce a model that represents the information of interest and importance to the potential database users. A conceptual design is developed in part by many consultations with these users, and it is basically their needs that are represented by the design.

Physical models. Usually, a conceptual design cannot be directly implemented on a particular database system. Rather, the design must first be translated into a physical database design, or physical model, that conforms to the features of the particular DBMS being used. The reason for this is that each DBMS has its own particular set of data structures for storing and maintaining information, and there is often no direct relationship between these structures and those of a particular conceptual model. Thus, a conceptual design, which is built up from entity-types, relationships, constraints, and so on, must be recast into forms that can then be *directly* implemented on the DBMS. In other words, they must be recast into a suitable physical database design.

For example, many DBMS's are based on files, records, and fields. Physical database models that are designed for this type of DBMS must also be oriented around the same types of constructs.

As a crude analogy, we can compare the conceptual and physical models for a particular database design to two stages in the design of a new automobile. The first of these, corresponding to a conceptual design, would lay out the basic *functional* specifications of the machine: seats for four, engine, luggage area, and so on. The second phase would deal more with the actual details of the physical design, such as the materials and structures to be used for the different components. The purpose of this latter phase would be to translate the functional specifications arrived at in the first stage into a set of designs that were consistent with available materials, construction techniques, and so on.

Some aspects of a particular conceptual design may not be supportable by the particular DBMS being used. For example, certain types of *constraints* may not be directly enforceable. Alternatively, the DBMS may not be able to distinguish between required and optional data elements. When situations like this occur, the database designer must modify the conceptual design, choosing whatever compromise solutions are appropriate. For example, the designer might opt to develop application programs to run in conjunction with the DBMS for the purpose of enforcing constraints.

DBMS categories: relational and network models. Many different types of data structures are used by various DBMS's to store information. Nevertheless, most DBMS's fit nicely into one of a very small number of categories. Each category is defined by: (1) the way in which entities are represented in storage; and (2) the way in which relationships among entities are maintained. The two most common categories are known by the names **relational** and **network.** If a particular DBMS is a relational one, then it conforms to the **relational database model,** and similarly for the **network database model.**

This categorization of DBMS's is a convenience that allows general discussions to be made for each. However, it would be a mistake to jump to the conclusion that all relational DBMS's are fundamentally the same. On the contrary, there are usually many more differences than there are similarities between any two randomly chosen relational DBMS's. By the same token, two DBMS's, one of which is a relational type and the other of which is a network type, may have a great many characteristics in common.

It should be noted that some DBMS's are so unique that they are neither relational nor network. On the other hand, some are hybrids, exhibiting both relational and network qualities.

The rise of relational database systems. In this and the following chapter, we shall study the relational approach to database management, which has recently risen to preeminence in the computing world. This rapid growth in popularity has occurred because of several factors, most notably because of the ease with which users may interact with this type of system. In fact, nearly all microcomputer-based DBMS's claim to be relational.

Relational database systems offer a unified and straightforward approach to data management. The relational method includes a systematic procedure for designing databases with well-behaved characteristics, which we shall study in this chapter. Also included under the relational umbrella are sophisticated languages for performing complex database searches with minimal user effort.

Implementing a database on a relational DBMS. As mentioned earlier, if a particular DBMS is of the relational type, we say that it conforms to the relational database model. If we wish to implement a particular database on a relational DBMS, the physical design of the database must conform to the relational database model. That is, the design must be in terms of the type of data structures used by a relational DBMS. Thus, when we discuss the characteristics of the relational model, we are defining the rules that govern the physical design of any database that would be implemented on a relational DBMS.

In this chapter, the basic characteristics of the relational database model are defined, including a detailed discussion of how a conceptual design can be transformed into a corresponding relational design. Chapter 11 will provide more detail concerning the use of relational database systems. Subsequent chapters will deal in similar ways with database systems based on the network model, as well as other less common types of database systems.

The Relational Database Model

Basic Characteristics

Relational databases have certain characteristics that distinguish them from other types of databases. These are:

- A relational database consists of one or more two-dimensional tables of data values, with very simple rules defining the construction of a table. Each table corresponds to a conceptual entity-type that contains no repeating groups.
- Relationships between two or more tables are established by virtue of common data values contained in the corresponding tables.
- A systematic methodology has been developed for transforming a set of entity-types (representing a conceptual design) into a corresponding set of tables. The goal of this methodology is the generation of a group of tables in which data duplication is minimized, and in which certain problems associated with the maintenance of the tables are eliminated.
- High-level query languages are usually associated with relational database systems, to facilitate database searching and updating in as flexible a manner as possible.

The first two of these items are really the heart of the relational model—they define the basic characteristics that distinguish this model from others. Although the last two items are usually considered to be part of the relational model, they are not unique to it, and in fact they may often be used to great advantage with other types of DBMS's.

Figure 10.1
Sample relational table
(also called a relation).

Table: EMPLOYEES

NAME	ID	CITY	AGE
Slocum, J.	00001	Boston	25
Mowat, F.	00005	Berkeley	36
Chiles, W.	99999	San Diego	54
Chichester, F.	00004	London	86

Definitions and Rules

The basic structure of a relational database design is the **table,** technically known as a **relation.** A sample table is shown in figure 10.1. Each table corresponds to a particular conceptual entity-type and is assigned an arbitrary name. Each **row** of a table, technically known as a **tuple,** contains the data for a particular instance of the entity-type represented by the table. Alternatively, each row may be thought of as representing a real-world fact. For example, each row of the table in figure 10.1 corresponds to a single employee. A row may also be thought of as being equivalent to a database record.

Each column of a table corresponds to a particular attribute of the corresponding entity-type. Alternatively, we may think of a column as representing a particular characteristic of the group of facts indicated by the rows. A column may also be thought of as being equivalent to a field of a record. The terms *attributes* and *columns* will be used interchangeably in discussing the relational model.

Table 10.1 lists the terminology associated with the relational model, along with the corresponding terms used in conceptual design and in conventional data-storage applications. Much of the terminology associated with relational design comes from work whose origins lie partially in mathematical set theory. Many of the terms of this specialized vocabulary, such as *tuple* and *relation,* have proven to be unpopular. Consequently, we shall normally use more common terminology in this text. For example, discussions will usually be in terms of tables and rows, rather than relations and tuples.

Rules for Table Construction

Part of the beauty of the relational model lies in the simplicity of the basic table design:

- Each row of a table must be unique, that is, no two rows may have identical data for all attributes. This is because each row represents a distinct fact, and the presence of two identical rows would be redundant.

Table 10.1	List of Terminology Equivalences		
	Relational Model	**Conceptual Model**	**Common Storage Terminology**
	Table (Relation)	Entity-type	File
	Row (Tuple)	Instance of an entity-type	Record
	Attribute (column)	Attribute	Field

- Each entry in a table, corresponding to a particular combination of row and attribute, must be single-valued. In other words, each entry reflects a single characteristic about a particular fact.
- The order of the rows in a table is irrelevant, again reflecting the correspondence between a group of rows and a set of facts, which are usually not ordered.
- Each attribute is given an arbitrary name, usually chosen to reflect the corresponding real-world characteristic.

Notation for table design. In discussing tables, it will be convenient to use the same shorthand notation that was employed for describing entity-types. For example, the table shown in figure 10.1 could be described as follows:

EMPLOYEES [NAME, ID, CITY, AGE]

In addition, a particular attribute of this table, such as NAME, may be referred to as EMPLOYEES (NAME).

Attributes and Domains

An attribute of a table represents a particular characteristic of the set of facts represented by the table. A related concept that is very useful is the **domain** of an attribute, which is defined as all of the possible values that may be assumed by the attribute.

As an example, the domain of the NAME attribute in figure 10.1 would be the names of all employees of a particular company. Normally, one does not list the complete set of possible values that make up a domain. Instead, it is usually sufficient to make a general statement of the logical range encompassed by the domain.

Domain compatibility. The concept of domain is particularly useful when working with two or more attributes from different tables, all of which represent the same physical characteristic of a set of facts. When this is the case, the attributes are said to be **domain compatible.** In other words, each of the attributes has the same domain. For example, consider the following tables:

EMPLOYEE_SALARY [EMPLOYEE_NAME, GROSS_SALARY]
EMPLOYEES [NAME, ADDRESS, Phone]

If EMPLOYEE_NAME and NAME both represent names of the same group of people, then the two attributes are domain compatible.

Keys

The design of relational tables makes heavy use of keys, and it is important that the related basic concepts are clearly understood.

Each table must have a primary key (or simply *key* for brevity), whose purpose is to identify *uniquely* each row of the table. Keys may take several forms, but in the simplest case a key consists of a single attribute. This attribute must be unique in the sense that no two rows of the table have the same value for that attribute. As an example, consider the table in figure 10.1. If no two employees have the same ID value, then ID may be considered to be the key of the table.

In writing down a table description, the key of the table is often indicated by underlining the appropriate attribute. For example, the table in figure 10.1 would be written as:

EMPLOYEES [NAME, ID, CITY, AGE].

Frequently, more than one attribute within a table may be unique. When this occurs, each of these attributes is called a **candidate key,** and one of them is arbitrarily chosen as the table key. The remaining unique attributes are then called **alternate keys.**

As an example, consider again the EMPLOYEES table. If no two employees have identical names, then either ID or NAME could be the key of the table—they are both candidate keys. If ID is chosen to be the key, then NAME becomes an alternate key, and vice versa.

Concatenated keys. Often, a table exists in which no single attribute is unique. When this is the case, the key must be the concatenation of more than one attribute. As an example, consider the ORDERS table shown in figure 10.2. Each row of this table represents a particular item associated with a given order. An inspection of the table reveals that no single attribute may be used as a key, because no attribute is unique. However, the combination of attributes ORDER_ID and ITEM_NUMBER is unique, in that no two rows will have the same set of values for these two attributes. Therefore, this combination of attributes may be chosen as the table key. This type of key is called a **concatenated**

Figure 10.2
Table requiring a
concatenated key:
ORDER_ID + ITEM_
NUMBER.

Table: ORDERS

(Key) ORDER_ID	(Key) ITEM_NUMBER	QUANTITY
A3544	H9123	15
A2543	L3233	25
A2543	M1125	500
A2543	H3324	40
A1624	M1124	250

key, and it is written as ORDER_ID + ITEM_NUMBER. Thus, the key value for the first row of the ORDERS table is "A3544H9123." A concatenated key may consist of a combination of several attributes, and the following discussion will furnish a guide for choosing the key of a table.

The significance of keys. There is a simple relationship between the key of a table and the set of facts represented by the table. The following rule describes this relationship:

(R–1)

> The primary key of a table is that attribute, or set of attributes, whose values *uniquely* identify each of the facts represented by the table. The remaining attributes furnish additional information about these facts.

As an example of this rule, consider the EMPLOYEES table shown in figure 10.1. Each row of this table represents a particular employee, and the attribute that uniquely identifies each employee is ID (assuming that names are not unique). Therefore, ID may be chosen as the key of the table. On the other hand, if employee names were unique, then NAME could alternatively be chosen as the table key. In this case, the choice between NAME or ID would be arbitrary, possibly based on other considerations. In either case, the remaining nonkey attributes of the table furnish additional information about each employee.

As a second example of how keys may be chosen, consider again the ORDERS table in figure 10.2. The unique fact represented by each row is that a particular item has been included within a specific shipment. Therefore, the two attributes, ORDER_ID and ITEM_NUMBER, are both needed to uniquely specify each fact. The remaining attribute, QUANTITY, gives additional information about each fact.

Figure 10.3
A relational table.

STUDENT_ID	NAME	YEAR	GPA
01234	Harris, J.	FR	3.4
22346	Ferret, A.	SO	3.1
21452	Johnson, P.	SO	2.9
11349	Sampson, P.	SN	3.7
08349	Clive, X.	SN	3.9
03472	Peters, W.	JU	3.1
33461	Wilson, W.	SO	2.9

Functional Dependency and Determinants

Consider the following table, for which sample data is shown in figure 10.3:

STUDENTS [<u>STUDENT_ID</u>, NAME, YEAR, GPA]

Each row represents data for an individual student, and a likely choice for the table key is STUDENT_ID (assuming non-unique student names). With respect to this table, the following is true: given a particular value for STUDENT_ID, the value of NAME is automatically determined. For example, specifying "21452" as a value for STUDENT_ID *automatically* determines the value "Johnson, P." for the NAME attribute. This follows directly from the real-life facts: the identification number "21452" corresponds to the student "Johnson, P." NAME is said to be **functionally dependent** on STUDENT_ID. This is an example of the following general definition:

(R–2)

> An attribute B is functionally dependent on attribute A if every value of A uniquely determines the value of B. In this case, attribute A is called the **determinant** of B.
>
> The notation for this functional dependency is:
>
> $$A \rightarrow B$$

Using this definition, we see that the attributes YEAR and GPA are also functionally dependent on STUDENT_ID. That is, STUDENT_ID is the determinant of NAME, YEAR, and GPA. These dependencies may be written as follows:

$$\text{STUDENT\_ID} \rightarrow \text{NAME}$$

or

$$\text{STUDENT\_ID} \rightarrow \begin{array}{l} \text{NAME} \\ \text{YEAR} \\ \text{GPA} \end{array}$$

Symmetric and nonsymmetric dependencies. Functional dependencies are not necessarily symmetric, in that

$$A \rightarrow B$$

does not necessarily imply

$$B \rightarrow A$$

Thus, in the STUDENTS table, a particular value of STUDENT_ID uniquely determines a value for the GPA, but a specific value for GPA may be associated with none, one, or several students.

If two attributes, A and B, are *both* candidate keys for the same table, then they are mutually functionally dependent, which may be written as follows:

$$A \longleftrightarrow B$$

A functional dependency may involve more than two attributes. As an example, consider the ORDERS table shown in figure 10.2, in which the key is the concatenation of ORDER_ID and ITEM_NUMBER. An examination of this table reveals only one functional dependency, which is the following:

$$\text{ORDER\_ID} + \text{ITEM\_NUMBER} \rightarrow \text{QUANTITY}$$

Thus, for a particular row the value of QUANTITY is *not* dependent either on ORDER_ID or ITEM_NUMBER alone, but only on the *combination* of ORDER_ID and ITEM_NUMBER.

In the preceding examples, the nonkey attributes are all functionally dependent on the key. We shall see later that in general, this is a desirable feature for most tables.

Table Normalization

Having described the basic features of relational tables, we are now in a position to attack the major problem confronting a database designer:

Given a conceptual design for a system, translate that design into a set of relational tables that have reasonable properties with respect to data management. Exactly what these properties are will be demonstrated by examples.

Experience has shown that poorly designed tables exhibit predictable data-management difficulties. Many of these difficulties can be extremely costly in terms of both data-storage requirements and personnel time needed to work with the databases. To help eliminate these problems, a systematic technique has been developed for translating a conceptual design into a set of well-designed tables. This technique is known as **normalization.**

We shall approach the study of normalization by examining a series of simple table examples. Each of these will exhibit specific types of problems, and the elimination of these problems will be steps in the normalization process. The result of these analyses will be the development of a systematic procedure for the design of relational tables.

Normal forms.   Tables may be categorized according to certain characteristics, and different combinations of these characteristics define what are known as **Normal Forms.** That is, if a table has a particular set of well-defined characteristics, it is said to be in a specific Normal Form.

There are several standard Normal Forms, and each of them has been designed to remove a particular difficulty associated with relational tables. In fact, the normalization of a set of tables is a series of transformations whereby each table is changed from one Normal Form to another. The objective of this process is a set of tables that has as many desirable features as possible.

First Normal Form

The starting point in the normalization process is usually a conceptual design for a particular real-world system. The heart of this design is a set of entity-type definitions, such as that shown for Jellybeans, Inc. in figure 9.4. Normalization begins with the transformation of each of these definitions into a corresponding relational table definition, which *must* be in **First Normal Form,** defined as follows:

(R-3)

First Normal Form
A table is in First Normal Form if: • No two rows are identical, and • Each table entry is single-valued

Notice that this definition corresponds to the first two of the items listed on pages 276–77.

The definition of an entity-type can be directly translated into a corresponding relational table provided the following conditions are met:

- It must be possible to specify a unique key for each entity-type. This follows from the first requirement for First Normal Form
- Each attribute of the entity-type must be single-valued, which follows directly from the second part of the definition of First Normal Form. The only entity-types that do not meet this requirement are those that contain repeating groups

As an example, consider the following entity-type definition:

CUSTOMERS [NAME, CUSTOMER_ID, ADDRESS]

The transformation of this definition into a relation table is simple, since CUSTOMER_ID is unique, and every attribute is single-valued. Of course, the designer has the option of changing the names of the table itself or of any of the attributes. Thus, a table definition corresponding to CUSTOMERS might be the following:

CUSTOMER [NAME, ID, ADDRESS]

Entity-types with Repeating Groups

If an entity-type definition contains a repeating group, the transformation of the entity-type into a relational table in First Normal Form is more complicated, because by definition a repeating group is a set of one or more attributes that is multi-valued. This violates one of the basic requirements of relational tables. Consider the following entity-type definition:

(1) CUSTOMERS [NAME, ID, ADDRESS, (ORDER_NO, ORDER_DATE)]

Each instance of this entity-type represents a single customer and the repeating group represents all of the orders associated with that customer.

Before translation into a relational table can take place, the CUSTOMERS definition must itself be decomposed into entity-types that do not contain repeating groups. This process, which was discussed in chapter 8, is based on the fact that a repeating group always represents a one-to-many relationship. Thus, the CUSTOMERS entity-type in (1) may be decomposed into the following definitions:

(2) CUSTS [NAME, ID, ADDRESS]
ORDERS [ORDER_NO, CUSTOMER_ID, ORDER_DATE]

Each of these two definitions contains only single-valued attributes, and because each can be assigned a unique key, they can be translated directly into relational table definitions, as follows:

(3)

CUSTS [NAME, <u>ID</u>, ADDRESS]
ORDERS [<u>ORDER_NO</u>, CUSTOMER_ID, ORDER_DATE]

Synopsis. We may summarize our progress up to this point as follows. The first step in designing a set of relational tables is to translate the corresponding conceptual design into a set of tables in First Normal Form. Each entity-type of the conceptual design can be translated directly into a relational table unless it contains a repeating group, in which case a preliminary decomposition must be made to eliminate the repeating group.

Second Normal Form

Tables in First Normal Form often have characteristics that render them difficult to use. These characteristics are recognizable, and they are usually eliminated by one or more transformations of the tables.

Consider the following table, which contains information describing students and their classes, and which is in First Normal Form:

(4)

STUDENTS_CLASSES [NAME, <u>STUDENT_ID</u>, GPA,
<u>CLASS_ID</u>, GRADE]

We shall interpret this as follows: Each row represents a student enrolled in a class. If a particular row has a value for GRADE, then the student has completed that class. Otherwise, the student is currently taking the class. Figure 10.4 illustrates sample data for this table. The first three attributes contain information that is student-specific, and the next one is class-specific. The last attribute represents the grade attained by the student in that class, to be left blank if the class is currently in progress.

Data Redundancy

An examination of this table reveals several serious problems, the first of which is that a great deal of information is stored redundantly. For example, the values of NAME, STUDENT_ID, and GPA are stored three times for the student "Harris, J.". Other duplications exist as well.

Whenever possible, unnecessary data duplication should be avoided, for a variety of reasons:

- **Data-storage space.** Duplicated information requires extra storage space, usually on magnetic-disk devices. Although the cost of disk devices is

Figure 10.4
Sample data for the
STUDENTS_CLASSES
table.

Table: STUDENTS_CLASSES

NAME	(Key) STUDENT_ID	GPA	(Key) CLASS_ID	GRADE
Harris, J.	01234	3.4	Phys-1A	A
Ferret, A.	22346	3.1	Phys-1A	B
Sampson, P.	11349	2.8	Chem-2B	A
Harris, J.	01234	3.4	Chem-2B	A
Clive, X.	08349	3.9	Music-5	B
Peters, W.	03472	3.1	Art-3A	-
Ferret, A.	22346	3.1	Chem-1A	C
Harris, J.	01234	3.4	Music-5	B
Wilson, W.	33461	2.9	Art-3A	-
Peters, W.	03472	3.1	Music-1	-

dropping rapidly, it is still not free, and a good database design always strives for the minimum amount of required storage space to satisfy users' requirements.

- **Data-entry costs.** A great deal of database information must be manually entered by data-entry personnel. The existence of redundant data usually implies extra data-entry time, which in the last analysis translates into additional costs.
- **Database inconsistencies.** If information is entered redundantly, the chances for inconsistencies are correspondingly increased. For example, the GPA for "Harris, J." is entered three times into the STUDENTS_ CLASSES table, thereby tripling the probability that an incorrect entry will be made for this data item.

Modification Anomalies

The presence of data redundancy is nearly always accompanied by several predictable difficulties; these become apparent when information within the table is manipulated. These problems, known collectively as **modification anomalies,** are encountered during data updating, deletion, and insertion.

Update anomalies. Suppose that the GPA for the student "Harris, J." is changed from 3.4 to some other value, perhaps as the result of a course grade change. Because the GPA value is stored in several rows of STUDENTS_ CLASSES, the entire table must be searched, with changes made to each occurrence of the GPA for "Harris, J." This search-and-change procedure is not only time-consuming, but it offers opportunity for inconsistencies—either from human error if it is performed manually, or from system sources, such as a hardware interruption during the updating process. In either case, the result would be a table with inconsistent information.

In any case, the alteration of a *single* fact—the change in value of a GPA, requires the modification of *several* table entries, which is both time-consuming and error-prone. This type of situation is known as an **update anomaly,** and its existence suggests that the design of the table could be improved.

Deletion anomalies. Suppose that a student who has only recently enrolled in school drops all of his or her classes but does not drop out of school. All of the rows for that student must be deleted from the STUDENTS_CLASSES table. However, when this is done the basic information about that student, such as name and ID number, is lost from the table. In other words, as far as the database is concerned, the student no longer exists, even though in fact the student is still registered. The information in the database no longer corresponds to the real-world facts, and we say that a **deletion anomaly** has occurred.

Insertion anomalies. Suppose that a new student enrolls in the school but for various reasons does not immediately register for a class. Because of the design of the STUDENTS_CLASSES table, each row represents a student enrolled in a class. Therefore, each row should contain a value for CLASS_ID. However, the row for the new student can be entered with a special value for CLASS_ID, indicating that the student is not taking any classes. Later, when the student actually registers for courses, this original row becomes a liability in the database and would have to be removed. In fact, allowing this type of special row to exist complicates nearly all operations with the table.

This type of situation is called an **insertion anomaly:** the real-world fact, in this case the registration of a new student, cannot be conveniently described within the database because of its design.

The Source of Modification Anomalies

The various types of modification anomalies described are not impossible problems to deal with, but they can seriously complicate the efficient use of a database. It would be preferable if the anomalies could be eliminated, and in fact they can, by studying the fundamental source of the difficulties. We shall see that the anomalous behavior is directly related to the presence of data redundancy: both problems arise from the way in which the STUDENTS_CLASSES table is structured, and both can be eliminated by a suitable transformation of the table.

To attack the problem, ask the following question: What are the basic facts represented by the STUDENTS_CLASSES table? The answer is simply that each table row represents a particular student enrolled in a specific class. There is, however, a second independent fact contained in each row: the very existence of the student. That is, each row contains information that is specific to the student, such as GPA, and this data is independent of the classes represented in each row. This is the heart of the matter: when more than one row corresponds to a particular student, the student-specific data is repeated in each row.

In view of this statement, and by studying the table data in figure 10.4, the following conclusion is reached:

The problems of data redundancy and update anomalies in the STU-DENTS_CLASSES table arise specifically because each row of the table contains *two* independent facts.

Another point of view. Before illustrating the table transformation that eliminates both data redundancy and modification anomalies, we readdress the same situation from a different perspective: that of keys and functional dependencies. This approach will provide a much more abbreviated and direct way of dealing with the same issues in the many examples to be discussed further on in this chapter. Consider the following two questions:

1. What is the key of the STUDENTS_CLASSES table?
2. What functional dependencies exist within this table?

Because each row represents a particular combination of class and student, a reasonable choice for the key is the combination of STUDENT_ID + CLASS_ID, as indicated in (4).

We next list all of the functional dependencies that exist among the table attributes:

(F–1)
(F–2)

$$\text{STUDENT\_ID} + \text{CLASS\_ID} \rightarrow \text{GRADE}$$
$$\text{STUDENT\_ID} \rightarrow \begin{array}{l} \text{NAME} \\ \text{GPA} \end{array}$$

Partial functional dependencies. Although GRADE is functionally dependent on the *entire* key, NAME and GPA are dependent on only part of the key, as indicated in (F–2). These latter are known as **partial functional dependencies,** or simply **partial dependencies:**

(R–4)

> A partial functional dependency is said to exist between two table attributes A and B if:
> - B is functionally dependent on A, and
> - A is only part of the table key

The presence of these dependencies implies that NAME and GPA are *independent* of the full table key. To demonstrate this, consider the first and fourth rows of the table in figure 10.4. The key values for each of these rows are (by necessity) different, and yet the values of NAME and GPA do not change, which means that they are *independent* of the principal fact of each row. Since this is true, then either NAME and GPA are completely superfluous to the table, or they are associated with some secondary fact that is independent of the main fact implied by the key value.

In actuality, the dependencies shown in (F–2) indicate the presence of the set of facts that represent the existence of the group of students. This same set of secondary facts was discovered in the earlier discussion.

In summary, the following observation can be made:

(R–5)

> The existence of a partial functional dependency within a table implies that a set of facts is represented within the table *in addition* to those represented by the primary key.

Thus, looking for partial dependencies within a table is equivalent to looking for secondary sets of facts. As discussed earlier, the existence of this secondary set leads to data redundancy and anomalous behavior.

Removing partial dependencies.   The elimination of the partial dependencies in the STUDENTS_CLASSES table will remove the redundancy and anomaly problems. This is accomplished by *splitting off* these dependencies into a separate table, thus creating the following new tables:

(5)
(6)

STUDENT [NAME, <u>STUDENT_ID</u>, GPA]
STUDENT_CLASS [<u>STUDENT_ID</u>, <u>CLASS_ID</u>, GRADE]

Figure 10.5 shows the same data as in figure 10.4, now split into the two new tables. For each of these tables, the functional dependencies shown in (F–1) and (F–2) still hold because they are based on the realities of the student-class situation. However, (F–1) now applies only to the STUDENT table and (F–2) only to STUDENT_CLASS.

For each of the new tables, every nonkey attribute is functionally dependent on the entire key. A table that has this characteristic is said to be in **Second Normal Form.**

Figure 10.5

The result of splitting
the STUDENTS_
CLASSES table in
figure 10.4 into two
tables, each of which is
in Second Normal Form.

Table: STUDENT_CLASS

(Key) STUDENT_ID	(Key) CLASS_ID	GRADE
01234	Phys-1A	A
22346	Phys-1A	B
11349	Chem-2B	A
01234	Chem-2B	A
08349	Music-5	B
03472	Art-3A	-
22346	Chem-1A	C
01234	Music-5	B
33461	Art-3A	-
03472	Music-1	-

Table: STUDENT

NAME	(Key) STUDENT_ID	GPA
Harris, J.	01234	3.4
Ferret, A.	22346	3.1
Sampson, P.	11349	2.8
Clive, X.	08349	3.9
Peters, W.	03472	3.1
Wilson, W.	33461	2.9

Second Normal Form

(R–6)

A table is in Second Normal Form if:
• It is in First Normal Form, and
• Each nonkey attribute is functionally dependent on the entire key

Now examine the two new tables, STUDENT and STUDENT_CLASS, to see if any of the problems associated with the original STUDENT_CLASS table have improved. One immediate change that can be seen is that the data redundancy situation has been greatly improved. In particular, the basic data for each student now appears only once, in the STUDENT table.

It might appear that there still exists some redundancy in the new tables. For example, a STUDENT_ID value of "01234" appears three times in STUDENT_CLASS. However, this is an unavoidable consequence of the fact that this student is associated with three classes. One of the objectives of the normalization process is to reduce the amount of data redundancy to the absolute minimum, and this has been accomplished with the STUDENT and STUDENT_CLASS tables.

The splitting of the STUDENTS_CLASSES table has also eliminated the possibility of the modification anomalies already discussed. Each of the types of anomalous behaviour discussed earlier is reexamined in light of the new tables. As you read the following sections, a review of the corresponding earlier discussions concerning modification anomalies might be helpful.

Update anomalies. If the GPA value for a particular student must be changed, only a single row in the STUDENT table must be altered. Recall that in the original table, many entries for each student might have to be modified.

Deletion anomalies. If a student drops all of his or her courses but still remains registered, an entry can still exist in the STUDENT table, even though no entries exist for that student in STUDENT_CLASS.

Insertion anomalies. The earlier possibilities for insertion anomalies have also disappeared: an entry can be made in the STUDENT table for a new student who has not yet enrolled in any courses. As new courses are added for that student, corresponding entries can be made in the STUDENT_CLASS table.

Third Normal Form

In the previous example, a table in First Normal Form (STUDENTS_CLASSES) was split into two tables in Second Normal Form in order to eliminate problems associated with data redundancy and anomalous behavior. However, some tables in Second Normal Form can nevertheless exhibit problems of redundancy and anomalies. These problems may be removed by transformations that result in tables that are said to be in **Third Normal Form.** The following example illustrates this procedure.

Adding Instructors Data

Suppose that we wish to modify the database design embodied in the STUDENT and STUDENT_CLASS tables in (5) and (6), in order to include the names and office numbers of instructors who teach classes. Since the STUDENT_CLASS table in (a) already contains data on classes, it would seem to be the most likely place to include information on instructors. The following modification to STUDENT_CLASS accomplishes our goal:

(7)   STUDENT_CLASS_INSTR [STUDENT_ID, CLASS_ID, GRADE, INSTRUCTOR, OFFICE]

We have renamed the table to indicate its contents. Figure 10.6 shows sample data for this table.

Figure 10.6
Sample data for the
STUDENT_CLASS_INSTR
table.

Table: STUDENT_CLASS_INSTR

STUDENT_ID	CLASS_ID	GRADE	INSTRUCTOR	OFFICE
01234	Phys-1A	A	Weiner, N.	M11
22346	Phys-1A	B	Weiner, N.	M11
11349	Chem-2B	A	Pauling, L.	CT2
01234	Chem-2B	A	Pauling, L.	CT2
08349	Music-5	B	Harris, R.	M22
03472	Art-3A	-	Harris, R.	M22
22346	Chem-1A	C	Pauling, L.	CT2
01234	Music-5	B	Harris, R.	M22
33461	Art-3A	-	Harris, R.	M22
03472	Music-1	-	Harris, R.	M22

Keys and Functional Dependencies

Let us analyze the table in (7) in terms of keys and dependencies, as we did for
the previous example. The key of the table remains the same as before, namely
STUDENT_ID + CLASS_ID, because the basic fact contained in each row is
still a particular combination of student and class. The functional dependencies
of the table are the following:

(F-3)   STUDENT_ID + CLASS_ID → GRADE

(F-4)   CLASS_ID   → INSTRUCTOR
                                            OFFICE

As before, GRADE is functionally dependent on the combination STU-
DENT_ID + CLASS_ID. However, INSTRUCTOR is functionally dependent
only on CLASS_ID, because each class uniquely determines the instructor, regardless of the students enrolled in the class. Similarly, OFFICE is functionally
dependent only on CLASS_ID, because a particular class uniquely determines
an office, namely that of the instructor teaching the class.

Which normal form? Because the functional dependencies in (F-4) are partial,
the STUDENT_CLASS_INSTR table is not in Second Normal Form. Again,
this is because two basic facts are represented by each row: the student/class
fact is the same as before, but another slightly hidden fact also exists: *each class
exists independent of the enrolled students.*

Transforming to Second Normal Form

Because of these partial dependencies, the STUDENT_CLASS_INSTR table will exhibit the same types of redundancy and anomaly problems discussed earlier. This may be verified from a study of the sample data shown in figure 10.6. As in the preceding example, these difficulties may be removed by splitting off the partial dependencies, resulting in the following new tables:

(8)
STUDENT_CLASS [STUDENT_ID, CLASS_ID, GRADE]
(9)
CLASS_INSTR [CLASS_ID, INSTRUCTOR, OFFICE]

Notice that the splitting has resulted in the recreation of the earlier STUDENT_CLASS table shown in (6) which was in Second Normal Form. Focusing our attention on CLASS_INSTR, we note that it is also in Second Normal Form because of the functional dependencies shown in (F–4). That is, each of the nonkey attributes is fully dependent on CLASS_ID, which is the key.

Data Redundancy and Anomalous Behavior

By studying sample data for CLASS_INSTR, as illustrated in figure 10.7, note that even though the table is in Second Normal Form, there is still considerable data redundancy: the names and office numbers of some of the instructors appear more than once. Furthermore, the table exhibits the same types of modification anomalies that were discussed earlier:

Update anomalies. If a particular instructor moves from one office to another, several entries in the table may have to be modified. This is another example in which the change of a single fact, namely the association of an instructor and an office, requires alterations to several table entries. This modification anomaly is undesirable for reasons discussed earlier.

Deletion anomalies. Suppose that an instructor loses all of his or her classes because of lack of student attendance. When all of the corresponding entries in the table are removed, so is the information about that instructor's office number. That is, because the instructor has no classes, the database loses the information relating the instructor to an office. This is a deletion anomaly, and it is clearly undesirable.

Insertion anomalies. Suppose that a new instructor joins the faculty, but does not yet have any assigned classes. It will not be possible to add the name and office number of this person to the table because CLASS_ID is the table key. It does not make sense to have a table entry with no key value, because two such entries would result in two rows having the same key value, which violates a basic rule of relational tables. Of course, a fake key value could be concocted so that the instructor data could be entered as a separate row, but the potential problems associated with this procedure are sufficiently gruesome to deter this type of solution.

Figure 10.7

The result of splitting
the STUDENT_CLASS_
INSTR table in figure
10.6 into two new
tables, each of which is
in Second Normal Form.

Table: CLASS_INSTR

(Key) CLASS_ID	INSTRUCTOR	OFFICE
Phys-1A	Weiner, N.	M11
Music-1	Harris, R.	M22
Chem-2B	Pauling, L.	CT2
Chem-1A	Pauling, L.	CT2
Music-5	Harris, R.	M22
ART-3A	Harris, R.	M22

Table: STUDENT_CLASS

(Key) STUDENT_ID	(Key) CLASS_ID	GRADE
01234	Phys-1A	A
22346	Phys-1A	B
11349	Chem-2B	A
01234	Chem-2B	A
08349	Music-5	B
03472	Art-3A	-
22346	Chem-1A	C
01234	Music-5	B
33461	Art-3A	-
03472	Music-1	-

Transitive Functional Dependencies

We seem to have found that although CLASS_INSTR is in Second Normal Form, it has exactly the same types of problems that existed with our earlier examples of tables that were in First Normal Form. In fact, the reason for these problems is also similar to that uncovered earlier: there is a further functional dependency within the table which we failed to note in (F–3) and (F–4). This dependency arises from the reality that although OFFICE is functionally dependent on CLASS_ID, it is also completely functionally dependent on INSTRUCTOR:

(F–5) $$\text{INSTRUCTOR} \rightarrow \text{OFFICE}$$

This dependency may be observed by studying the data in figure 10.7, noticing that the values of OFFICE are completely linked to values of INSTRUCTOR.

The relationship in (F–5) is an example of a **transitive functional dependency,** which is defined as follows:

(R–7)

> A **transitive functional dependency** is said to exist between two table attributes A and B if:
> - One of the two attributes is functionally dependent on the other, and
> - Neither of the attributes is part of the table key

The transitive dependency and its associated problems of data redundancy may be eliminated by the same technique used to remove partial dependencies—by splitting off the dependency into a separate table, as follows:

(10)   CLASS_INSTR [<u>CLASS-ID</u>, INSTRUCTOR]
(11)   INSTRUCTORS [<u>NAME</u>, OFFICE]

Each of these tables is said to be in Third Normal Form, which has the following definition:

> ### Third Normal Form
>
> A table is in Third Normal Form if:
> - It is in Second Normal Form, and
> - It has no transitive dependencies

(R–8)

As a result of the table splitting, the data in figure 10.7 becomes that shown in figure 10.8, and an examination of these two tables reveals that the problems of redundancy and anomalous behavior have been eliminated.

The Best Normal Form

The Normal Forms that have been presented so far, as well as those that will be discussed later, are in a sense, ideals for the designer to bear in mind. However, it is not absolutely essential that a table be in any particular form in order to be usable. For example, the STUDENTS_CLASSES table in figure 10.4 could be used as is for storing, retrieving, and modifying data. The designer, however, should be aware of the potential difficulties involving modification anomalies and extra required storage for redundant data.

To Split or Not to Split?

Frequently, a choice may deliberately be made not to transform a table into Third Normal Form, but rather to leave it in one of the lower forms. Consider the following example:

(12)   CUSTOMERS [<u>NAME</u>, STREET, CITY, STATE, ZIP, Phone]

Figure 10.8

The result of splitting
CLASS_INSTR (figure
10.7) into two tables,
each of which is in
Third Normal Form.

Table: CLASS_INSTR

(Key) CLASS_ID	INSTRUCTOR
Phys-1A	Weiner, N.
Music-1	Harris, R.
Chem-2B	Pauling, L.
Chem-1A	Pauling, L.
Music-5	Harris, R.
ART-3A	Harris, R.

Table: INSTRUCTORS

(Key) NAME	OFFICE
Weiner, N.	M11
Harris, R.	M22
Pauling, L.	CT2

This table is not in Third Normal Form because there are transitive dependencies between several of the attributes:

(F–6)

$$ZIP \rightarrow CITY$$
$$STATE$$

(There may also be a transitive dependency between CITY and STATE, depending on whether the city names within the database are unique.) In order to remove these partial dependencies, the CUSTOMERS table would have to be split into the following:

(13)

CUSTS [NAME, STREET, ZIP, Phone]

ZIPS [CODE, CITY, STATE]

For reasons of convenience, however, the design in (12) would often be chosen over that in (13). To illustrate this, suppose that we are interactively searching a database for information concerning one or more customers. If our database consists of the single table represented by the design in (12), all of the information regarding each customer can be found with a single search.

On the other hand, suppose that our database consists of the two tables represented by (13). In this case, a two-step process must be used for each customer:

1. Locate the correct entry in the CUSTS table
2. Using the value found for ZIP, search the ZIPS table for the appropriate entry, which contains the corresponding city and state

In choosing the design in (12) over that in (13), a compromise is being made between (1) convenience of use; and (2) the problems associated with using a table containing transitive dependencies. In this particular example, the anomaly problems are hardly significant, because the relationships between zip codes, cities, and states are unlikely to change. Furthermore, there probably would be no interest in knowing the city and state for a particular zip code if there were no customer living within that zip location. Consequently, the existence of a separate ZIPS table would not enhance the usefulness of the database.

The only real disadvantage of using the design in (12) rather than (13) is the presence of redundant data. In this particular example, many designers would gladly pay the price for the convenience gained.

Third Normal Form is a useful goal, but the designer may often be faced with the choice of sacrificing the ideal for the practical.

Boyce-Codd Normal Form

For most situations, tables in Third Normal Form are usually free from the problems of data redundancy and anomalies. Occasionally, odd situations arise in which tables in Third Normal Form may nevertheless be problematical. Because of this, several still higher forms for tables have been defined in order to pinpoint the sources of the difficulties and to clarify the methods for their elimination. **Boyce-Codd Normal Form (BCNF)** is the first of these.

One of the more subtle types of difficulties that can occur with tables is illustrated by the following example, which involves information concerning students, sports in which they participate, and their coaches. For the purposes of this example, we assume that the following rules apply to students, sports, and coaches:

1. Each student may participate in one or more sports
2. For each sport in which a student participates, (s)he has a different coach
3. Each sport may have several coaches
4. Each coach works with only one sport

The following table definition could be used to describe the various players in this drama:

(14)   STUDENT_SPORT_COACH [STUDENT, SPORT, COACH]

Each row of this table represents a student's participation in a specific sport, as well as the coach guiding the student in that particular sport. Figure 10.9 illustrates some sample data for this design.

Keys and Functional Dependencies

We shall analyze this table in the usual way, that is, by finding the appropriate key, and identifying the various functional dependencies. In this way, we can determine the Normal Form of the table.

The choice of key for the table depends on what basic fact is represented by each row, and in this example there may be more than one point of view. First, we could say that the combination of a particular student and a given sport represents an independent fact, so that the key is STUDENT + SPORT.

```
Table: STUDENT_SPORT_COACH
--------------------------------------
(key2)
(key1)              (key2)
(key1)      (key1)
STUDENT     SPORT       COACH
```

STUDENT	SPORT	COACH
Peters, N.	Baseball	Ruth, B.
Harris, R.	Soccer	Boer, N.
Rogers, L.	Volleyball	Ives, C.
Lofgren, P.	Baseball	Ruth, B.
Alben, J.	Volleyball	Harris, R.
Smythe, Q.	Soccer	Boer, N.
Portola, Y.	Baseball	Ruth, B.

```
The table has two alternate keys:
    1. STUDENT + SPORT
    2. STUDENT + COACH
```

On the other hand, the combination of a particular student and a coach is also an independent fact, so that STUDENT + COACH could also be a key. This is an example of a situation in which there are two candidate keys, each of which happens to also be a concatenated key.

We shall arbitrarily choose STUDENT + SPORT as the table key for the present analysis. (Later, we shall see the effect of choosing STUDENT + COACH.) In order to see what normal form the table has, we list the functional dependencies, which follow directly from the four ground rules listed previously:

(F–7) $$\text{STUDENT} + \text{SPORT} \rightarrow \text{COACH}$$

(F–8) $$\text{COACH} \qquad\qquad \rightarrow \text{SPORT}$$

The dependency in (F–7) follows directly from the first two rules already listed: a particular pair of values for STUDENT and SPORT automatically determine the value of COACH, because each student has a specific coach for each of his or her sports. The dependency in (F–8) follows directly from the fourth rule: each coach is connected with only one sport.

As a result of (F–7) and (F–8), we conclude that the STUDENT_SPORT_ COACH table contains no partial dependencies, and is therefore in Second Normal Form. Note that although the dependency in (F–8) may appear at first glance to be a partial dependency, this is in fact not the case. This can be seen by reviewing the precise definition of partial dependencies, given in (R–4). Moreover, the table contains no transitive dependencies, so that the table is also in Third Normal Form. You might wish to verify this by reviewing the definition of transitive dependencies in (R–7).

Figure 10.10
The result of splitting
the STUDENT_SPORT_
COACH table (figure
10.9) into two tables,
each of which is in
Boyce-Codd Normal
Form.

```
Table: STUDENT_COACH                Table: COACH_SPORT
-------------------------           -------------------------

(key)             (key)            (key)             (key)
STUDENT           COACH            COACH             SPORT

Peters, N.        Ruth, B.         Ruth, B.          Baseball
Harris, R.        Boer, N.         Boer, N.          Soccer
Rogers, L.        Ives, C.         Ives, C.          Volleyball
Lofgren, P.       Ruth, B.         Harris, R.        Volleyball
Alben, J.         Harris, R.
Smythe, Q.        Boer, N.
Portola, Y.       Ruth, B.
```

Redundancy and Anomalies

In spite of the fact that STUDENT_SPORT_COACH is in Third Normal Form, the familiar problems of data redundancy and anomalous behavior rear their ugly heads. This may be seen by studying the sample data for the table, shown in figure 10.9. For example, the fact that "B. Ruth" coaches baseball is listed three times (data redundancy). Moreover, if those three students corresponding to "B. Ruth" drop out of school, the data relating "Ruth, B." to "Baseball" will be lost from the database (deletion anomaly). Other types of anomalous behavior also exist.

As before, these difficulties can be traced to a functional dependency that reflects the existence of more than one fact within each row. The functional dependency in question is that shown in (F–8), but in this case it is neither a partial nor a transitive dependency. Nevertheless, it is this dependency that causes the anomalous behavior.

One way to eliminate the difficulties is to follow the method used in prior examples and remove the offending functional dependency by splitting the STUDENT_SPORT_COACH table into two tables:

(15)

STUDENT_COACH [<u>STUDENT</u>, <u>COACH</u>]

COACH_SPORT [<u>COACH</u>, SPORT]

The original data now appears in two separate tables, as shown in figure 10.10. By comparing this data with that of the original table in figure 10.9, we see that the problems of redundancy and anomalies have again been eliminated.

Each of the new tables in (15) is said to be in Boyce-Codd Normal Form, which has the following formal definition:

(R–9)

> ### Boyce-Codd Normal Form (BCNF)
>
> A table is in Boyce-Codd Normal Form if:
> - It is in Third Normal Form, and
> - Each determinant is either the key or an alternate key

Note that the original STUDENT_SPORT_COACH table (14) is not in BCNF by virtue of the dependency in (F–8): COACH is a determinant, but it is neither the key nor an alternate key.

Trade-offs

Although the two new tables in (15) have eliminated the problems of redundancy, they introduce a different type of troublesome behavior. For example, suppose that we wish to determine the sports in which a particular student participates. In order to do so, the following two-step process must be carried out:

1. The entries for the student in question must be found in the STUDENT_COACH table
2. Using each value of COACH found in the first step, the COACH_SPORT table must be searched for the corresponding entry. This in turn yields the corresponding value of SPORT.

For interactive searching, this two-step process would be tedious. In fact, using the original STUDENT_SPORT_COACH table for this type of search would be much more efficient—requiring only one step instead of two.

To split or not to split. In this example, the designer is again faced with a design trade-off choice: the ease of database searching offered by STUDENT_SPORT_COACH, as opposed to the elimination of data redundancy and associated modification anomalies offered by STUDENT_COACH and COACH_SPORT. Many factors may ultimately determine which design is more appropriate.

Another Point of View

As mentioned earlier, there is an alternate way of analyzing the STUDENT_SPORT_COACH table, namely by choosing the key to be the combination STUDENT + COACH. With this choice, the functional dependencies are the following:

(F–9)
(F–10)

$$\text{STUDENT} + \text{COACH} \rightarrow \text{SPORT}$$
$$\text{COACH} \qquad\qquad \rightarrow \text{SPORT}$$

These should be contrasted with the dependencies shown in (F–7) and (F–8). Note that (F–9) and (F–7) are two different ways of expressing the same physical reality. In fact, from the point of view of (F–10), (F–9) is not only superfluous, it is in a sense incorrect!

From the point of view of (F–10), along with the choice of STUDENT + COACH as the key, we see that the STUDENT_SPORT_COACH table has a transitive dependency, because SPORT is dependent on only part of the key. As before, this dependency can be split off into a separate table, and when this is done the result is again the pair of tables shown in (15). Thus, we see that regardless of which of the possible alternate keys is chosen, the end result is the two tables in (15), which are in Boyce-Codd Normal Form. This is not too surprising, if one considers the logic behind the concepts of alternate keys and functional dependencies.

Fourth Normal Form

As a further example of the possible complexities that may arise in dealing with different types of designs, we consider the following modification to the previous STUDENT_SPORT_COACH situation:

1. Each student may participate in many sports
2. Each student may be assigned several coaches, any of whom may assist the student in any sport.

This example differs from the previous one in that there is no longer a functional dependency between COACH and SPORT. In other words, given a particular coach, there is no specifically related sport. Consequently, there is no longer a one-to-one correspondence between the coaches and sports for a given student.

Let us now investigate the design of the STUDENT_SPORT_COACH table, which is repeated below for convenience, with a sample set of data shown in figure 10.11.

(16)

STUDENT_SPORT_COACH [STUDENT, SPORT, COACH]

We shall analyze this table first with respect to functional dependencies and possible keys. A discussion then will be made of data redundancy, modification anomalies, and other possible difficulties associated with the use of the table.

Figure 10.11
A table with two multi-valued dependencies.

```
           Table: STUDENT_SPORT_COACH
           ------------------------------------

             (Key)            (Key)           (Key)
           STUDENT            SPORT           COACH

         +--------------------------------------------------+
         | Peters, N.       Baseball      Ruth, B.          |
         | Peters, N.       Baseball      Williams, T.      |
         | Rogers, L.       Football      Harris, R.        |
         | Rogers, L.       Soccer        Harris, R.        |
         | Smythe, Q.       Football      Williams, T.      |
         | Smythe, Q.       Baseball      Williams, T.      |
         | Smythe, Q.       Football      Dimaggio, D.      |
         | Smythe, Q.       Baseball      Dimaggio, D.      |
         +--------------------------------------------------+
```

Multi-valued Dependencies

Because of the basic assumptions of this situation, there are no simple functional dependencies between any of the attributes. However, there are two **multi-valued dependencies,** denoted as:

(F–11)

$$\text{STUDENT} \longrightarrow \text{SPORT}$$

$$\text{STUDENT} \longrightarrow \text{COACH}$$

A multi-valued dependency between attributes A and B is defined as follows:

Multi-valued Dependencies

(R–10)

A multi-valued dependency is said to exist between two attributes A and B if for each value of attribute A there is one or more associated values of attribute B.

Keys

By studying the data in figure 10.11, and remembering that a key must be unique, we conclude that the key for the STUDENT_SPORT_COACH table must be the combination of all three attributes: STUDENT + SPORT + COACH. This follows from the fact that no single attribute or combination of two attributes produces unique values.

By examining the contents of the table in figure 10.11, we can see that a good deal of redundancy exists. In addition, various types of anomalous behavior can be uncovered. For example, suppose that the student "Rogers, L." is assigned a new coach, "Jones, J." What value of SPORT is to be used in the table? It could be either "Football," "Soccer," a blank value, or possibly both "Football" and "Soccer." Furthermore, there is no reason to use any one value in preference to another.

Another type of anomaly shows up if the student "Smythe, Q." drops out of football. In that case, two entries must be deleted from the table, even though only a single fact changed.

As a final example, consider what occurs if the student "Peters, N." drops out of baseball. When the corresponding rows are deleted from the table, the fact that this student was assigned two coaches, "Ruth, B." and "Williams, T.," will also be lost from the table.

Again, as in previous examples, these deficiencies are due to the fact that each row of the table contains more than one independent fact. However, in this example the exact form of the table that causes the problem is different from that of any previous examples—the table contains multiple multi-valued dependencies, as shown in (F–11).

In fact, the STUDENT_SPORT_COACH design makes little sense to begin with, because there is no connection whatsoever between the two facts in each row: the STUDENT_SPORT and STUDENT_COACH relationships. The attempt to combine these two types of relationships into a single table is akin to the classical combination of apples and oranges. In fact, the table design in (16) should never have been developed at all. The design may be salvaged however, by using the same techniques developed in previous examples: the table must be split into two new ones, each of which represents only one of the relationships embodied in (F–11):

(17)

$$\text{STUDENT\_SPORT [} \underline{\text{STUDENT}}, \underline{\text{SPORT}} \text{]}$$

$$\text{STUDENT\_COACH [} \underline{\text{STUDENT}}, \underline{\text{COACH}} \text{]}$$

The corresponding data is shown in figure 10.12, and by comparing this data with that in figure 10.11, notice that a great deal of the redundancy has been eliminated. Similarly, all of the anomalous behavior has been eliminated.

Figure 10.12

The result of splitting the STUDENT_SPORT_ COACH table (figure 10.11) into two tables, each of which is in Fourth Normal Form.

Table: STUDENT_SPORT
- -

(key) STUDENT	(key) SPORT
Peters, N.	Baseball
Rogers, L.	Football
Rogers, L.	Soccer
Smythe, Q.	Football
Smythe, Q.	Baseball

Table: STUDENT_COACH
- -

(key) STUDENT	(key) COACH
Peters, N.	Ruth, B.
Peters, N.	Williams, T.
Rogers, L.	Harris, R.
Smythe, Q.	Williams, T.
Smythe, Q.	Dimagio, D.

The STUDENT_SPORT and STUDENT_COACH tables are said to be in Fourth Normal Form, which has the following technical definition:

(R–11)

Fourth Normal Form

A table is in Fourth Normal Form if:
- It is in Boyce-Codd Normal Form, and
- It does not contain multiple multi-valued dependencies

Still Higher Forms

Several other table forms have been identified, each of which removes a special type of difficulty. However, we shall not discuss any of these because the problems that are eliminated by using these forms are extremely rare. In fact, nearly all problems related to redundancy and anomalous behavior are eliminated by tables in Third Normal Form.

Combining Tables

All of the normalization procedures studied to this point involve processes by which a table was split into two or more new tables. However, it often happens that a design may be simplified by the reverse process, that is by combining two or more tables into a single one. Consider for example, a database consisting of the following two tables:

(18)

CLIENT_DATA [NAME, ADDRESS, Phone]

CLIENT_BALANCE [CLIENT_NAME, BALANCE_DUE]

The first table contains basic client information, and the second contains information strictly related to client financial matters. Assuming that NAME and

CLIENT_NAME are domain compatible, each client name will appear twice in the database—once in each table. This data redundancy can be eliminated by combining the two tables in (18) into a single one, as follows:

(19)

CLIENT_TOTAL_INFO [<u>NAME</u>, ADDRESS, Phone, BALANCE_DUE]

For reasons of security or convenience, it might be desirable not to transform the tables in (18) into that of (19). However, *in principle,* the transformation into (19) results in the elimination of data redundancy.

We may generalize this procedure as follows. Given two tables, Table1 and Table2, and their respective attributes:

> Table1 [<u>KEY1</u>, att12, att13, ...]
> Table2 [<u>KEY2</u>, att22, att23, ...]

and assuming that *only* the following functional dependencies exist:

(F–12)

$$KEY1 \rightarrow att12, att13, ...$$

$$KEY2 \rightarrow att22, att23, ...$$

Then if KEY1 and KEY2 are domain compatible, the two tables may be combined to form a new table, Table3, without introducing any modification anomalies.

> Table3 [<u>KEY</u>, att12, att13, att22, att23, ...]

where KEY is either KEY1 or KEY2.

Combining tables that have keys that are not domain compatible is more problematical, often leading to a resultant table with worse characteristics than the original pair. Consider the following pair of tables:

> Table3 [<u>KAT1</u>, <u>KAT2</u>, att3, att4]
> Table4 [<u>KAT1</u>, att5, att6]

with the following functional dependencies:

KAT1 + KAT2	$\rightarrow$	att3, att4

(F–13)

KAT1	$\rightarrow$	att5, att6

Suppose that Table3 and Table4 are combined into a single table, as follows:

> Table5 [<u>KAT1</u>, <u>KAT2</u>, att3, att4, att5, att6]

By virtue of (F–13), we have created a table with a partial functional dependency, whereas the original two tables were in Fourth Normal Form. Thus, table combination must be carried out carefully, to ensure that the final result does not introduce more problems than it eliminates.

Relationships and Relational Tables

Within the framework of relational tables, one of the qualities inherent in relationships is that *they are implicit in the data.* That is, a relationship between two tables exists by virtue of two domain compatible attributes.

The translation of a conceptual design into a set of relational tables usually retains any relationships that were part of the conceptual design. However, the normalization process frequently introduces new relationships into the design. Often, when a table is split into two tables in order to eliminate an undesirable dependency, a one-to-many relationship will exist between the two new tables. This can be seen with most of the examples of splitting used in this chapter.

One-to-Many Relationships

One of the most commonly encountered types of conceptual relationships is the one-to-many, and it fits very naturally into the relational model. Consider the following pair of tables:

(20)
$$\text{INSTRUCTORS} \quad [\text{ NAME, } \underline{\text{IDENT}}, \text{ OFFICE }]$$
$$\text{CLASSES} \quad\quad [\underline{\text{CLASS\_ID}}, \text{ TIME, ROOM, INSTRUCTOR\_ID }]$$

The relationship between INSTRUCTORS and CLASSES is one-to-many: for each row in INSTRUCTORS there may be zero, one, or several corresponding rows in CLASSES. The relationship is implicitly maintained by virtue of common values contained in the attributes IDENT and INSTRUCTOR_ID. Note that although their names are different, INSTRUCTOR_ID and IDENT are domain compatible, in that they both represent the same set of possible values—instructor identification numbers.

Foreign keys. The attribute INSTRUCTOR_ID is called a **foreign key** of the CLASSES table, because it is domain compatible with an attribute that is the key of another table, namely IDENT. INSTRUCTOR_ID is also called a secondary key of CLASSES.

Other Types of Relationships

Any of the types of relationships that were discussed in the context of conceptual models may also exist within the framework of a set of relational tables. Whatever the nature of the relationship, it is maintained by means of domain compatible attributes that contain common values, as discussed above for the one-to-many relationship.

For example, a many-to-many relationship is usually represented by three individual tables, among which there exist two one-to-many relationships. Some of the review problems at the end of this chapter will deal with this subject.

Figure 10.13
Summary of the
normalization process.

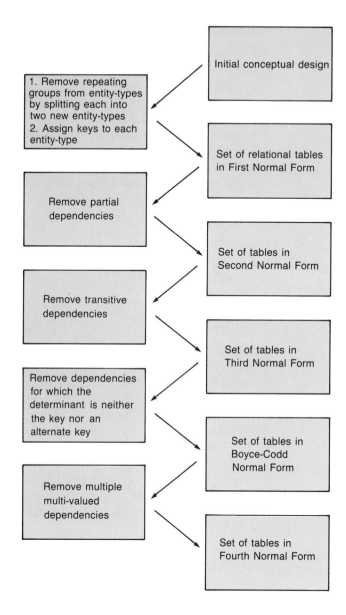

Normalization Summary

Figure 10.13 summarizes the steps involved in transforming a conceptual design into a set of relational tables suitable for implementation. Usually, each conceptual entity-type definition is worked with individually. Each is transformed into one or more relational tables in First Normal Form, splitting off any repeating groups into separate tables. Each table is then transformed into whatever normal form is appropriate. If a split results in two new tables at some stage in the process, each of these tables must then be normalized separately.

Starting with a table in First Normal Form, each step in the process uses the same fundamental approach for dealing with undesirable table qualities:

- Determine whether each row in the table contains any secondary facts that are independent of the principal fact represented by the row. This can be accomplished by the following: (1) a careful study of the meaning of each attribute and the functional dependencies among the attributes of the table; and (2) creating a sample table of data, which can then be studied carefully, looking for data redundancy and associated modification anomalies. If either of the latter is found, there is a good chance that a hidden dependency exists.
- Split off each offending functional dependency into a separate table. When this is done, usually only one attribute of the dependency remains in the original table, and in most cases it is the determinant of the dependency.

A Relational Design for Jellybeans, Inc.

Using the normalization techniques presented in the preceding sections, we shall now develop a relational design for Jellybeans, Inc. The starting point for the design will be the conceptual design developed in chapter 9, and embodied in figure 9.4, repeated in figure 10.14 for your convenience.

Each entity-type listed in figure 10.14 will be transformed separately into one or more tables using the scheme outlined in figure 10.13. Unless otherwise stated, all tables will be transformed into Fourth Normal Form. If new relationships are established as a result of table splitting, they will be specifically pointed out.

This section merits careful study, since it embodies most of the principles discussed in this chapter. As you study the transformation of each entity-type, it might be helpful to review the basis for its original design in chapter 9, in order to refamiliarize yourself with the precise meanings of each entity-type, its attributes, and the relationships with other entity-types.

CUSTOMERS, STOCK_ITEMS, ACC_PAYABLE, PAYMENTS_OUT

We begin the relational design for Jellybeans, Inc. with four entity-types (figure 10.15). For each of these, the transformation into a relational table is a straightforward process, inasmuch as each table has only single-valued attributes. In fact, only a key must be chosen for each table to complete the transformation of each entity-type into a First Normal Form table.

Since none of the tables in First Normal Form contain any partial dependencies, transitive dependencies, or multiple multi-valued dependencies, each is also in Fourth Normal Form, as shown by the final table definitions (T–1) through (T–4) in the figure. It is worthwhile to become familiar with the style developed in figure 10.15, because it will be used repeatedly in following figures.

Figure 10.14
Summary of entity-
types for conceptual
database design for
Jellybeans, Inc.

```
CUSTOMERS        [ NAME, IDENT, ADDRESS, Phone                    ]  (E-1)


                 [ CUSTOMER_ID, CUSTOMER_NAME, ADDRESS, Phone,    ]
                 [ ORDER_ID, ORDER_DATE, ORDER_STATUS             ]
ORDERS_IN                                                            (E-2)
                 [ (FLAVOR, PRICE_PER_LB, AMOUNT, TOTAL_PRICE,    ]
                 [ ITEM_STATUS )                                  ]


                 [ FLAVOR, QUANTITY_ON_HAND, UNIT_PRICE           ]
STOCK_ITEM                                                           (E-3-A)
                 [ REORDER_AMOUNT, REORDERED                      ]


                 [ SHIPMENT_ID, CUSTOMER_ID, CUSTOMER_NAME,       ]
SHIPMENTS_OUT    [ ADDRESS, Phone, SHIPMENT_DATE,                 ]  (E-4)
                 [ (FLAVOR, AMOUNT, TOTAL_PRICE)                  ]


                 [ CUSTOMER_ID, CUSTOMER_NAME, ADDRESS,           ]
ACC_RECEIVABLE   [ Phone, BALANCE_DUE, LAST_BILLING_DATE,         ]  (E-5)
                 [ LAST_PAYMENT_DATE                              ]


                 [ CUSTOMER_ID, CUSTOMER_NAME, AMOUNT,            ]
PAYMENTS                                                            (E-6)
                 [ DATE_RECEIVED                                  ]


                 [ NAME, ID, ADDRESS, Phone                       ]
SUPPLIERS                                                           (E-7)
                 [ (FLAVORS_STOCKED, PRICE_PER_POUND)             ]


                 [ ORDER_ID, SUPPLIER_ID, SUPPLIER_NAME,          ]
                 [ ADDRESS, Phone, ORDER_DATE, ORDER_STATUS,      ]
ORDERS_OUT                                                          (E-8)
                 [ (ORDER_ITEM, ITEM_AMOUNT, ITEM_COST,           ]
                 [ ITEM_STATUS)                                   ]


                 [ SHIPMENT_NO, SUPPLIER_ID, SUPPLIER_NAME,       ]
SHIPMENTS_IN     [ ADDRESS, Phone, SHIPMENT_DATE,                 ]  (E-9)
                 [ (FLAVOR, AMOUNT, TOTAL_COST)                   ]


ACC_PAYABLE      [ CREDITOR_NAME, ADDRESS, Phone, AMOUNT_OWED ]  (E-10)


PAYMENTS_OUT     [ NAME, ADDRESS, Phone, AMOUNT, PAYMENT_DATE ]  (E-11)
```

Figure 10.15
Relational design for
Jellybeans, Inc.

```
        I. Entity-types:

CUSTOMERS    [ NAME, IDENT, ADDRESS, Phone            ]

STOCK_ITEM   [ FLAVOR, QUANTITY_ON_HAND, UNIT_PRICE, ]
             [ REORDER_AMOUNT, REORDERED             ]

ACC_PAYABLE  [ CREDITOR_NAME, ADDRESS, Phone,        ]
             [ AMOUNT_OWED                           ]

PAYMENTS_OUT [ NAME, ADDRESS, Phone, AMOUNT,         ]
             [ PAYMENT_DATE                          ]

   Repeating groups: none
```

```
   II. First Normal Form Tables:

CUSTOMERS    [ NAME, IDENT, ADDRESS, Phone            ]

STOCK_ITEM   [ FLAVOR, QUANTITY_ON_HAND, UNIT_PRICE, ]
             [ REORDER_AMOUNT, REORDERED             ]

ACC_PAYABLE  [ CREDITOR NAME, ADDRESS, Phone,        ]
             [ AMOUNT_OWED                           ]

PAYMENTS_OUT [ NAME, ADDRESS, Phone, AMOUNT,         ]
             [ PAYMENT_DATE                          ]

     Alternate keys:          none[1]

     Partial dependencies:    none[2]

     Transitive dependencies: none
```

Notes
1. If customer names were unique, then NAME would be an
   alternate key for CUSTOMERS. We shall assume that
   customer names are not unique
2. A partial dependency can occur only if a table key consists of the
   concatenation of more than one attribute. Henceforth, partial
   dependencies will be cited only if a concatenated key exists

Figure 10.15
[*Continued*]

```
┌─────────────────────────────────────────────────────────────────────┐
│                                                                       │
│       III.  Fourth  Normal  Form  Tables⁽³⁾                           │
│                                                                       │
│   CUSTOMERS      [ NAME, IDENT, ADDRESS, Phone          ] (T-1)       │
│                                                                       │
│   STOCK_ITEM     [ FLAVOR, QUANTITY_ON_HAND, UNIT_PRICE, ] (T-2)      │
│                  [ REORDER_AMOUNT, REORDERED            ]             │
│                                                                       │
│   ACC_PAYABLE    [ CREDITOR NAME, ADDRESS, Phone,       ] (T-3)       │
│                  [ AMOUNT_OWED                          ]             │
│                                                                       │
│   PAYMENTS_OUT   [ NAME, ADDRESS, Phone, AMOUNT,        ] (T-4)       │
│                  [ PAYMENT_DATE                         ]             │
│                                                                       │
└─────────────────────────────────────────────────────────────────────┘
```

Notes

3. Tables will be transformed into Fourth Normal Form unless
   otherwise stated

ACC_RECEIVABLE

This entity-type, which represents those persons or companies owing money to Jellybeans, Inc., has no repeating groups, and because it has a suitable key (CUSTOMER _ID), it can be converted directly into a First Normal Form table (figure 10.16). In addition, it is also in Fourth Normal Form because of the lack of any partial or transitive dependencies.

By comparing the definition of ACC_RECEIVABLE in figure 10.16 with the definition of CUSTOMERS shown in figure 10.15, we see that the CUSTOMERS table is actually a subset of ACC_RECEIVABLE and is therefore entirely superfluous. The CUSTOMERS table from figure 10.15 is therefore removed from the set, and ACC_RECEIVABLE is renamed CUSTOMERS, as shown in figure 10.16.

SUPPLIERS

This entity-type, which represents suppliers of jellybeans, has a repeating group that must be removed as part of the transformation process (figure 10.17). As discussed earlier in this chapter, this is accomplished by splitting off the repeating group from SUPPLIERS and forming the following new entity-types:

SUPPLIERS   [NAME, ID, ADDRESS, Phone]

SUPPLIER_FLAVORS [SUPPLIER_ID, FLAVOR_STOCKED,
                    PRICE_PER_LB]

Figure 10.16
Relational design for
Jellybeans, Inc.
(continued).

I. Entity-type:

```
                    [ CUSTOMER_ID, CUSTOMER_NAME, ADDRESS,      ]
ACC_RECEIVABLE      [ Phone, BALANCE_DUE, LAST_BILLING_DATE,    ]
                    [ LAST_PAYMENT_DATE                          ]

        Repeating groups: none
```

II. First Normal Form Table:

```
                    [ CUSTOMER ID, CUSTOMER_NAME, ADDRESS,      ]
ACC_RECEIVABLE      [ Phone, BALANCE_DUE, LAST_BILLING_DATE,    ]
                    [ LAST_PAYMENT_DATE                          ]

        Alternate keys:           none

        Transitive dependencies: none
```

III. Fourth Normal Form Table:

```
            (1)     [ CUSTOMER ID, CUSTOMER_NAME, ADDRESS,      ]
CUSTOMERS           [ Phone, BALANCE_DUE, LAST_BILLING_DATE, ] (T-1)
                    [ LAST_PAYMENT_DATE                          ]
```

Notes
1. The CUSTOMERS table in (T-1) replaces the CUSTOMERS table shown
   in figure 10.15. See discussion in the text.

Figure 10.17
Relational design for
Jellybeans, Inc.
(continued).

```
┌─────────────────────────────────────────────────────────────────┐
│                   I. Entity-type:                                 │
│                                                                   │
│ SUPPLIERS        [ NAME, ID, ADDRESS, Phone              ]        │
│                  [ (FLAVORS_STOCKED, PRICE_PER_POUND)    ]        │
│                                                                   │
│    Repeating groups: (FLAVORS_STOCKED, PRICE_PER_POUND)           │
├─────────────────────────────────────────────────────────────────┤
│             II. First Normal Form Tables:                         │
│                                                                   │
│ SUPPLIERS        [ NAME, ID, ADDRESS, Phone                       │
│                                                          ]        │
│ SUPPLIER_FLAVORS [ SUPPLIER ID,FLAVOR STOCKED,PRICE_PER_LB]       │
│                                                                   │
│    Alternate keys: NAME(1)                                        │
│                                                                   │
│    New relationships: (2,3)                                       │
│                                                                   │
│           (a) SUPPLIERS/SUPPLIER_FLAVORS : 1/M                    │
│           (b) STOCK_ITEM/SUPPLIER_FLAVORS : 1/M                   │
│                                                                   │
│    Partial dependencies: none                                     │
│                                                                   │
│    Transitive dependencies: none                                  │
├─────────────────────────────────────────────────────────────────┤
│            III. Fourth Normal Form Tables:                        │
│                                                                   │
│ SUPPLIERS        [ NAME, ID, ADDRESS, Phone         ] (T-5)       │
│                                                                   │
│ SUPPLIER_FLAVORS [ SUPPLIER_ID, FLAVOR_STOCKED,                   │
│                                         PRICE_PER_LB] (T-6)       │
└─────────────────────────────────────────────────────────────────┘
```

Notes
1. Assuming that supplier names are unique, NAME is an alternate key
   for SUPPLIERS; ID is arbitrarily chosen as the key
2. The splitting off of a repeating group normally results in a
   one-to-many relationship between the two new tables. In this case,
   the tables are SUPPLIERS and SUPPLIER_FLAVORS
3. An additional consequence of splitting off of the repeating group
   is that the original many-to-many relationship between the entity-
   types SUPPLIERS and STOCK_ITEMS has been replaced by the two
   one-to-many relationships listed above. SUPPLIER_FLAVORS is called
   an intersection table, because it represents the association of a
   particular supplier and a specific flavor

Each of these definitions can be directly converted into a table in First Normal Form, provided that a suitable key can be found for each table. This is shown in figure 10.17 under the heading "First Normal Form Tables". Notice that the key for SUPPLIER_FLAVORS must be a concatenated key. This is typical of a table created as the result of splitting off a repeating group.

Transforming a Many-to-Many Relationship

The original SUPPLIERS entity-type had a many-to-many relationship with STOCK_ITEMS, as discussed in the preceding chapter, and shown in figure 9.5. However, as a result of the splitting off of the repeating group in SUPPLIERS, the original many-to-many relationship is replaced with two one-to-many relationships, each involving the new entity-type SUPPLIERS_FLAVORS. Thus, for each row of STOCK_ITEM, there may be many corresponding rows in SUPPLIERS_FLAVORS; and similarly for each row of SUPPLIERS. In other words, each row of SUPPLIERS_FLAVORS corresponds to a particular flavor supplied by a particular supplier.

Because there are no partial or transitive dependencies in either of the new tables, they are also in Fourth Normal Form so no further changes are necessary.

ORDERS_IN

This entity-type, representing customer orders for jellybeans, contains a repeating group that must be split off. This results in the two tables ORDERS_IN and ORDER_ITEM shown under the heading "First Normal Form Tables" in figure 10.18.

Again, because of the splitting, ORDER_ITEM has a concatenated key. In addition, ORDER_ITEM has a partial dependency, in that PRICE_PER_LB is dependent on FLAVOR, which is only part of the table key. When this dependency is split off, the result is the new table ITEM_PRICE, which is shown under the heading "Fourth Normal Form Tables" in the figure. By comparing this table with the definition of STOCK_ITEM, table (T-2) in figure 10.15, we see that ITEM_PRICE is actually a subset of STOCK_ITEM. Therefore, because ITEM_PRICE is entirely redundant, it is not included in the set of tables.

Focusing our attention on ORDERS_IN, we find that a transitive dependency exists within the definition: several attributes are dependent on CUSTOMER_ID, which is a nonkey attribute. When removed, the dependency forms a new table, CUSTOMERS, shown under the heading "Fourth Normal Form Tables" in figure 10.18. This table is also redundant, being a subset of the CUSTOMERS definition shown in figure 10.16. It is therefore not included in the list of tables.

Figure 10.18
Relational design for
Jellybeans, Inc.
(continued).

I. Entity-type:

```
ORDERS_IN      [ CUSTOMER_ID, CUSTOMER_NAME, ADDRESS, Phone,]
               [ ORDER_ID, ORDER_DATE, ORDER_STATUS        ]
               [        (FLAVOR, AMOUNT, TOTAL_PRICE,       ]
               [           ITEM_STATUS, PRICE_PER_LB )      ]
```

Repeating groups:

(FLAVOR, AMOUNT, TOTAL_PRICE, ITEM_STATUS, PRICE_PER_LB)

II. First Normal Form Tables:

```
ORDERS_IN      [ CUSTOMER_ID, CUSTOMER_NAME, ADDRESS, Phone,
               [ ORDER_ID, ORDER_DATE, ORDER_STATUS ]

ORDER_ITEM (1) [ ORDER_ID, FLAVOR, AMOUNT, TOTAL_PRICE, ]
               [ ITEM_STATUS, PRICE_PER_LB ]
```

New relationships: [2,3]

        (a) ORDERS_IN/ORDER_ITEM : 1/M
        (b) STOCK_ITEM/ORDER_ITEM : 1/M

Alternate keys: none

Partial dependencies:

        FLAVOR ---> PRICE_PER_LB

Transitive dependencies:

        CUSTOMER_ID ---> CUSTOMER_NAME, ADDRESS, Phone

Notes
1. The unique key for ORDER_ITEM must consist of the combination of
   ORDER_NO and FLAVOR: neither attribute by itself is unique for this table
2. The splitting off of a repeating group normally results in a one-to-many
   relationship between the two new tables

Figure 10.18
[*Continued*]

```
        III. Fourth Normal Form Tables:

ORDERS_IN      [ ORDER_ID, CUSTOMER_ID, ORDER_DATE,     ](T-7)
               [ ORDER_STATUS                           ]

ORDER_ITEM     [ ORDER_ID, FLAVOR, AMOUNT, TOTAL_PRICE, ](T-8)
               [ ITEM_STATUS                            ]

ITEM_PRICE⁽⁴⁾  [ FLAVOR, PRICE_PER_LB                   ]

CUSTOMERS ⁽⁵⁾  [ NAMF, IDENT, ADDRESS, Phone            ]
```

3. Because of the splitting off of the repeating group, the original M/N relationship between ORDERS_IN and STOCK_ITEMS is replaced by the two one-to-many relationships indicated
4. The partial dependency is split off, resulting in the new table ITEM_PRICE. It is not included in the set of tables, as it duplicates part of the definition in STOCK_ITEM (relational table T-2)
5. The transitive dependencies involving CUSTOMER_ID lead to the new table CUSTOMERS, which has already been defined above in relational table (T-1)

PAYMENTS

In order to transform the PAYMENTS entity-type (figure 10.19) into a First Normal Form table, a suitable key must be found. In this case, CUSTOMER_ID is not sufficient because there may be several payments corresponding to each customer. However, it is unlikely that two payments will be received from the same customer on the same date, so a good choice for the key is the combination CUSTOMER_ID + DATE_RECEIVED.

Choosing Not to Split

A partial dependency exists within the PAYMENTS table in that CUSTOMER_NAME is dependent on CUSTOMER_ID, which is only part of the key. In this case, however, we choose *not* to split off the dependency because when scanning the PAYMENTS table it will be convenient to be able to immediately identify a particular payment with the name of a customer, rather than with a customer identification number. We make this choice with the knowledge that the price to be paid will be a certain amount of extra secondary storage in order to accommodate the data redundancy. Note that a one-to-many relationship exists between the tables CUSTOMERS and PAYMENTS.

Figure 10.19
Relational design for
Jellybeans, Inc.
(continued).

```
                 I.  Entity-type:

PAYMENTS          [ CUSTOMER_ID, CUSTOMER_NAME, AMOUNT, ]
                  [ DATE_RECEIVED                        ]

       Repeating groups: none
```

```
          II.  First  Normal  Form  Table:

PAYMENTS          [ CUSTOMER_ID, CUSTOMER_NAME, AMOUNT, ](T-9)
                  [ DATE_RECEIVED                        ]

       Partial dependencies:
            CUSTOMER_ID ---> CUSTOMER_NAME
```

Notes

1. The CUSTOMER_NAME field represents redundant data, also appearing
   in the CUSTOMERS table in (T-1). However, it is left as part of the
   table definition, for convenience. Therefore, the table is left in
   in First Normal Form.

SHIPMENTS_OUT

SHIPMENTS_OUT has a repeating group, which when removed results in the
tables SHIPMENTS_OUT and SHIPMENT_ITEM listed under "First Normal
Form Tables" in figure 10.20. As in previous situations, this splitting has the
following consequences:

- A one-to-many relationship exists between the two tables created as a
  result of the splitting
- The original many-to-many relationship between SHIPMENTS_OUT
  and STOCK_ITEM is replaced by two one-to-many relationships. These
  are listed under "new relationships" in the figure.

Note that there is also a transitive dependency in the First Normal Form table
SHIPMENTS_OUT; and the splitting off of this dependency results in two tables, one of which is discarded because it is redundant with the CUSTOMERS
table shown in figure 10.16. The remaining table, SHIPMENTS_OUT, is shown
in (T–10) of figure 10.20.

SHIPMENTS_IN and ORDERS_OUT

The transformation of each of these entity-types (figures 10.21 and 10.22) par-
allels that for SHIPMENTS_OUT already given. The splitting off of each repeating group results in two relational tables and two new one-to-many
relationships. The splitting off of each transitive dependency results in a simpler
definition for each of the final tables because of redundant tables that may be
discarded.

Figure 10.20
Relational design for
Jellybeans, Inc.
(continued).

```
                    I. Entity-type:

SHIPMENTS_OUT [ SHIPMENT_ID, CUSTOMER_ID, CUSTOMER_NAME, ]
              [ ADDRESS, Phone, SHIPMENT_DATE,            ]
              [ (FLAVOR, AMOUNT, TOTAL_PRICE)            ]

    Repeating groups: (FLAVOR, AMOUNT, TOTAL_PRICE)
```

```
          II. First Normal Form Table:

SHIPMENTS_OUT [ SHIPMENT_ID, CUSTOMER_ID, CUSTOMER_NAME, ]
              [ ADDRESS, Phone, SHIPMENT_DATE            ]

SHIPMENT_ITEM [ SHIPMENT_ID, FLAVOR, AMOUNT, TOTAL_PRICE ]

   New relationships: (1,2)

        (a) SHIPMENTS_OUT/SHIPMENT_ITEM: 1/M
        (b) STOCK_ITEM/SHIPMENT_ITEM : 1/M

   Alternate keys: none

   Partial dependencies: none

   Transitive dependencies:

        CUSTOMER_ID ---> CUSTOMER_NAME, ADDRESS, Phone
```

```
       III. Fourth Normal Form Tables:

SHIPMENTS_OUT [ SHIPMENT_ID, CUSTOMER_ID, SHIPMENT_DATE ] (T-10)

SHIPMENT_ITEM [ SHIPMENT_ID, FLAVOR, AMOUNT, TOTAL_PRICE ] (T-11)
```

Notes
1. The splitting off of a repeating group normally results in a one-
   to-many relationship between the two new tables

2. Creation of SHIPMENT_ITEM results in the original M/N relationship
   between SHIPMENTS_OUT and STOCK_ITEM being replaced by two 1/M
   relationships. SHIPMENT_ITEM is the intersection table, each row of
   which represents a particular item in a given shipment.

Figure 10.21
Relational design for
Jellybeans, Inc.
(continued).

I. Entity-type:

```
SHIPMENTS_IN  [ SHIPMENT_NO, SUPPLIER_ID, SUPPLIER_NAME, ]
              [ ADDRESS, SHIPMENT_DATE, (FLAVOR, AMOUNT,  ]
              [ TOTAL_COST)                               ]


     Repeating groups: (FLAVOR, AMOUNT, TOTAL_COST)
```

II. First Normal Form Tables:

```
SHIPMENTS_IN  [ SHIPMENT_NO, SUPPLIER_ID, SUPPLIER_NAME, ]
              [ ADDRESS, SHIPMENT_DATE                   ]

ITEM_IN       [ SHIPMENT_NO, FLAVOR, AMOUNT, TOTAL_COST  ]

    Alternate keys: none

    New relationships:

         (a) SHIPMENTS_IN/ITEM_IN : 1/M
         (b) STOCK_ITEM/ITEM_IN : 1/M

    Partial dependencies: none

    Transitive dependencies:
```

SUPPLIER_ID	SUPPLIER_NAME, ADDRESS

III. Fourth Normal Form Tables:

```
SHIPMENTS_IN [ SHIPMENT_NO, SUPPLIER_ID, SHIPMENT_DATE ](T-12)

ITEM_IN      [ SHIPMENT_NO, FLAVOR, AMOUNT, TOTAL_COST ](T-13)

SUPPLIERS⁽¹⁾ [ SUPPLIER_ID, SUPPLIER_NAME, ADDRESS     ]
```

Notes
1. This table results from the splitting off of the transitive
   dependency shown; but it has already been defined in relational
   table (T-5)

Figure 10.22
Relational design for
Jellybeans, Inc.
(continued).

I. Entity-type:

```
ORDERS_OUT        [ ORDER_ID, SUPPLIER_ID, SUPPLIER_NAME,    ]
                  [ ADDRESS, ORDER_DATE, ORDER_STATUS,       ]
                  [ (ORDER_ITEM, AMOUNT, ITEM_COST,          ]
                  [ ITEM_STATUS)                             ]


        Repeating groups: (ORDER_ITEM, AMOUNT, ITEM_COST, ITEM_
                           STATUS)
```

I. Second Normal Form Table:

```
ORDERS_OUT        [ ORDER_ID, SUPPLIER_ID, SUPPLIER_NAME,    ]
                  [ ADDRESS, ORDER_DATE, ORDER_STATUS        ]

ITEM_OUT          [ ORDER_ID, ORDER_ITEM, AMOUNT, ITEM_COST, ]
                  [ ITEM_STATUS                              ]

        New relationships:(1)


                ORDERS_OUT/ITEM_OUT : 1/M
                STOCK_ITEM/ITEM_OUT : 1/M

        Alternate keys:            none

        Partial dependencies:      none

        Transitive dependencies:

                SUPPLIER_ID ---> SUPPLIER_NAME, ADDRESS
```

III. Fourth Normal Form Tables:

```
ORDERS_OUT        [ ORDER_ID, SUPPLIER_ID, ORDER_DATE,   ] (T-14)
                  [ ORDER_STATUS                         ]

ITEM_OUT          [ ORDER_ID, FLAVOR, AMOUNT, ITEM_COST, ] (T-15)
                  [ ITEM_STATUS                          ]

SUPPLIERS(2)      [ SUPPLIER_ID, SUPPLIER_NAME, ADDRESS  ]
```

Notes
1. The attribute ORDER_ITEM is domain compatible with the attribute
   FLAVOR: both attributes refer to jellybeans of a particular flavor
2. This table, which results from the splitting off of the functional
   dependency, has already been defined in relational table (T-5)

Design Summary

The relational design for Jellybeans, Inc. is summarized in the table definitions (T–1) through (T–15) and associated relationships described in figures 10.15 through 10.22. However, these definitions and relationships are only the backbone of a complete design. This would include a good deal more, including a full description of each attribute, as well as a listing of all significant constraints, such as was presented in figure 9.7. In addition, a data structure diagram would enhance the clarity of the overall design.

With one exception, the tables developed were put into Fourth Normal Form. Many of these came about as a result of splitting off partial and transitive functional dependencies. There were no instances either of multiple multi-valued dependencies or determinants that were neither keys nor candidate keys.

Summary

In contrast to a conceptual database model, which is an idealization of a real-world system, a physical database model conforms to the data structures of a particular type of DBMS. Each of the major types of database systems may be characterized by a particular type of physical model. One of the most popular of these is the relational model, which describes the basic data structures utilized by relational DBMS's.

The basic data structure of a relational DBMS is the table, which is a two-dimensional array of values. Each table consists of rows and columns. Each row represents a real-world fact, whose characteristics are described by the table columns, also referred to as attributes. Although a good deal of specialized terminology has accompanied the inception of relational systems, much of it has given way to more commonly-used terms.

The rules to which relational tables must conform are fairly straightforward: each row must be unique, the order of the rows is not significant, and the intersection of a row and a column must be single-valued. Each attribute is characterized by a domain, which refers to the range of possible values for that attribute, and different attributes referring to the same physical quantities are said to be domain compatible.

Each table must have a primary key, which uniquely identifies each row. A key may consist of one or more attributes, and it is possible for a table to have more than one possible key, referred to as candidate keys.

Some particular types of table designs produce undesirable data management characteristics, such as unnecessary data redundancy and various types of anomalous behavior. These poor qualities, which are identified with different table structures called Normal Forms, can be eliminated by a process known as normalization. This procedure involves a set of table transformations from one normal form into another, the end result being a group of tables in which the undesirable qualities are absent or at least minimized. Tables are characterized by functional dependencies and determinants. Various types of dependencies are associated with particular types of poor table characteristics, and the identification of these dependencies leads to successful normalization.

In most situations, it is desirable to transform tables into Fourth Normal Form; although there are sometimes reasons for leaving a table in First or Second Normal Form.

The process of transforming a conceptual design into a relational physical design takes several steps, the first of which is the splitting off of any repeating groups from each entity-type, usually generating a new entity-type for each group split off. The result is a set of relational tables in First Normal Form, which are in turn transformed into tables in higher Normal Forms.

Although the design principles developed in this chapter have been couched in the relational database framework, they may often be applied with success to non-relational database situations. Thus, for example, data redundancy is an undesirable characteristic of any database design, and the identification of the equivalent of partial or transitive functional dependencies may be valuable in many types of data management settings.

Many approaches to database management continue to flourish in addition to the relational one, and the design principles developed in this chapter will often prove to be of value for these systems—even when the data structures do not resemble those used in the relational approach.

Chapter Review

Terminology

alternate key	partial functional dependency
attribute	physical model
candidate key	primary key
determinant	redundancy
domain	relation
domain compatible	relational database model
functional dependency	relational table
modification anomaly	table column
multi-valued dependency	table row
normal forms	transitive functional dependency
normalization	tuple

Review Questions

1. Define *database model*. Distinguish between conceptual and physical models.
2. List the main features that define relational tables.
3. Why is a repeating group incompatible with the concept of relational tables?

4. Which rule governing table construction is consistent with the requirement that each table have a primary key? Explain your answer.
5. Define the differences between *primary, candidate,* and *alternate* keys.
6. Define the term *domain.* Explain how two attributes with different names, and in two different tables, can have the same domain.
7. Explain why every table must have a primary key.

Problems

1. A small school has a student body in which no two students have the same name. Given the following table describing basic student information:

   STUDENT [IDENT, NAME, ADDRESS, PHONE]

   a. List the candidate keys for the table
   b. Which of these keys would be the least likely choice as the primary key? Why?
   c. List the functional dependencies of the table.

2. Suppose that all of the customers of a particular business live in states for which each city name is unique. Given the following table design for customer data:

   CUSTOMER [NAME, IDENT, STREET, CITY, STATE, ZIP, Phone]

   a. List the most likely candidate for the primary key
   b. List the functional dependencies, along with the type of each (partial, etc.)
   c. What is the Normal Form of the table?
   d. How should the table be split in order to transform it into Third Normal Form? Would this be a desirable design?

3. A certain school has a group of dormitories in which students live. The school also has several clubs, and each student may belong to one or more of these. Consider the following tables, which describe the situation:

   STUDENT_DORM [STUDENT_ID, DORM, DORM_YEARLY_FEE]
   STUDENT_CLUB [STUDENT_ID, CLUB, CLUB_YEARLY_FEE]

   a. For each table, list (1) the key; (2) each functional dependency; (3) the Normal Form.
   b. Transform each table into Third Normal Form.

4. Suppose that the design for a CUSTOMERS entity-type includes orders information, as follows:

   CUSTOMERS [ID, NAME, ADDRESS, PHONE,
              (ORDER_DATE, FLAVOR, AMOUNT)]

Transform this into two relational tables. Note that this is somewhat different from the example in the text, in that orders do *not* have individual identification numbers. Your main challenge will be to find suitable keys for the tables that result from the splitting.

5. Suppose that a table has two alternate keys, KEY1 and KEY2. Why is it true that these two attributes are mutually functionally-dependent?

6. Suppose that a table has a concatenated key, KEY1 + KEY2. Is it possible for KEY1 to be functionally dependent on KEY2? Explain your answer.

7. Consider the two tables shown in (15) of this chapter which are the result of splitting the table shown in (14).

    a. Suppose that a user wishes to query these two tables in order to find all sports engaged in by a particular student. Describe the search process that would be necessary.

    b. Suppose that in order to simplify the above type of search process, the original table in (14) were split as follows, instead of the split shown in (15):

STUDENT_SPORT [STUDENT, SPORT]

COACH_SPORT [COACH, SPORT]

      1. Does this in fact simplify the search process described in part a?

      2. Using the above design, how would a user find the coach for a student in a particular sport?

      3. How could the design be altered to simplify the search problem described in part a and *at the same time* solve the problem addressed in 2?

8. Consider the STUDENTS_CLASSES table shown in (4) of this chapter:

STUDENTS_CLASSES [NAME, STUDENT_ID, GPA, CLASS_ID, GRADE]

    a. What groups of real-world facts are represented by this table?

    b. What is the relationship between these groups?

    c. Can you draw any conclusions regarding this type of relationship and the problems of redundancy and modification anomalies?

9. A group of doctors lives in a small town. Each doctor has several patients, but each patient visits only one doctor.

    a. Design a *single* entity-type to represent this situation, using only the following attributes:

DOCTOR_NAME	PATIENT_ADDRESS
DOCTOR_ADDRESS	PATIENT_PHONE
DOCTOR_PHONE	BALANCE_DUE
PATIENT_NAME	

b. What groups of real-world facts are represented by this table?

c. Transform the entity-type into one or more relational tables, each of which is in *at least* Third Normal Form. For each table, indicate the key, the functional dependencies (including their type), and the Normal Form.

10. Suppose that in a nearby town, the situation is slightly different from that described in problem 9: each doctor has several patients, but each patient may see several doctors.

a. What type of relationship exists between doctors and patients?

b. Using only the attributes listed in problem 9, develop a set of entity-types to represent the doctors and their patients.

c. Transform the design developed in part b into one or more relational tables each of which is in *at least* Third Normal Form. For each table, indicate the key, functional dependencies, and the Normal Form.

d. Do the final designs of this problem and the previous one reflect the differences in the doctor-patient relationships?

11. Draw a complete data structure diagram for the final relational design for Jellybeans, Inc., based on figures 10.15–10.22.

12. A movie studio wishes to institute a database to manage their files of movies, actors, and directors. The following facts are relevant:

• Each actor has appeared in many movies
• Each director has directed many movies
• Each movie has had one director, and one or more actors
• Each actor and director may have several addresses and telephone numbers

Design a set of tables for the studio, using only the following attributes:

ACTOR_NAME ADDRESS PHONE_NUMBER DIRECTOR_NAME
MOVIE_TITLE AGE PRODUCTION_COST YEAR_RELEASED

Show that each table in your final design is in at least Third Normal Form.

13. A family has several children, each of whom has several PETS (dogs, cats, rabbits, etc.), with the following restrictions:

• Each pet belongs to a particular child
• Each pet is very fussy and eats only particular types of pet food
• Each type of pet food may be eaten by more than one pet

Design a set of tables to describe the children and their pets, using only the following attributes:

CHILD_NAME   PET_NAME   PET_FOOD_TYPE
PET_TYPE   PET_AGE   CHILD_AGE
NUMBER_OF_PETS_OWNED FOOD_COST_PER_LB

Show that each table in the final design is in at least Third Normal Form.

14. Suppose that a single table represents a many-to-many relationship between two sets of real-world facts.
    a. Show that the table key must be a concatenation of at least two attributes.
    b. Show that in general, one would expect the table to contain one or more partial functional dependencies.
    c. Show how the transformation of the table into Third Normal Form will generally result in three separate tables.

Chapter Eleven

Working with Relational Systems

Introduction

Database management systems are proliferating at an astonishing rate, particularly in the microcomputer arena. Each month, at least one new product is announced, and the vast majority of these are called relational database management systems (often abbreviated to **relational systems** or **RDBMS's**) by their designers. In a way, this is an unfortunate situation because the term *relational database system* originally had a very precise meaning. Because so many different types of DBMS's are being called "relational" however, the term is in danger of losing meaning. (This is not unusual in the computer field: the precise definitions of many words are not clear because of the rapidly changing technology.)

Relational systems first came into existence in the early l970s, initially as experimental projects. In the past few years, they have developed into commercial products that cover the complete spectrum of computers, from small microcomputers to large mainframes. Relational database systems have inherent weaknesses as well as strengths. The biggest criticism is that certain types of operations tend to require relatively long execution times, compared to other types of database systems. On the positive side, the relational approach offers a degree of flexibility that is unequalled by other types of DBMS's.

The general concensus among database professionals is that relational systems are here to stay, although the exact forms that will evolve are still not clear. Already, many commercial database systems have combined the positive qualities of the relational approach with desirable features of other types of systems. Indeed, it seems likely that relational features will play an important part in the future development of the database industry.

This chapter and the next are devoted to some of the practical aspects of working with relational database management systems. These features are of interest not only to those involved with database design and implementation, but also to end-users as well. Although this chapter is oriented around relational database systems, many of the features to be discussed are relevant to a wide variety of DBMS's.

Distinguishing Characteristics

Database systems differ from one another in a great many ways, and in fact no two DBMS's are ever truly identical. However, certain fundamental features uniquely distinguish relational database systems from all other types. Following is a summary of these features.

Relational Tables

Within a relational DBMS, each database is defined in terms of one or more relational tables, which by definition must be at least in First Normal Form: each table consists of a two-dimensional array of elements, each of which is single-valued. The order of the rows and columns in a table is immaterial.

One of the cornerstones of relational philosophy is that the user's *perception* of each table within a database is a simple two-dimensional array of values. However, the actual manner in which the data is physically maintained need not be of concern to the user. The database system is free to store the data in whatever way is most convenient, as long as it appears *logically* to the user as a simple two-dimensional array.

If a relational database consists of several tables, then relationships among data in the various tables are implicit by virtue of common data values. This is another unique feature of relational systems. With other types of DBMS's, such as hierarchical and network systems, relationships are often maintained with physical linkages.

Query Languages

Relational database systems are also characterized by the types of query languages used for searching and manipulating information. Relational-type query languages are **nonprocedural** in nature and are often referred to as **higher-level** languages. One of the outstanding features of these languages is the ability of a single query command to effect a search for related information in several tables.

Because of their nonprocedural nature, relational query languages are extremely powerful, and their use often eliminates the necessity for writing complex application programs. The subject of relational query languages is an important one and a large part of this chapter will be devoted to it.

Nearly Relational DBMS's

Many database systems are characterized as relational because of the way in which data is represented in tables and the manner in which relationships are represented. Nevertheless, these DBMS's are not considered to be "true" relational systems because they do not possess a relational-type query language as previously described. Many of these database systems do in fact utilize some form of non-procedural query language, but it is capable of querying only one table (or file) at a time. At best, such systems can be called *nearly relational,* a term that applies to many of the current microcomputer-oriented database systems.

It may seem that this issue of database system classification is unnecessarily picky. After all, what difference does it make what we call a particular DBMS, as long as it has desirable characteristics? The answer lies in the philosophy behind the concept of standards—if the same word is used to describe apples and oranges, then it becomes impossible to distinguish between the two. By the same token, if we are not consistent about the definition of *relational,* it will cease to have any meaning. From the inception of the development of relational systems, it has been a consistant assumption within the industry that a truly relational DBMS must contain a query language that has the aforementioned qualities, and it is desirable and even necessary to continue with that philosophy.

Other Important Features

A relational database goes through many stages during its lifetime. It begins as a set of ideas that develop over a period of time—first as a conceptual database design, and then into a physical design consisting of relational tables, relationships, and so on. These design phases have been the subject of the preceding two chapters.

After a database design has been completed, it is then implemented on a DBMS. This involves writing down the exact database description in a language that can be understood by the DBMS. After suitable testing and debugging, the database is put into the users' hands, where it begins the functional part of its life cycle. During this stage, various processes occur: database information is added, deleted, and modified; users make queries of the database in order to extract information. Also, as users' requirements change, the very structure of the database may also have to be altered accordingly. Finally, various types of safeguards are employed to guarantee the safety and consistency of the database information.

All of these processes involve the use of various DBMS tools, or features, some of which are outlined in the following paragraphs. Some of these features are then explored in some depth in this and the following chapter. Although this group of features acts as a kind of "wish list" for database management systems, most relational systems have some of these characteristics to some degree.

Database definition facility. Every DBMS must give users a facility for defining the detailed structure of each database. This includes tables, columns, and other characteristics necessary to completely define a database. The specialized language used to write down these details is known as the **Data Definition Language (DDL).**

Database restructuring. As users become familiar with a database and its associated DBMS, their horizons may expand in terms of expectations from the system. Because of this, it is important that a DBMS contain some type of facility to modify an existing database structure with a minimum of inconvenience to the database designers and users. Typical structural changes would include the addition of new columns to a table, the addition of new tables to a database, and the modification of existing column characteristics. Ideally, this type of restructuring should be possible *without the need for rewriting existing programs, and without affecting the way in which users interact with the database.* When this is the case, the database system is said to have a high degree of **data independence.**

User views. Database users are often interested in looking at data in ways other than how it happens to be logically structured. A powerful DBMS feature is one that allows the creation of a logical database picture, or **view,** that suits a user's needs, but which may be quite different from the actual database structure. The user then interacts with the database as though it had the logical structure as presented by the view. Ideally, a different view would be created for each type of user. Views will be discussed in more detail in chapter 12.

Index creation. Indexes are powerful tools that can greatly enhance the performance of relational systems. An index can be useful for speeding up searches, as well as for quickly obtaining information sorted in particular ways.

Integrity controls. Information contained within a database may be subject to many different limitations, dictated by the real-world system represented by the database. An important DBMS capability is to be able to validate incoming data with respect to these various limitations, so that the database is as consistent as possible with the corresponding real-world system.

Database dictionary. Frequently, all of the information *about* a database is contained in a centralized location known as the **database dictionary.** This dictionary may be maintained by the DBMS, or it may be an entirely independent software package. This latter type of package can be an invaluable tool during the design, implementation, and use of a database.

Interactive and batch processing. It is often important to have the capability of interacting with a database in either the interactive or batch mode. Batch processing is accomplished by the use of application programs, written either in a language specific to a particular DBMS, or in a host language such as COBOL, BASIC, or FORTRAN.

Report generation. Much of the usefulness of database systems derives from their ability to produce reports in a large variety of output formats and *in an easy and flexible manner.* There are a great many ways in which users can create database reports, and modern database systems offer a great deal of flexibility in this area.

Transaction processing. A transaction may be defined as a set of changes to a database that constitute a single logical operation. A powerful DBMS feature is one that prevents only part of a transaction from being entered into a database. If a transaction fails during execution, those portions of the transaction that were executed up to the moment of the failure can be removed from the database, thus maintaining the database in a consistent state.

Backup and restoration procedures. A vital part of any database system is the ability to recover from software or hardware failures with a minimum of data loss. The procedures necessary for this type of protection can be quite complex and can require a great deal of system overhead, but they are vital for any type of serious database application.

Security controls. Many types of data must be protected against unauthorized access through various types of security controls, including data encryption, the use of passwords, and others.

Multiple-user access and concurrency control. A powerful feature is the ability to allow the simultaneous access to a database by several users. This capability must be accompanied by **concurrency control,** which is a technique used to prevent possible conflicts arising from the simultaneous access to data by several users.

Defining and Modifying Database Structures

This section is devoted to a discussion of DBMS features dealing with database structures. These include methods for the initial creation of databases, modifications to database structures during the database life cycle, and the use of indexes.

Database Definition

Every DBMS must contain a facility which may be employed by a user to define a new database. This part of the database system is sometimes referred to as the **database definition facility.** It may be a separate subsystem or module of the DBMS, or it may be integrated with the rest of the system. In either case, the user accesses the facility by issuing appropriate DBMS commands.

The process of database definition is one in which all of the details of a new database are communicated to the DBMS, so that they may be stored for subsequent use. These details include the following:

- **Table definition.** Each database consists of one or more tables, each of which is usually given a distinct name. The definition of each table includes the specification of every attribute to be included.

- **Attribute definition.** The definition of each attribute within a table must include the exact specifications of the type of data to be stored in the attribute. For example, if a particular attribute is to contain alphanumeric data, then the length of the attribute (number of bytes per data item) would have to be specified if the database system uses fixed-length attributes.

- **Constraints.** Many DBMS's allow the specification of different types of restrictions to be applied to information stored in a database. These constraints could apply to individual attributes, or to conditions between two or more attributes. For example, a constraint on a salary attribute could state that no value exceed 50,000. The general subject of constraints was discussed in chapter 9 and will be referred to again in chapter 12.

Techniques for Entering Database Definitions

Most database definitions are written in one of two ways. The first of these, DBMS screen prompting, is extremely simple to use, normally requiring no prior knowledge of the DBMS. With this technique, a DBMS prompts the user for the name and characteristics of each attribute that is to be part of a new table. This type of facility is suitable when the kinds of information required for a database definition are limited. It is utilized by nearly all microcomputer-based DBMS's. Figures 2.3 and 2.4 illustrated this type of database definition facility.

A more general type of database definition requires that the user write down all of the details necessary to describe a database by using a database definition language (DDL), which can be understood by the DBMS. With this technique, a database definition is first written down, usually by utilizing a text editor. The definition is then read and processed (translated) by the database system, in a manner analogous to the compilation of a FORTRAN or Pascal computer program. The results of this translation are stored in an internal form, often in a data dictionary. They are used as a template, or guide, for all operations or interactions between the database system and the database. This type of database definition process is illustrated in figure 11.1.

Figure 11.1

The creation of a
database definition. The
final database definition
is stored in the
database dictionary.

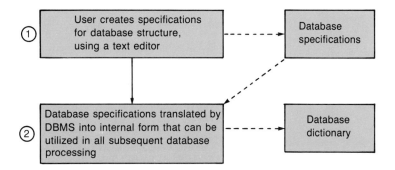

A Sample Database Definition

Figure 11.2 shows a typical database definition for a two-table database named
ENROLLMENT. The syntax used in this figure is not based on any particular
DBMS, but it is typical of the type of language normally used in database def-
initions. The **ENROLLMENT** database consists of two tables, STUDENTS and
STUDENT_CLASS. Each table definition contains specifications for the indi-
vidual attributes of the table, and two types of data are specified, namely CHAR-
ACTER and INTEGER. In addition, various types of constraints are contained
in the definition:

- **Single attribute constraints.** The NOT NULL clause attached to an
  attribute indicates that the attribute is required—each row must be given
  a value for that particular attribute.
  The DEFINE INTEGRITY statements indicate value restrictions on
  particular attributes. For example, values for STUDENT_NUMBER
  must lie in the range 1–999,999.
- **Inter-table constraints.** The REFERENCE INTEGRITY statement
  requires that for each row in the STUDENT_CLASS table, a
  corresponding row must exist in the STUDENT table. The
  correspondence is established by the attributes STUD_NUM and
  STUDENT.

The definition in figure 11.2 would be created with a text processor, then stored
in a temporary file, and finally processed by the DBMS. The final result would
be an internal form of the information, stored in the database dictionary for **EN-
ROLLMENT.**

Figure 11.2

A sample database
definition, including
various types of
constraint
specifications.

```
DEFINE DATABASE = ENROLLMENT

TABLE = STUDENT
        STUDENT-NUMBER:        INTEGER, NOT NULL
        STUDENT-NAME:          CHARACTER (25)
        MAJOR:                 CHARACTER (15)
        GRADE-LEVEL:           CHARACTER (2), NOT NULL
        AGE:                   INTEGER

        DEFINE INTEGRITY ON GRADE-LEVEL:
        GRADE-LEVEL IN ( 'FR' , 'SO' , 'JU' , 'SN' )

        DEFINE INTEGRITY ON STUDENT-NUMBER:
        ( STUDENT-NUMBER    0 ) AND ( STUDENT-NUMBER    1000000 )

END TABLE STUDENTS:

TABLE = STUDENT-CLASS
        CLASS-NUM:             CHARACTER (15), NOT NULL
        STUD-NUM:              INTEGER, NOT NULL
        GRADE:                 INTEGER

        REFERENCE INTEGRITY ON STUD-NUM:
        STUDENT-NUMBER IN TABLE = STUDENTS

END TABLE STUDENT-CLASS

END DATABASE DEFINTION
```

Database Dictionaries

Often, all of the information *about* a database is stored in the database dictionary
for that database. Like many other terms in the data processing vocabulary, *database dictionary* has come to refer to virtually any type of centralized repository
of database information. As a result, there is often considerable confusion over
its meaning. In this section, we shall discuss the two common types of database
dictionaries: (1) an internal dictionary, which is an integral part of a database
system; and (2) an external dictionary, which is an independent software package
that is used in conjunction with a database system.

Internal Dictionaries

An **internal database dictionary** is a centralized collection of all information concerning a particular database, maintained by the database system *primarily for
its own use.* The dictionary is available to every part of the DBMS, as shown in
figure 11.3, and all references to the database must be coordinated with the dictionary. Unfortunately, many database systems use the term *database dictionary*
to refer to the collection of information about a database, whether or not the
information is centralized, and this practice has helped to muddy the meaning
of the term.

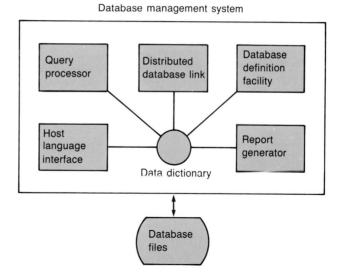

Figure 11.3
The central role of a
data dictionary. This
dictionary is utilized by
all DBMS modules
when referencing the
database.

An internal dictionary usually includes *at least* the following information:

- Names of tables for each database
- For each table, a list of the names and attributes, including the following:
  (a) Type of attribute data, such as alphanumeric, numeric, etc.

  (b) Length of data, if applicable (alphanumeric, for example)

  (c) Synonyms for that attribute since more than one name may be used to refer to a particular column

  (d) Constraints, or restrictions, that apply to the data contained in that attribute

  (e) Security controls. This is usually a list of valid passwords for reading, modifying, and so on;
- A list of current indexes for each table
- The name and definition of each database view (see pp. 380–84 for a discussion of views).

An internal database dictionary may also contain the information about where the database itself is physically stored, such as disk addresses, and so on. This part of the dictionary is called the **database directory.**

Whenever any action is taken against a database, or any reference is made to it, the database dictionary is used to obtain the required information about the database. For example, when a user attempts to enter a new row of data into a database table, the database dictionary is used to ascertain whether the user has authorized access, whether the data violates any constraints, where to store the new data, and so on.

Figure 11.4
Typical dBASE III
output in response to
the DISPLAY
STRUCTURE
command.

```
Structure for database : B:STUDENTS
Number of data records : 13
Date of last update    : 08/14/85

Field  Field name  Type         Width Dec
    1  STUDENTNUM  Numeric          6
    2  STUDNAME    Character       25
    3  MAJOR       Character       15
    4  GRADE       Character        2
    5  AGE         Numeric          6
```

A database user may often be able to access the dictionary with various **DBMS** commands, in order to determine various things of interest about the database. For example, when working with a database in the dBASE III system, the DIS-PLAY STRUCTURE command shows the user a list of names and attributes of a given table, as well as other information. An example of dBASE III output is shown in figure 11.4.

External Dictionaries

The term *database dictionary* also has a very different meaning from that already described—it can refer to a type of *independent* software package that is physically and logically distinct from any particular DBMS. This type of package is often designed and marketed by independent vendors, although many **DBMS** vendors also design their own independent dictionary packages. Some database dictionaries are designed for use with particular DBMS's, whereas others are strictly *stand-alone* systems. The latter have no physical connections with a particular DBMS and are therefore capable of being used with virtually any of them.

External database dictionaries are distinctive in that they themselves are a very specialized type of database system. They have many of the features normally associated with ordinary database systems, but they are designed specifically for the creation of *databases about databases*. They invariably contain characteristics such as data definition facilities, query languages, report generators, and so on. Their principal function is to assist in all aspects of the design, development, and use of large, highly complex databases. These databases can involve so many details that their design can easily become unmanageable. They can involve a great many tables and hundreds of attributes; each attribute may have several synonyms; there may be dozens of different relationships, countless constraints, and a great many associated applications programs.

External database dictionaries offer the facility for managing the myriad details of a complex database design and include many features intended to assist the database designers and users. These include easy-to-use query languages and report writing capabilities, which give convenient access to any particular subset of information about a database. For example, some typical reports that might be of interest to various users of a database would be:

- A list of all table names for the database
- A list of all attribute names, their characteristics, and their synonyms for a particular database table
- A list of all constraints applied to the database. This would include both constraints applied to individual attributes, as well as those involving several attributes and tables
- A list of all application programs used with the database, along with the table and attribute names used by each program
- A list of all column names associated with the database, along with a list of application programs that reference each column.

This list is by no means inclusive; it is merely representative of the kinds of information that can be obtained from a database dictionary. Also, because there are no industry standards for database dictionary design, every product has its own features.

Active and Passive Dictionaries

As mentioned, many of the external dictionaries implemented during the design, development, and use of a database are entirely stand-alone. Dictionaries of this type are called **passive** and are utilized by database designers and users as a kind of super-indexed filing system, which can be used for reference during all phases of a database life cycle.

In contrast, there are some external dictionaries designed to be integrated, or interfaced, with a particular database system, and the various components of the database system interact directly with the dictionary. In this type of situation, as shown in figure 11.5, the dictionary has two types of interactions: one with the users, and the other with the database system itself. When the degree of integration between the dictionary and the database system is very high, every interaction between a human and the database, whether it is a design process or a user action, is channelled through the dictionary. This helps to ensure that the database as *implemented* is as consistent as possible with the database as *designed*. Database dictionaries that are interfaced in this way are known as **active** dictionaries.

Microcomputer database systems and dictionaries. The term *database dictionary* is conspicuously absent from the literature dealing with microcomputer-oriented database systems. These systems certainly incorporate dictionary-like functions, such as the descriptions of tables, attributes, and so on. However, these functions are usually not grouped together into a centralized area known as a

Figure 11.5
The role of an
integrated data
dictionary. This
dictionary is utilized by
both the database
management system
and the database
users. If the degree of
integration of the
dictionary is very high,
all references to the
database will be
referenced through the
dictionary.

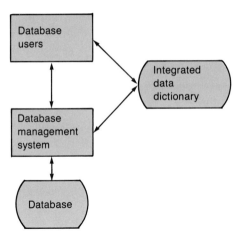

database dictionary. Rather, they are simply incorporated into the overall DBMS and are referenced by commands directly to the DBMS. This distinction is a technical one, and is of no particular importance to the microcomputer user.

Database Restructuring

A powerful feature associated with database systems is the ability to modify the structure of an existing database at any time. One type of structure modification is the addition of one or more new tables to a database. Another type is the addition of new attributes or the modification of existing attributes within a table. Often, these types of modifications are unapparent to the users: the way in which users perceive the database remains unchanged. Also, many types of structural changes can be made without the need to rewrite applications programs that interact with the database.

As already mentioned, when changes to database structures can be made with little or no impact on the users or application programs, the DBMS is said to exhibit a high degree of data independence. This separation of the functions of *data management* and *data usage* is one of the chief advantages of database systems. Although the ideal is that each activity can proceed independently of the other, in practice, 100% data independence is never achieved.

Many types of structural changes involve a complex data manipulation process known as **unload/reload,** which consists of the following steps (see figure 11.6):

- **Database unloading.** Data from the relevant tables is copied to a temporary file. This is a *data only* transfer process—nothing about the database *structure* itself is transferred. The purpose of this step is to preserve the database information externally, while the original database structure is altered. The unloading process is often limited to those tables to which structural changes are to be made.

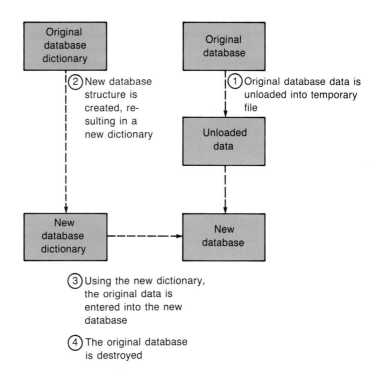

Figure 11.6
Restructuring a
database.

The diagram shows the following boxes and steps:

Original database dictionary → (2) New database structure is created, re-sulting in a new dictionary → **New database dictionary**

Original database → (1) Original database data is unloaded into temporary file → **Unloaded data**

New database dictionary - - - → **New database**

(3) Using the new dictionary, the original data is entered into the new database

(4) The original database is destroyed

- **Database restructuring.** A new database structure is defined, consisting of the original database structure with whatever changes are needed. This is essentially the definition of a new database whose structure happens to be similar to the old one.
- **Database reloading.** The data unloaded in the first step is read back into the newly defined database.
- **Removal of old database.** The original database tables are no longer of use, and are therefore destroyed.

For the database reloading process to be successful, the new database definition must be compatible with the data that is to be reloaded. For example, suppose that the definition of a particular attribute was changed from alphanumeric to numeric. If the original data for that attribute contained nonnumeric characters, then the new definition would be inconsistent with the original data for that attribute. Figure 11.7 illustrates an example of this type of incompatibility. Many other types of inconsistencies can occur, so the unload/reload process must be very carefully thought out.

Because the unload/reload cycle can be extremely time-consuming and tedious and involves the possibility of catastrophic errors, many database systems have automated the process to some degree. This not only eliminates much of the manual work on the part of the user, but it also reduces the chances of errors occurring. Using this type of automatic facility, a table may be restructured by

Figure 11.7
A table redefinition, in
which the new
definition is
incompatible with parts
of the original data,
making the data
reloading process
awkward.

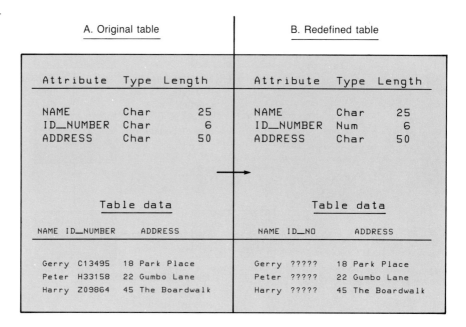

A. Original table | B. Redefined table

Attribute	Type	Length
NAME	Char	25
ID_NUMBER	Char	6
ADDRESS	Char	50

Attribute	Type	Length
NAME	Char	25
ID_NUMBER	Num	6
ADDRESS	Char	50

Table data

NAME	ID_NUMBER	ADDRESS
Gerry	C13495	18 Park Place
Peter	H33158	22 Gumbo Lane
Harry	Z09864	45 The Boardwalk

Table data

NAME	ID_NO	ADDRESS
Gerry	?????	18 Park Place
Peter	?????	22 Gumbo Lane
Harry	?????	45 The Boardwalk

simply entering the new table definition into the database system. In turn, the DBMS automatically takes care of whatever physical data manipulations are necessary to fit the data into the new structure. This process may involve an unloading type of procedure, or some other type of data movement technique that is invisible to the database designer.

Table Addition and Deletion

Because of the independence of each table in a relational database, it is usually possible to add new tables or delete existing ones without going through any type of unload/reload process. For example, a new table concerned with details on classes might be added to the database defined in figure 11.2, with the following commands:

```
ATTACH DATABASE = 'STUDENT_ENROLLMENT'
CREATE TABLE = CLASSES
      CLASS_ID:        CHARACTER(10), NOT NULL
      INSTRUCTOR:      CHARACTER(20)
      ROOM:            CHARACTER(10)
      TIME:            CHARACTER(6)
END TABLE
```

As before, the syntax is *representative* only. The first command specifies the name of the database to be accessed, and the second command indicates that a new table is to be attached to the database. The remainder of the lines spell out the table details.

Similarly, a table can usually be deleted with a simple command, such as

DELETE TABLE = 'CLASSES'

The effect of this command would be the deletion of all data stored in the CLASSES table, as well as the removal of the table structure definition from the database dictionary.

Index Creation

An extremely useful DBMS feature is the ability to create and destroy indexes at any point during the lifetime of a database. In the absence of indexes, any type of relational database searching must be sequential; for large files this can be extremely time-consuming. If searching can be done with the aid of appropriate indexes, the total time necessary to effect the searches may be reduced by orders of magnitude. The ability to create a temporary index is a particularly valuable feature, because the index utilizes disk space only for as long as it is needed.

As an example, suppose that a large number of searches of the STUDENTS table in figure 11.2 have to be done, based on STUDENT_NAME. A temporary index on STUDENT_NAME could be created for the duration of the searching process, and a typical set of database commands would look like the following:

CREATE INDEX = "NAME" ON STUDENT
(STUDENT_NAME)
|searching commands based on STUDENT_NAME|
DELETE INDEX = "NAME"

The first of these commands creates an index on the STUDENT_NAME attribute of the table, and the last command destroys the index after the searching is done. If the STUDENTS table contains a large number of rows, the index creation process could take many minutes. However, this could be paid back many times over when the actual searching was done.

Often, an index can be based on the concatenation of two or more attributes. For example, consider the following command:

CREATE INDEX = "NAME" ON STUDENT
(MAJOR, STUDENT_NAME)

This would build an index that sorts the STUDENTS table first by MAJOR and secondarily by STUDENT_NAME. This would be useful if searches of the table were done on the combined basis of major subject and student name.

Most relational database systems offer some form of indexing capability, but the flexibility varies enormously from one system to another. Some DBMS's require that all indexes for a database be defined at the time that the database definition itself is created. This is a particularly annoying restriction, given that users' needs change with time and it is impossible to foresee all of the ways in which a database will be utilized in a dynamic working environment. Interestingly enough, the ability to create temporary indexes is not particularly exclusive to larger DBMS's. Many microcomputer-oriented systems have this feature, whereas some of those for larger machines do not.

Relational Query Languages

One of the distinguishing characteristics of relational database management systems is their ability to perform complex and flexible queries against a database by using query languages with a high degree of versatility and sophistication. These languages are an integral and vital part of relational systems, and they form the subject of the remainder of this chapter.

Relational query languages have several outstanding characteristics. The most significant has already been mentioned: the fact that they are nonprocedural. That is, a query contains no specification of sequences, loops, or any other types of logic designation. The query indicates in detail *what* result is desired, but not *how* it is to be obtained. From this standpoint, relational query languages are often called **fourth generation languages,** because they take a giant leap beyond the step-by-step logic of traditional programming languages such as FORTRAN, COBOL, and Pascal.

Another special quality of these languages is that the subject of each query is one or more entire relational tables, rather than one or more individual table rows. That is, a query specifies which tables are to be searched, as well as the criteria used to conduct the search. Moreover, the final result of a query is itself always another relational table. This power means that a single relational query may be the equivalent of a lengthy program written in an ordinary programming language. In fact, each query must be translated by the database system into a set of procedural programs that are then used to search the specified table or tables. This translation and search process is completely invisible to the user.

In chapter 5, several examples of relational-type queries were given, including some that involved complex Boolean logic. These examples were relational in style, in that they were non-procedural. However, they were also limited in scope, in that each query referenced only a single table. The types of queries that were discussed in chapter 5 are typical of many microcomputer-oriented database systems that claim to be relational: the queries are nonprocedural and therefore quite powerful, but a single query is limited to one table. In the following sections, more powerful types of relational query languages will be discussed. A review of the material on queries given in chapter 5 would be helpful before reading the following sections.

Fundamental Table Operations: RELATIONAL ALGEBRA

To aid in understanding some of the principles underlying the execution of relational queries, we shall introduce a group of fundamental table operations that collectively come under the heading of **relational algebra** (although they bear little resemblance to the type of arithmetic algebra commonly encountered). Each of these operations is characterized by the fact that it conceptually operates on a *complete table at one time,* rather than row by row. Thus, each relational algebra operation may be the equivalent of a reasonably-sized program in an ordinary programming language. The major operations are discussed in the following paragraphs.

Table Union

Under certain conditions, two tables may be combined to form a new table that is the composite of the originals. This process is known as a **union,** an example of which is shown in figure 11.8: the union of the UNDERGRADUATES and GRADUATES tables results in the ALL_STUDENTS table.

Figure 11.8
(a) Two student tables;
(b) the union of the tables.

(a)

Table: UNDERGRADUATES

NAME	ID_NO	CLASS
Harris, J.	34521	FR
Smith, P.	98237	SO
Peterson, W.	34917	SN
Richards, X.	22981	FR
Myers, H.	10102	JU

Table: GRADUATES

STUDENT_NAME	STUDENT_ID	CLASS
Rogers, J.	33341	G1
Cuthbert, Y.	16371	G3
Ryan, D.	66231	G1
Englebert, H.	01537	G1
York, S.	33772	G2

(b)

Table: ALL_STUDENTS

NAME	ID_NO	CLASS
Harris, J.	34521	FR
Smith, P.	98237	SO
Peterson, W.	34917	SN
Richards, X.	22981	FR
Myers, H.	10102	JU
Rogers, J.	33341	G1
Cuthbert, Y.	16371	G3
Ryan, D.	66231	G1
Englebert, H.	01537	G1
York, S.	33772	G2

The union of two tables can be performed only if they are **union compatible.** That is, each column in one table must be domain compatible with the corresponding column in the other. For example, referring to the tables in figure 11.8, both the NAME and STUDENT_NAME columns refer to the same group of values, which is the group of student names at a particular school.

It is possible that two tables involved in a union may have one or more rows in common, so that the resultant table will have duplicate rows. By the strict definition of relational tables, duplicate rows are not allowed to exist (they serve no useful purpose), so in principle the duplicates would have to be removed. However, in practice, many database systems allow duplicate rows to exist and in fact often require the user to explicitly state that duplicates must be removed.

Table Difference

The **difference** of two tables A and B is defined to be a new table that contains all of the rows of A that are *not* in B. Again, the two original tables must be union compatible. For example, referring again to the tables in figure 11.8, the difference between the ALL_STUDENTS and GRADUATES tables is the UNDERGRADUATES table.

Table Intersection

The **intersection** of two tables A and B is defined as a new table that contains all of the rows *in common* between A and B. Again, the two tables involved in an intersection must be union compatible. Figure 11.9 shows an example of the intersection of two tables.

Selection

The selection operation on a table produces a subset of rows from the table on the basis of a specified **selection criterion.** As an example, consider the STUDENTS table shown in figure 11.10. A **selection** of this table based on the criterion that (GPA > 3.0) would result in the new table shown in figure 11.11.

Projection

Projection produces a subset of columns from a table. Considering again the STUDENTS table in figure 11.10, the projection over the columns (NAME, ID_NO) would result in the table shown in figure 11.12.

(a)

Figure 11.9
(a) Two student tables;
(b) the intersection of
the tables.

Table: 1983 Student roster

NAME	ID_NUMBER
Harris, P.	01253
Jones, Q.	22153
Smythe, X.	99203
Rawlins, L.	29038
Laredo, Y.	33885
York, S.	90231
Mattel, T.	29405
Lewis, U.	29406
Ginsburg, H.	30571
Crawford, P.	01726
Hunt, R.	48261

Table: 1984 Student roster

NAME	ID_NUMBER
Peters, L.	11348
Lawford, P.	33158
Morris, P.	12349
Harris, P.	01253
Jones, Q.	22153
Hunt, R.	48261
York, S.	90763
Laredo, Y.	33885
Lewis, U.	29406
Easley, L.	88334
Mattel, T.	29405
Ginsburg, H.	30571

(b)

NAME	ID_NUMBER
Harris, P.	01253
Jones, Q.	22153
Hunt, R.	48261
Laredo, Y.	33885
Lewis, U.	29406
Mattel, T.	29405
Ginsburg, H.	30571

Table Join

Table join is one of the most powerful and useful operations for performing complex relational queries. In order for two tables to be joined to form a new table, there must exist a *common column* in both tables. The column names may be different, but they must be domain compatible. The join of tables A and B is as follows. Each row of table A is concatenated with every row of table B to form a row of the new table, *provided that the values in the two common columns are identical.*

As an example, the STUDENTS and STUDENT_CLASS tables of figure 11.10 may be joined on the basis of the common columns ID_NO and STUDENT_ID. The resultant table is shown in figure 11.13. Each row of the new table is the concatenation of one row from STUDENTS and a row from

Figure 11.10
Sample relational
tables.

Table: STUDENTS

NAME	ID_NO	CLASS	GPA
Harris, J.	34521	FR	3.2
Smith, P.	98237	SO	3.7
Peterson, W.	34917	SN	2.9
Richards, X.	22981	FR	3.1
Lomax, Z.	88721	SO	1.7
Alberts, R.	33312	SO	3.2
Jeffers, R.	77154	JU	3.1
Myers, H.	10102	JU	2.8
Rogers, J.	33341	G1	4.0
Cuthbert, Y.	16371	G3	3.1
Ryan, D.	66231	G1	2.7
Englebert, H.	01537	G1	3.7
York, S.	33772	G2	3.9

Table: STUDENT_CLASS

STUDENT_ID	CLASS_ID
33772	Physics-1A
10102	Chem-2B
22981	Physics-1A
33772	Music-5
34521	Chem-2B
10102	Music-5

Table: CLASSES

CLASS_ID	INSTRUCTOR	ROOM	HOURS
Physics-1A	Weiner	H123	MWF2-3
Chem-2B	Pauling	M337	MWF8-9
Music-5	Harris	P774	TTh9-11
French-2	Pasteur	H337	MWF3-7

Figure 11.11
Result of a selection
process applied to the
STUDENTS table in
figure 11.10.

NAME	ID_NO	CLASS	GPA
Harris, J.	34521	FR	3.2
Smith, P.	98237	SO	3.7
Richards, X.	22981	FR	3.1
Alberts, R.	33312	SO	3.2
Jeffers, R.	77154	JU	3.1
Rogers, J.	33341	G1	4.0
Cuthbert, Y.	16371	G3	3.1
Englebert, H.	01537	G1	3.7
York, S.	33772	G2	3.9

Figure 11.12
Result of a projection
process applied to the
STUDENTS table in
figure 11.10.

NAME	ID_NO
Harris, J.	34521
Smith, P.	98237
Peterson, W.	34917
Richards, X.	22981
Lomax, Z.	88721
Alberts, R.	33312
Jeffers, R.	77154
Myers, H.	10102
Rogers, J.	33341
Cuthbert, Y.	16371
Ryan, D.	66231
Englebert, H.	01537
York, S.	33772

Figure 11.13
Table resulting from the
join of the STUDENTS
and STUDENT_CLASS
table in figure 11.10.

NAME	ID_NO	CLASS	GPA	CLASS_ID
Harris, J.	34521	FR	3.2	Chem-2B
Richards, X.	22981	FR	3.1	Physics-1A
Myers, H.	10102	JU	2.8	Chem-2B
Myers, H.	10102	JU	2.8	Music-5
York, S.	33772	G2	3.9	Physics-1A
York, S.	33772	G2	3.9	Music-5
York, S.	33772	G2	3.9	French-2

STUDENT_CLASS with the same student identification number. The columns of the new table are the combination of those of the original tables, except that STUDENT_ID has been removed because it is a duplicate of the ID_NO column. This type of join, in which the duplicate column is removed, is technically known as an **equi-join.**

The relational algebra operations described above are seldom used individually when working with relational tables. However, they form the basis for several types of even higher-level query languages, some of which have become quite popular. In the following sections, we shall explore two of the most common of these languages.

SQL

Currently, there is not a great deal of standardization among relational query languages, as each vendor strives independently to produce a language that will be as attractive as possible to users. Nevertheless, a few languages have managed to become quite popular, and one or more of them may eventually become the basis for an industry standard. One of the most likely candidates is **SQL,** which is an acronym for structured query language. Its syntax is particularly clear and simple, and it has been used as a model for query languages developed by several commercial RDBMS's. In the following sections, we shall use SQL to illustrate the power of relational query languages. This is not because SQL is necessarily the best of all languages, but simply because it is a good vehicle for demonstrating the kinds of queries that can be effected with relational database systems.

There are many dialects of SQL, because different database system developers have tailored the language to their own individual partialities. In the following examples, we have drawn freely from more than one of these dialects whenever it was felt necessary to illustrate a particular point.

It should be mentioned that the relational algebra operations described earlier in this chapter do not appear explicitly in SQL queries. However, many of these queries contain algebra-like components. An understanding of the various algebra operations, such as join and project, will help in appreciating the content and power of SQL queries.

In the following examples, we shall first consider queries that apply only to single tables, and then consider those that apply to two or more tables. Many of these examples will refer to the tables in figure 11.10.

Single-table Queries

General form. The first set of examples illustrate SQL queries against single tables, and have the following general form:

> **SELECT** | *list of column names* |
> **FROM** | *search table* |
> **WHERE** | *search conditions* |

The result of each query of this type will be another table, which we shall call the **result table.** The FROM clause denotes the name of the table to be searched. The SELECT clause specifies the list of columns to appear in the result table, and any combination of columns from *search table* may be specified. The WHERE clause specifies the search conditions that must be satisfied by a row in *search table* in order for it to appear in the result table. *Search conditions* may contain any combination of conditions applied to one or more of the columns in *search table.*

In terms of the relational algebra operations, the SELECT clause causes a projection of *search table* over the specified list of column names, and the WHERE clause initiates a selection over this table, based on *search conditions*.

Example 1: A simple search. Referring to figure 11.10, suppose that we wish to find the names of all the students who are in their first year of classes. The following query will produce the desired list:

```
SELECT   NAME
FROM     STUDENTS
WHERE    CLASS = 'FR'
```

This query designates that the STUDENTS table is to be searched. The WHERE clause specifies that only those rows are to be chosen for which the value of CLASS is 'FR'. Finally, the result table is to consist of the single column of names of students who satisfy the WHERE clause. Note that the query does not contain any logic. Rather, it is nonprocedural: it merely states *what* is wanted. It is up to the database system to translate the query into a set of procedures to search the entire STUDENTS table for the appropriate rows. To appreciate the complexity of this, you may wish to translate the above query into a program in a procedural language such as FORTRAN, BASIC, or Pascal.

When this query is executed, the following result table is generated:

NAME

| Harris, J. |
| Richards, X. |

Contrasting with dBASE III. As a point of comparison, the above query is shown rewritten in dBASE III syntax:

```
USE     STUDENTS
LIST    NAME;
FOR     CLASS = 'FR'
```

In fact, the dBASE III syntax is very close to that of SQL! The only significant difference is that the dBASE III query consists of two statements instead of one (the LIST . . . FOR . . . is a single statement).

Example 2: Choosing all columns. In the preceding example, the result table consists of only a single column. We can modify the query so that the result table contains all of the columns of the table being searched, as follows:

```
SELECT  *
FROM    STUDENTS
WHERE   CLASS = 'FR'
```

The use of an asterisk in the SELECT clause is a shorthand used by many SQL dialects to indicate "all columns." The result table becomes:

NAME	ID NO	CLASS	GPA
Harris, J.	34521	FR	3.2
Richards, X.	22981	FR	3.1

Example 3: No search criteria. Suppose that we wish to obtain a list of all student names in the table, as well as their GPA's. The following query accomplishes this:

```
SELECT  NAME, GPA
FROM    STUDENTS
```

In this query, the WHERE clause has been omitted, so that no selection criteria is specified. Therefore, all rows of the STUDENTS table are included in the result table, but only the NAME and GPA columns appear:

NAME	GPA
Harris, J.	3.2
Smith, P.	3.7
Peterson, W.	2.9
Richards, X.	3.1
Lomax, Z.	1.7
Alberts, R.	3.2
Jeffers, R.	3.1
Myers, H.	2.8
Rogers, J.	4.0
Cuthbert, Y.	3.1
Ryan, D.	2.7
Englebert, H.	3.7
York, S.	3.9

Example 4: Removing duplicate rows. We wish to produce a list of all of the courses for which any student is enrolled. This can be done by searching the STUDENT_CLASS table with the following query:

```
SELECT  UNIQUE CLASS_ID
FROM    STUDENT_CLASS
```

The SELECT UNIQUE clause eliminates duplicates from the result table, which becomes the following:

CLASS_ID

Physics–1A
Chem–2B
Music–5
French–2

Example 5: Complex search conditions. The WHERE clause of a query may contain arbitrarily complicated search conditions, combining any of the standard Boolean (AND, NOT, OR) and logical ($=$, $>$, etc.) operators. For example, the following query will generate a list of names and GPA's of all first-year graduate students who have a GPA > 3.5:

```
SELECT  NAME, GPA, CLASS
FROM    STUDENTS
WHERE  (CLASS = "G1") AND (GPA > 3.5)
```

The result table generated from this query is the following:

NAME	CLASS	GPA
Rogers, J.	G1	4.0
Englebert, H.	G1	3.7

The CLASS column could have been omitted, since it merely verifies part of the search conditions.

Example 6: Another complex search. Suppose that we wish to obtain a list of all undergraduates whose GPA is greater than 3.5. One way to accomplish this is with the following query:

```
SELECT  NAME, GPA
FROM    STUDENTS
WHERE   NOT (CLASS='G1' OR CLASS='G2' OR CLASS='G3')
        AND (GPA > 3.5)
```

The NOT operator applies to the expression that immediately follows in parentheses: the expression will therefore be true *only* if the value of CLASS is neither 'G1' nor 'G2' nor 'G3' .

The preceding WHERE clause may appear a bit confusing, and an alternative WHERE clause that may seem more straightforward is:

```
WHERE   CLASS = 'FR' OR CLASS = 'SO' OR CLASS = 'JU'
        OR CLASS = 'SN'.
```

Figure 11.14
Standard SQL
functions.

Function name	Result of computation
COUNT (*)	Number of rows
AVE(*col-name*)	Average of column values
MIN(*col-name*)	Minimum of column values
MAX(*col-name*)	Maximum of column values
SUM(*col-name*)	Sum of column values

This is an example of how a complex set of search conditions may often be written in several different ways; the choice is usually a matter of which seems clearest to the user.

Built-in functions. Many dialects of SQL include a variety of functions for performing various types of common numerical operations as part of a query. These functions are listed in figure 11.14. Most of them require an **argument,** which specifies the column to which the function applies. The particular rows to which a function applies depends on the context in which it is used. The following examples will help to clarify this.

Example 7: Computing an average. We can use a query to obtain the average GPA of all students in the table, by using the AVE function as follows:

> SELECT AVE (GPA)
> FROM STUDENTS

The FROM clause specifies that the STUDENTS table is to be used, and the SELECT AVE (GPA) clause specifies that the average of the GPA values for every row in the table is to be calculated. The result of this query is a single value. Technically, it is a table with a single column and a single row, but this is really quibbling:

AVE (GPA)

3.2

Notice that it would not make sense to include the name of any other column in the SELECT clause (what would the result table look like?). In general, when a function is used in a SELECT clause, no other column names may be included there. (Some special exceptions to this rule exist and will be discussed in later examples.)

Example 8: Computing the average of a subset. A function may be applied to a subset of rows in a table. For instance, as a variation of the preceding example, we can compute the average GPA of only freshmen with the following query:

```
SELECT  AVE (GPA)
FROM    STUDENTS
WHERE  CLASS = 'FR'
```

The WHERE clause specifies the particular subset of rows to be included. In this case, the SELECT AVE (GPA) clause specifies that the average of the GPA column values is to be calculated for *only* those rows specified by the WHERE clause. The result is the following table:

AVE (GPA)

3.15

Example 9: Using a function as part of a condition. Many of the standard functions can be used to help specify the search conditions. For example, we can use the following query to obtain a list of students whose GPA is greater than or equal to the average GPA:

```
SELECT  NAME
FROM    STUDENTS
WHERE  GPA >= AVE (GPA)
```

Here, the AVE function is applied to *all* rows in the table before the WHERE clause is applied. The WHERE clause is then applied to choose those rows for which the value of GPA is at least that of the overall average. If this ordering of events is not obvious, ask yourself how else AVE (GPA) could make sense in the context of the query.

Example 10: Counting the rows of a table. The COUNT function is different from the others, in that it does not need an argument, because it does not refer to a particular column. Instead, it counts rows. For example, the following query counts the number of freshmen listed in the database:

```
SELECT  COUNT
FROM    STUDENTS
WHERE  CLASS = 'FR'
```

In this case, the COUNT function applies only to those rows that satisfy the WHERE clause. Again, the result of this query is a single value.

Groupings. The built-in functions may be applied simultaneously to several subsets of rows within a table. This is accomplished by the use of a GROUP BY clause, as illustrated in the following examples.

Example 11: Computing the average GPA for each class. The following query will calculate the average GPA of each class of students (FR, SO, etc):

```
SELECT  CLASS, AVE (GPA)
FROM    STUDENTS
GROUP   BY CLASS
```

This query is processed in the following manner.

- Arrange the rows of the table into groups, each of which corresponds to a different value of CLASS
- Calculate the average GPA for each group
- Generate the result table, applying the SELECT clause individually to each group:

CLASS	AVE. GPA
FR	3.15
SO	2.8
JU	2.95
SN	2.9
G1	3.47
G2	3.9
G3	3.1

Notice that the result table must include two columns: one is the column specified in the GROUP BY clause, and the other is the result of the function applied to each group. The following general rule applies:

> When a function is used in conjunction with a "GROUP BY *column name*" clause, both the function and *column name* must appear in the SELECT clause.

Example 12: Conditions on rows within groups. In the last example, every row of each group contributed to the final results. For example, every FR row contributed to the calculation of the average GPA for freshmen. In some cases, it may be desirable to form groups using only subsets of the rows. For example, we might wish to find the number of students in each class whose GPA is greater than the average overall GPA. The following query would accomplish this:

```
SELECT  CLASS, COUNT
FROM    STUDENTS
WHERE   GPA > AVE (GPA)
GROUP   BY CLASS
```

Here, AVE (GPA) applies to *all* rows of the table. The GROUP BY clause forms groups by value of CLASS, as in the last example, but the members of each group are *only* those rows that satisfy the WHERE condition. Finally, the SELECT CLASS, COUNT clause counts the number of rows in each group, producing the following result table:

CLASS	COUNT
FR	1
SO	1
JU	0
SN	0
G1	1
G2	1
G3	0

Example 13: Imposing conditions on groups. We may wish to specify that a result consist only of those groups that satisfy certain conditions. For example, the following query will list only those classes for which the average GPA is greater than 3.0:

```
SELECT   CLASS, AVE (GPA)
FROM     STUDENTS
GROUP    BY CLASS
HAVING   AVE (GPA) > 3.0
```

The HAVING clause specifically refers to groups, rather than to individual rows. The sequence of events relating to the execution of this query is the following:

- Group all rows based on the value of CLASS
- Calculate the average GPA for each group
- Eliminate groups for which the average GPA is less than 3.0
- Generate the result table, consisting of data for the remaining groups:

CLASS	AVE. GPA
FR	3.15
G1	3.47
G2	3.9
G3	3.1

Many of the types of queries illustrated in previous examples can be accomplished with microcomputer-based "relational" systems that are available in today's market, though the exact syntax will vary quite a lot from one system to the next. As an example of this , we shall rewrite the query shown in Example 10, using the syntax of dBASE III to count the number of freshmen in the STUDENTS database:

USE STUDENTS
COUNT FOR (CLASS = 'FR')

The first command selects the table to be searched, and the second specifies the search conditions to be imposed (CLASS = 'FR'), as well as the fact that a count is to be made of those rows that satisfy the search condition.

Multiple-table Queries

The real power of relational query languages comes into play when two or more tables are simultaneously searched for specific results. SQL-type languages have two different techniques for performing multiple-table searches: the **subquery** and the **direct join** methods. With the first of these, a complete query is subdivided into two or more parts, or subqueries, each of which refers to a single table. With the direct join method, all of the tables to be searched are joined to form a single table, using suitable **join conditions.** The resultant table is then searched. In this section, illustrative examples of each method are given.

The subquery method. **Example 14: A two-file search.** Again referring to figure 11.10, suppose that we wish to produce a list of all names and GPA's of students who are enrolled in Physics-1A. The difficulty with this lies in the fact that the appropriate list of student identification numbers can be obtained from the STUDENT_CLASS table, but the correspondence between identification numbers and student names is contained in the STUDENTS table. In other words, the information that we wish to obtain resides in two different tables.

We could obtain the result by a rather lengthy two-step process:
STEP 1:

Generates a list of STUDENT_ID values.

SELECT STUDENT_ID
FROM STUDENT_CLASS
WHERE CLASS_ID = "Physics-1A"

STEP 2:

Perform once for each value of STUDENT_ID found from Step 1

SELECT NAME
FROM STUDENTS
WHERE ID_NO = *STUDENT_ID*

This entire process could become unbearably laborious: if 20 students were enrolled in Physics-1A, step 2 would have to be performed 20 times. One might well choose to use a rolodex file instead of a database.

Fortunately, this whole process can be condensed into a single query involving both tables:

SELECT NAME, GPA
FROM   STUDENTS
WHERE   ID_NO IN
        SELECT   STUDENT_ID
        FROM   STUDENT_CLASS
        WHERE   CLASS_ID = 'Physics–1A'

Subquery

This query is processed "from the inside out," as follows. The lower half of the query constitutes a **subquery.** This subquery is processed first, and the result is the following *intermediate* table:

STUDENT_ID

33772
22981

The top half of the query is then processed. The crucial clause here is **WHERE ID_NO IN.** This part of the query may be translated as follows: select only those STUDENT rows for which the value of ID_NO is included in the intermediate table generated by the subquery. The final result is the following table:

NAME	GPA
York, S.	3.9
Richards, X.	3.1

It is important to realize that for this entire query to make sense, the ID_NO and STUDENT_ID columns must refer to the same domain, which in this case is the list of all student identification numbers. Most relational systems do not support the concept of domain compatibility. In this case, for instance, the system would probably not "know" that ID_NO and STUDENT_ID were domain compatible. For example, suppose that this query were incorrectly written, with the clause WHERE NAME IN substituted for WHERE ID_NO IN. The database system would happily check the NAME value of each STUDENT row against the list in the temporary table, eventually concluding that no rows satisfied the search condition! Clearly, the user must be extremely careful when constructing complex queries, to ensure that the use of the IN operation connects domain compatible columns.

Example 15: A three-level query using subqueries. Subqueries may be nested to several levels, depending on the number of tables involved in the query. Suppose that we wish to generate a list of students who are taking any class with the instructor whose name is Weiner. Before attempting to construct a query to satisfy this, the tables that are likely to be involved should be studied in order to decide: (1) which table contains which pieces of the required information; and (2) the order in which the tables should be queried. In this example, we deduce the following strategy:

1. From the CLASSES table, a list of CLASS_ID values can be obtained for those classes taught by Weiner.
2. From the STUDENT_CLASS table, a set of rows can be obtained whose values of CLASS_ID are contained in the list generated in 1. From this set of rows, a list of corresponding values of STUDENT_ID can then be generated.
3. Using the STUDENTS table, a set of rows can be found, each of whose ID_NO value is contained in the list generated in 2. Finally, the list of student names can be generated from this last set of rows.

The complete query is given below. It is divided into the main query, a subquery, and a sub-subquery. These correspond to steps 3, 2, and 1, above. It may be easiest to study the sections of the complete query in the order just described.

(Query)

```
SELECT   NAME
FROM     STUDENTS
WHERE    ID_NO IN
```

(Subquery)

```
      SELECT   STUDENT_ID
      FROM     STUDENT_CLASS
      WHERE    STUDENT_CLASS.CLASS_ID IN
```

(Sub-subquery)

```
            SELECT   CLASSES.CLASS_ID
            FROM     CLASSES
            WHERE    INSTRUCTOR = 'Weiner'
```

The result of this query is the following table:

NAME

York, S.
Richards, X.

Qualified names. In constructing the preceding query, we have made use of column name **qualifiers,** which are table names prefixed to column names. Qualifiers are used to avoid ambiguities when two or more columns have the same name. For example, because CLASS_ID is the name of columns in two different tables, we use the term CLASSES. CLASS_ID refers to the CLASS_ID column in CLASSES; the qualifier is CLASSES. A qualifier must be used whenever an ambiguity exists because of duplicate column names. In addition, a qualifier may optionally be used whenever it would enhance the clarity of a query.

The direct join method. In each of the above examples using the subquery method, the result table consisted of one or more columns from a *single* table. Thus, in the last example, the result table consisted of the NAME column from STUDENTS. Frequently, situations arise in which the desired result table consists of columns from more than one table. In such cases, the subquery method does not work, because the top (main) part of a query of this type refers only to a single table.

The direct join method offers an alternative that circumvents this limitation. With this method, the tables of interest are first joined to form an intermediate table, using one or more join conditions. This table is then searched for those rows that satisfy the specified search conditions, and the final result table is constructed. The following examples illustrate this technique.

Example 16: A two-file search. As a first example of the direct join technique, we shall obtain the same result as in Example 14—a list of names and GPA's of students who are enrolled in Physics-1A. The following query accomplishes this:

SELECT	STUDENTS.NAME, STUDENTS.GPA
(Direct join) ⟶ FROM	STUDENTS, STUDENT_CLASS
(Join condition) ⟶ WHERE	STUDENTS.ID_NO = STUDENT_CLASS.STUDENT_ID
AND	STUDENT_CLASS.CLASS_ID = 'Physics-1A'

The FROM clause contains the names of the tables that are involved in the query. Because two tables are named, SQL assumes that they are to be joined, using a join condition to be specified in the WHERE clause. Recall that a join is a concatenation of the rows of two tables based on the equality of values of two columns—one from each of the tables.

The result of the join is a temporary table constructed in accordance with the join condition: each row from STUDENTS will be concatenated with every row from STUDENT_CLASS that has a matching value of STUDENT_ID. Figure 11.15 shows the temporary table. The STUDENT.ID_NO column has been removed from this table because it is identical to the STUDENT_CLASS. STUDENT_ID column and therefore serves no useful purpose.

The second part of the WHERE clause specifies which rows from this temporary table are to be part of the final result table. The SELECT clause specifies the columns to be part of this table. Note that in this query, every column name has been qualified with its corresponding table name. This has been done because more than one table is referenced in the query. Name qualification helps in understanding the precise meaning of the query by directly identifying each column name with its corresponding table.

Figure 11.15
Temporary join table for
example 16.

NAME	ID_NO	CLASS	GPA	CLASS_ID
Harris, J.	34521	FR	3.2	Chem-2B
Richards, X.	22981	FR	3.1	Physics-1A
Myers, H.	10102	JU	2.8	Chem-2B
Myers, H.	10102	JU	2.8	Music-5
York, S.	33772	G2	3.9	Physics-1A
York, S.	33772	G2	3.9	Music-5
York, S.	33772	G2	3.9	French-2

The result table is shown below, and as expected, it is the same as that shown in Example 14:

NAME	GPA
York, S.	3.9
Richards, X.	3.1

Example 17: Sorting the results of a query. The results of a query can be sorted by specifying the column on which the sorting is to be done. For example, if we wish to have the results of the previous query sorted by student name, the query could be modified by the addition of an ORDER BY clause, as follows:

```
SELECT      STUDENTS.NAME, STUDENTS.GPA
FROM        STUDENTS, STUDENT_CLASS
WHERE       STUDENTS.ID_NO = STUDENT_CLASS.STUDENT_ID
 AND        STUDENT_CLASS.CLASS_ID = 'Physics-1A'
ORDER BY    STUDENTS.NAME
```

The result table would then become the following:

NAME	GPA
Richards, X.	3.1
York, S.	3.9

Example 18: A three-table query. In this example, we illustrate how the direct join technique can be used to search several tables. We shall construct a query to produce a list of students, each of whom is enrolled in one or more classes. In addition, the instructors for each of these students will also be listed at the same time.

Figure 11.16
Temporary join table for
example 18.

NAME	ID_NO	CLASS	GPA	CLASS_ID	INSTRUCTOR	ROOM	HOURS
Harris, J.	34521	FR	3.2	Chem-2B	Weiner	M337	MWF8-9
Richards, X.	22981	FR	3.1	Physics-1A	Weiner	H123	MWF2-3
Myers, H.	10102	JU	2.8	Chem-2B	Weiner	M337	MWF8-9
Myers, H.	10102	JU	2.8	Music-5	Harris	P774	TTh9-11
York, S.	33772	G2	3.9	Physics-1A	Weiner	H123	MWF2-3
York, S.	33772	G2	3.9	Music-5	Harris	P774	TTh9-11
York, S.	33772	G2	3.9	French-2	Pasteur	H337	MWF3-7

Before attempting to write down the query, we should first decide which tables must be involved. First, the instructor names appear only in the CLASSES table, so CLASSES must clearly be included in the query. Next, student names appear only in the STUDENTS table, so that table must also be involved. Finally, the STUDENT_CLASS table must be included in the query because it acts as a double link: (1) between student names and their classes (via the student identification numbers); and (2) between class names and their associated instructors (via the CLASS_ID values).

The complete query is the following:

SELECT STUDENTS.NAME, CLASSES.INSTRUCTOR
FROM STUDENTS, STUDENT_CLASS, CLASSES
(Join condition #1) WHERE STUDENTS.ID_NO = STUDENT_CLASS.STUDENT_ID
(Join condition #2) AND STUDENT_CLASS.CLASS_ID = CLASSES.CLASS_ID

In this case, three tables are specified in the FROM clause. Therefore, SQL will join all of them, two at a time, to form a temporary table, shown in figure 11.16. Thus, two join conditions must be specified in the WHERE clause, one for each pair of tables to be joined.

Since no other search condition is specified in the query, the final result table will be a simple projection of the intermediate table over the NAME and INSTRUCTOR columns:

NAME	INSTRUCTOR
Harris, J.	Pauling
Richards, X.	Weiner
Myers, H.	Harris
Myers, H.	Pauling
York, S.	Weiner
York, S.	Harris
York, S.	Pasteur

Summing up multiple-table queries. The two methods for querying multiple tables each has its advantages. In particular, the direct join method must be used if the result table is to consist of rows from more than one of the tables being searched. From a syntax point of view, some users may find one method easier to understand and work with.

Because each method operates very differently from the other, it would be expected that they would differ in terms of time required to perform queries. Thus, one method might perform much faster than the other for certain types of queries, and vice-versa. In general, a user must experiment with each method to determine which gives the best performance for the particular types of queries of interest.

Interactive and Embedded Queries with SQL

Database query languages may be utilized in two distinct ways. In the more common approach, a user enters query commands directly at the computer or terminal, much like any other type of DBMS command would be entered. This mode of operation has become almost universally popular with users of microcomputer-based systems, because the users get immediate feedback from the DBMS to whatever particular queries seem important at the moment. Thus, in order to execute a particular database search, a user might enter an SQL query, in a form identical to the examples discussed earlier. The DBMS would interpret the query, perform the search, and return the results immediately to the user.

For complex, multiple-line queries, a text editor is sometimes used to construct the entire query in a text buffer. This method gives a user the option to read over the query after it has been entered, and to make any necessary corrections. When the query has been checked for accuracy, it is then sent to the database system for execution. The results from an interactive query may be sent to the monitor, to a printer, or to some other type of output device.

Another method for using relational queries exists, in which the queries are contained within a program, written either in a so-called host language such as FORTRAN, or in a programming language that is an inherent part of the DBMS. Often, the syntax of these embedded queries is virtually identical to that used in the direct entry method already described. When this is the case, DBMS users need to learn only one query language syntax, which can be used for either mode of operation.

As an example of how embedded queries are used, a simple FORTRAN program containing SQL and other database commands is shown in figure 11.17.

An understanding of the details of this program, or for that matter, of FORTRAN itself, is not important in this example. The significant point is the way in which the various DBMS commands, including queries, appear within the program. In particular, the SQL command shown in lines 21–23 are quite familiar-looking, except that the names of variables that refer to column values are prefixed with a $.

Figure 11.17
A simplified FORTRAN
program containing
embedded SQL and
other DBMS
commands.

```
1.        PROGRAM GETREC

2.    C   Inputs a value for CUSTOMER_ID from a user,
3.    C   then searches the JELLYBEANS database for the
4.    C   corresponding record.

5.    C   NOTE: All database commands are preceded with
6.    C         a $; all variables used directly by
7.    C         the database begin with $ .

8.    C   Variable definitions

9.        INTEGER*4     CUSTOMER_NO
10.       INTEGER*4     $NAME, $ID
11.       CHARACTER*13 $PHONE
12.       CHARACTER*1   ANS
13.       STATUS        $S1

14.   $   OPEN DATABASE JELLYBEANS FOR READING

15.   C   Get the customer number from the user

16.   1 PRINT * 'Please enter the customer I-D
17.       number:'
18.       READ *, CUSTOMER_NO

19.   C   Search the CUSTOMERS database table for the
20.   C   corresponding record

21.   $   SELECT $NAME, $PHONE
22.       FROM CUSTOMERS
23.       WHERE $ID = CUSTOMER_NO

24.   C   The DBMS returns the outcome of the search in
25.   C   variable $S1:
26.       IF $S1 = 0 THEN
27.          PRINT 'Customer name: ',$NAME
28.          PRINT 'Customer phone: '$PHONE
29.       ELSE
30.           PRINT 'No such customer exist in
31.           database.'
32.       ENDIF

33.       PRINT *, 'Another input? (Y/N)'
34.       READ *, ANS
35.       IF (ANS = 'Y') .OR. (ANS = 'y') THEN
36.          GO TO 1
37.       ELSE
38.           STOP
39.       ENDIF
40.       END
```

The purpose of the program in figure 11.17 is to search the CUSTOMERS table of the JELLYBEANS database for records corresponding to user-supplied identification numbers. If a record is found, selected portions are output by the program. The variable $S1 is a status flag whose value is set by the DBMS, indicating the outcome of a particular operation. Thus, in this example, $S1 is set to 0 if a database search is successful.

Other SQL-type Query Languages

The query examples in the last section were based on the model of SQL, a language rapidly gaining popularity in the relational database world. Many other relational-type query languages exist, and nearly all of them are non-procedural. In general, a query in any of these languages includes the following:

- The name of the table or file to be queried (some relational systems use the term *file* instead of *table*)
- The search conditions to be used in generating the result

Most query languages may include specifications of where and how the results are to be reported. For example, a typical dBASE III query would take the following form:

USE STUDENTS
DISPLAY ALL FOR (GPA > 3.0) FIELDS NAME, GPA

The first statement selects the STUDENTS table. The second statement includes the search conditions, the fields to be included in the result, and the output device. (DISPLAY specifies the standard output device, usually the terminal and possibly the printer as well.)

There is not room in this book to include all of the possible variations of query language syntax that exist. For the most part, they follow the preceding pattern. There is one interesting exception, which is briefly described in the following section.

Query by Example

Nearly all query languages have in common the fact that the commands are written in some form or other of stylized English. In other words, learning to write queries in a particular language is the equivalent of acquiring familiarity with a very specialized dialect. In recent years, there has been an increasing trend away from prose, and towards graphical utilization of computers. Examples of this trend are the popularity of the "mouse" and the use of "windows" for controlling the operations of computer programs.

Figure 11.18
A QBE example to find
all sophomores in the
STUDENTS table.
(a) An empty form to be
filled-in by the user;
(b) the filled-in form;
(c) result of the query.

(a)

STUDENTS	NAME	ID_NO	CLASS	GPA

(b)

STUDENTS	NAME	ID_NO	CLASS	GPA
	P.XXX		SO	

(c)

NAME
Smith, P.
Lomax, Z.
Alberts, R.

One type of query language that follows this graphical trend is **query by example (QBE)**. This language was developed by M. M. Zloof,[1] originally for IBM-oriented relational database systems, but its style has been used by many other DBMS's. With a QBE-like language, a user creates a query by filling in an empty "form" that appears on the computer monitor. We illustrate this with some simple examples, using the STUDENTS table shown in figure 11.10.

Suppose that a user wishes to obtain a list of all sophomores in the table. This would be accomplished by first issuing a statement to the DBMS that the STUDENTS table was to be selected. The system would respond by creating a display similar to that shown in figure 11.18a. The user would then make the entries as shown in figure 11.18b. The SO value placed in the CLASS column specifies that only those rows for which the CLASS value is equal to SO are to be chosen. The entry in the NAME column consists of two parts. First, the underlined part, XXX, indicates that the value of this column is to be chosen from each result row; the P. part of the entry indicates that the column is to be output. (A value other than P. would indicate another type of operation: for example, D. would indicate deletion.)

The XXX entry can be interpreted to mean "the value of this column for each row that is selected". Usually, *any* arbitrary choice of underlined characters would do. The result of this query would be the table shown in figure 11.18c. This would appear directly on the screen, or perhaps on a printer, depending on the user's specifications.

[1]M. M. Zloof, "Query by Example: A Database Language," *IBM Systems Journal*, VA, 1977.

Figure 11.19
A QBE example to find
the students whose
GPA is greater than 3.0.
(a) An empty form to be
filled-in by the user;
(b) the filled-in form;
(c) result of the query.

(a)

STUDENTS	NAME	ID_NO	CLASS	GPA

(b)

STUDENTS	NAME	ID_NO	CLASS	GPA
	P.XXX	P.XXX		XXX > 3.0

(c)

NAME	ID_NO
Harris, J.	34521
Smith, P.	98237
Richards, X.	22981
Alberts, R.	33312
Jeffers, R.	77154
Rogers, J.	33341
Cuthbert, Y.	16371
Englebert, H.	01537
York, S.	33772

Another QBE-type example is illustrated in figure 11.19, which shows a query for listing the names and identification numbers for students whose GPA is greater than 3.0. The entry XXX > 3.0 is the selection criterion, namely "rows for which the value of this column is greater than 3.0".

These two short examples are not intended to illustrate the complete capabilities of QBE-like languages, but merely to hint at their general style. These languages are quite easy to learn because of the lack of syntax-like rules to follow. Some of them contain advanced features, such as the ability to perform joins for multiple-table querying.

No database management system is complete without the capabilities of adding and modifying information. These activities are often included under the general heading of "queries." Each DBMS has its own set of commands for performing these operations, and it should come as no surprise that little standardization exists in this area. Nevertheless, we can make one or two generalizations concerning the nature and style of these types of commands.

Data Entry

Data entry can take place in any of the following styles, depending on the particular system:

Prompting: The database system automatically prompts the user for each column value to be input

Edited input: The user prepares one or more rows of data with the assistance of a line or screen editor. The user then sends the data to the DBMS

Batch input: Input is prepared and written to a separate file. At some later time, an application program is run, which reads the input file and sends the data to the database system.

The following information *must* be supplied for each set of data to be added to a database:

- The name of the table to which the data is to be added
- Values for all required columns for each row to be added, in addition to any other columns. Recall that some database systems permit the specification of required columns; others do not, placing the burden either on user-written application programs or on data-entry staff.

Data Modification

The following information must be supplied for each modification, or set of modifications, to be made:

- The name of the table to be accessed
- The search conditions that specify which subset of rows is to be modified
- The modifications to be applied to each row specified by the search conditions.

As an example, we shall modify data in the STUDENTS table shown in figure 11.10, using syntax that is available with many SQL-type languages. Specifically, we shall demonstrate commands for changing the value of CLASS to sophomore for all students listed as freshmen:

```
UPDATE STUDENTS
SET      CLASS = "SO"
WHERE  CLASS = "FR"
```

In this example, the first line specifies the table to be accessed. The third line gives the search conditions, that is, the specific rows to be altered. Finally, the second line specifies the changes to be made to the appropriate rows. Notice the power of this simple command to modify many rows at once.

By way of contrast, the following dBASE III command accomplishes the same set of modifications:

```
USE       STUDENTS
REPLACE  CLASS WITH "SO" FOR CLASS = "FR"
```

Of course, a single row can also be modified, such as the following SQL-type command to delete the row for a specific student:

```
DELETE
FROM STUDENTS
WHERE NAME = "Lomax, Z."
```

Again, there are many variations on each modification theme, depending on the language used.

Summary

Relational database systems have become an important part of contemporary database management. Although RDBMS's are by no means completely dominant in the database field, many of the ideas and concepts originally associated with relational systems have been adopted by a large number of different types of DBMS's. For example, the ideas behind table normalization are often applied to non-relational types of databases. Moreover, the types of higher-level query languages discussed in this chapter have found their way into the majority of DBMS's now in use.

Relational systems are characterized by three distinct qualities: (1) the tabular structure of database information, and the rules that must be adhered to in the construction of these tables; (2) the fact that relationships within data are maintained by virtue of common data values; and (3) the high-level nature of the query languages. In particular, a DBMS is considered to be truly relational only if its query language is capable of searching multiple tables simultaneously.

Table 11.1

Summary of Relational Database Features

Feature or Facility	Unique to Relational DBMS's
Tabular form of data	No*
The way in which relationships are maintained	Yes*
High-level query language	No*
Database definition facility	No
Database restructuring	No
Index creation	No
Built-in integrity controls	No
Database dictionary	No
Both interactive and batch processing	No
Transaction processing	No
Report generation	No
Backup and restoration procedures	No
Security controls	No
Multiple-user access and concurrency control	No

*By definition, a relation DBMS must have all three of these characteristics

In addition, relational systems have many features in common with nonrelational DBMS's. Table 11.1 summarizes these, as well as those specific qualities described in the preceding paragraph. Some of the features listed in this table have been dealt with in this chapter and in chapter 10; others will be discussed in chapter 12.

Every database system, whether or not it is relational, must allow users a facility for defining the structure of a database, including such items as details of each row and column, and constraints. This database definition is stored internally, often in a specific part of the DBMS known as the database dictionary. The latter is used for all interactions between the database and the DBMS.

The term *database dictionary* also refers to a particular type of stand-alone software package used to assist in the design, implementation, and utilization of databases. These packages are themselves specialized types of DBMS's, designed to contain databases *about* databases.

Two features that are particularly useful in working with databases are: (1) the ability to redefine the structure of an existing database with minimal impact on users; and (2) the capability to create and destroy indexes at any time during the life cycle of a database. Both of these characteristics help keep up with the changes in users' needs that inevitably accompany continued exposure to a database system.

Query languages are one of the strongest features of relational database systems, giving users tremendous flexibility in performing database searching and updating operations. Many different types of these query languages exist, but they all have in common the quality that a single user-generated query may reference one or more entire relational tables. The logic necessary to perform these searches is generated automatically by the DBMS and is completely hidden from the user. Two of the most popular languages of this type are SQL and QBE, both of which exist in a large variety of flavors.

Chapter Review

Terminology

data definition language	QBE
database definition facility	query language
database dictionary	relational algebra
database restructuring	selection
difference	SQL
intersection	union
join	union compatible
nonprocedural language	unload/reload
projection	

Review Questions

1. What are the features that distinguish relational DBMS's?
2. How does a nonprocedural query language differ from a program written in a language such as Pascal?
3. Define as many terms as you can in table 11.1.
4. What major types of information must appear in a database definition?
5. What are the two most common methods for entering a database definition? Give examples of each type.
6. Explain the difference between internal and external database dictionaries.
7. What is the meaning of *database restructuring?* Explain each of the steps involved in the restructuring process.
8. Define the term *union compatible.* Can two tables be union compatible even though they have different attribute names?
9. Explain how the term *select* has quite different meanings in relational algebra and in SQL. Give an example of each.

Problems

1. Consider the CUSTOMERS and PAYMENTS definitions shown in figure 10.14. Assuming that they refer to relational tables, create a database definition for them, using the style and syntax shown in figure 11.2.

2. With respect to the students and classes represented by the database definition in figure 11.2, the following table definition may be used to describe the individual classes:

CLASSES [CLASS_ID, ROOM, TIME, INSTRUCTOR] .

Make the necessary changes to figure 11.2 in order to add this table definition to the database. Be sure to take into account the relationship between CLASSES and STUDENT_CLASS when modifying the database definition.

3. Referring to figure 11.7, suppose that the original ID_NUMBER data consists of the following values, instead of those shown in the figure:

ID_NUMBER

13495
33158
09864

Would this data still be incompatible with the redefined table in part B of the figure?

Problems 4 through 6 refer to the following tables:

Table: DOGS

DOG_NAME	AGE	OWNER
Fido	4	Billie
Bowser	6	Tommie
Rex	5	Sarah
Rover	2	Billie
Mollie	1	Patti
Beauregard	14	Carol
Sundae	6	Carol

Table: CATS

CAT_NAME	AGE	OWNER
Mimi	2	Peter
Poco	7	Gerry
Babyface	8	Carol
Tomasina	7	Carol
Fifi	3	Tommie

4. Justify the statement that the above two tables are union compatible. Write down the results of each of the following operations on the DOGS and CATS tables:

a. union
b. difference
c. intersection

5. Write down the results of the following operations on the DOGS table:

    a. **Projection** over (DOG_NAME, OWNER)

    b. **Selection** for all animals over 3 years old

6. Write down the join of DOGS and CATS based on the OWNER attribute. Can you think of any useful reason for performing this join?

7. Referring to the ALL_STUDENTS table in figure 11.8, write down SQL queries to find each of the following:

    a. The names of all freshmen

    b. The names and ID numbers of all freshmen

    c. The names of all freshmen and sophomores

    d. The names of all students *except* seniors. (Write two different queries for this one.)

    e. The names of all freshmen whose ID numbers are greater than 30000

    f. The entire table

8. Assume that ALL_STUDENTS exists as an ordinary file of records. Write a program either in BASIC or Pascal to perform the search equivalent to part a in problem 7.

The following tables will be used for problem 9:

Table: CUSTOMERS

CUST_ID	NAME	STREET	CITY	STATE	ZIP	BALANCE
1156	Andersen, Tim	9532 Clark Pl.	Albany	CA	94661	327.13
1894	Baker, James	1 Cyle Road	Berkeley	CA	94704	125.15
4985	Clark, Kent	7 Hidden Way	Pittsburg	CA	94882	395.15
5093	Drue, Ellen	55 Pork Place	Albany	CA	94666	3527.98
2246	Gregory, Robert	357 Mission St.	Berkeley	CA	94704	1857.32
9124	Harris, Peter	19 Taraval St.	Oakland	CA	94620	155.75
4590	James, Jesse	39 Trout Gulch	Newark	CA	95061	532.87
3333	LaRue, Elaine	7244 52nd St.	Berkeley	CA	94169	955.00
4501	Norman, Samuel	339 40th Ave.	Oakland	CA	95123	0
2298	Smith, Alfred	18 Center St.	Oakland	CA	95543	0
1579	Smith, Jennifer	123 Hayes St.	Berkeley	CA	94704	0

Table: ORDERS_IN		
ORDER_NO	CUST_ID	ORDER_DATE
05528	1156	04/11/85
02340	4501	07/22/85
04873	3333	06/01/85
08923	1156	03/15/85
08744	2246	05/19/85
01587	1156	03/12/85
09942	4501	04/03/85
03342	1156	02/19/85

Table: ORDER_ITEM		
ORDER_NO	FLAVOR	QUANTITY(lbs)
02340	ORANGE	75
02340	LICORICE	25
02340	MINT	50
09942	CHERRY	125
09942	ORANGE	30
04873	MINT	80
04873	ORANGE	200
01587	ORANGE	150

9. Referring to the above tables, write SQL queries to obtain each of the following sets of data:

   a. The names and addresses of all customers who owe more than $500

   b. The total number of customers in the file

   c. The list of order numbers for the customer whose ID number is 1156

   d. The list of order numbers for the customer "Norman, Samuel". Assume that you do *not* know the correspondence between customer names and their ID numbers. Write two separate queries for this problem: one using the subquery method, and the other using the direct join method

   e. The list of flavors contained in order number 9942

   f. The list of all flavors for all orders submitted by "Norman, Samuel"

   g. The list of customers who live in Berkeley and who also have ever ordered ORANGE jellybeans

   h. The total amount of jellybeans ordered for *all* flavors (summed over all orders)

   i. The total amount of each flavor of jellybeans ordered (summed over all orders)

   j. The maximum amount of any flavor of jellybeans ordered in a single order

Chapter Twelve

Information Protection and Confidentiality

Introduction

Computerized information has become one of the mainstays of our society. In fact, this decade is often referred to as the "age of information." As our dependency on machine-readable information has increased, so has the need to protect this data. Because most computerized information is stored in some form of a database, it is important to discuss the subject of information protection in this text.

Computerized data is vulnerable to many types of damage and abuse. Consequently, in planning for the design and implementation of a database, it is essential that preparations be made to deal with any conceivable situation that could result in data loss. The various types of circumstances that could lead to unexpected loss include hardware and software failures, human errors, and even unlikely catastrophic events (earthquakes, meteors, etc).

One important area of database protection, of increasing concern in recent years, deals with the issue of confidentiality. Often, computerized information is sensitive, in that it must be protected against unauthorized access. Various methods have been developed to help ensure that access to sensitive information is safely under the control of the data management software.

A topic that is closely related to the area of database protection has to do with the maintenance of a database in a consistent state. Many types of safeguards can be implemented to help ensure that information placed into a database is as free as possible from errors, and that it is consistent with previously stored data. In fact, a great many different types of data errors can be detected *before* information becomes a part of a database, thus maximizing the degree to which a database accurately reflects the real world.

Computerized information is a valuable resource, and often this value is related to how well the data is kept confidential. There are different degrees of confidentiality, and the extent to which information must be guarded depends to some extent on how sensitive it is. For example, the salary information within a company should be kept out of reach of all but a very few persons. Even telephone numbers and addresses may be considered private enough to be kept reasonably inaccessible. Most financial information is also considered confidential, whether it is bank account data for individuals or corporate profit and loss statements. In some cases, financial confidentiality may be vital to the success of an institution's operation.

Another side to the security picture is the need to protect information against malicious mischief, sometimes known as "computer crime." The news media have described many incidents in which various databases have been penetrated, with varying degrees of resulting damage. Most of these incidents were the result of harmless "hackers," whose only intention was to "beat the system." Nevertheless, serious harm occasionally results from the destruction or corruption of valuable data, or from large-scale theft by the manipulation of a database to an individual's advantage. The field of computer crime prevention is in its infancy, and a full-scale struggle seems to be blossoming between those who try to protect valuable database information and others who are determined to circumvent whatever protection schemes are devised.

An important function of a DBMS is the ability to offer various types of mechanisms for providing database security. Only a handful of protection methods are in common use, and different database systems offer various degrees of security protection. Many of the smaller microcomputer-oriented DBMS's provide no protection whatsoever. On the other hand, DBMS's for larger machines often devote a significant portion of their software to database security.

The most common methods for providing for database security are the following: (1) password protection, (2) user views, and (3) application programs. Each of these techniques is described in the following sections.

Password Protection

With password protection, each authorized user is given a password that allows access to a particular database. Moreover, a particular password may restrict the manner in which that user may interact with the database. For example, password protection may apply to one or more of the following levels.

- **Computer level.** Often, a user must possess a valid password in order to be given access to *any* part of a computer system. This is often referred to as a **log on password,** which lets the user "enter the front door," so to speak. However, additional passwords may be necessary in order to access any particular software package within the system.

- **DBMS level.** Often, a special password is needed to gain access to a database management system residing within the computer. Thus, even though a user were allowed to log on to the computer, (s)he might not be able to access the DBMS.
- **Database level.** Each individual database might be assigned its own set of valid passwords.
- **Table level.** In addition to any of the preceding, each individual table or file may have its own set of access passwords. Thus, each database user can be given privileges only to specific portions of a total database.
- **Column level.** A user might have access only to selected columns from one or more database tables. This is another way to restrict access to part of a database.
- **View level.** Instead of being given access to a table or a set of columns, a user might have access to one or more particular database views. The use of views is an important mechanism for limiting database access, and it is discussed in a later section of this chapter.

Password protection may exist for any or all of these levels. The first two of these are under the control of the computer's operating system; the remaining ones, if they exist, are maintained by the database system. The term **granularity** is sometimes used to describe the degree to which a database system offers password protection. Thus, protection on the column level would be an example of fine granularity, whereas protection only on the database level would be an example of coarse granularity. Clearly, as the degree of granularity goes from coarse to fine, the amount of software necessary to support the activity increases.

Types of Password Authorization

Users may be granted different types of access to all or part of a database. For example, one particular user might be granted **read-only access** to one or more database tables: this user could inspect the data but could not modify it in any way. On the other hand, another user might have **read/write access** to the same data. Some DBMS's allow a user with read/write access to perform any type of data modification, whereas other DBMS's differentiate between access for insert, modify, and delete operations.

For those database systems that offer multiuser access to a database, other types of password authorization are possible. For example, a user who is modifying a table might be granted **exclusive access** to that table—no other users may be granted access at the same time to that data. This type of authorization is discussed in more detail in the section on concurrency control.

Examples of password authorization methods. There are many different schemes for implementing password protection. With some database systems, simple commands are used to assign levels of password authorization. These commands would be issued directly at a computer console. For example, consider the following set of commands:

GRANT READ ACCESS TO STUDENTS FOR PASSWORD=
     'ST_READER'
GRANT WRITE ACCESS TO CLASSES FOR PASSWORD=
     'CL_WRITER'

The first of these commands would allow read access to the STUDENTS table for the password 'ST_READER', while the second command would grant write access to the CLASSES table for 'CL_WRITER'.

Another method for implementing password protection on both the table and column level is to include the password specifications as part of the database definition. An example of this type of mechanism is shown in figure 12.1. It is the same as the database definition shown in figure 11.2, but with the inclusion of the password specifications.

Referring to the PASSWORDS specifications in this figure, the passwords 'README', 'WRITEME', and 'READGRADE' are defined to be equivalent to the numbers 1, 2, and 3 respectively. Throughout the remainder of the figure, each table and column definition ends with the clause **[N1/N2]**, where N1 and N2 are integers. These two integers indicate the valid read access and write access values for the table or column. For example, consider the following entry in figure 12.1:

TABLE = STUDENTS [1/2]

The password that corresponds to the number 1 (README) is given read access to data contained in this table. On the other hand, the password that corresponds to the number 2 (WRITEME) is given write access to the table data. Similarly, with respect to the GRADE column in the STUDENT_CLASS table, the 'READGRADE' password is given read access to this column of data and the 'WRITEME' password is given write access.

When a database system supports password protection, a list of valid passwords is maintained for each database table and/or column, often in the data dictionary. A typical set of entries might resemble the **authorization table** shown in figure 12.2, which represents the set of password authorizations defined for the STUDENT_CLASS table shown in figure 12.1.

When a user issues a database system command to access a particular column within a table, that user's password is checked against the appropriate authorization table to verify that the desired use is authorized. Clearly, if *every* single database activity is accompanied by this type of checking, a significant amount of CPU time can be involved. It is often a necessary price to be paid for maintaining database security.

Figure 12.1
A database definition
with the inclusion of
specifications for read
and write password
protection, both on the
table and column
levels.

```
DEFINE DATABASE = ENROLLMENT

PASSWORDS:    READ:      'README'    = 1
                         'READGRADE' = 3
              WRITE:     'WRITEME'   = 2

TABLE = STUDENT [ 1/2 ]
        STUDENT_NUMBER:    INTEGER, NOT NULL     [ 1/2 ]
        STUDENT_NAME:      CHARACTER(25)          [ 1/2 ]
        MAJOR:             CHARACTER(15)          [ 1/2 ]
        GRADE_LEVEL:       CHARACTER(2), NOT NULL [ 1/2 ]
        AGE:               INTEGER                [ 1/2 ]

        DEFINE INTEGRITY ON GRADE_LEVEL:
            GRADE_LEVEL IN ( 'FR' , 'SO' , 'JU' , 'SN' )

        DEFINE INTEGRITY ON STUDENT_NUMBER:
            ( STUDENT_NUMBER > 0 ) AND
              ( STUDENT_NUMBER < 1000000 )

END TABLE STUDENT

TABLE = STUDENT_CLASS      [ 1/2 ]
        CLASS_NUM:         CHARACTER(15), NOT NULL [ 1/2 ]
        STUD_NUM:          INTEGER, NOT NULL       [ 1/2 ]
        GRADE:             INTEGER                 [ 3/2 ]

        REFERENCE INTEGRITY ON STUD_NUM:
            STUDENT_NUMBER IN TABLE = STUDENT

END TABLE STUDENT_CLASS

END DATABASE DEFINITION
```

Figure 12.2
A typical authorization
table for the STUDENT_
CLASS table defined in
figure 12.1.

Column or table name	Valid Passwords	
	READ_ONLY	READ/WRITE
STUDENT_CLASS	README	WRITEME
CLASS_NUM	README	WRITEME
STUD_NUM	README	WRITEME
GRADE	READGRADE	WRITEME

Many other methods exist for creating database password protection. In general, there are no standards; each DBMS has its own particular way of implementing this feature. Regardless of the method used, the objective is to limit database access to authorized users.

Database Views

As was discussed in the previous chapter, a convenient way to limit a user's access to specific portions of a database is to create a database **view.** This is a logical picture of a database that does not necessarily correspond to the physical structure of the actual database tables. The effect of a view is to give a particular user access only to the specific information of interest.

In this section, we shall first discuss a general technique used by many relational database systems for creating views. The way in which views may be used for controlling database access will then be outlined.

A view may be a projection of a specific table, a selection of particular rows from a table, or a combination of both. Moreover, a view may be a combination of specific rows and columns from two or more tables. In addition, one or more of the columns of a view may be **virtual.** A virtual column is one whose values do not exist in the database. Instead, the values are the composite of values from two or more actual columns. In essence, a view is a "virtual table" that is built up from bits and pieces of the actual database tables.

View Examples

We shall illustrate some examples of defining user views, utilizing a common technique that employs an SQL-type of syntax. This is by no means the only way of defining views, but its syntax is relatively easy to understand, and it illustrates the basic concepts.

Figure 12.3 shows several examples of view definitions. The first of these illustrates a view named STUDENT_GPA, which is defined to be a simple projection over the STUDENTS table shown in figure 11.10. A user accessing this view would see only the NAME and GPA columns of the STUDENTS table. Furthermore, these columns have been renamed in the view definition to STUDENT and GRADE_AVE.

When the STUDENT_GPA view has been defined, its structure is permanently stored in the database dictionary. The view itself does not contain any data. When a query is made against it, the STUDENTS table is queried, and the appropriate data is accumulated to form the result table.

Figure 12.3
Several different view
definitions.

```
CREATE VIEW STUDENT-GPA (STUDENT, GRADE-AVE)

    AS SELECT NAME, GPA
       FROM STUDENTS
```

(a) A projection over the STUDENTS table

```
CREATE VIEW UNDERGRADS (STUDENT, YEAR, GPA)

    AS SELECT NAME, CLASS, GPA
       FROM STUDENTS
          WHERE CLASS = 'FR' OR CLASS = 'SO'
          OR CLASS = 'JU' OR CLASS = 'SN'
```

(b) A projection and a selection over the STUDENTS table

```
CREATE VIEW STUDENT-SITUATIONS
    (STUDENT-NAME, GPA-DIFF)

    AS SELECT NAME, ( GPA - AVE (GPA) )
       FROM STUDENTS
       ORDER BY NAME
```

(c) A view with a virtual column, GPA-DIFF

```
CREATE VIEW STUD-CLAS (NAME, CLASS)

    AS SELECT STUDENTS.NAME, STUDENTS-CLASS.CLASS-ID
       FROM STUDENTS, STUDENT-CLASS
       WHERE STUDENTS.ID-NO = STUDENT-CLASS.STUD-ID
```

(d) A view involving two tables

The STUDENT_GPA view may be queried in exactly the same way as an ordinary table. For example, the following query could be used to generate a list of all students and their GPA's:

```
SELECT  *
FROM STUDENT_GPA
```

To satisfy this query, the database system refers to the definition of STUDENT_GPA in the database dictionary, notes that the STUDENTS table is involved, and obtains the relevant data from that table. Finally the following result table is generated:

STUDENT	GRADE_AVE
Harris, J.	3.2
Smith, P.	3.7
Peterson, W.	2.9
Richards, X.	3.1
Lomax, Z.	1.7
Alberts, R.	3.2
Jeffers, R.	3.1
Myers, H.	2.8
Rogers, J.	4.0
Cuthbert, Y.	3.1
Ryan, D.	2.7
Englebert, H.	3.7
York, S.	3.9

Alternatively, if a user wishes to see a list of names of only those students whose GPA was greater than 3.0, the following query could be used:

```
SELECT  STUDENT
FROM    STUDENT_GPA
WHERE   GRADE_AVE > 3.0
```

Notice that the search condition is in terms of the name of the column in the *view,* GRADE_AVE, as opposed to the name of the original column, GPA.

Some DBMS's allow any type of normal table operation to be performed on a view (including data addition, modification, and deletion) provided that a user has the appropriate access authorization. For example, if a user were to specify that the value of GRADE_AVE be changed for a particular row in STUDENT_GPA, the value of GPA for the corresponding row in the STUDENTS table would actually be changed.

The issue of deleting rows within a view raises some sticky issues. For example, suppose that an instruction is made to delete a particular row in STUDENT_GPA. Should the *entire* corresponding row in STUDENTS be deleted, or only the NAME and GPA values? Some DBMS's avoid this problem by disallowing deletions. Other systems set up specific rules regarding the effect of deletions from views. Once again, there are few standards in this area.

Figure 12.3 illustrates other types of view definitions. Part (b) of the figure shows the creation of a view named UNDERGRADS, in which the only rows visible from the STUDENTS table are those that correspond to undergraduates.

Figure 12.3(c) creates a view that contains the virtual column GPA_DIFF. Each value for this column is computed to be the difference between a student's GPA and the average GPA for all students. Note that there is no data stored in the database for the GPA_DIFF column. Instead, values are computed by the system at the moment that they are needed.

A view may be used to define an aspect of a database that encompasses more than one table. For example, figure 12.3(d) defines the STUD_CLAS view, which combines data from both the STUDENTS and STUDENT_CLASS tables. This view essentially creates a direct list of students (by name) and their associated classes. A user could utilize this view to obtain a list of students enrolled in "Physics-1A" with the following simple query:

```
SELECT NAME
FROM STUD_CLAS
WHERE CLASS = 'Physics-1A'
```

This query example illustrates a great advantage of using views from the standpoint of the users: a predefined view can take most of the work out of creating a query, in that the difficult parts can be built into the definition of the view. For example, compare the preceding query with the equivalent direct query of the two tables:

```
SELECT  NAME
FROM    STUDENTS
WHERE   ID_NO IN

        SELECT  STUDENT_ID
        FROM    STUDENT_CLASS
        WHERE   CLASS_ID = 'Physics-1A'
```

Using Views to Restrict Access

There are many reasons for using a view to restrict a user's access to a specific portion of a database. One of these is convenience: a view may be defined so that a user *automatically* sees only that data of interest. The user does not need to be concerned with the details involved with a complex query, nor does (s)he need to be aware of the actual structure of the database. The only database picture that the user need be concerned with is that of the particular view of interest, and this is invariably a simple table with a few column names.

Another important use of views is to control access to information for security reasons. When a user is restricted to a particular view, *only* that part of the database is available. By creating different views for different classes of users, a high degree of access control is automatically attained.

Types of View Access

Different types of access authorization may be granted for a particular view. Thus, one user might be given read access: the information accessible through the view could be read, but not altered. On the other hand, another user might be granted both read and write access. These authorizations would be made by assigning different passwords to a view, in the same way as described earlier for tables. For example, with respect to the database shown in figure 11.10, suppose that a specific user is to be given read access to only the NAME and GPA columns of the STUDENTS table. This could be accomplished as follows. First, a view is defined that includes only the NAME and GPA columns, such as the STUDENT_GPA view shown in figure 12.3(a). A password with read access is then defined for that view, possibly by a command such as the following:

GRANT READ ACCESS TO STUDENT_GPA FOR
PASSWORD = 'SG_READ'

Other Techniques for Defining Views

The preceding examples utilized SQL-type syntax for defining database views. Many other techniques exist, but they all have the same general purpose: to limit access to a database to specific portions of interest, either for reasons of convenience, security, or both.

Application Programs

The use of application programs is a common technique for providing database security. Most mainframe-oriented database systems, as well as a small number of micro-based systems, support the use of application programs. These are usually written in a standard procedural language such as COBOL or FORTRAN, but a few database systems support their own internal procedural language. Application programs can be written in any of these languages to perform a variety of tasks in conjunction with the use of a database. Many examples of this were given in chapter 6.

If a database system does not support password protection, or if the amount of built-in security is inadequate, the deficiencies can often be overcome with user-written application programs. Thus, a program can act as an interface between a data-entry person and a database, providing built-in security protection.

In essence, an application program can perform virtually *any* type of desired password protection. However, a program of this type is usually fairly complex, involving: (1) the maintenance of an authorization list for each database table and (2) checking every request for database access to ensure proper authorization.

Data Encryption

Password protection works up to a point, but for many types of database information, this form of security is often inadequate. Passwords act as protection only as long as they remain secret, and experience has shown that nearly any password protection scheme can be breached if enough effort is put to the task.

For information that is sufficiently sensitive to warrant protection beyond the password level, a second line of defense is offered by data encryption. This is a technique in which database information is encoded in such a way that it is unintelligible without the decryption key. A great deal of research has been devoted to encryption, and many methods have been developed. The simplest type of system involves a character-for-character replacement, and the amount of computer time necessary for the encoding is trivial. On the other hand, this type of code is easily broken and is therefore seldom used.

Some types of encryption are virtually invulnerable to deciphering, but they unfortunately involve enormous amounts of computer time. Usually, compromise methods are employed: these are reasonably secure against deciphering, and they involve only modest amounts of computer time.

A few database systems have built-in encryption and decryption packages that may be invoked at the discretion of the user. For those systems that do not offer this type of capability, many independent vendors offer packages that can be used to encode virtually any type of database file, with various levels of sophistication and complexity.

Database Integrity

In the previous section, we discussed the protection of databases from a "need-to-know" point of view. Databases must also be protected from corruption due to the presence of poor quality information, which can be defined to be data that is either invalid or inconsistent. Data errors can arise at any time, from the moment the data is first generated up to the instant it is entered into the computer, and a great many types of errors are possible. Fortunately, many of these can be guarded against by suitable data-validation techniques. For example, if the value for an AGE field were accidentally entered as 141, instead of 41, the error could be detected with a validation check on all AGE values to ensure that they were within reasonable limits. On the other hand, if an AGE value were incorrectly entered as 29 instead of 39, the error probably could not be detected. In the following sections, we shall study the various methods used to help ensure database integrity.

Constraints

In general, many different types of tests can be made on incoming data, in order to assure that the data is valid. A condition or restriction that is imposed on a particular set of data is often called a **constraint** or **integrity control.** Constraints may apply either to (1) individual columns; (2) the relationship between two different columns, usually in different tables; or (3) the rows of one or more tables. When an attempt is made to enter a new row of data that violates the conditions specified by any constraint, the data will not be allowed into the database. Several types of constraints are shown in figure 12.1. These were discussed in chapter 11.

Automatic and Programmed Constraints

In figure 12.1, constraints are specified in the database definition for each table. Presumably then, the enforcement of these constraints would be carried out by the database system *automatically,* as each new piece of data was entered. If a constraint were violated, the data would be rejected by the system.

A constraint that is managed in this way has the very definite advantage of being extremely easy to use, requiring only that the designer enter the appropriate lines in the database definition. The problem with relying on this type of automatic constraint enforcement is that most DBMS's have very limited capabilities in this area, and many offer none at all. A few systems actually give the user enormous flexibility in constraint specifications, but these systems are few and far between.

There is another type of mechanism for specifying constraints that is far more flexible, but which requires the expenditure of large amounts of energy on the part of the database designers and implementers. This method involves the use of application programs to control the input of all information to a database. As each piece of data is received by a program, it is checked for whatever constraint rules are built into the program. This approach has the advantage that virtually any type of constraint whatsoever can be built into data-entry programs. The disadvantage is that writing and debugging programs of this type are often time-consuming processes.

Often, the two types of constraint-enforcement mechanisms are combined. For example, an application program might check input data for a certain set of constraints, such as range constraints for certain columns. The data would then be passed on to the DBMS, which in turn might check for other types of controls, such as referential constraints.

The enforcement of constraints is an important tool for controlling the consistency and validity of a database, and the designer usually tries to include as many integrity controls as possible in a database implementation.

Transaction Processing

A concept frequently associated with database security and protection is that of a database **transaction,** which can be defined as follows. When a modification is made to a database, it reflects a change to the real-world system represented by that database. Often, the modification may involve the addition or alteration of several individual database items. This complete set of database changes is known as a transaction.

In order for a database to remain consistent, *all* of the database changes that are part of a transaction must be made at the same time. If only some of these changes are made, and the processing of that transaction aborts, the database will be in an inconsistent state. This abort could be due to any number of things: software or hardware failure, human error, or a catastrophic event. From the standpoint of database consistency, the cause is irrelevant: an aborted transaction may result in an inconsistent database.

Many DBMS's allow users to define the beginning and end of a complete transaction, so that the system knows exactly when a transaction begins and ends. Then, if a transaction is aborted for any reason, the DBMS can subsequently remove those database changes that were made up to the instant of the abort, thereby returning the database to a consistent state. Database systems that support this type of activity are said to have the capability of **transaction processing.**

An Example of Transaction Processing

As an example of transaction processing, consider the ENROLLMENT database defined in figure 12.1, which contains information dealing with students and their classes. Suppose that an existing student drops out of school. In order to accurately reflect this dropout, the following changes must be made to the database: (1) the appropriate row in the STUDENTS table must be deleted, and (2) all corresponding rows in the STUDENTS_CLASS table must also be deleted. If only some of these changes are made, the database will be inconsistent in that it will not accurately reflect the status of that student.

Assuming that the ENROLLMENT database is implemented on a DBMS that supports transaction processing, the following is a typical set of database commands that might be used to define the complete transaction representing the student's dropout:

1. ACCESS DATABASE = "ENROLLMENT"
2. **BEGIN TRANSACTION**
3. *Statements to delete the appropriate row from the STUDENTS table*
4. *Statements to delete the appropriate rows from the STUDENT_CLASS table*
5. **END TRANSACTION**

Statements 2 and 5 define the boundaries of the transaction. When statement 2 is entered, the DBMS notes that a transaction has begun. If the system aborts for any reason during either steps 3 or 4, the database system will note that an END TRANSACTION statement was not received for this transaction. When the DBMS eventually recovers from the abort, it can undo all of the changes for the transaction up to the point of the abort, thus eliminating any trace of the transaction from the database. The entire transaction (steps 2 through 5) can then be resubmitted at some later time.

In order to be able to support transaction processing, a DBMS makes use of a technique known as **transaction logging,** in which a record is kept of every single change made to a database. Transaction logging is discussed in a subsequent section of this chapter.

If a database system does not support transaction processing, then it may be the responsibility of the data-entry personnel to keep a record of transactions that do not go to completion—a dangerous practice. If transaction logging is not part of a DBMS, it is often necessary to use application programs to simulate the process.

Database Recovery

Computerized information is sensitive to a wide range of events that can result in irretrievable damage. These range from simple human errors to natural catastrophic phenomena. Because today's society has come to depend heavily on computers for the maintenance of information, both individuals and large organizations expect that this information is safe and secure, and that it is always reliably available when needed. It is therefore vital that procedures exist to guarantee that these expectations can be met.

Regardless of how or why a database is damaged, methods must exist for restoring nearly all (99.99 + %) of the information. Usually, a database cannot be returned precisely to the same state that existed at the instant of failure. However, it is nearly always possible to determine what activities were being performed by the DBMS when a failure occurred. That information can subsequently be used to restore a database to the consistent condition that was known to exist at some time before the failure.

Sources of Failure

A great deal of effort has gone into the design and implementation of techniques for dealing with various types of computer failures that might result in damage to stored information. In a sense, designers of hardware and software systems must be extreme pessimists, dreaming up as many different ways as possible in which disasters might occur, and planning for ways to cope with these possibilities. Some of the various types of circumstances that could result in database damage are summarized in the following paragraphs.

Hardware Breakdowns

Many computer components are highly sensitive to environmental changes and are quite easily damaged. Some parts are temperature sensitive—a 20 degree rise is often enough to cause failure. Other electronic components have predictable failure rates due to a wide range of random changes.

Various mechanical elements, such as the platters and read/write arms of disk units, are subject to deterioration due to physical wear. In fact, one of the most common sources of database damage is so-called "head crashes," events during which a disk read/write head comes in physical contact with the platter, causing permanent damage to the platter, the data, and occasionally the database user's peace of mind. Power failures or surges can sometimes cause unpredictable damage to stored information, and many installations are equipped with power regulators and backup power supplies to minimize risks from these sources.

Software Problems

Both operating systems and database management systems are enormously complex conglomerations of programs. Occasionally, unexpected circumstances may arise that cause one or the other of these systems to break down, possibly resulting in unpredictable damage to various data files. This may seem a bit surprising, because one might expect these software systems to be completely error free. Unfortunately, this is rarely the case in practice; unusual circumstances (especially in multiuser environments) may often cause software breakdowns.

Human Errors

People are considerably more error prone than machines, and there are endless ways in which human errors may result in damage to a database. For example, a computer operator might give an inappropriate command either to the operating system or the DBMS, resulting in unexpected actions leading to destruction of data. Or, a database user might accidentally destroy a file by an improper set of DBMS commands (it's remarkably easy). In addition, computer hardware can be easily damaged by physical abuse: one sticky finger accidentally placed in contact with a floppy disk can wreak an unbelievable amount of havoc.

Recovery Techniques

Various methods exist for restoring a corrupted database to an undamaged state. The type of recovery technique used in a particular situation depends on various factors, including the following:

- The extent of the damage to the database. For example, a single record is found to contain bad data; the recovery technique is trivial compared to the restoration procedure needed following a head crash.
- The activity level of the database. Recovery techniques are fairly easy to implement for databases that are modified on a relatively infrequent basis. By contrast, it is much more difficult and expensive to design recovery techniques for continuously-updated databases. If a database is continuously updated, then by implication it is heavily depended upon, so that rapid recovery is critical.

- The nature of the database information. For some types of data, the loss of a small amount of information may not be particularly critical. In other situations, such as financial databases, no amount of loss, no matter how small, is acceptable. The two types of circumstances require very different approaches to reliability and recovery.

Database Backups

In order to effect *any* type of database restoration, periodic **database backups** must be made. This is a process in which an exact copy of the database is written onto a magnetic device physically separate from that on which the database itself is stored. On larger systems, this is usually a magnetic tape. On micro-based systems, it could be either a cassette tape or one or more floppy disks. Usually, during the time that a backup is being generated, all other database activity must be stopped.

Often, more than one backup copy is made, and they are stored far away from the computer and from each other. The rationale for this is that if any type of physical catastrophe were to destroy the computer, at least one of the backup tapes would not be damaged by the same event. Often, for critical databases, such as banking information, at least one backup is stored many miles from the computer facility. Furthermore, it is not uncommon for several generations of backups to be kept as an extra level of protection.

A Simple Recovery Method

The simplest type of database recovery scheme is the following. Periodically, perhaps once a day, a database backup is made. Starting from the time that each backup is made, a physical list, or **log,** is kept manually of all subsequent changes made to the database. If the database crashes, that is, is damaged or destroyed, the following sequence of events is used to effect recovery:

- Repair whatever hardware or software problem caused the crash
- Restore the database with the most recently generated backup. Note that this does *not* restore the database to its state at the instant the damage occurred
- Manually reenter the database changes made since the backup, using the log

A schematic of this process is shown in figure 12.4, which depicts the events surrounding a particular database crash and its subsequent recovery. In this figure, the "logging" procedure refers to the process of maintaining the list of database changes.

Figure 12.4
Schematic for
restoration of a lost
database.

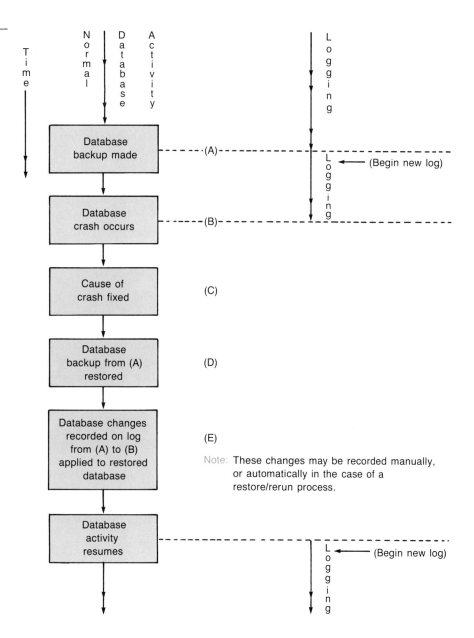

This type of recovery technique is practical only for databases having a very small amount of update activity between backups, because of the amount of work needed to maintain the list of database changes and to reenter these changes. Consequently, this method has limited usefulness. For reasonably active databases, that is, those with more than a few changes per day, other recovery methods must be employed.

Transaction Logging and Restore/Rerun

An extension to the preceding technique is to *automatically* maintain on a computer file the list of database changes made between backups. This computerized list is known as a **transaction log,** and it is invariably maintained on a different physical device from that on which the database itself is stored. Usually, a magnetic tape unit or separate disk device is utilized for this purpose. The reason for using a separate device is simply that if the database is damaged, the cause is not likely to affect data on a separate physical device.

The way in which a transaction log is used to assist in a database restoration is identical to that already described, except for the last step. In this case the restoration of the transactions on the log is performed by a DBMS utility routine, bringing the database back to a state that existed just prior to the moment of the crash. This entire process is often referred to as **restore/rerun,** and figure 12.4 shows the process. In this case, the "logging" in the figure refers to the *automatic* recording of each transaction on the log. Also, step (E) is performed automatically.

The key to the successful use of a transaction log lies in the ability of the DBMS to recognize the beginning and end of each transaction, as discussed earlier in this chapter. For each database transaction, the log contains "Beginning-of-transaction" and "End-of-transaction" markers, in addition to a record of the individual database changes made for that transaction. The "End-of-transaction" marker is recorded on the log by the DBMS *only after the successful conclusion of the transaction.* Thus, if a crash interrupts the processing of a transaction, no "End-of-transaction" will appear on the log. When a restore/rerun is done, only completed transactions will be restored from the log, and a printed report can be made, indicating which transactions were not completed and therefore not entered into the database.

For extremely active databases, the restore/rerun technique may prove to be inadequate because the reprocessing of the log may take several hours, during which time the database is unavailable for regular activity. If a database is very active, this unavailability will probably be intolerable, and other restoration techniques must be used.

Rollback Recovery

Rollback recovery is useful in situations in which database processing is interrupted, but the database itself is not damaged in any way. An example of this would be some type of failure that results in an abnormal termination of the DBMS execution. Transactions in progress might be aborted before completion, and the associated records might be left in unknown states, but the rest of the database would be unaffected.

The rollback recovery technique requires that the transaction log contain **before-images** of each database record to which changes have been made since the last backup. A before-image is a copy of a record immediately *prior* to its being modified as part of a transaction.

The process of rollback recovery involves the following. After the DBMS has been placed back in operation, with the undisturbed database just as it was when the interruption occurred, the transaction log is processed. For every *incomplete* transaction noted in the log, each before-image is used to replace the current version of the corresponding record in the database. Thus, each database record that was modified as part of an incomplete transaction is returned to its state before the beginning of the transaction. The result of this process is the removal from the database of all traces of the incomplete transactions, that is, those that were in process when the crash occurred. Figure 12.5 illustrates the rollback process.

Notice that for rollback recovery to work, the transaction log must contain "Beginning-of-transaction" and "End-of-transaction" markers for each transaction. When a rollback recovery process is carried out, incomplete transactions can be detected by the absence of an "End-of-transaction" marker.

The amount of effort necessary to carry out a rollback recovery may be far less than that needed for a restore/rerun recovery. For example, suppose that 1000 transactions have been recorded on a log between the time of the last backup and the moment of a failure (one that does not damage the database). Let us also suppose that at the instant of failure, 5 transactions are in process. With restore/rerun, the database must be restored from the last backup, and then 995 transactions will have to be reprocessed. On the other hand, a rollback recovery will start with the database as it is, simply undoing the effects of the 5 incomplete transactions.

Rollforward Recovery

Rollforward is another type of recovery mechanism, often used when a database has been damaged and must therefore be restored from a backup. It is similar in flavor to the rollback technique, and it also has the advantage of being much faster than the restore/rerun method. It requires that the transaction log contain **after-images** of each database record to which changes have been made since the last backup. An after-image is a copy of a record immediately *after* it has been modified as part of a transaction.

In its simplest form, rollforward recovery consists of the following steps:

- Following an abort that results in damage to a database, the last backup is used to restore the database
- The log is processed, starting at the point at which the last backup was made. For every *completed transaction* noted in the log, each after-image is used to replace the current version of the corresponding record in the database

Figure 12.6 illustrates the rollforward process.

The rollforward technique is considerably faster than the restore/rerun method, because the replacement of a record with its after-image takes much less time than the recreation of the entire database process involved with the change to the record.

Figure 12.5
Rollback recovery using
the transaction log.

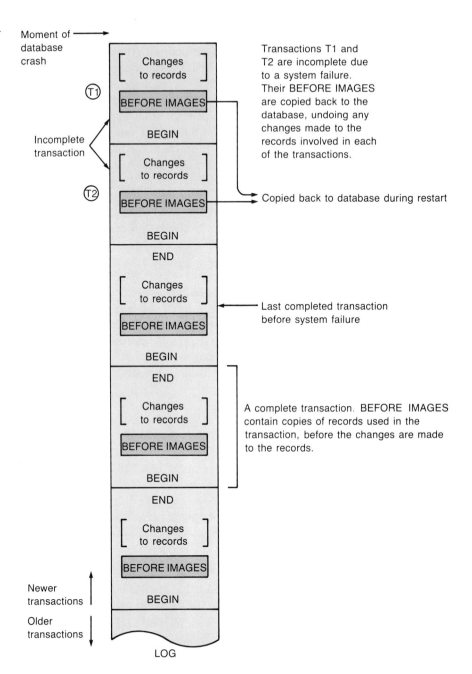

Moment of
database
crash

Transactions T1 and
T2 are incomplete due
to a system failure.
Their BEFORE IMAGES
are copied back to the
database, undoing any
changes made to the
records involved in each
of the transactions.

Incomplete
transaction

Copied back to database during restart

Last completed transaction
before system failure

A complete transaction. BEFORE IMAGES
contain copies of records used in the
transaction, before the changes are made
to the records.

Newer
transactions

Older
transactions

LOG

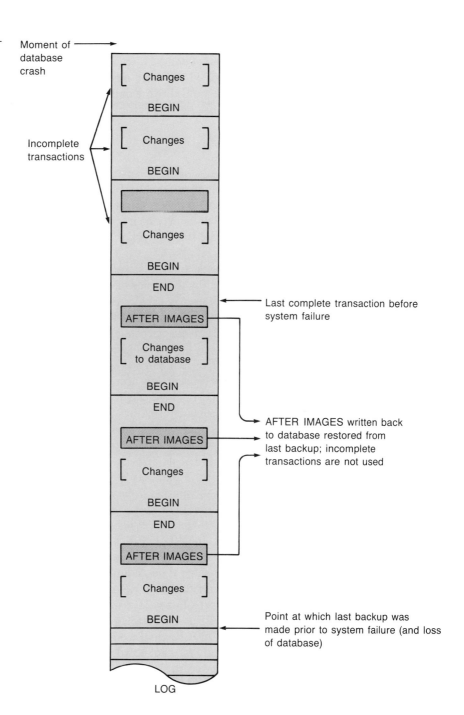

Figure 12.6
Rollforward recovery
using the transaction
log.

Moment of
database
crash

Incomplete
transactions

Changes

BEGIN

Changes

BEGIN

Changes

BEGIN

END

AFTER IMAGES

Changes
to database

BEGIN

END

AFTER IMAGES

Changes

BEGIN

END

AFTER IMAGES

Changes

BEGIN

LOG

Last complete transaction before
system failure

AFTER IMAGES written back
to database restored from
last backup; incomplete
transactions are not used

Point at which last backup was
made prior to system failure (and loss
of database)

There are several variations on the basic rollforward method, designed to further improve the speed of database recovery. For example, the entire set of after-images can first be sorted by record number. Then, only the *last* after-image for each record has to be applied to the database. For those records to which several changes are reflected in the log, this can represent a tremendous saving in processing time.

Concurrency Control

Many database systems are capable of handling multiple users concurrently.[1] In some situations, each user may interact with a different database, while in other circumstances, many users may be interacting with the same database. Thus, in figure 12.7, users A and B each work with separate databases, while users C and D share another.

Very large databases, such as those associated with airline reservation systems, may be accessed by thousands of users at the same time. Even in extreme cases like these, each user is usually unaware that others may be sharing the same data. The operating system and the DBMS both share the responsibility of keeping track of the messages passing between users and the appropriate databases. In this context, a *user* could refer either to a real person sitting at a terminal or computer, or to a batch program interacting with a database.

When several users concurrently access a database, various types of data-usage conflicts potentially exist. These conflicts might occur, for instance, if one user was attempting to modify information that other users were trying to read. Alternatively, two users could simultaneously be attempting to update the same record; or worse yet, one user could be trying to read a record while another user was trying to delete it! The database system must ensure that conflicts such as these are resolved in ways that satisfy the needs of the different users without creating confusion in the process. This type of DBMS activity is known as **concurrency control.**

To illustrate in more depth the types of conflict that might arise, suppose that two users, READER and WRITER, are concurrently working with the same database. READER issues a request for a transaction to read a particular record; at approximately the same time, WRITER issues a transaction to modify the same record. The result that user READER sees will depend on which of the two transactions happens to be acted upon first by the database system. If the transaction of READER is completely processed first, the old version of the record will be sent to READER. On the other hand, if the transaction of WRITER is completely processed first, the record will be modified, and READER will see the new version of the record.

---

[1] The word *concurrent* is used as opposed to *simultaneous,* to denote the subtle distinction that a computer actually deals with one user at a time, but that it goes from one user to another very rapidly.

Figure 12.7

Concurrent database
access. Users A and B
each interact with
separate databases;
users C and D share a
common database.

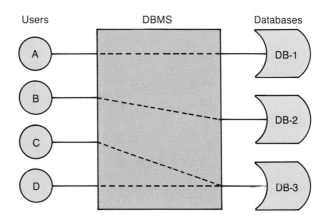

Note that users' transactions are not necessarily processed in the order in which
they are chronologically issued. A transaction may be issued by READER several seconds before one is issued by WRITER, and yet the transaction of
WRITER may be completed first. This possibility exists because a transaction
may consist of many different parts, each of which is processed separately. Because of the operational complexities of both the operating system and the DBMS,
it is quite possible for transaction A to be started before transaction B, and yet
for B to be completed before A.

Resource Locking

In the preceding example, it seemed that chance determined which version of the
record was finally sent to READER, but this is not necessarily true. To illustrate
this, consider the following situation. Suppose that the two transactions, which
we shall call READER and WRITER, are both received at nearly the same instant by the DBMS, and suppose that by chance, the processing of WRITER is
begun first. If the first action within this transaction is a **record locking** command,
then the record in question will be made inaccessible to READER (or to any
other transaction) until WRITER is finished. On the other hand, if WRITER
did *not* lock the record, then even though WRITER was begun first, it would
still be quite possible for READER to read the old copy of the record. These two
possible scenarios are illustrated in figures 12.8 (a) and (b).

Note that it is still true that chance determines whether or not WRITER is
acted on before READER. However, because of record locking, whenever a
WRITER type of transaction does begin first, the READER transaction will be
delayed long enough to ensure that it reads the latest possible version of the record. Therefore, record locking can significantly improve the performance of a
database, particularly a very active one.

Figure 12.8

The processing of two requests against the same database record (a) *without* record locking; and (b) with record locking.

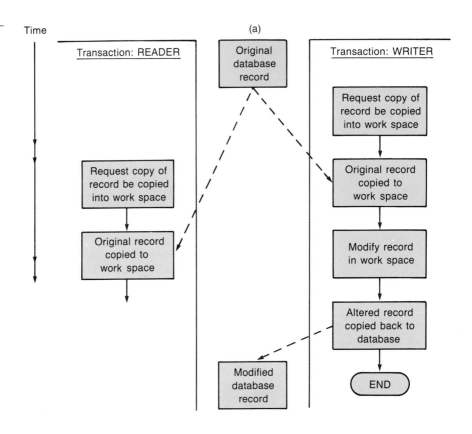

READER is processed immediately, retrieving the original version of the record, before WRITER has finished modifying the record

Levels of Resource Locking

Database resources may be locked on several different levels. The extent to which resources are locked is referred to as the locking granularity. For example, an entire database may be locked by a transaction during an update (coarse granularity). On the other hand, only the actual data items being modified within a single record may be locked (fine granularity).

Types of Locking

It is sometimes possible to specify the precise way in which transactions are locked out. The two most common types of locking are the following:

No access: all other users are locked out of the data for the duration of the transaction

Read-only access: users may read the data while it is being modified

Figure 12.8
[*Continued*]

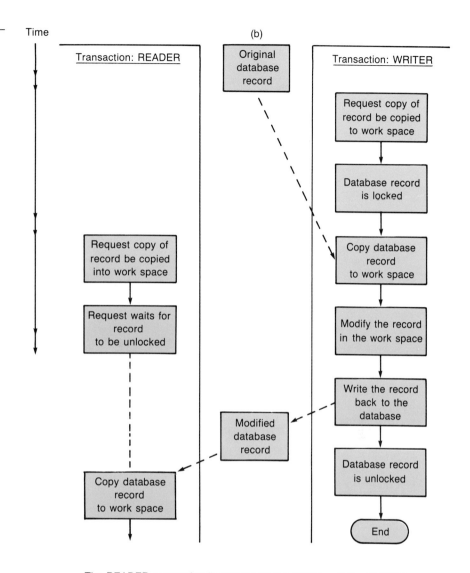

The READER transaction is delayed by the DBMS until the WRITER request to alter the record has been finished; READER will then read the updated version of the record

The latter type of access would most likely be chosen for very active databases, that is, those with a very high frequency of transactions of all types. In this type of situation, complete record lockout could degrade the performance of the system to unacceptable levels.

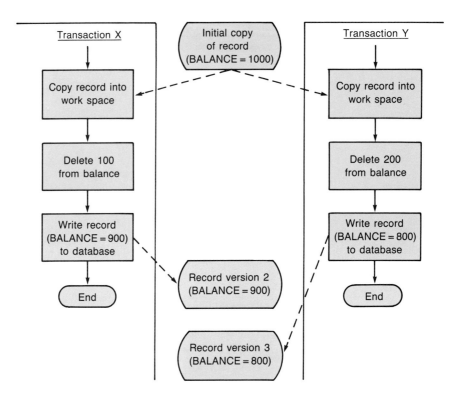

Figure 12.9
Concurrent updates
without any
concurrency control.
Both transactions
proceed concurrently,
and the results of
transaction X are lost.

Concurrent Updating

In some instances, resource locking is absolutely essential for maintaining database integrity. As an example of this type of situation, suppose that users X and Y each issue a request for a transaction against the same bank account record, at nearly the same instant. In addition, suppose that:

1. Both transactions are withdrawals, the first for $100, and the second for $200
2. The initial balance field within the record is $1000
3. Both transactions are received by the DBMS at nearly the same instant, and processing for both also begins at nearly the same instant

If the transactions are begun close enough together, the scenario shown in figure 12.9 could well occur: transaction X causes a copy of the record to be placed into the **work space** X. (A work space is a small region of primary storage where any changes involved with a transaction are done.) Within this work space, the BALANCE field is decreased from 1000 to 900. While this is occurring, transaction Y causes another copy of the *same* record to be read into the work space Y. In this work space, the BALANCE field is decreased from 1000 to 800.

Meanwhile, the final copy of the record in the work space X is written back to the database, showing a BALANCE value of 900. Finally, the record copy in work space Y is written back to the database, *overwriting the BALANCE value of 900 with a new value of 800.*

The final value of the BALANCE field should be 700, but instead it is 800! The reason for this disaster is that both *update* transactions were allowed to proceed together indiscriminately, and the effect of transaction X has been lost in the shuffle. The way to prevent this type of intolerable situation lies in having one of the transactions lock the record against any other type of update activity while the transaction is being processed. Thus, if transaction X locks the record, then transaction Y cannot proceed until transaction X is finished, as shown in figure 12.10.

This is all well and good, but suppose that both transactions begin at *exactly* the same instant? In that case, will they both lock each other out, or if not, what exactly will occur? The answer to this lies in the fact that in the current world of computers, only one instruction can execute at a time. Because a database system is a program that runs by executing instructions, one transaction *must* precede another. That is, the transaction that happens to be initiated first will lock out any others.

The Deadly Embrace Problem

A single database transaction may involve the updating of several records. Because of this, various types of concurrency control problems can occur that require special handling by database systems. A favorite example used to illustrate this type of problem is that of the **deadly embrace,** also known as **deadlock,** illustrated in figure 12.11. In this situation, two transactions, X and Y, are involved, and both begin at approximately the same time. By chance, both transactions involve the updating of records A and B. Transaction X is initiated first by the DBMS, and the first few of its instructions to the DBMS are the following:

X–1. Lock record A
X–2. Read a copy of record A into work space X
X–3. Update the copy of the record in the work space
X–4. Write the updated version of A back to the database
X–5. Lock record B
X–6. Read a copy of record B into the work space

.
.
.

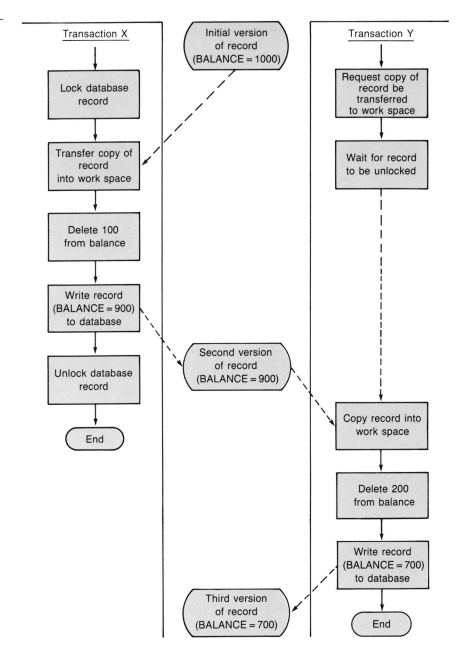

Figure 12.10
Concurrent updates with concurrency control. Transaction X locks the record; transaction Y proceeds only after the conclusion of transaction X. The final record contains the effects of both transactions.

Transaction X

Initial version of record (BALANCE = 1000)

Lock database record

Transfer copy of record into work space

Delete 100 from balance

Write record (BALANCE = 900) to database

Unlock database record

End

Second version of record (BALANCE = 900)

Third version of record (BALANCE = 700)

Transaction Y

Request copy of record be transferred to work space

Wait for record to be unlocked

Copy record into work space

Delete 200 from balance

Write record (BALANCE = 700) to database

End

Figure 12.11
A deadly embrace
situation.

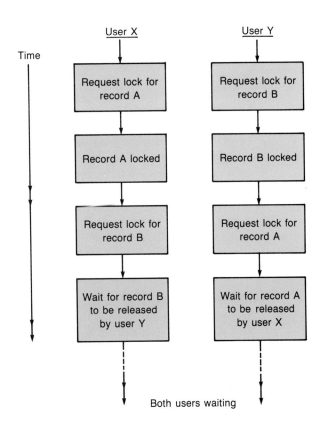

We now suppose that transaction B is initiated sometime during the preceding steps, and also that this transaction must access record B *before* it accesses record A. The first few instructions for this transaction are the following:

Y–1. Lock record B
Y–2. Read a copy of record B into work space Y
Y–3. Update the copy of the record in the work space
Y–4. Write the updated version of B back to the database
Y–5. Lock record A
Y–6. Read a copy of record A into the work space

.
.
.

Now suppose that instruction Y–1 occurs *after* instruction X–1 and (the critical point) *before* X–5. When transaction X reaches X–5, it will be unable to proceed, because record B has been locked by transaction Y.

Meanwhile, transaction Y proceeds until it reaches instruction Y–5, at which point it must wait, because transaction X has locked record A. At this point, each transaction is hung up, waiting for a record to be unlocked by the other, and neither can move. This situation is known as a deadly embrace, and were it not for DBMS intervention, both transactions would patiently wait until the next system crash.

Unlocking a deadly embrace. Several methods have been proposed for dealing with the deadly embrace problem. Strangely enough, the one that has proved to be the most successful allows the deadly embrace to occur. Many DBMS's can detect the existence of a deadly embrace situation by keeping a constant check on which resources are being requested by each transaction in process. When a deadlock is detected, the database system resolves it by terminating one of the transactions. To do this, those portions of the transaction that have already been carried out must be reversed. This can be done by a rollback process using *before images,* as described earlier in this chapter.

Local Area Networks and Concurrency

A very recent advance in the microcomputer arena is the development of the **local area networks.** In this type of situation, two or more microcomputers are linked by a *network* to common resources, such as a printer or hard disk device. This type of situation is depicted in figure 12.12; typically the network consists of a simple two-conductor cable, plus specialized hardware and software to make it all hang together.

Within the framework of a local area network, it is possible for several individual copies of the same DBMS to concurrently access a particular database, as depicted in figure 12.13. Here, each copy of the DBMS runs on a separate microcomputer, *independent* of the others. In this type of situation, there may still exist the same types of concurrency control problems discussed earlier such as concurrent update and so on. However, the solutions to these problems must take somewhat different forms because of the independence of each DBMS.

For example, record locking is still a necessity, but in this case the fact that a copy of the DBMS has locked a given record will not automatically be known by the other DBMS's. Some mechanism *external to all of the DBMS's* must be provided for indicating which records or files are locked at any moment.

The rapid developments in local area networks have forced micro-based DBMS's to reevaluate their products. As a result, many of these have been redesigned for proper use in the multi-user environment. Much work in this area still needs to be done, since most micro-based DBMS's are still written for single-user database access. Unfortunately, although these may often seem to run well in a multi-user setting they often have disastrous results.

Figure 12.12
A local area network.
As shown, different
microcomputers share
common resources
such as a printer and
hard disk.

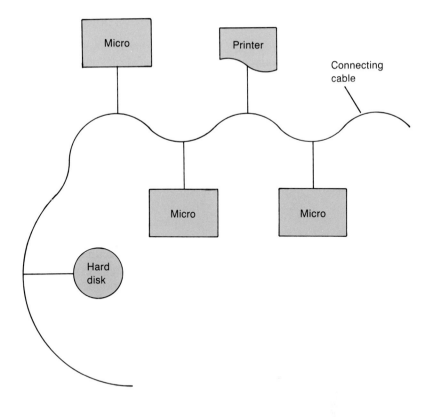

Figure 12.13
Concurrent database
access in the
environment of a local
area network. Each
DBMS accesses the
same database via the
network.

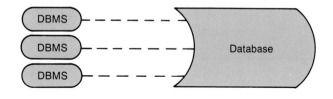

Distributed Database Environments

Distributed processing is a situation in which various portions of a database are maintained in different physical locations, usually quite far removed from one another. Although distributed systems are difficult to implement, they are becoming more and more popular because of the advantages they offer. For example, each local site (sometimes referred to as a *node*), is responsible for maintaining that part of the total database that is of direct interest to its own staff. Access to that local information is often much faster than it would be were the data to be maintained at a remote site. Also, if a local computer goes down, it does not necessarily affect the operations at other locations. A good example of this is a multi-branch bank, where each branch is responsible for maintaining its own data, as well as having access to the information at the other locations.

When a database is physically distributed among several locations, the problems of concurrency control become enormously more complicated because of many factors, and many of these issues have not yet been fully resolved. Consider, for example, the complications that can arise when some parts of a database are duplicated for convenience in several locations. Two users may be working concurrently with different copies of the same data, each making different changes to that information! The problem of simply keeping the various copies synchronized is far from trivial.

Complicating the problem of concurrency control are many issues associated with the field of data communications. For example, electronic messages take significant amounts of time to go from one location to another, partially because of the various types of switching activity involved with the transfers. Under these circumstances, the very concept of concurrency takes on an entirely different dimension. These issues are mentioned here simply because distributed database processing is becoming an important topic within the field of database management and it is therefore important to be aware of its existence.

Summary

The protection of computerized information has become an increasingly important aspect of database management as more reliance is placed on computers for information storage and retrieval. Protection of data takes many forms, one of which is the guarding against unauthorized access. This is accomplished in a variety of ways, including password protection, data encryption, and the creation of user views.

Many database systems provide built-in password security. For those that do not, application programs may need to be written in order to achieve a reasonable level of protection. Password protection may exist on a variety of levels, ranging from an entire computer system to a single column within a table. For situations demanding even more stringent forms of protection than that offered by passwords, data encryption is often utilized. Many types of encryption schemes have been developed. The level of security offered by any particular method is strongly dependent on the amount of computing power required by the method.

Database views provide a convenient means for limiting users' access to specific portions of a database. A defined view can combine parts of one or several tables, including virtual columns, which are the result of combining values from several actual columns. Views not only limit access for security reasons; they also furnish users with extremely simple tools for accessing databases within which complex relationships exist.

The combination of passwords and views results in strongly controlled access to a database, limiting specific users not only to the *amount* of a database that is visible, but also to the *type* of access.

Maintaining database integrity is also an important issue. One aspect of this is input data validation, based on constraints arising from various real-world conditions. Some DBMS's offer a wide range of built-in constraint-enforcement procedures; others require user-written programs for the validation of input data.

Database failures may occur from a wide variety of sources, including hardware, software, and human. When the level of database activity is not very high, an occasional database crash is not significant, because the database can be rebuilt from a recent backup and a record of transactions made to the database since the backup. However, for active databases, it is often imperative that recovery following a crash be effected as quickly and as accurately as possible. To this end, many DBMS's provide a number of sophisticated tools, usually including a set of built-in routines for automatically rebuilding a database from backups and transaction logs. The exact type of recovery techniques used for a particular database depend to some extent on various factors, including the activity level of the database, and the speed with which the database must be recovered.

Multi-user access to a database introduces a special set of problems dealing with database consistency. The possibility of more than one user attempting simultaneously to modify the same data, as well as other scenarios along these lines, creates the need for a variety of software controls. Resource locking, for example, ensures that each user obtains the necessary database access without creating conflicts within the system. Resource locking is a vital part of multi-user database management because without it, database integrity could rapidly be destroyed. The ability to lock out database resources, however, requires a great deal of DBMS software, and consumes a large amount of CPU time. The types of concurrency control problems that can arise are accentuated when a database is distributed over several physical locations.

The issue of concurrent access has recently begun to affect the world of microcomputer-oriented databases, because of the emergence of local area networks. In an effort to stay competitive, many micro-based DBMS's are being converted to multi-user systems. Inevitably, concurrent database use will play an important role in the microcomputer world.

Terminology

after image
before image
concurrency control
concurrent access
data validation
deadly embrace (deadlock)
distributed processing
encryption
granularity
local area network
password protection

read-only access
read/write access
resource locking
restore/rerun
rollback
rollforward
transaction
transaction log
transaction processing
view
virtual column

Review Questions

1. Give several examples of different types of sensitive data, that is, information that for some reason should not be indiscriminantly available to public access.
2. Summarize the various techniques used to provide database security protection against unauthorized access.
3. Outline the various levels at which password protection may be invoked. Suggest the types of users for whom each level of protection would be appropriate.
4. With respect to password protection, explain why fine granularity requires more overhead than coarse granularity.
5. How does a database view differ from password protection in terms of the types of confidentiality provided?
6. How does a database transaction differ from the process of simply adding a new record or modifying an existing one? How is the concept of a transaction useful in preserving database integrity?
7. List at least three different types of databases for which it would be necessary to guarantee *complete* recovery following a database crash.
8. Explain the difference between a rollback recovery and a rollforward recovery. Also, what are the similarities between the two techniques?
9. In what ways are the problems of concurrency control different in the local area network environment, in comparison to the situation of a single DBMS servicing multiple users?

Problems

1. With respect to the database in figure 12.1, suggest what types of users might be given each of the three passwords shown. For example, would the president of the college necessarily be authorized to modify student data?

2. Again with respect to figure 12.1, suppose that a particular user is to be given the following type of access authority:

   a. Read-only access to all student-related information, except for the following:

   b. Read/write access to any data pertaining specifically to classes attended by students

Modify the database definition in figure 12.1 to provide access for this user.

3. This problem references the Jellybeans, Inc. database design shown in figure 9.4. Using the SQL-type of syntax shown in figure 12.3, create views to satisfy the needs of each of the following users.

USER1: limited to the identification number and phone number of customers.

USER2: limited to customer names and their payments.

4. With respect to the school database shown in figure 11.10, create a single view to provide easy access to students' names, the classes taken by each student, and the instructor teaching each of the classes.

5. Using a simple flowchart or pseudo code, outline a program that would provide both read-access and write-access password protection into a particular database. Assume that the following programs are used *exclusively* for reading and writing the database:

READDB: Used to read information from the database.
WRITEDB: Used to read and write database information.

6. Why must the NOT NULL clause be included with the definition of STUDENT_NUMBER in the STUDENTS table in figure 12.1?

7. Modify the database definition shown in figure 12.1 to include the following constraint: the value of MAJOR must contain one of the following values:

      ["PHYS", "CHEM", "MUSIC", "C-S", "ART", "PSYCH"]

8. a. Modify the definition in figure 12.1 to include the following table:

      CLASSES [CLASS_NUM, TIME, ROOM, INSTRUCTOR]

   b. Add a constraint to the definition in order to guarantee that for every row that is added to the STUDENT_CLASS table, there will exist a corresponding row in the CLASSES table.

9. Suppose that you were implementing the database shown in figure 12.1, but that the DBMS did not allow automatic constraint specifications, such as those shown in the figure. Outline a data-entry program that would check input data, accepting only those rows that conformed with the constraints defined in the figure.

10. Suppose that a particular database system does not support built-in transaction processing. Would it be possible to guarantee complete database recovery following a crash of this DBMS? Explain your answer.

11. With respect to the database defined in figure 12.1, suppose that the school assigns a new identification number to a particular student. Define the scope of a database transaction that would be used to modify the database accordingly. In other words, list the individual database activities that would be included within the transaction.

12. A particular DBMS makes periodic backups, and also maintains a transaction log. Suppose that at time A a backup is made, such as illustrated in figure 12.4. What would be a reasonable thing to do with the log made up to time A, *after* the backup? For example, one possibility might be to destroy the log, in order to free up the tape or disk for the new log that begins at time A. In deciding on a course of action, put yourself in the position of the database administrator, who has to guarantee the security of the database under all conceivable circumstances.

13. A particular DBMS utilizes both rollforward recovery in some circumstances and rollback recovery in others. Using a schematic diagram similar to those shown in figures 12.5 and 12.6, show how a single transaction log could be used to serve both purposes. In other words, what information would have to be stored on the log?

14. Suppose that the purpose of a particular database transaction is to modify an existing record.
    a. Why must the very first activity of the transaction be to lock the record?

    b. Must the record be locked against *any* other types of transactions? If not, what types of other transactions might be given access to the record during the modification?

15. Devise a scenario in which three separate transactions are mutually deadlocked.

Chapter Thirteen

Data Structures for Database Management Systems

Introduction

Computerized information is useful because of the fact that a variety of methods exist for connecting and accessing the bits and pieces of stored data in some logical manner. Any *physical* means by which logically related data items are linked together is known as a data structure, and many different types of these structures exist. In this text, several of these have already been discussed.

For example, a data record consists of a group of one or more fields among which some logical connections exist; the fields represent a set of qualities about the particular real-world entity represented by the record. The logical connection among the fields is maintained by their physical relationship, or data structure, within the storage medium. That is, usually an entire record is physically stored contiguously, so that when a particular field within a record is accessed, the other fields are immediately available, because a record is normally read as a unit. In this case, the data structure is the record itself.

Another general type of data structure to which we have had considerable exposure in this text is the file. Usually, a set of records is grouped together into a file because there is some type of logical connection among them. In addition, for each type of file there exists at least one method for moving from one record to another within the file, and the file is in effect a type of data structure. As a simple example, the records in a sequential file are arranged in such a way that as each record is read, the next one is immediately accessible.

An index is another type of data structure that we have explored to some degree in preceding chapters. It is a mechanism that facilitates the accessing of records within a file, often in some particular order.

In general, we may summarize the qualities of a data structure as follows:

- It consists of a group of logically related data items that are *physically* organized into some type of cohesive unit
- A method exists for accessing and/or manipulating these data items

411

Within the field of database management, many types of data structures are utilized, and in this chapter we shall examine the most commonly-used ones. The first of these is the data record itself, and a brief description will be given of the various forms in which records can exist. Next, a fundamental structure known as the **chain** will be studied. This is a building block frequently used in other types of data structures, some of which will also be investigated in this chapter. Finally, we shall study complex structures that involve records from several files. Using these structures, relationships among different record-types can be built into the data itself, furnishing a convenient means of accessing related groups of records.

Records

Up to this point in the text, we have tacitly been assuming that records are fixed-length, and furthermore that each field within a record is also fixed-length. Although the records used by most DBMS's do in fact conform to these restrictions, there are other types of records with more complex structures.

Fixed-length Records

As a point of comparison, we shall first review some of the properties of fixed-length records. Figure 13.1(a) illustrates a group of records, each of which contains four fixed-length fields. This simple type of record structure is commonly used by database systems because of the ease with which the records can be stored and retrieved. That is, since all records are the same size, secondary-storage space management is relatively simple. Also, because all fields are in predetermined positions within the record, they are quite easy to access.

The biggest disadvantage with fixed-length records is that the length of each field must be made large enough to accommodate the largest possible value that could reasonably be expected to be entered in that field. Because of this, a considerable amount of storage space is often wasted. Thus, for example, even though the average length of a city name might be 10 characters, the largest name might be 25. On the average, then, 15 bytes of storage would be wasted for each stored record.

Variable-length Records

By definition, if a file contains records whose lengths are not all the same, the records are said to be **variable-length.** This type of record may arise from the following:

- One or more record fields are variable-length
- One or more fields are multiply-occurring
- A combination of the above

Figure 13.1
(a) Fixed-length
records; (b) variable-
length records with field
delimiters; (c) variable-
length records with field
counters.

(a)

NAME	STREET	CITY	STATE	ZIP
J. Harrison	123 Market St.	Boston	MA	02146
R. Ricci	1452 10th Ave	New York	NY	34687
L. Shapiro	1 Park Place	Trenton	NJ	22194
A. Peterson	152 Penn St.	Boston	MA	02148

(b)

```
44J. Harrison$123 Market St.$Boston$MA$02146

43R. Ricci$1452 10th Ave.$New York$NY$34687

42L. Shapiro$1 Park Place$Trenton$NJ$22194

40A. Peterson$152 Penn St.$Boston$MA$02148
```

Each field terminates with a delimiter ($) and each record is
immediately preceded by its byte count

(c)

```
4511J. Harrison14123 Market St.6Boston2MA502146

438R. Ricci141452 10th Ave.8New York2NY534687

4310L. Shapiro121Park Place7Trenton2NJ522194

4211A. Peterson\152 Penn St.\Boston\MA\02148
```

Each field is preceded by its byte count and each record is preceded
by its total byte count

Variable-length Fields within Records

Because of the wasted-space problem often associated with fixed-length records,
some DBMS's allow one or more fields within a record to be established as
variable-length. For each field of this type, the length is automatically adjusted
to accommodate whatever value is contained in the field. For instance, using the
CITY field in figure 13.1 as an example, "Boston" would take up 6 bytes of
storage, while "Trenton" would occupy 7.

Several techniques exist for constructing variable-length fields, and two of the most common of these—the use of either field delimiters or counters, are illustrated in figure 13.1 (b) and (c).

Field delimiters. As illustrated in figure 13.1(b), fields may be separated by a special character known as a **delimiter.** With this method, each field takes up only the space needed for the contained value plus one byte for the delimiter. An empty field is indicated by two adjacent delimiters. In order to access a field within a record, a scan must be made for that particular delimiter within the record. For example, the CITY field is located by scanning the record for the second delimiter. All of the following characters up to the next delimiter make up the value of the CITY field.

When this type of method is utilized, the total byte count of each record is usually placed at the beginning of the record. This often simplifies the arithmetic when working with multiple records. For example, if the system wishes to skip over an entire record, the total byte count furnishes the number of bytes to be skipped. By contrast, if the byte count were not present, the system would have to perform a character-by-character scan through the record, counting delimiters in order to determine the record's endpoint.

It is possible to combine fixed- and variable-length fields within a record structure. This helps to improve the process of record scanning, and a byte is saved here and there. For example, if the STATE and ZIP fields in figure 13.1(b) were established as fixed-length fields, delimiters would not be needed after each of these data fields because the system would automatically know the exact field lengths.

Field counters. A variation on the delimiter theme is to place the actual byte count of each field at the beginning of the field, as shown in figure 13.1(c). Each counter consists of a fixed number of bytes, usually two or three. Again, each record is preceded by its total byte count. Regardless of which method is used for dealing with variable-length fields, the objective is the same—to minimize the amount of storage needed for each record.

Multiply-Occurring Fields

Some database systems have built-in provisions that allow one or more fields to be established as multiply-occurring. Thus, in figure 13.2 the PHONE field in each record may be given any number of values. With this type of structure, each record must contain the following additional information:

- The count of the number of occurrences for each multiply-occurring field
- The total length of the record, which is determined in part by the number of occurrences of each field

Figure 13.2
A record-type with
multiply-occurring
fields.

NAME	PHONE	CITY	STATE	ZIP
J. Kilroy	(415) 882-3461	Albany	CA	94156
A. Markham	(415) 987-1298 (415) 987-1274 (408) 225-8719	Berkeley	CA	94707
P. Grimes	(818) 337-4224	Los Angeles	CA	91356
R. Harris		Oakland	CA	94616

The PHONE field may have zoro, one, or several occurrences

A multiply-occurring field may be either fixed- or variable-length. If it is the latter, then each occurrence must be delineated by one of the methods already described.

Pros and Cons

Although variable-length record structures offer the advantage of conserving secondary storage, there are prices to be paid, such as the fact that secondary-storage space management is considerably more complicated. For example, when fixed-length records are used, the system knows that every record occupies the same amount of storage space. By contrast, with variable-length records the system must keep track of how much space is occupied by each record and each field. Another disadvantage of variable-length records is that when a record is deleted, its vacated space may lie unused, because it may be difficult to find a new record small enough to fit the space.

By definition, true relational DBMS's do not allow multiply-occurring fields. Consequently, if a conceptual design calls for a multiply-occurring attribute within a particular entity-type, the relational design must translate the entity-type into two tables, between which exists a one-to-many relationship. On the other hand, variable-length fields and records exist within some relational DBMS's.

Chains

The **chain,** often referred to as a **linked list,** or sometimes simply a list, is a specific mechanism by which various records within one or more files are grouped into a logical structure. For example, it might be convenient to connect all of the records in an ORDERS file that correspond to a particular customer. These connections would serve as convenient means by which any particular subset of ORDERS records could be rapidly accessed.

Table 13.1

Sample ORDERS File

RELATIVE ADDRESS	CUSTOMER_ID	ORDER_ID	ORDER_DATE	ITEM_NO	QNTY
1	12122	33148	1/15/82	P3442	15
2	22143	11358	9/18/81	S9874	75
3	8233	22184	11/15/81	P3442	5
4	12122	22984	12/05/81	S9874	25
5	98344	98712	2/27/82	L357	62
6	22143	33091	10/07/81	P3442	1
7	12122	24981	4/05/82	S9874	100
8	8233	20971	9/25/81	L357	65
9	98344	10006	4/28/82	P3442	2
10	12122	92836	2/02/82	S9874	15

The chain is one of the basic tools used in constructing more complex data structures. We shall introduce this tool by a specific example. Consider a file of customer ORDERS records, represented by the data in table 13.1.

In this table, the column RELATIVE ADDRESS refers to the address of each record *relative* to the beginning of the file. This is a common and convenient method of specifying record addresses, as opposed to using physical addresses. The latter are usually considerably more complicated, because they involve the specification of such items as sector number, track number, and so on. The relative address of a record can be easily converted to a physical address, by means of a separate table. Relative addresses are also convenient to use because a file of data can be displaced from one part of a disk to another without the need for changing the relative addresses.

In this chapter, we shall use the term *address* as a shorthand term for the relative address of a record. Also, for simplicity we shall refer to a record by its relative address. Thus, the record at relative address 1 will be called "Record 1."

Using Chains

Suppose that we wish to find all of the ORDERS records corresponding to a particular CUSTOMER_ID, say 12122. In order to accomplish this, it is necessary to search the entire ORDERS file, examining each record to see if the value of the CUSTOMER_ID field is equal to 12122. If the file contains many

Table 13.2

ORDERS File with Pointers

RELATIVE ADDRESS	CUSTOMER_ID	ORDER_ID	ORDER_DATE	ITEM_NO	QNTY	PNTR	
1	12122	33148	1/15/82	P3442	15	4	←head
2	22143	11358	9/18/81	S9874	75	6	←head
3	8233	22184	11/15/81	P3442	5	8	←head
4	12122	22984	12/05/81	S9874	25	7	
5	98344	98712	2/27/82	L357	62	9	←head
6	22143	33091	10/07/81	P3442	1	—	
7	12122	24981	4/05/82	S9874	100	10	
8	8233	20971	9/25/81	L357	65	—	
9	98344	10006	4/28/82	P3442	2	—	
10	12122	92836	2/02/82	S9874	15	—	

hundreds or thousands of records, the search time can be inordinately large, even if the records are grouped in such a way that many of them can be read into primary storage with a single disk access.

The amount of effort required to accomplish this search can be reduced significantly by creating a series of chains within the ORDERS file, as illustrated in table 13.2. This table is similar to table 13.1, except that a new column labelled PNTR has been added, representing the addition of a new field to each ORDERS record. The contents of this field is a quantity known as a **pointer**, which contains a value corresponding to a record address. Thus, a pointer is a data item that points to a particular record. For example, in table 13.2, the value of PNTR for record 1 is 4. Consequently, *it points to the record whose relative address is 4.*

The records illustrated in table 13.2 are organized by the various pointers into a series of chains, or sets of records, and each of these chains is associated with a particular value of CUSTOMER_ID. For instance, consider record 1 in the table, which represents an order belonging to a customer whose ID value is 12122. By scanning through the table, we see that records 4, 7, and 10 are also associated with the same customer. Furthermore, by examining the values of the PNTR field for these records, we see that the pointer of each record gives the address of the next one corresponding to CUSTOMER_ID = 12122.

Figure 13.3
Set of chain heads
corresponding to the
ORDERS file in table
13.2.

Value of CUSTOMER_ID	Chain head
8233	3
12122	1
22143	2
98344	5

Record 10 is the last one associated with CUSTOMER_ID = 12122. Therefore, its pointer has no record to which to point, and this is indicated in the table by the dashed line. We say that this pointer has a **null value.**

Records 1, 4, 7, and 10 form a chain, or linked list, and the pointer values connect the links in the chain. In a similar manner, each of the records in the ORDERS file is connected to a chain corresponding to a particular value of CUSTOMER_ID. Thus, if the file contains records for 25 different customers, then there will be 25 distinct chains threading the file.

Locating Chains

The first record of a chain may be located by means of a **chain head,** which is a special memory location containing a pointer to that record. Each chain must have its own head, and the entire group of chain heads must be stored in such a way that the first member of any particular chain is easily accessible. Figure 13.3 illustrates conceptually a simple way in which a group of chain heads might be stored. Notice that the entries are sorted by value of CUSTOMER_ID, so that a simple search algorithm can be used to quickly locate any particular entry. In practice, chain heads are stored in a variety of ways, depending on the particular application.

Chain Traversing

The chain is a powerful tool, because the pointers may be utilized by programs—either DBMS utilities or user-written—to move about easily from one record to another. For example, suppose that we wish to display all of the records corresponding to CUSTOMER_ID = 12122. Figure 13.4 illustrates a simple algorithm for accomplishing this. The process of accessing successive members of a chain, as outlined in the figure, is called chain **traversing.** This may be done for many different purposes, such as the display, deletion, or modification of one or more of the records.

Figure 13.4

Algorithm for finding and outputting members of a particular chain.

```
1. POINT  <---- Contents ( Chain Head )

2. Read the record from the address contained in POINT
   into a holding BUFFER

3. Output the record in BUFFER

4. POINT <---- Value of the PNTR field of the record
   in BUFFER

5. IF   Contents ( POINT ) = NULL

   THEN Terminate this algorithm

   ELSE Go to Step 2
```

Notes

STEP 1: The contents of the chain head (an address) is stored in the variable named POINT

STEP 2: The record at the address given by the contents of POINT is read into BUFFER, a temporary holding area in primary storage

STEP 3: The record in BUFFER is output

STEP 4: With respect to the record in BUFFER: If the contents of the PNTR field is NULL, the searching process ends. Otherwise, the contents are copied into POINT, and the process continues.

Chain Diagrams

When discussing record chains, it is often convenient to use diagrams that depict the physical connections among the records in one or more chains. Figure 13.5 illustrates this type of diagram for the chain corresponding to CUSTOMER_ID = 12122 in table 13.2. In this figure, each rectangle represents an ORDERS record. The top half of a rectangle represents user data for that record, and the bottom half denotes that part of the record reserved for pointers. The lines with arrows indicate the connections between records via the pointers. Numbers in parentheses in the figure indicate record addresses. The oval shape in the figure represents the chain head.

Note that the records in figure 13.5 are shown to be next to each other. In fact, the records may be widely scattered about the disk, being physically far removed from one another. For this reason, the type of diagram shown in the figure may be thought of as a *logical* representation of the chain.

Figure 13.5

A chain diagram:
pictorial of the ORDERS
records shown in table
13.2 corresponding to a
CUSTOMER_ID value of
12122.

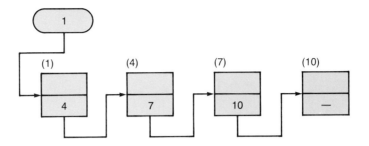

Working with Chains

When the records in a file are grouped into chains by sets of pointers, any changes to the file are likely to be accompanied by alterations to one or more pointers. In this section, we shall investigate the ways in which chains must be altered to reflect file changes.

Adding records. Suppose that a new record for CUSTOMER_ID = 12122 is to be added to the ORDERS file. This addition can be looked at as a two-step process, the first of which is the *physical* writing of the record to the file; we shall assume that the record is written to address 11. After the record has been written, it must be *logically* attached to the chain corresponding to CUSTOMER_ID = 12122, shown in figure 13.5.

Referring to this figure, the decision must be made as to where on the chain the new record should be attached. Because the chain simply represents all of the ORDERS records corresponding to CUSTOMER_ID = 12122, it would seem reasonable to assume that the new record could be placed *anywhere* in the chain. If we recall that chain heads are always accessible, we may conclude that the simplest place to add the record is at the start of the chain, because the address of the first chain member is given directly by the corresponding chain head.

Figure 13.6(a) gives a simple algorithm for adding the new record to the chain, and figure 13.6(b) illustrates the chain after the addition of the record.

Notice that by adding records in this manner, a chain traversal will access the records in reverse historical order—the last record to be added to the chain will be the first one accessed, and so on. Also, in this particular example, the logical position of each ORDERS record in the chain is immaterial, since the purpose of the chain is merely to serve as a tool for rapidly locating all of the records corresponding to a particular customer. Thus, each new record is placed at the beginning of a chain simply as a matter of convenience. In some circumstances, however, the logical ordering of the chain members is significant, as we shall see later in this chapter.

The insertion of a record into a chain is strictly a matter of setting pointer values. That is, the logical position of a record in a chain is independent of the actual physical location of the record in the file. This independence between physical and logical positions is an important one, because it allows the same group of records to be accessed in many different ways.

Figure 13.6
Adding a new record to a chain. (a) Algorithm; (b) a new record added to the chain shown in figure 13.5.

1. Get the address of the first record in the chain from the appropriate chain head

2. Place this address in the PNTR field of the new record (Record 11)

3. Replace the value of the chain head with the address of the new record

(b)

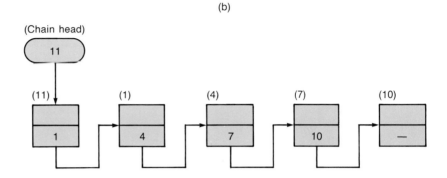

The original value of the chain head has been replaced with the address of the new record

Figure 13.7
Deletion of record 7 from its chain. The dotted arrow indicates the new connection established by the new pointer value in record 4. Note that record 7 is logically deleted from the chain, even though it may still be physically present in the file.

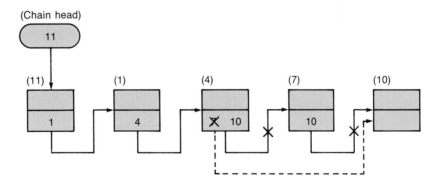

Deleting records. Suppose that we wish to delete record 7 from the ORDERS file shown in figure 13.6. Again, this can be looked at as a two-step process, the first of which is to remove record 7 from its chain, as shown in figure 13.7. This is accomplished simply by changing the pointer of the record immediately preceding record 7, namely record 4. The new pointer value is set to the address of the record immediately following record 7: record 10.

Record 7 must also be deleted from the file. The exact manner in which this is done is highly system-dependent. In some cases, the space occupied by the record is immediately made available for use. Other systems set an "erased" bit or byte in the record—the record is logically removed from the file, but the space is unavailable until a system reorganization of the file is performed.

Modifying existing records. The modification of an existing record may or may not involve alteration to existing pointers, depending on which field is to be modified. If any field other than CUSTOMER_ID is to be changed, the record remains where it is in its chain. However, if the value of CUSTOMER_ID must be modified (which would usually occur because an incorrect value was originally entered) the record must be removed from the existing chain and added to the chain corresponding to the new value of CUSTOMER_ID. This would involve changing pointers as described in the preceding sections.

Sorted Chains

In the preceding example, the chain was formed without any regard for record ordering: each new record was added to the beginning of the chain. This approach is suitable for those situations where the order in which records are retrieved is immaterial. However, there are many situations in which it is desirable to retrieve records in some particular order. This can be accomplished using slight modifications to the techniques discussed for creating and maintaining chains.

As an example, suppose that we wish to be able to access the ORDERS records for each customer, sorted by the date of order. This can be accomplished as follows. As each new record is added to a particular chain, it is *not* added to the beginning of that chain. Instead, it is placed in a logical position so that the chain of records is sorted by the values of the ORDER_DATE field. Thus, the record with the smallest value of ORDER_DATE is kept at the beginning of the chain, the record with the next smallest value is put next in the chain, and so on.

Table 13.3 shows the same file of ORDERS records used in previous examples, but in this case, each chain is sorted by the value of ORDER_DATE. The top part of figure 13.8 illustrates the set of records shown in figure 13.5, rearranged so that they are sorted by ORDER_DATE. Note that the *physical* ordering of the records remains the same; only the pointers have been altered.

Adding and deleting records. When adding records to sorted chains, the techniques described earlier for dealing with pointers must be modified. As an illustration, let us assume that a new record is to be added to the chain for CUSTOMER_ID = 12122 shown in figure 13.8, and that the value of ORDER_DATE for this record is 1/28/82. We also assume that the address of the new record is 11.

Table 13.3

ORDERS File with the Records Sorted by ORDER_DATE

RELATIVE ADDRESS	CUSTOMER_ID	ORDER_ID	ORDER_DATE	ITEM_NO	QNTY	PNTR	
1	12122	33148	1/15/82	P3442	15	10	
2	22143	11358	9/18/81	S9874	75	6	←head
3	8233	22184	11/15/81	P3442	5	—	
4	12122	22984	12/05/81	S9874	25	1	←head
5	98344	98712	2/27/82	L357	62	9	←head
6	22143	33091	10/07/81	P3442	1	—	
7	12122	24981	4/05/82	S9874	100	—	
8	8233	20971	9/25/81	L357	65	3	←head
9	98344	10006	4/28/82	P3442	2	—	
10	12122	92836	2/02/82	S9874	15	7	

Figure 13.8
The chain shown in figure 13.5, sorted by ORDER_DATE. Also, record 11 is shown being added to the appropriate place in the chain, indicated by dotted lines.

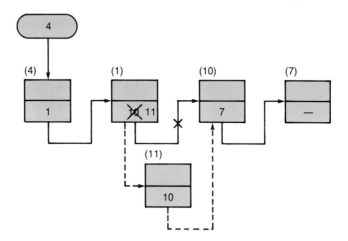

Before record 11 can be added to the chain, its exact position in the chain must be determined. This is accomplished by traversing the chain from the beginning, looking for the first record with a value of ORDER_DATE greater than that of the new record. In this example, record 11 must go between records 1 and 10. The changes that must then be made to the chain pointers are the following:

- The pointer of record 11 is set to the pointer value currently in record 1: 10
- The pointer of record 1 is changed to the address of the new record: 11

Figure 13.8 illustrates this process.

A record may be deleted from a chain by reversing this process. Again, the deletion involves two steps: the logical deletion from the chain, and the deletion from the file itself.

Independence between logical and physical ordering. As in previous examples, the order of records in a sorted chain is completely independent of the physical locations of those records in the file: the chain order is a logical sequence created by the particular values of the PNTR field for that group of records. In the previous example, the sequence was determined by the values of the ORDER_DATE field. In this respect, the chain structure is similar in its effect to that of an index, which also allows access to a group of records in a particular order.

Extensions to the Simple Chain Structure

Many variations exist on the simple chain structure previously described. The purpose of these variations is to enhance the flexibility with which a file of records may be accessed. In this section, we shall examine some of these variations.

As an introduction to more complex types of chains, we shall reconsider the problem of deleting records from chains. Suppose that the ORDERS file shown in table 13.2 is being casually scanned by a user, and for some reason (s)he decides to delete record 10. As discussed earlier, the pointer of the record that logically precedes 10 in the chain must be altered. Exactly how can that preceding record be located? The answer is that with the structure as shown in figure 13.5, the chain must be traversed from the beginning, constantly keeping track of the address of the record previous to the one being examined. When record 10 is located, the address of its previous record will then be known, and its pointer can thus be altered as necessary. Note that the appropriate chain head can be found by using the value of CUSTOMER_ID for record 10.

For long chains, this traversal process can be quite costly in terms of both time and resources, due to the large number of disk accesses required. Consequently, it would be extremely desirable to avoid this process by finding a direct method for accessing the record that logically precedes the one being accessed.

Table 13.4

ORDERS File with Reverse Pointers

RELATIVE ADDRESS	CUSTOMER_ID	ORDER_ID	ORDER_DATE	ITEM_NO	QNTY	POINTERS		
						FWRD	RVRSE	
1	12122	33148	1/15/82	P3442	15	10	4	
2	22143	11358	9/18/81	S9874	75	6	—	←head
3	8233	22184	11/15/81	P3442	5	—	8	
4	12122	22984	12/05/81	S9874	25	1	—	←head
5	98344	98712	2/27/82	L357	62	9	—	←head
6	22143	33091	10/07/81	P3442	1	—	2	
7	12122	24981	4/05/82	S9874	100	—	10	
8	8233	20971	9/25/81	L357	65	3	—	←head
9	98344	10006	4/28/82	P3442	2	—	5	
10	12122	92836	2/02/82	S9874	15	7	1	

Doubly-linked Chains

One common solution to the traversal problem described above is to introduce a second set of pointers, commonly known as **reverse pointers.** The use of this type of pointer is illustrated in table 13.4, which shows the same ORDERS data as table 13.3, but with the addition of a new field that contains the reverse pointers. To distinguish between the two different types of pointers, the original ones will be referred to as **forward pointers,** because each one refers to the *next* logical record in the chain. By contrast, each reverse pointer refers to the *previous* record in a chain.

A chain that contains both forward and reverse pointers is said to be **doubly-linked.** By contrast, a chain containing only forward pointers is called a **singly-linked chain.** Doubly-linked chains are frequently used because of the ease with which records can be deleted from the chains. They are also useful when it is desirable to traverse a chain in reverse order, a not uncommon situation. For example, if it were desired to locate a particular record that was known to be near the end of a chain, it would make sense to search the chain from the end rather than from the beginning, particularly if the chain contained a large number of records.

The chain diagram for the set of ORDERS records corresponding to CUS-TOMER_ID = 12122, with the inclusion of both forward and reverse pointers,

Figure 13.9
A chain with both
forward and reverse
pointers.

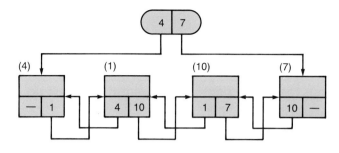

Figure 13.10
Logical deletion of
record 10 from the
chain shown in figure
13.9. Even though
record 10 may
physically remain in the
file, it has been
removed from the
chain.

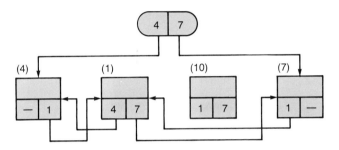

is shown in figure 13.9. Notice that the chain head now contains two pointers, one for the beginning of the chain, and the other for the end.

Deleting records. Referring once again to the problem of deleting record 10, we can now demonstrate how the presence of reverse pointers greatly simplifies the task. As mentioned above, the record immediately preceding 10 in the chain must have its forward pointer changed. Because of the reverse pointer in record 10, the preceding record is directly accessible, and its forward pointer can be changed to a value of 7, which is the address of the record in the chain directly after 10. However, since each record contains backward pointers, the reverse pointer of record 7 must also be changed to a value of 1. The result of this logical deletion process is illustrated in figure 13.10.

Adding records. The addition of a new record to an existing doubly-linked chain also involves the alteration of several pointers. Figure 13.11 illustrates the process of adding a new record, record 11, to the chain shown in figure 13.9. Both the forward pointer of record 1 and the reverse pointer of record 10 must be changed to a value of 11. The forward and reverse pointers of record 11 must be set to 10 and 1, respectively.

Figure 13.11
Addition of a record to
the doubly-linked chain
shown in figure 13.9.

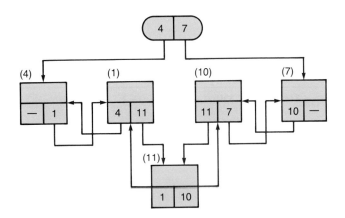

Pros and cons of doubly-linked chains. The use of doubly-linked chains offers greatly increased speed for record deletion, and the advantage of being able to choose the direction in which a chain is searched. As usual, there is a price to be paid, which in this case is: (1) the extra storage needed for the reverse pointers, and (2) the time required to adjust the second set of pointers whenever a chain update is made. The amount of storage needed for each pointer is system-dependent, but a typical value is two bytes per pointer per record. Usually, the price is more than offset by the advantages, and most DBMS's that use chains utilize the doubly-linked variety.

Rings

Another improvement to the structures discussed so far would be the ability to *completely* traverse a chain starting from *any* record in that chain. For example, we might be doing a record-by-record scan of the ORDERS file. Having come across a record of interest, we might then wish to view all other ORDERS records for that customer.

This type of capability can be accomplished by a minor variation of the chain structure, namely one in which the forward pointer of the last record in the chain is set to the address of the first record in the chain. Similarly, the reverse pointer of the first record in the chain is set to the address of the last record in the chain. By making these simple alterations, a doubly-linked chain becomes a doubly-linked **ring.** Figure 13.12 and table 13.5 illustrate this type of structure.

Singly- and doubly-linked rings are important tools for traversing sets of records. They are also useful when dealing with structures involving records from several files. This subject will be discussed later in the chapter. Throughout the remainder of this chapter, the term *chains* will be used to include the special case of rings, unless specifically stated otherwise.

Table 13.5

ORDERS File with End Pointers That Form Rings

RELATIVE ADDRESS	CUSTOMER_ID	ORDER_ID	ORDER_DATE	ITEM_NO	QNTY	POINTERS FWRD	RVRSE	
1	12122	33148	1/15/82	P3442	15	10	4	
2	22143	11358	9/18/81	S9874	75	6	6	←head
3	8233	22184	11/15/81	P3442	5	8	8	
4	12122	22984	12/05/81	S9874	25	1	7	←head
5	98344	98712	2/27/82	L357	62	9	9	←head
6	22143	33091	10/07/81	P3442	1	2	2	
7	12122	24981	4/05/82	S9874	100	4	10	
8	8233	20971	9/25/81	L357	65	3	3	←head
9	98344	10006	4/28/82	P3442	2	5	5	
10	12122	92836	2/02/82	S9874	15	7	1	

Figure 13.12
A doubly-linked ring structure. Records at each end of the chain have their pointers set to allow direct access to the opposite end.

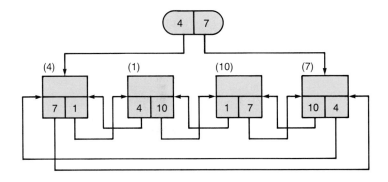

ORDERS File with a Second Set of Pointers

RELATIVE ADDRESS	CUSTOMER_ID	ORDER_ID	ORDER_DATE	ITEM_NO	QNTY	FORWARD POINTERS	
						CUST_ID	ITEM_NO
1	12122	33148	1/15/82	P3442	15	4 ←head	3 ←head
2	22143	11358	9/18/81	S9874	75	6 ←head	4 ←head
3	8233	22184	11/15/81	P3442	5	8 ←head	6
4	12122	22984	12/05/81	S9874	25	7	7
5	98344	98712	2/27/82	L357	62	9 ←head	8 ←head
6	22143	33091	10/07/81	P3442	1	2	9
7	12122	24981	4/05/82	S9874	100	10	10
8	8233	20971	9/25/81	L357	65	3	5
9	98344	10006	4/28/82	P3442	2	5	1
10	12122	92836	2/02/82	S9874	15	1	2

Multilists

In the examples given so far, the chains of ORDERS records have been grouped according to the values of the CUSTOMER_ID field. That is, all records corresponding to a particular customer are linked together via pointers. In a very real sense, the CUSTOMER_ID field is a secondary key for the ORDERS file: given a particular value of CUSTOMER_ID, all of the associated ORDERS records can be quickly located by using the appropriate chain.

Frequently, it is desirable to access a file by more than one secondary key. For example, we may wish to find all of the ORDERS records that correspond to a particular order item (note that in all of the examples used in this chapter, each ORDERS record contains a single order item). This may be accomplished by extending the methods developed so far: namely, by the addition of a second set of pointers to each ORDERS record, with a corresponding set of chain heads. These pointers logically group the ORDERS records according to the value of ITEM_NO, as illustrated in table 13.6. In this table, only forward pointers are shown, and each chain is closed into a ring.

Each record in the ORDERS file has become a member of more than one chain. This is commonly known as a **multiple-chain,** or **multilist** structure.

Figure 13.13

A subset of records
from table 13.6. Each
record is a member of
two chains, one
corresponding to
CUST_ID, and the other
to ITEM_NO. Only
forward pointers are
shown.

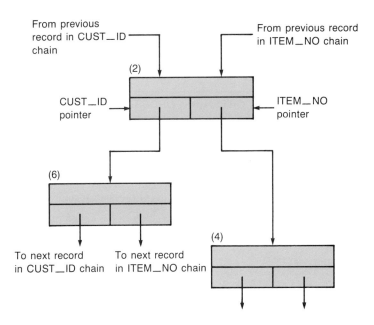

Figure 13.13 illustrates the logical connections for a small subset of records from table 13.6. Because each record is a member of two distinct chains, one based on CUSTOMER_ID, and the other based on ITEM_NO, it is possible to perform complex file searches. For example, we might traverse a particular chain based on CUSTOMER_ID in order to find a specific record. Once that record has been located, the corresponding chain based on ITEM_NO could then be traversed, so that we could locate all orders corresponding to that particular item.

Overhead costs.   In principle, records in a file may belong to as many chains as desired, possibly one for each record field. Each chain may be singly-linked, doubly-linked, or closed into rings. In practice, a secondary key on a particular field is established when it is known that the records will need to be accessed frequently by that field. However, for each chain type (that is, for each secondary key) there is the usual price to pay—the extra disk storage needed for the pointers. For example, with the commonly-used doubly-linked chains, an average of four bytes per record are needed for each type of chain that is established. As in many other situations, the trade-off is between speed of data access and required disk storage, and usually the former overshadows the latter.

Comparison between Chains and Indexes

In chapter 4, the subject of indexes (sometimes referred to as inverted lists) was discussed at some length. In principle, indexes and chains have two important functions in common: (1) they both are tools that allow rapid access to a group of one or more records; and (2) they allow access to a file of records in different sequences. In this section, we shall briefly discuss the major advantages of each type of data structure. In some sense, this comparison is academic because the user rarely has the choice of which type of data structure to use in a particular application. On the other hand, the comparison has value in that it helps to focus on some of the important issues, such as data storage requirements.

Overhead Costs

The basic structure of both indexes and chains involve the use of record pointers. With chains, the pointers are included with each record, whereas all of the pointers of an index are kept together in a separate file. For greatest efficiency, chains are usually doubly-linked, thus requiring two pointers per record per chain. Indexes, on the other hand, have no need of anything equivalent to backward pointers, since all of the pointers are grouped together in a single area. From this point of view, indexes have a space-saving advantage. On the other hand, large indexes are commonly built in multiple levels in order to avoid excessive disk accesses (see chapter 4). These levels introduce additional storage requirements, often equalling or exceeding twice the amount of storage needed for an equivalent single-level index.

Because these two factors affect storage requirements in different ways, it is difficult to say that one type of data structure has a clear advantage over the other in terms of required secondary storage.

Producing ordered lists. When one or more complete subsets of records from within a file are to be accessed, there is no clear advantage of one type of data structure over the other. For chains then, there will be approximately as many disk accesses needed as there are members in the chain. On the other hand, using an index to access a subset of records is a little more costly in terms of number of disk accesses, because the index itself usually resides on the disk. Therefore, the number of disk accesses necessary to read a given number of records will be equal to that number of records, *plus* additional disk accesses needed to read the index itself. However, the design of indexes is normally optimized so that the latter is a very small incremental increase.

Locating specific records. Suppose that we wish to locate a particular OR-DERS record, known to belong to a specific customer. If a chain is being used as the basic data structure for record access, the chain head for that customer must first be located. The chain is then traversed until the desired record is found. On the average, the number of disk accesses needed to find the record will be equal to one-half the number of records in the chain. For large chains this obviously can be quite costly.

Using an index to locate a particular record is quite a different matter. Because of the structure of an index, and also because of the efficiency of searching algorithms, only a small number of disk accesses are required to locate a particular index entry, regardless of the number of records in the file. In general, an index is a much more efficient mechanism for finding individual records.

Adding records. The cost of adding a new record to a chain depends greatly on whether or not the records are maintained in an ordered manner on the chain. If the records are unordered, each new addition to a chain can be added to the beginning of the chain, and only a small number of disk accesses are needed to accomplish this. In terms of number of accesses, this process is comparable to the adding of a new entry to an index. This is because searching an index to find the appropriate position for a new entry is virtually identical to searching for an existing entry in the index—only a small number of accesses are required.

On the other hand, if a chain is being used to maintain records in a specific order, then the addition of a new record requires a traversal of the chain in order to find the appropriate position for the new entry. On the average, the required number of disk accesses will be equal to one-half of the number of records in the chain. Again, in this case the index structure offers considerable advantage over the chain.

Deleting and modifying records. From the preceding discussions, we can see that whenever a specific record must be accessed by using a chain, many disk accesses may be required, the exact number depending on the length of the chain. On the other hand, an index allows any particular record to be found with very few disk accesses, regardless of the size of the file.

Error recovery. Chains offer one definite advantage over indexes: recovery following accidental data loss. If, for any reason, one pointer in a doubly-linked chain is lost, the entire chain is still accessible by using the other half of the chain. Furthermore, the lost pointer can even be reconstructed. By contrast, if a pointer within an index is lost, the entire index must be reconstructed, and for large files this may require a considerable amount of time.

Table 13.7 outlines the relative merits of chains and indexes.

Chains for Single Files: An Overview

Chains are extremely valuable for minimizing the processing times associated with handling single data files. The tasks of searching, reporting, and updating can all be greatly enhanced by the use of chains. Doubly-linked chains are much more commonly used than singly-linked ones, because they allow for greater flexibility in maneuvering within a file.

Almost invariably, chains are maintained by the database management system. As records are added, deleted, and modified, the DBMS is responsible for updating pointers as needed. In addition, a DBMS usually includes utility routines for navigating through record chains, under the control of the user. Thus, a user may issue commands equivalent to "Find the beginning of a particular chain," "Display each record in the chain," and so on. Each command invokes one or more DBMS utilities to perform the required task.

Invariably, the database designer has the option of specifying which fields are to be maintained as secondary indexes in the form of chains. Sometimes the designer may even have the option of choosing whether singly- or doubly-linked

Table 13.7	Relative Merits of Chains and Indexes

Item	Chains Versus Indexes*
Secondary storage requirements	No clear advantage for either
Accessing complete subsets of records	No clear advantage for either
Locating a specific record	Indexes superior to chains
Adding a new record: unordered chains	No clear advantage for either
Adding a new record: ordered chains	Indexes superior to chains
Deleting and modifying records	Indexes superior to chains
Recovery of a lost pointer	Possible with doubly-linked chains; not possible with indexes

*Major differences due to numbers of required disk accesses.

chains are to be maintained by the DBMS. Beyond that, however, database users are usually completely unaware of the existence of the underlying data structures.

For some data manipulation processes, indexes are clearly superior to chains. Why then are chains ever used in preference to indexes? The answer lies in the fact that chains are extremely advantageous in building structures consisting of more than one record-type, which forms the subject of the following section.

Multiple-file Data Structures

In the previous sections, we have discussed some of the basic data structures commonly used for dealing with single data files. In general, however, a database may consist of several files, often with many relationships among them. In this section, we shall extend the data structure concepts described earlier to deal with multiple-file situations. It will be seen that using chains, records of many different types can be logically connected in a variety of ways. In particular, a one-to-many relationship between two files can be directly represented with a chain structure, and this fact forms the basis of many complex structures.

Representing a One-to-Many Relationship

In order to demonstrate the various ways in which chain structures are utilized, we shall use the example of the CUSTOMERS/ORDERS database discussed in previous chapters (see chapter 7, for example). Recall that a one-to-many relationship exists between CUSTOMERS and ORDERS: each customer may have zero, one, or several associated orders, whereas each order is associated with exactly one customer.

Table 13.8

CUSTOMERS and ORDERS Files
with Connecting Pointers

	CUSTOMERS		
RELATIVE ADDRESS	CUSTOMER_ID	CUSTOMER DATA	CHAIN HEAD*
101	12122		4
102	22143		2
103	8233		8
104	98344		5

			ORDERS			
RELATIVE ADDRESS	CUSTOMER_ID	ORDER_ID	ORDER_DATE	ITEM_NO	QNTY	PNTR
1	12122	33148	1/15/82	P3442	15	10
2	22143	11358	9/18/81	S9874	75	6
3	8233	22184	11/15/81	P3442	5	—
4	12122	22984	12/05/81	S9874	25	1
5	98344	98712	2/27/82	L357	62	9
6	22143	33091	10/07/81	P3442	1	—
7	12122	24981	4/05/82	S9874	100	—
8	8233	20971	9/25/81	L357	65	3
9	98344	10006	4/28/82	P3442	2	—
10	12122	92836	2/02/82	S9874	15	7

*Each value points to the start of the ORDERS chain corresponding to the value of CUSTOMER_ID.

A singly-linked chain can be used to logically connect related records in the two files. Table 13.8 shows how this is accomplished, using a set of sample data for the two files. As in previous examples, a separate chain of ORDERS records is established for each customer. However, in this case the CUSTOMERS file contains links to the ORDERS file, by virtue of the values contained in the column labelled CHAIN HEAD. Each value in this column is a pointer to the start of the corresponding chain of ORDERS records. We have thus discovered a natural resting place for the chain heads that were discussed in the previous section!

Figure 13.14
Record chains involving
records from two
distinct files.

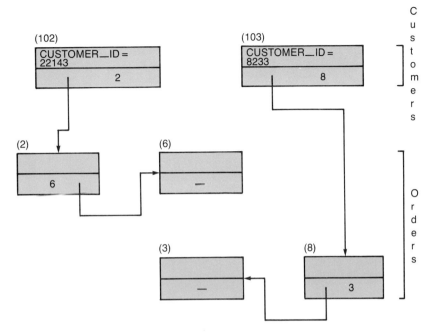

Figure 13.14 illustrates a diagram for a few of the records shown in table 13.8. As shown, each CUSTOMERS record is the start of the chain for all associated ORDERS records.

The complete set of chains linking the two files of records form the physical implementation of the one-to-many relationship that logically exists between the files. To illustrate the usefulness of this, suppose that we wish to find all of the ORDERS records for CUSTOMER_ID = 12122. This can be accomplished by the following procedure:

1. Search the CUSTOMERS file for the record corresponding to a CUSTOMER_ID value of 12122
2. When the record is found, read the value in the CHAIN_HEAD field
3. Find the ORDERS record at the address given in CHAIN_HEAD
4. Traverse the ORDERS chain

If the CUSTOMERS file is large, step 1 could be quite lengthy. In order to reduce the search time, a CUSTOMERS index could be created on the CUSTOMER_ID field (many DBMS's allow both chain and index structures to be used).

Terminology. In terms of the preceding data structures, each CUSTOMERS record is called a **parent** record, and each of the ORDERS records associated with a particular parent is called a **child** record. Thus, referring to table 13.8, the CUSTOMERS record with CUSTOMER_ID = 12122 is the parent to the four associated ORDERS records (the children). All of the children records related to the same parent are referred to as **siblings.**

Figure 13.15
Closing the rings of the
chains in figure 13.14.

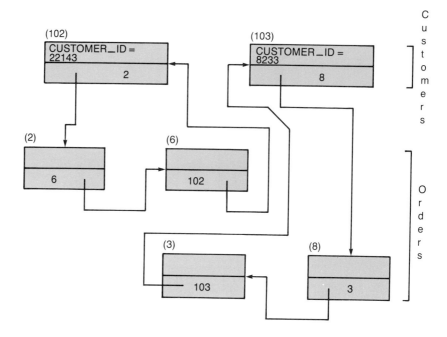

Additional Data Structures

Although the data structure shown in figure 13.14 allows easy access to all of the ORDERS records corresponding to a given CUSTOMERS record, the converse is not true. For example, suppose that during a casual scan of the ORDERS file, we have come across a particular record that seems to be interesting, and we would like to view the corresponding CUSTOMERS record. Using the data structure in figure 13.14, there is no simple way to accomplish this. Consequently, we search for additional structures to facilitate this type of flexibility. Two commonly-used approaches are discussed in the following section.

Closing the chain. A useful ring structure can be created by modifying the chains illustrated in figure 13.14, as follows: for each ORDERS chain, the address of the corresponding parent CUSTOMERS record is placed in the pointer field of the last record in the chain. Thus, when an ORDERS record is located by *any* means, the corresponding parent record can be accessed by traversing the chain to the end, and then back to the parent record. Figure 13.15 illustrates the resulting ring structure.

A common extension is the doubly-linked ring, as shown in figure 13.16. The advantages to this type of structure were discussed earlier in this chapter.

Parent pointers. The primary disadvantage of using ring structures to locate parent records is that for long rings, a great many disk accesses are necessary in order to complete a traversal back to the parent. This problem can be solved by

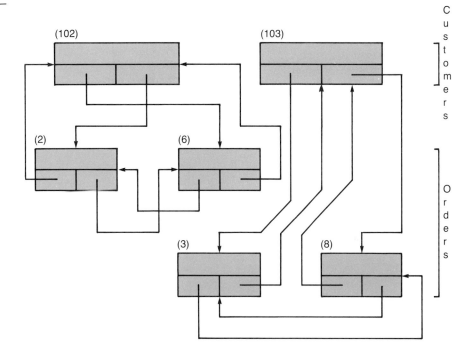

Figure 13.16
Doubly-linked rings
involving records from
two files.

the addition of a **parent pointer** to each ORDERS record, which contains the address of the corresponding parent record. Figure 13.17 illustrates this data structure.

With the inclusion of parent pointers, any ORDERS record can be used to access directly its parent record. As usual, the price is the additional storage space necessary for the pointers. Nevertheless, parent pointers are commonly utilized in database systems, because of the frequent need to access a parent record from one of its children.

Summary of Two-file Data Structures

Chains, rings, and parent pointers are all data structures commonly used for maintaining one-to-many relationships between pairs of files, and these structures allow rapid access to related records in the files. It is the task of a database designer to indicate to a DBMS that a one-to-many relationship exists between two files. It is then the task of the DBMS to maintain the necessary pointers. In addition, the various search processes of interest to users are usually carried out by programs that are an integral part of a DBMS. These processes would include locating all children of a particular parent, finding the parent of a particular child, and so on. These types of tasks are normally initiated by user-generated commands to the DBMS.

Figure 13.17
Doubly-linked rings
involving records from
two files, with the
inclusion of parent
pointers.

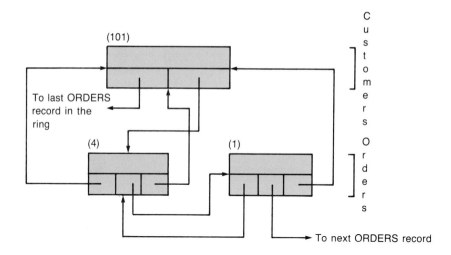

Structure of ORDERS records:

User data		
Reverse pointer	Forward pointer	Parent pointer

Trees

Using the tools just described, complex data structures involving many different files can be constructed. In the following sections, we shall describe the most common types of these structures, the first of which is the **tree.**

Also known as a **hierarchy,** a tree is a general type of data structure consisting of various elements, or **nodes.** Many different kinds of objects can be described by tree structures, including record-types and individual records.

Rules for Tree Structures

A typical tree structure is shown in figure 13.18. The following rules govern the relationships that can exist among the various nodes in a tree, regardless of what the nodes represent.

- The nodes are divided into **levels.** The node at the highest level is called the **root** node. Thus, in figure 13.18, A is the root.
- Nodes may be divided into groups. One member of each group is called the **parent,** and it is one level above the others, which are called the **children** of that parent. Thus, node A is a parent to nodes B and C.

Figure 13.18
A typical tree structure.
Each node represents a
particular record-type.
Each connected pair
represents a one-to-
many relationship.

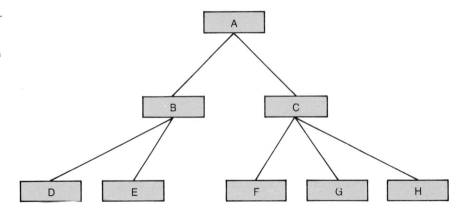

- Each parent node may have zero, one, or several child nodes. On the other hand, any single node may have only one parent node.
- A particular node may be the parent to several other nodes and at the same time be the child of yet another node. For instance, B is a child to A and also a parent to D and E.
- In principle, there is no limit to the number of levels that may exist in a tree structure (in figure 13.18 there are 3).

Using Trees to Represent Complex Relationships

Tree structures are well suited for representing groups of record-types among which there exist various one-to-many relationships. Figure 13.18 illustrates such a grouping if we interpret each individual node to represent a record-type. The figure is then known as a data-structure diagram. The relationship between a parent and each of its children is one-to-many. Typically, data-structure diagrams of this type use straight lines to connect pairs of record-types. If no arrows are drawn on the lines, it is understood that each connected pair represents a one-to-many relationship.

Using Trees to Represent a Structure Occurrence

A tree structure may also be used to describe one or more occurrences of part of a structure diagram. For example, figure 13.19 shows occurrences of part of the structure shown in figure 13.18. Thus, A1 is a particular record of type A. It has two children of type B: B1 and B2. It also has three children of type C. Record B1 has two children of type D and three of type E.

Figure 13.19
Specific occurrences of
part of the structure
shown in figure 13.18.
Each node represents a
single record.

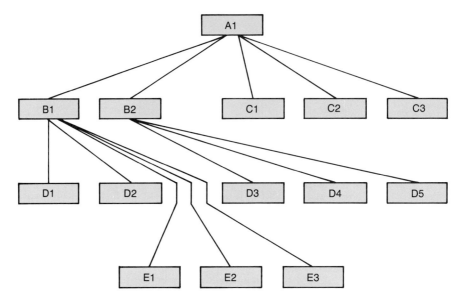

Thus, we have used tree structures in two entirely different contexts. In one case (figure 13.18), the general relationships among a group of record-types is represented; in another, (figure 13.19) a group of specific records is represented, along with the relationships among them.

The Physical Representation of Trees

The structure shown in figure 13.19 illustrates the logical relationships among a specific group of records, but it does not indicate how the relationships are actually implemented. In this section, we shall indicate the more common ways of creating the physical links between records.

Using chains to represent trees. The various forms of a chain, described in earlier sections, are the most commonly-used structures for representing trees. As an example, a subset of the records depicted in figure 13.19 is shown in figure 13.20, illustrating the physical links between records. The arrows in this figure represent pointer values that lead from one record to another. For the purposes of this example, only forward chain pointers have been shown. However, in practice many of the other extensions to simple forward pointer chains are also commonly used to implement record trees. These include the following: (1) reverse pointers, linking a record with its prior sibling in a chain; (2) parent pointers, linking a record with its parent; (3) rings, formed by pointers in the first and last members of a chain, referring back to the parent record.

Figure 13.21 illustrates the various types of pointers that could be contained within a single record, B1, from figure 13.20. Two pointers are used for referring to children records of types D and E. Two additional pointers refer to the next

Figure 13.20
Records shown in
figure 13.19, illustrating
logical record
connections via
pointers. For simplicity,
only child and sibling
pointers are shown—
parent and reverse
pointers are omitted.

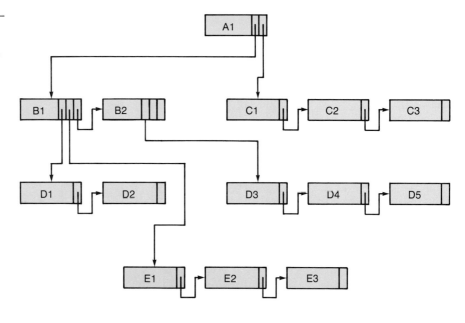

Figure 13.21
Details of the structure
of record of type B,
from figure 13.20,
showing both data and
pointer fields.

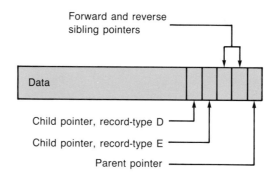

Forward and reverse
sibling pointers

Data

Child pointer, record-type D

Child pointer, record-type E

Parent pointer

and prior sibling records in the same chain as B1. Finally, a parent pointer contains the address of the parent record of B1.

Chains are one of the most common way of implementing tree structures. However, other techniques are occasionally used.

Multiple-child pointers. The set of records shown in figure 13.19 is again used as an example, and figure 13.22 illustrates the physical implementation using multiple-child pointers. With this type of structure, each parent record has a variable number of child pointers, one for each child record. One of the difficulties with this type of structure is that each record must either be variable-length, or else fixed-length with enough room to accommodate the largest possible number of children. For this and other reasons, multiple-child pointers are not frequently used.

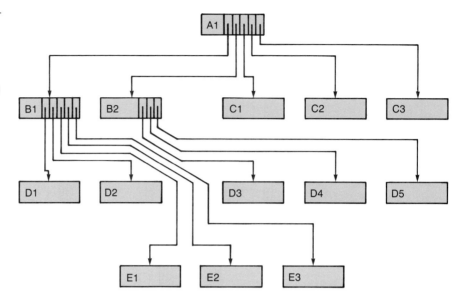

	A_1	D_1	D_2	D_3	D_4	D_5	E_1	E_2	E_3	E_4	E_5
B_1	1	1	1	0	0	0	1	1	1	0	0
B_2	1	0	0	1	1	1	0	0	0	1	1
C_1	1	0	0	0	0	0	0	0	0	0	0
C_2	1	0	0	0	0	0	0	0	0	0	0
C_3	1	0	0	0	0	0	0	0	0	0	0

Bit maps. A technique known as **bit mapping** is occasionally used to represent trees. Figure 13.23 shows a bit map corresponding to the tree in figure 13.19. As in the case of multiple-child pointers, bit maps are difficult to work with because they require a variable amount of storage.

Using indexes to represent trees. Indexes may be used to represent trees, and there are many different forms that these indexes can take. They all have in common the fact that the pointers for the various record-types are *not* embedded in the records themselves. Instead, they are gathered together in separate files. Some of the more common forms of indexes were discussed in chapter 4. In order to represent a particular tree structure, a separate index must be maintained for each one-to-many relationship. As discussed earlier, in certain situations indexes offer definite advantages over chains for representing relationships between record-types.

Figure 13.24
A logical structure that
does not conform to the
rules for trees.

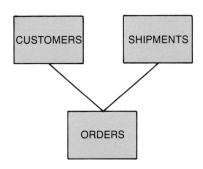

Limitations of Tree Structures

Tree structures have many important applications within the field of computing, and they are often useful for representing relationships among sets of record-types. However, there are many real-life situations that cannot be gracefully modelled by tree structures. For example, suppose that we wish to construct a data model consisting of the following three record-types:

    CUSTOMERS   [NAME, CUSTOMER_ID, ADDRESS]
    SHIPMENTS   [SHIPMENT_ID, SHIPMENT_DATE]
    ORDERS   [ORDER_NO, CUSTOMER_ID, SHIPMENT_ID]

Assuming that each customer may be associated with many orders, and that each shipment may contain many different orders for various customers, the following relationships exist:

        CUSTOMERS/ORDERS : 1/M
        SHIPMENTS/ORDERS : 1/M

The natural structure that exists among these record-types is shown in figure 13.24. A little study will reveal that this is not a valid tree structure, because the ORDERS record-type has two parent record-types. Although it is possible to model this structure with a set of trees, the resultant structures are inefficient and require considerably more storage space than other representations. In the following section, we shall examine another type of data model that is better suited to representing the types of structures shown in figure 13.24.

Networks

As mentioned earlier, a tree structure is defined in part by the restriction that each record-type may have only a single parent. However, other data structures exist that do not impose this limitation; they are collectively called **networks.**

In general, a network may be said to be *any* type of data structure involving two or more files, in which relationships exist between pairs of files. If each relationship is either a one-to-many or one-to-one, the structure is called a **simple network.** On the other hand, if the structure contains one or more many-to-many relationships, it is referred to as a **complex network.**

Figure 13.25
Occurrences of the
structure shown in
figure 13.24. Each
CUSTOMERS and
SHIPMENTS record is a
parent to zero or more
ORDERS records. A
straight line indicates
parent-child
relationships.

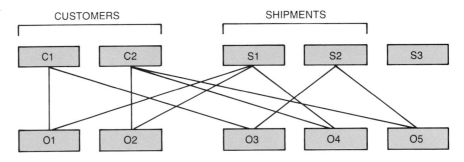

Simple Networks

Figure 13.24 illustrates an elementary example of a simple network, involving three record-types. Again, by convention, a one-to-many relationship is indicated by a straight line connecting a pair of record-types. In this example, both CUS-TOMERS and SHIPMENTS are parents to the ORDERS record-type: each customer may have many related orders, and each shipment may contain several orders.

A set of occurrences of this structure is shown in figure 13.25. Each CUS-TOMERS record is associated with a set of ORDERS records, and the same is true for each SHIPMENTS record. Furthermore, each ORDERS record may be associated with both a CUSTOMERS and a SHIPMENTS record (if an order has not yet been shipped, it will not be related to a SHIPMENTS record). For example, customer C1 is associated with orders O1 and O3; and shipment S1 is associated with orders O1, O2, and O4.

Representing simple networks with chains.   One of the most common methods of creating physical links to represent simple networks is with chains and parent pointers. An example of this is shown in figure 13.26, in which the record oc-currences shown in figure 13.25 are connected with singly-linked chains. For clarity of illustration, reverse pointers, parent pointers, and ring-closing pointers are not shown, although in practice they are frequently employed. Thus, a single ORDERS record could contain several pointers, in addition to data fields, as shown in figure 13.27. Because an ORDERS record can belong to two chains, one for CUSTOMERS and the other for SHIPMENTS, there must be a set of pointers (forward and reverse) for each. In addition, if parent pointers exist, there will be one for each of the two parent records.

The fundamental techniques used to build network structures are the same as those for tree structures. That is, a set of chains, along with other related pointers, is used to represent each one-to-many relationship. The basic difference between the two types of structures is that for trees, each child record has a single set of pointers (forward, backward, and parent) corresponding to its parent. Within a network, on the other hand, a child record has a set of pointers for each of its parents.

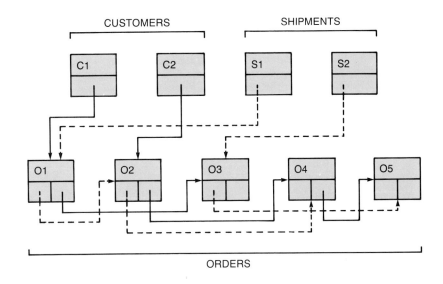

Figure 13.26
The records and
relationships shown in
figure 13.25,
implemented with
chains. Each ORDERS
record may belong to
two chains—one for a
CUSTOMER and the
other for a SHIPMENT.

CUSTOMERS

SHIPMENTS

ORDERS

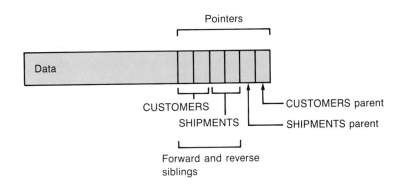

Figure 13.27
Structural details of an
ORDERS record.

Pointers

Data

CUSTOMERS

SHIPMENTS

CUSTOMERS parent

SHIPMENTS parent

Forward and reverse
siblings

Another example of a simple network is shown in figure 13.28 which shows the relationships among the following record-types:

DEPARTMENT   [DEPT_NAME, MANAGER, LOCATION]
EMPLOYEE   [EMP_NAME, ADDRESS, AGE, PHONE]
POSITION_HISTORY   [JOB_TITLE, START_DATE, END_DATE,
                         LAST_SALARY]
PROJECTS   [PROJ_TITLE, LEADER, PERCENT_TIME]

Each department has several employees, each of whom has a job history within the company. Also, an employee may be involved in several projects (one employee per project). Finally, each department is responsible for various projects. Again, the relationships between any two record-types are one-to-many, and each of these can be represented physically by a set of chains.

Figure 13.28
A simple network
structure.

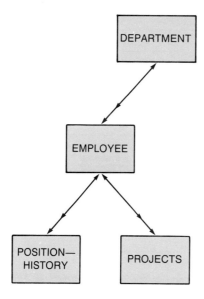

In principle, a network structure may allow any number of children record-types for a given parent record-type, and also any number of parents for each child. Furthermore, there is no inherent concept of levels, inasmuch as a one-to-many relationship can exist between *any* pair of record-types. An example of these ideas is shown in figure 13.29.

In practice, most database management systems place various types of restrictions on the structures that can be represented. For example, there is usually a maximum number of children record-types allowed per parent record-type, and vice versa. Some DBMS's permit only two levels of structure: record-types on the top level are parents, and those on the lower level are children. These and other limitations will be discussed in chapter 14, when specific types of implementations are discussed.

Complex Networks

A complex network is one in which there exists one or more many-to-many relationships. The simplest example of this is a two-file structure, such as that shown in figure 13.30(a). Most DBMS's cannot directly and/or economically represent this relationship. Instead, it is usually transformed by the designer into two one-to-many relationships, generally by the introduction of intersection record-types, as discussed in earlier chapters. Thus, the structure in figure 13.30(a) is normally replaced by that shown in figure 13.30(b), in which STUDENT_CLASS is the intersection record-type. As before, a connecting straight line indicates a one-to-many relationship.

Figure 13.29
A simple network
involving many record-
types. Each straight
line indicates a one-to-
many relationship. For a
general network
structure, the concept
of levels is
meaningless.

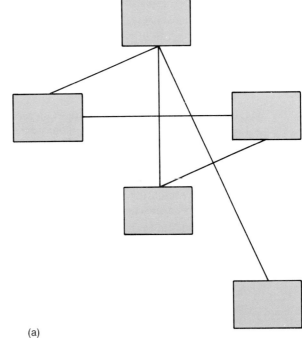

Figure 13.30
(a) Two record-types
involved in a many-to-
many relationship, and
(b) the reduction into
two one-to-many
relationships by the
introduction of the
STUDENT_CLASS
intersection record-
type.

(a)

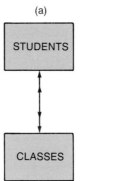

(b)

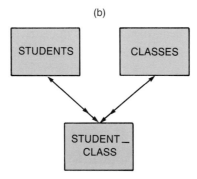

Another example of a complex network was shown in figure 9.6. Many different relationships exist in this structure; some are one-to-many, and others are many-to-many. In practice, each of the latter would need to be transformed into two one-to-many relationships.

Cycles and Loops

Often, real-world situations arise which cannot be modelled by the types of structures described. In such cases, it may be necessary to enhance a DBMS by a great deal of user programming, in order to obtain an overall model that does justice to the actual situation of interest.

There are, however, simple extensions to the network models that are adequate for representing some types of real-world circumstances. These extensions are known as **cycles** and **loops,** and each of these models is described in the following paragraphs.

Cycles

A cycle is a network type of structure in which a circular path exists among the record-types. As an example, consider the following set of record-types:

DEPARTMENT	[MAJOR, CHAIRMAN, BUILDING]
FACULTY	[FAC_NAME, DEPARTMENT, LOCATION]
STUDENT	[STUD_NAME, MAJOR, ADDRESS, GPA]

Each department has several faculty members, each of whom belongs to only one department. Also, each faculty member has several student "advisees." Finally, each student may have more than one major. The structure diagram for these record-types is shown in figure 13.31(a).

Thus, suppose that N. Weiner is an instructor in physics, and that he is an advisor of a student named G. Portnoy. Finally, assume that Mr. Portnoy has a physics major. A circular path exists, starting with the physics DEPARTMENT record, to the FACULTY record for N. Weiner, to the STUDENT record for Mr. Portnoy, and finally back to the physics record again.

Notice that because there is a many-to-many relationship between DEPARTMENT and STUDENT, an intersection record-type will usually have to be created in the actual implementation, as shown in figure 13.31(b).

Loops

A loop is a special case of a cycle, namely one in which associations exist within records of the same type. For example, consider all of the students at a given school:

STUDENTS [STUDENT_NAME, STUDENT_ID, ADDRESS, GPA]

Figure 13.31
A cycle structure.
(a) General structure
diagram; and
(b) addition of the
STUD_DEPT
intersection record-type
to remove the many-to-
many relationship
between DEPARTMENT
and STUDENT.

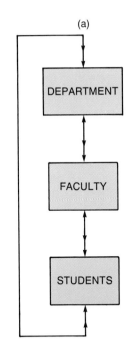

(a)

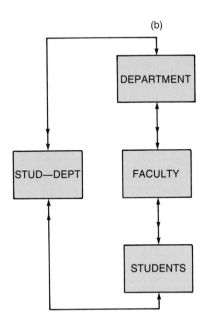

(b)

Figure 13.32
A loop structure.
(a) Structure diagram,
indicating a many-to-
many relationship
among the STUDENTS
records; (b) introduction
of FRIENDS intersection
record-type to eliminate
the many-to-many
relationship.

(a)

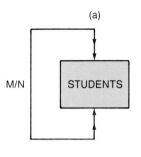

(b)

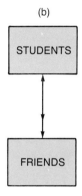

Each student will have a group of other students that (s)he considers close friends. The structure diagram for this situation is depicted in figure 13.32(a). Notice that the relationship is many-to-many. In order to implement this, an intersection record-type will usually have to be created:

FRIENDS [STUDENT_ID, FRIEND_ID]

The relationship between STUDENTS and FRIENDS is one-to-many, as depicted in figure 13.32(b).

Note that most of the data structures discussed in this chapter have not been previously mentioned in conjunction with relational database systems. In fact, most relational DBMS's depend almost exclusively on three types of data structures: records, files, and indexes. In the following chapter, we shall examine various types of DBMS's that do in fact depend heavily on chains, networks, and other related structures.

Summary

Data structures play a significant role in database management. Each type of structure is characterized by the particular way in which logically related data items are connected.

Records and files are commonly-used structures, and each has many possible variations. Within the field of database management, both fixed-length and variable-length records are used. In general, the latter occur with DBMS's that utilize either variable-length fields, multiply-occurring fields, or a combination of both.

One particularly important type of data structure is the chain, which furnishes a basic mechanism by which groups of related records can be quickly accessed. This access is accomplished in part by the use of various types of pointers, which form the links between individual records in a chain.

Several different types of chains exist, and one or more of them are often used as the basis for more complex data structures. In particular, a chain may be used to represent a one-to-many relationship between two record-types. This, in turn, forms the basis for tree and network structures, each of which is used to represent various types of real-world situations.

Trees and simple networks are similar types of data structures, in that both are built from groups of record-types consisting of one or more one-to-many relationships. The simple network structure has much more flexibility than the tree in representing different types of real-world situations. Its implementation is correspondingly more difficult because many different sets of pointers must be maintained. Because of its usefulness, however, the simple network model is the basis for a great many database systems.

A complex network structure differs from a simple network in that it may include many-to-many relationships. However, most network-oriented DBMS's cannot directly implement complex networks, requiring the database designer to reduce each many-to-many relationship to a pair of one-to-many relationships.

Each particular network-type database system has its own set of restrictions concerning what forms the networks can take. For example, some DBMS's allow any number of record-types, with relationships defined arbitrarily among them. On the other hand, other DBMS's impose very strong restrictions on the degree of complexity that may exist within a given structure. In general, the database designer must always work within the limitations of the available DBMS, and frequently considerable programming must be done in order to accommodate these limitations to the real-world situation.

Terminology

bit map
chain
chain head
complex network
cycle
delimiter
doubly-linked chain
field delimiter
hierarchy

linked list
loop
multilist
node
pointer
ring
simple network
tree
variable-length record

Review Questions

1. Define the term *data structure*. Within the context of this definition, how are records and chains similar?
2. What are the advantages of fixed-length records over variable-length? What are the disadvantages?
3. Give one or two examples of record-types where it would be highly advantageous to employ variable-length records.
4. What is the meaning of *null value?* In table 13.2, this value is indicated by the – symbol. What value should be used by a DBMS to represent a null value?
5. Explain the difference between the *physical* location of a record within a file, and the *logical* location of that record within a chain.
6. Explain the difference between the *logical* deletion of a record from a chain, and its *physical* deletion from a file.
7. What is the major advantage of a ring structure over a doubly-linked chain? Why is it necessary to include a chain head even in a ring structure?
8. What is the major advantage to each record within a file having several sets of pointers (such as shown in figure 13.13 and table 13.6)?
9. Explain the major differences between:
     a. Tree and simple network structures;
     b. Simple network and complex network structures.
10. Explain why the use of multiple-child pointers (as shown in figure 13.22) is difficult to implement.

Problems

1. Referring to figure 13.1(b), why are $ delimiters not shown at the end of each record?
2. With respect to figure 13.1(c), notice that the total record count is followed immediately by the count for the first field. How is it possible to avoid possible ambiguities in these two counts? For example, in the first record, could the number "4511" imply the following?
   a. Total record count: 451
   b. First field count: 1
3. State two ways in which a pointer field differs from an ordinary field.
4. How many values are contained in each chain head for a doubly-linked chain?
5. Referring to the chain shown in figure 13.5, suppose that it has been discovered that the CUSTOMER_ID value of record 4 is not 12122, but is actually 22143. Outline the steps necessary to place this record into the proper chain.
6. Suppose that a group of ORDERS records belongs to the chain represented by the diagram in figure 13.9. Using any convenient notation, write down an algorithm for finding and deleting any particular record of the chain. Assume that the appropriate chain head is known or can be easily found.
7. Consider the chain of sorted records shown in figure 13.8 and table 13.3. A new record, whose ORDER_DATE value is 12/25/81, is to be added to the chain. Write down the steps necessary to add the record.
8. Suppose that during the traversal of a doubly-linked ring, it is discovered that the forward pointer of one of the records has been damaged, perhaps due to a cosmic ray. Devise an algorithm for restoring the value of the lost pointer.
9. Suppose that the CUSTOMERS and ORDERS records all belong to sets of doubly-linked chains, such as shown in figure 13.17. Outline the steps needed to add a new ORDERS record to the proper chain.
10. Consider a *logical* tree structure consisting of the record-types A, B, C, and D shown in figure 13.18. This structure is implemented *physically* by chains, as shown in figure 13.20. Devise an alternate physical implemention, by using a group of indexes instead of chains.
11. The text states that network-type relationships, such as that shown in figure 13.24, cannot be "gracefully" modelled using trees. Devise a tree structure, however ungraceful, to model the relationships shown in this figure. You may find that your solution involves some data redundancy.

12. Show that in order to directly represent a many-to-many relationship with chains, it is necessary to use one of the following:
    a. Variable-length records
    b. Fixed-length records, with the condition that there is a *maximum* number of records to which any given record may be related.
13. Suppose that the logical structure in figure 13.28 is implemented with singly-linked chains. Draw an instance of the structure using a chain diagram, consisting of the following:

    • One DEPARTMENT record, D1
    • Two EMPLOYEE records, E1 and E2, both related to D1
    • Two PROJECTS records, P1 and P2. Both are related to E1, and in addition P1 is also related to D1.

14. Using a chain diagram, draw an instance of the STUDENTS_FRIENDS relationship shown in figure 13.32, consisting of records ST1, FR1, and FR2.

Chapter Fourteen

Other Types of Data Management Systems

Introduction

In previous chapters, we have studied the processes used for developing databases to represent real-world systems. We saw that the first step in this type of process involves the development of a conceptual design, which is expressed in terms of entities, relationships, and constraints. The second step consists of translating the conceptual design into a physical database design that is compatible with the database system to be used for implementation.

The emphasis up to this point has been on relational database systems, and this has been done for a number of reasons. First, the subject of database management is most easily introduced in the context of the relation model, because the associated concepts are relatively simple (compared to other types of DBMS's). Also, a great deal of the new development work in the field of database management is being done in the context of the relational approach, and most systems being developed are utilizing relational concepts. Finally, nearly all microcomputer-oriented database systems are relational, or at least have that flavor. Therefore, students are far more likely to be exposed to this type of system than to any other.

This is not to say that relational database systems are the only type of DBMS worth considering or discussing; on the contrary, many other types of database systems exist. These range from very simple software packages for microcomputers to enormously complex ones for larger machines. The purpose of this chapter is to survey the various types of database systems, other than relational ones, that are presently in common use, both for small and large computers. Because this chapter is intended as a survey, we shall not go into great depth with respect to any particular type of DBMS. Instead, discussions will be limited to those features that distinguish each general category of database system.

The first part of the chapter deals with DBMS's that are primarily oriented around larger computers. The latter part of the chapter focuses on those systems that are particularly popular in the microcomputer arena.

Up to now, we have emphasized database systems that are based on the relational model. One of the fundamental characteristics of these systems is that each table within a database is *physically* independent of the others. If a one-to-many relationship (or any other type of relationship) exists between two tables, it is contained *implicitly* within the data. In this section, we shall explore database systems of quite a different nature. Their common characteristic is that relationships among groups of records are maintained *explicitly* by direct connections between the records. Most database systems having this type of feature are known as either **network** or **hierarchical.**

General Background and History

In order to introduce the concept of direct record connections, we begin by reviewing the way in which relational systems operate, namely *without* direct connections. Consider the two-file database consisting of CUSTOMERS and ORDERS records, illustrated in figure 14.1. Part (a) of this figure illustrates the one-to-many relationship between the two record-types. Part (b) shows a few records from the database, as they would exist under the management of a relational-type database system. Note that several ORDERS records are related to the CUSTOMERS record for "J. Abercrombie." Recall that the relationship among these records exists implicitly by virtue of the common value in the CUSTOMER_ID fields.

To illustrate direct record connections, the records in figure 14.1(b) are shown again in figure 14.2. However, in this case each group of related records is logically connected into a circular chain, as indicated by the arrows in the figure. These chains are constructed in such a way that a database system can directly navigate from one record to the next. This allows all related records to be quickly and directly accessed, either for reporting, modification, or any other reason.

Structures of the type shown in figure 14.2 are referred to as **sets,** and play an important role in two general classes of database systems known as hierarchical and network. The distinction between these two types of systems is based on the kinds of database structures that each can support. In this section, a bit of historical background will be given concerning each of these types of database systems. The major features of each will then be discussed.

The general concept of database management goes back to the early 1960s, when the bulk of business-oriented programming was done in COBOL. Early database systems were conceived to be groups of routines that could be called from COBOL programs, for the purposes of assisting in the manipulation of data files. Much of the data being processed was seen to fall into groups of related records, in which one record of a given type was associated with several records of a second type. At this time, early systems were experimenting with linking groups of related records together into chains. This approach proved to be quite successful, and the emergence of full database systems quickly followed.

Figure 14.1
A two-file database
consisting of
CUSTOMERS and
ORDERS. (a) The
general relationship;
and (b) sample records
from the database.

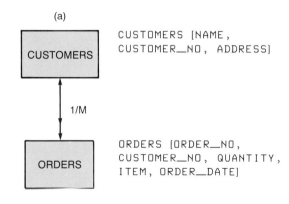

(a)

CUSTOMERS [NAME,
CUSTOMER_NO, ADDRESS]

1/M

ORDERS [ORDER_NO,
CUSTOMER_NO, QUANTITY,
ITEM, ORDER_DATE]

(b)

CUSTOMERS:

| Abercrombie, J. | 13579 | 32 14th St. Boston, MA 02146 |

ORDERS:

| ORD-1734 | 13579 | 25 | CLEAVERS | 5/15/85 |

| ORD-2105 | 13579 | 70 | HAMMERS | 07/21/85 |

| ORD-1518 | 13579 | 5 | AWLS | 01/29/85 |

| ORD-3964 | 13579 | 35 | SHOVELS | 07/01/85 |

Records are related by virtue of common values in the
CUSTOMER_ID fields

The Hierarchical Approach

One of the first commercially successful database systems was Information Management System (IMS), developed for IBM machines in the mid-1960s. This system was the first hierarchical DBMS, so-called because database information is structured in a hierarchical manner (we shall illustrate the nature of these structures later on). IMS has gone through many changes since the original version, and it has had tremendous staying power in spite of the fact that the hierarchical approach has several major shortcomings. A great many data processing installations continue to use IMS, primarily because of the investment in hardware, existing databases and programs, and programming expertise.

Figure 14.2
The group of records
shown in figure 14.1
connected into a SET.
Heavy arrows indicate
direct connections
between records.

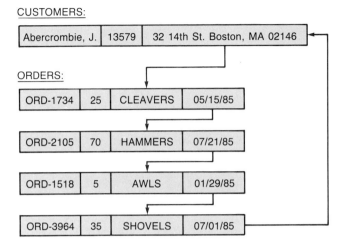

CUSTOMERS:

| Abercrombie, J. | 13579 | 32 14th St. Boston, MA 02146 |

ORDERS:

ORD-1734	25	CLEAVERS	05/15/85
ORD-2105	70	HAMMERS	07/21/85
ORD-1518	5	AWLS	01/29/85
ORD-3964	35	SHOVELS	07/01/85

One other highly successful database system utilizing the hierarchical approach is System 2000/80, marketed by INTEL Systems Corporation. Like IMS, this system has developed over several years, and it has many highly complex and sophisticated features. It runs on a variety of large computers, including those of IBM, UNIVAC, and CDC.

The Network Approach

At the same time that IMS was being developed, other efforts along vaguely similar lines were developing within the growing computing industry. Beginning in the late 1960s, a national committee known as CODASYL (Committee on Data System Languages) began work on an attempt to develop guidelines that could act as a set of standards for emerging database management systems. The actual work was done by a subcommittee of CODASYL, known as the Data Base Task Group (DBTG). Members of the DBTG recognized that the approach to database management adopted by IMS had several major shortcomings, and they worked to develop standards that would eliminate many of these. Between 1969 and 1981,[1] the DBTG issued several important documents, containing the **CODASYL DBTG guidelines.**

The DBTG guidelines are extremely complex, containing a large number of details concerning a great many aspects of the design of database management systems. Of particular interest is the fact that the guidelines set out specifications for what are known as network database structures, which are significantly more flexible than those allowed by the IMS-type hierarchical approach. These guidelines have strongly influenced the development of database systems since the early

[1]*See* CODASYL Data Base Task Group Report (April 1971). Available from the Association of Computing Machinery, New York. Also, CODASYL Data Description Language Committee (1978). DDL Journal of Development, Hull, Canada.

part of the 1970s, particularly those for larger computers. A large number of database systems currently exist that follow the guidelines to at least some degree. Many of these are referred to either as CODASYL or DBTG database systems, because of the high degree to which they conform to the DBTG suggestions.

On the other hand, many systems have adopted the network-type database structure, but have not followed the DBTG guidelines to any great extent. These systems are known simply as network DBMS's.

With very few exceptions, network-oriented database systems have been designed for larger computers. The primary reason for this is that these systems are by nature quite complex. Until recently, this amount of complexity was inconsistent with the resources available for microcomputers. Even with recent improvements in microcomputer speed and memory capacity, there has been little movement of network-based DBMS's towards these machines. The one outstanding exception to this is MDBS III,® a network-type microcomputer-based database system marketed by Micro Data Base Systems, Inc. The designers of this system claim that it is the best small-machine database system for complex scientific and business database applications. In fact, compared to many micro-oriented systems, MDBS III is indeed a highly sophisticated system, and it requires the skill of a very competent programmer.

Network Database Systems

Network database systems are used on many different types of computers. They were one of the first types of DBMS's to gain widespread popularity, and they continue to enjoy a wide user base.

An Overview

In this section, we will give an overview of the particular qualities that distinguish network DBMS's from other types, including the following: (1) the types of database structures that are commonly used with this type of DBMS, and (2) the types of languages (data definition, query, etc.) normally encountered.

Many different types of network-oriented database systems exist. However, they all have several common characteristics, which are summarized below.

Structure

Files, records, and fields. As with previously described DBMS's, each database consists of a group of one or more record-types. Usually, all records of a given type are grouped together into a file. Each record consists of zero or more fields, and all records of a given type have the same structure. (Certain types of intersection record-types may contain no user-data fields, existing only to act as links between different records.) Some network DBMS's permit repeating groups within records.

Sets and networks. If a one-to-many relationship exists between two record-types, a set may be defined, consisting of these two record-types. This relationship is then *automatically* maintained by the DBMS for all records in A and B. Sets are maintained by chains and other similar structures; this is the crux of the importance of database structures within a network DBMS.

The set is a basic structural unit within a network-oriented database. Several sets may be combined to form more complex database structures, known as networks (hence the terminology *network database*).

Languages

- **Data definition language.** Each network-type DBMS contains a language for defining the details of each database, known as the data definition language (DDL). These details include (1) the definition of record-types in terms of fields; (2) the definition of sets; (3) security controls; and (4) constraints on the data. When the definition of a particular database is processed by the DBMS, a database dictionary is created for that database.

- **Data manipulation languages.** Each DBMS contains at least one language for searching and modifying databases, usually called a data manipulation language (DML). These languages are usually procedural, operating on a single record at a time (in contrast with relational-type query languages, which operate on a table at a time). Each DML is usually quite rich, consisting of many different types of commands for finding particular set occurrences and moving around within them.

- **Host languages.** Normally, DML commands are embedded within application programs, usually written in a host language such as COBOL, FORTRAN, or Pascal. Each application program communicates with the network DBMS by means of a **host language interface,** which is a built-in subsystem of the DBMS. Each different programming language requires a separate host language interface.

- **Nonprocedural query languages.** Many network-type DBMS's have additional facilities that make use of relational-type nonprocedural query languages for searching and updating databases. For the most part, these are separate software packages that have been added fairly late in the life cycle of the DBMS.

Overview Summary

Generally, the first step in using a network DBMS is to utilize the data definition to define a new database structure. The DBMS then processes this definition, creating a database dictionary for that database. A database may be defined with a great deal of internal structure, which basically defines different sets, or relationships among various record-types. These relationships are automatically maintained by the DBMS. Subsequent use of the database is usually by means of applications programs, in which data manipulation language commands are embedded. Each program has a particular function, such as adding new records to the database, searching for particular subsets of records, and so on.

Many network DBMS's also contain nonprocedural query languages, which allow users to perform flexible interactive queries and other types of database manipulations.

Database Structures

One of the distinguishing characteristics of network database systems is that they support various types of complex database structures. These structures facilitate movement within a database, allowing rapid access to groups of related records. In this section, we shall describe the various types of structures that may be built. Following sections will describe how these structures may be manipulated.

Sets: The Basic Building Blocks

As we mentioned, if a one-to-many relationship exists between two record-types, they can be defined to form a structure called a set.

Rules for sets. The construction and use of sets follow specific rules:

- A set may be defined between any two record-types, provided that a one-to-many relationship exists between them. Sets are defined at the same time as the overall database, using the database definition language. Thus, in addition to specifying record-types, fields, and so on, a user also identifies the sets that are to be part of the database.
- For the purposes of identification, each set is given an arbitrary name, usually chosen to indicate the nature of the relationship between the two record-types. One of the record-types is called the *owner,* and the other is the *member.*
- Each group of related records within a set is known as a **set occurrence.** The records within each occurrence are linked in such a way that they are easily accessible as a unit. These links are maintained by the DBMS. A set occurrence consists of a single owner record and zero or more related member records. The owner record of a set occurrence is said to "own" the related member records.
- A particular record-type may belong to more than one set. This is the basis upon which complex database structures can be built. The precise rules governing this aspect of database structures are highly dependent on the type of network DBMS.
- A particular record may have at most one owner *within a given set.* In other words, each record may be a member of only one occurrence of each set.

Example. To illustrate some of these ideas, consider the two-file database shown in figure 14.3(a). Because a one-to-many relationship exists between CUSTOMERS and ORDERS, the set named CUSTS_ORDERS has been defined (this specification would be made in the original database definition). CUSTOMERS is said to be the owner record-type of the set, and ORDERS is the member record-type.

An occurrence of the CUSTS_ORDERS set is illustrated in figure 14.3(b), and also in figure 14.2. This occurrence consists of a single CUSTOMERS record plus all of the related ORDERS records. The records that make up the occurrence are connected into a logical unit, as shown by the heavy arrows in figure 14.2. The actual implementation of the connections is usually accomplished by storing pointers within each record, as shown in figure 14.3(b).

Notice that unlike the ORDERS file shown in figure 14.1, the CUSTOMER_ID field is omitted from the records shown in figure 14.3(b). This is because the pointer in each ORDERS record furnishes the connection to the related CUSTOMERS record, so that the CUSTOMER_ID value is not required.

Using sets. One of the major reasons for the existence of sets is to facilitate the rapid location and manipulation of a particular group of related records. The following list includes some of the more common types of searches that are greatly assisted by the use of sets:

- Find one or more of the member records that belong to the same set occurrence as a particular owner record. This would be accomplished by navigating along the chain of member records, using the pointers contained within each record, until all of the desired records were located. For example, referring to figure 14.3, all of the ORDERS records related to "Abercrombie, J." could be found by following the chain beginning with the CUSTOMERS record for "Abercrombie, J." The process of navigation along record chains was discussed extensively in the previous chapter.
- Navigate forward or backward through a group of member records belonging to a particular set. Forward and reverse pointers attached to each member record are used for these purposes. In network DBMS terminology, these are often called *next* and *prior* pointers.
- Locate the owner record corresponding to any particular member record. This could be accomplished either by the use of a parent pointer contained within the member record, or by navigating along the chain of records until the parent was found. Again referring to figure 14.3, the CUSTOMERS record for "Abercrombie, J." could be found from any related ORDERS record by following the *next* pointers back to the CUSTOMERS record.

Figure 14.3
(a) The set formed by
the CUSTOMERS and
ORDERS record-types;
(b) the implementation
of direct connections
with pointer chains. The
records shown are
those in figure 14.2.

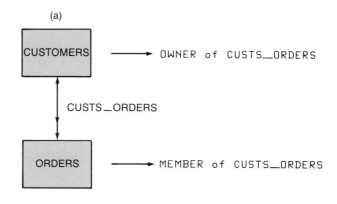

(a)

CUSTOMERS ⟶ OWNER of CUSTS_ORDERS

CUSTS_ORDERS

ORDERS ⟶ MEMBER of CUSTS_ORDERS

(b)

CUSTOMERS:

(25)

| Abercrombie, J. | 13579 | 32 14th St. Boston, MA 02146 | 137 |

ORDERS:

(137)

| ORD-1734 | 25 | CLEAVERS | 05/15/85 | 441 | ⟵ POINTERS

(441)

| ORD-2105 | 70 | HAMMERS | 07/21/85 | 287 |

(287)

| ORD-1518 | 5 | AWLS | 01/29/85 | 116 |

Each record contains a
pointer field, which
contains the address of
related record

(116)

| ORD-3964 | 35 | SHOVELS | 07/01/85 | 025 |

(1) Numbers in parentheses represent record addresses.

(2) The ORDERS records may be widely separated physically in the file.
The pointers furnish the means for directly accessing one record from
another.

Figure 14.4
A network consisting of
several sets.

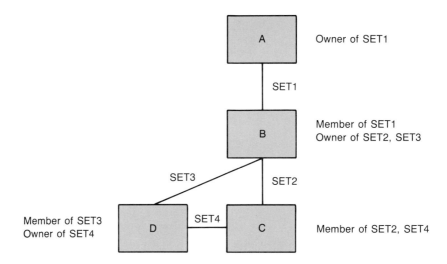

Defining and maintaining sets. It is important to understand the following point: a set is a logical entity that must be defined by the database designer as part of the database definition process. This is done using the data definition language. However, when records are added and deleted from the files during normal database activity, the DBMS is responsible for maintaining set occurrences by manipulating appropriate pointers within the records.

Networks

A single set consists of two record-types, one of which is the owner and the other the member. In addition, a single record-type may belong to more than one set. For example, as shown in figure 14.4, record-type A is the member of SET1 and the owner of SET2. On the other hand, record-type B is the owner of two sets, while C is the member of two.

Thus, many interesting and complex database structures can be built, using the set as the basic building block. In the following section, we shall give examples of some of the more common types of structures, in order to illustrate the wide variety of possibilities.

A simple network database structure. Consider the ZOO database whose structure is shown in figure 14.5(a). This database represents information about animals, their cages, and their attendants. The following assumptions are made with respect to the zoo:

1. Each cage may contain many animals;
2. Each zoo attendant is responsible for many individual animals;
3. Each animal has only one attendant; and
4. Each animal has only one cage.

As indicated in figure 14.5, these relationships may be represented by the following two sets: (1) the ABODES set, consisting of CAGES (owner) and ANIMALS (member); (2) the ATT_ANIMALS set, consisting of ATTENDANTS (owner) and ANIMALS (member).

The ZOO database is a modest example of a simple network, which is the most common type of database structure used by network DBMS's, and which is defined by the following rules:

Definition of a Simple Network Database Structure

1. The structure consists of one or more sets, each of which represents a one-to-many relationship
2. A record-type may belong to more than one set
3. A record-type may be the owner of one or more sets
4. A record-type may also be the member of one or more sets

Returning to the ZOO database of figure 14.5, we see that it falls within the definition of a simple network. Figure 14.5(b) shows a few set occurrences of the ZOO database. Notice that each animal has two connections: one to a particular cage, and the other to a specific attendant. On the other hand, each cage may be associated with many animals, and the same is true for each attendant. Thus, Elsie lives in cage C-14, and she is tended by Joe. We say that the "Elsie" record is owned by both the "C-14" and "Joe" records. Joe also tends Wailer and Tigressa, and we say that the "Joe" record owns both the "Wailer" and "Tigressa" records.

Again, we stress the fact that the lines in figure 14.5 represent record connections via pointers, which are maintained by the network DBMS.

A hierarchical structure. Another type of database structure commonly used by network DBMS's is illustrated by the SCHOOL database shown in figure 14.6, which contains information about departments, instructors, and classes within a given school. We assume that each department may have many instructors, and each instructor may teach several classes. The database consists of two sets, DEPT_INST and INST_CLASS. The first of these is made up of two record-types, DEPARTMENT (owner) and INSTRUCTOR (member). Similarly, the INST_CLASS set consists of INSTRUCTOR (owner) and CLASS (member).

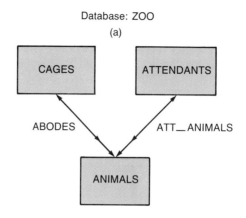

Figure 14.5
A database consisting of three record-types that form two sets.
(a) The general database structure;
(b) occurrences of the ZOO data structures.

Database: ZOO
(a)

```
                    Set membership

CAGES            : Owner  of ABODES
ATTENDANTS       : Owner  of ATT_ANIMALS
ANIMALS          : Member of ABODES,
                   -- " -- ATT_ANIMALS
```

```
            Structure of each record-type

CAGES            [ CAGE_ID, ZOO_SECTION ]

ATTENDANTS       [ NAME, ADDRESS, AGE, SEX, WEIGHT ]

ANIMALS          [ NAME, SPECIES, ATTENDANT, AGE,
                 CAGE_ID ]
```

The **SCHOOL** database is an example of a hierarchy. A database structure is said to be hierarchical if it conforms to the following rules:

Definition of a Hierarchical Database Structure

1. The structure consists of one or more sets, each of which conforms to the rules for sets that were described earlier
2. A record-type may be both an owner and a member, subject to the following limitations:
3. A record-type may be the owner of more than one set
4. A record-type may be the member of only a single set

Figure 14.5
[Continued]

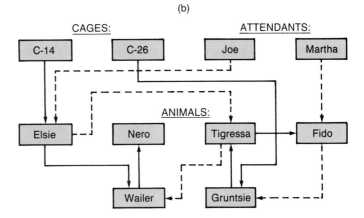

Solid lines represent connections between animals
in a particular cage

Dashed lines represent connections between animals
with a common attendant

By comparing the definitions of hierarchical and simple network structures, we can see that all hierarchical structures are subsets of the general simple network structure. Therefore, any network DBMS that supports simple network structures also supports hierarchies.

Figure 14.6(b) illustrates a few set occurrences for the SCHOOL database. Note that each particular INSTRUCTOR record is owned by only one DEPARTMENT record. On the other hand, each INSTRUCTOR record may own several different CLASS records. For example, the INSTRUCTOR record labelled "Harris" is owned by the single DEPARTMENT record labelled "Physics." On the other hand, "Harris" owns several CLASS records.

More complex structures. The databases shown in figures 14.5 and 14.6 represent the simplest possible structures that can be built with more than one set. Virtually unlimited extensions of each of these structures are possible. For example, we can extend the ZOO database discussed above by incorporating the following facts: (1) each cage is cleaned on a regular schedule, and (2) periodically, each animal is given a medical checkup. The following two new record-types could be incorporated into the database:

CLEANUPS [CAGE_ID, CLEANING_DATE, CLEANER]
CHECKUPS [ANIMAL_NAME, DOCTOR, CHECKUP_DATE,
COMMENTS]

Each CLEANUPS record corresponds to a specific cleaning of a particular cage. Therefore, each CAGES record may be associated with many CLEANUPS records. Thus, a new set can be defined in terms of these two record-types; we

Figure 14.6
A database built from
three record-types,
forming two set-types.
(a) The general
database structure and
(b) instances of the
database structure.

(a)

Database: SCHOOL

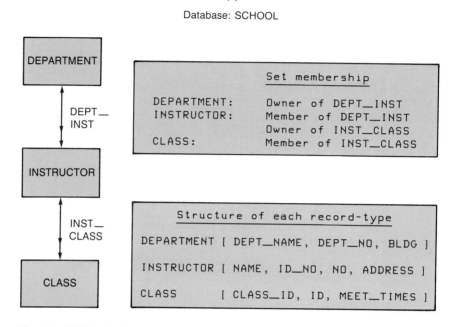

Note that INSTRUCTOR is a member of both sets

(b)

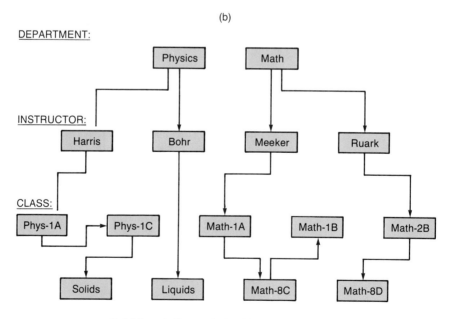

Solid lines indicate relationships among records

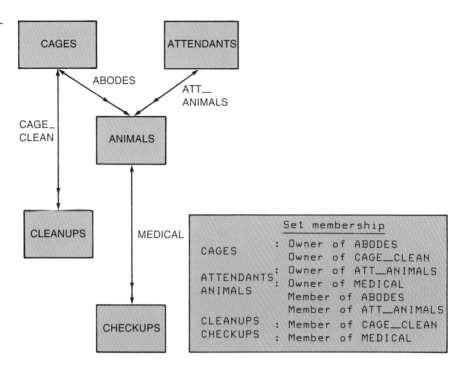

```
                                      Set membership
                   CAGES      : Owner of ABODES
                                Owner of CAGE_CLEAN
                   ATTENDANTS: Owner of ATT_ANIMALS
                   ANIMALS   : Owner of MEDICAL
                                Member of ABODES
                                Member of ATT_ANIMALS
                   CLEANUPS   : Member of CAGE_CLEAN
                   CHECKUPS   : Member of MEDICAL
```

```
              Structure of each record-type

    CAGES     [ CAGE_ID, ZOO_SECTION ]

    ATTENDANTS[ NAME, ADDRESS, AGE, SEX, WEIGHT ]

    ANIMALS   [ NAME, SPECIES, AGE, CAGE_ID, ATTENDANT ]

    CLEANUPS  [ CLEANING_DATE, CLEANER ]

    CHECKUPS  [ DOCTOR, CHECKUP_DATE, COMMENTS ]
```

have arbitrarily given this set the name CAGE_CLEAN. Similarly, another set, MEDICAL, can be defined in terms of ANIMALS and CHECKUPS. The new database structure incorporating these additional record-types and sets is shown in figure 14.7. This structure is considerably more complex than that of previous examples, since one record-type is a member of two sets, another record-type is the owner of two sets, and so on.

Representing many-to-many relationships. As we have mentioned in previous chapters, many types of real-world situations can be well-represented by many-to-many relationships. This type of relationship can be represented in a

Figure 14.8
The representation of
the relationship
between STUDENTS
and CLASSES record-
types. (a) The original
relationship and (b) the
representation by two
set-types.

(a)

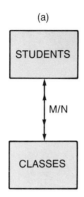

(b)

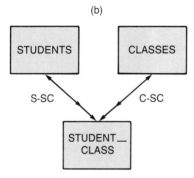

network-type database by the introduction of an intersection record-type. The original many-to-many relationship is replaced with two one-to-many relationships, and therefore with two sets.

We illustrate this technique by using the example of the STUDENTS/ CLASSES database, as depicted in figure 14.8. The relationship between STUDENTS and CLASSES is many-to-many, as illustrated in the first part of this figure. To represent this relationship, a third record-type, STUDENT_CLASS, is introduced. This is the intersection record-type, and it has the following very simple structure:

STUDENT_CLASS [GRADE]

The only data field needed in STUDENT_CLASS is GRADE, corresponding to the grade received by a particular student in a specific class. For each class taken by a particular student, there will be a single STUDENT_CLASS record. Thus, there are two one-to-many relationships: STUDENTS/STUDENT_CLASS, and CLASSES/STUDENT_CLASS. We may therefore define a set to represent each of these two one-to-many relationships, as shown in figure 14.8(b). These two sets, S_SC and C_SC, represent the original many-to-many relationship.

Figure 14.9
A few occurrences of
the database sets
shown in figure 14.8.
Each intersection
record represents a
combination of a
student and a class.
Solid lines represent
logical connections
between the various
records. Each
STUDENT_CLASS
record is associated
with one STUDENTS
record and one
CLASSES record.

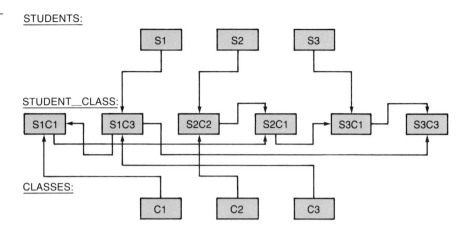

Figure 14.9 shows several set occurrences for this database. Each occurrence of the STUDENT_CLASS record-type represents a particular student-class combination. Each STUDENTS record is linked to all of its associated STUDENT_CLASS records to form a single set, indicated by solid lines in the figure. In a similar manner, solid lines also indicate the connections between each CLASSES record and its associated STUDENT_CLASS records.

It should be pointed out that the creation of the STUDENT_CLASS record-type is the responsibility of the database designer; it is not somehow automatically introduced into the design by the DBMS. In addition, each STUDENT_CLASS record must be separately entered into the database—one for each student class combination. In situations such as this, clever programming can often alleviate most of the data-entry tedium.

Other types of structures. The set can be used as a building block to create a large variety of complex database structures. These can be virtually any combination of sets, including some rather strange ones, such as a set in which a single record-type is both the owner and member![2]

Categorization of Network Database Systems

Having now explored the more common types of network structures that can be used for building databases, we are ready to describe the various types of network database systems, categorizing them according to the types of database structures used. In other words, each type of network DBMS is designed to handle only specific structural forms. Fortunately, these DBMS's divide nicely into the following three major categories: (1) simple network systems, (2) limited network systems, and (3) others.

---

[2]We shall not delve into these unusual structures, but the interested reader can find stimulating discussions on this subject in various references including: "The CODASYL Approach to Data Base Management," T.W. Olle, J. Wiley & Sons (1978).

Simple Network Systems

A simple network database is one in which the structure consists of one or more sets, following the rules for simple networks already outlined. A simple network database system is one that supports structures of this kind. Most network DBMS's that fall into this category have been more or less designed to follow the CODASYL DBTG guidelines, and they are consequently known as CODASYL or DBTG database systems (see the discussion earlier in this chapter for a brief history of CODASYL efforts). Database systems of this type are characterized by the rich variety of database structures that they can support, and many of these were illustrated in examples given in the preceding section.

In general, simple network database systems are quite complex. In addition, there is a tremendous variation among different systems (although the DBTG guidelines do tend to furnish some degree of standardization). Consequently, a detailed study of simple network DBMS's is well beyond the scope of this text. However, in later sections of this chapter, we shall provide a flavor for their nature by giving some examples of how typical network DBMS's are utilized.

Limited Network Systems

A few database systems have borrowed some of the ideas from the DBTG guidelines, but have severely limited the types of database structures that they can support. The most common type of restriction results in what is called the **limited network** database structure. Record-types within this type of structure are divided into two categories: *master* and *detail,* and there may be many record-types in each category. Each master record-type may be the owner of several sets, and each detail record-type may be the member of several sets. The basic limitation comes from the fact that a record-type may *not* be both a master and a detail type. This limitation has the effect of restricting database structures to two levels, as illustrated by the following example.

Figure 14.10 illustrates the ZOO database of figure 14.7, but recast into the limited network mold. Notice that in the original design (figure 14.7), the ANIMALS record-type is both the owner of one set and the member of another. Because this type of multiple membership is not permitted in the limited network model, the ANIMALS record-type of figure 14.7 must be represented by two different record-types, ANIMALS and ANIMALS_MAST, as indicated in figure 14.10. Notice also that there is a one-to-one correspondence between the ANIMALS and ANIMALS_MAST record-types.

At first glance, it would seem that the restrictions imposed by the limited network type of structure would severely limit the range of useful applications. In fact, this has not been the case, partially because most of the inherent limitations can be circumvented by such devices as the introduction of two record-types to represent a single class of entities (such as ANIMALS and ANIMALS_MAST in the previous ZOO example). In addition, aggressive marketing coupled with excellent product design and support have combined to produce two highly successful commercial products that utilize the limited-network model. These are

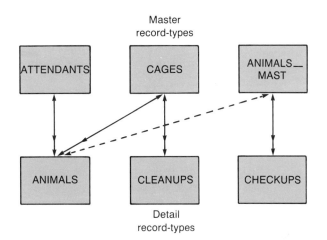

Figure 14.10
The ZOO database shown in figure 14.7 recast into a limited network structure. Record-types are in either MASTER or DETAIL categories. A set consists of one MASTER record-type and one DETAIL record-type.

Master record-types

ATTENDANTS	CAGES	ANIMALS— MAST

ANIMALS	CLEANUPS	CHECKUPS

Detail record-types

```
                    Record  structures

ATTENDANTS      [NAME, ADDRESS, AGE, SEX, WEIGHT ]
CAGES           [CAGE—ID, ZOO—SECTION]
ANIMALS         [ANIMAL—NAME, SPECIES, AGE, CAGE—ID,
                ATTENDANT]
ANIMALS—MAST    [ANIMAL—NAME]
CLEANUPS        [CAGE—ID, CLEANING—DATE, CLEANER]
CHECKUPS        [ANIMAL—NAME, DOCTOR, CHECKUP—DATE,
                COMMENTS]
```

(1) IMAGE/QUERY, a database system marketed by Hewlett-Packard for its own machines,[3] and (2) TOTAL, a database system from CINCOM Systems, Inc., which has been implemented for an extremely wide range of medium and large computers.[4]

Other Network Database Systems

In addition to the types of network DBMS's described, a smattering of other kinds have also been implemented. One of the most interesting of these is the previously mentioned MDBS III, marketed by Micro Data Base Systems, Inc. This database system is particularly unusual for two reasons. First, it is a network-type DBMS that runs on microcomputers, and secondly, it *directly* implements many-to-many relationships. It is also particularly interesting in that it

[3]Image/Query

[4]"Total Reference Manual," Cincom Systems Inc., Cincinnati, Ohio.

does not claim to be user-friendly. On the contrary, it is extremely complex, and requires as much programming skill as many DBMS's for large computers.[5]

A survey of some of the more popular network database systems is given in the Appendix. This covers not only network systems, but other types as well.

Data Definition Languages

Every database management system has some type of facility for defining the details of each database that is to be managed. Usually, this takes the form of a data definition language. There is very little syntactic uniformity among the DDL's of different database systems. The one exception to this includes those DBMS's that conform to the guidelines of the DBTG, which is a detailed set of specifications for the syntax rules of data definition languages.

Nevertheless, if you have seen one DDL, you have basically seen them all— it is usually fairly easy to figure out most of the meaning of any particular database definition, even with an unfamiliar DDL. This is because the purpose of all DDL's is to define the same type of information, such as field names and types, and so on.

Schemas and Their Contents

In the world of network database systems, the description of a database, written with a DDL, is referred to as a **schema.** Typically, a schema includes specifications regarding most or all aspects of a database. These include the following:

- Names of all record-types included in the database
- Structure of each record-type, including name, type, and other details about each field
- Inter-record and intra-record constraints
- Security controls, such as password specifications
- Definition of each set to be part of the database, including names of owner and member record-types, as well as any particular restrictions or conditions that apply to the set

A sample schema.   Figure 14.11 illustrates a simplified schema for the ZOO database originally shown in figure 14.7. The syntax used in this example is typical of the simplicity with which schemas are written.

This schema contains several major divisions, the first of which is the USER section, which lists the passwords that may give access to the database. Each password is identified with two short codes, one each for read and write access. These items are used to identify the portions of the schema that are accessible to each password, and their purpose. For example, records of type CAGES are given read access both to MANAGER and CLERK, whereas write access is given only to MANAGER.

---

[5]A brief overview of this system is given in "Data Base Management Systems," D. Kruglinski, Osborne, McGraw-Hill (1986).

Figure 14.11
A simplified schema for
the ZOO database
shown in figure 14.7.

```
                           USER SECTION

User is "MANAGER"
     Read access is (M)
     Write access is (M)

User is "CLERK"
     Read access is (C)
     Write access is (C)

                          RECORDS SECTION

Record name is CAGES,                Read access is (M,C),
                                     Write access is (M),

     CAGE_ID:        CHAR (8),
     ZOO_SECTION:    CHAR (4),
     Key is CAGE_ID,
     Duplicates not allowed;

Record name is ATTENDANTS,           Read access is (M,C),
                                     Write access is (M),

     NAME:           CHAR (20),
     ADDRESS:        CHAR (50),
     AGE:            NUM  (3),
     SEX:            CHAR (1),
     WEIGHT:         NUM  (3),
     Key is NAME,
     Duplicates not allowed;

Record name is ANIMALS,              Read access is (M,C),
                                     Write access is (M),

     NAME:           CHAR (15),
     SPECIES:        CHAR (20),
     ATTENDANT_NAME: CHAR (20),
     AGE:            NUM  (2),
     CAGE_ID:        CHAR (8),
     Key is NAME + CAGE_ID,
     Duplicates not allowed,
     Key is SPECIES,
     Duplicates allowed;

Record name is CLEANUPS,             Read access is (M,C),
                                     Write access is (M),

     CAGE_ID:        CHAR (8),
     CLEANING_DATE:  CHAR (8),
     CLEANER:        CHAR (20);

Record name is CHECKUPS,             Read access is (M,C),
                                     Write access is (M),

     ANIMAL_NAME:    CHAR (15),
     DOCTOR:         CHAR (20),
     CHECKUP_DATE:   CHAR (8),
     COMMENTS:       CHAR (300);
```

Figure 14.11
[*Continued*]

```
                          SETS SECTION

Set name is ABODES,
     Owner is CAGES
     Member is ANIMALS
          Set selection is by value of CAGE_ID in
               CAGES
          Insertion is manual

Set name is CAGE_CLEAN,
     Owner is CAGES
     Member is CLEANUPS
          Set selection is by value of CAGE_ID in
               CAGES
          Insertion is automatic

Set name is ATT_ANIMALS,
     Owner is ATTENDANTS
     Member is ANIMALS
          Set selection is by value of NAME in
               ATTENDANTS
          Insertion is manual

Set name is MEDICAL,
     Owner is ANIMALS
     Member is CHECKUPS
          Set selection is by value of NAME in ANIMALS
          Insertion is automatic
```

The RECORDS section of the schema specifies the details of every record-type in the database. For each record-type, every field is identified by a name, type, and length. The "Key is *field name*" clause defines *field name* to be a search key for the record-type in which the clause appears. In response to this clause, the DBMS establishes some type of direct access to records of that type, with *field name* as the key. This is usually either an index or a hashing scheme, based on *field name*. For example, in the sample schema, the field CAGE_ID is established as a search key for the CAGES record-type. Furthermore, the clause "Duplicates not allowed" specifies that no two CAGES records may have the same value for CAGE_ID. In essence, this defines CAGE_ID to be a primary key for CAGES.

Similarly, the "Key is SPECIES" clause within the ANIMALS record-type establishes SPECIES as a search key. However, in this case the accompanying clause "Duplicates allowed" also appears. In effect, SPECIES is defined to be a secondary key for ANIMALS. This would most likely be implemented by the use of an index on SPECIES. Notice that two different keys have been defined for ANIMALS. The first of these is NAME + CAGE_ID, and it is further specified to be a unique key. The implication is that no two animals in the same cage may have the same name. The second key for ANIMALS is defined to be the field SPECIES, but it is allowed to be nonunique, by virtue of the accompanying

"Duplicates allowed" clause. Thus, many animals of the same species may exist in the zoo. Clearly, uniqueness specifications are directly related to the real-world situation represented by the database. For example, in the case of the CAGES record-type, no two cages may have the same identification number.

The SETS section of the schema describes the details of each set that will be part of the database. For every set, owner and member record-types are specified. The other entries in this section determine the manner in which individual records are added to set occurrences.

To illustrate these ideas, we consider the ABODES set entry. Suppose that the following ANIMALS record is to be added to the database:

NAME:	Big nose
SPECIES:	Housecat
ATTENDANT_NAME:	Clark, Z.
AGE:	4
CAGE_ID:	C–17

The clause, "Set selection is by value of CAGE_ID in CAGES" dictates the choice of set occurrence for each new ANIMALS record. This is done as follows: the DBMS searches for the set occurrence that contains a CAGES record with a CAGE_ID value of C–17. The ANIMALS record will then be attached to that occurrence. Figure 14.12 illustrates this process.

Insertion clauses. The "Insertion is manual/automatic" clauses have to do with the way in which records may be added to sets. With many types of network database systems, a great deal of flexibility exists with regard to how records and sets are handled. For example, suppose that record-types A and B form a set, SETA. It is possible to add a record of type B to the database without adding it to any occurrence of SETA. In the ZOO example, suppose that a new animal comes to the zoo, but it has not yet been assigned a permanent cage. It would be desirable to be able to add a record to the database for the animal, but its addition to the ABODES set would need to be deferred until its cage assignment had been made. The "Insertion is manual" clause permits this to occur.

On the other hand, each CLEANUPS record represents a particular cleaning of a cage. Therefore, each record should belong to a specific occurrence of the set CAGE_CLEAN. Its set insertion is therefore made automatic: each new CLEANUPS record will automatically be added to the appropriate occurrence of the CAGE_CLEAN set.[6]

This discussion of schemas for network DBMS's has outlined the more common elements found in various data definition languages. As indicated earlier, there is very little uniformity in DDL syntax from one DBMS to another. In addition, the possible *content* of a schema will depend on the design options that are available to the database designer.

[6]This discussion of records and set occurrences has only scratched the surface; the subject is quite complex, and it is treated in detail in "The CODASYL Approach to Data Base Management," T. W. Olle, J. Wiley & Sons (1978).

Figure 14.12

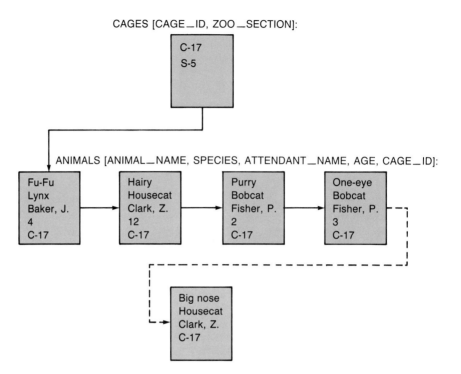

The addition of a new
ANIMALS record to the
appropriate occurrence
of the ABODES set. All
of the ANIMALS records
shown belong to the
same set occurrence,
corresponding to Cage
C-17. Solid lines
represent the linking of
the records in this
occurrence. Dotted line
indicates the new
connections that will be
made in order to add
the new record to the
set occurrence.

Subschemas

Many network-type systems have a facility by which different users may be given different views of a database. This concept is similar to that of user views discussed in chapter 12, and it may be helpful to review that material. A **subschema** is similar to a schema, in that it describes groups of record-types and sets. However, it differs from a schema in that it describes only part of a total database. The main purpose of a subschema is to give a particular group of users access only to that portion of a database that is of interest.

A subschema may create a particular view in which various fields, record-types, and sets are absent. Names used in a subschema may differ from the original names in the schema, and **virtual** record-types may sometimes be defined, consisting of various parts of the actual record-types defined in the schema. Many subschemas may be defined for one database, and they are normally stored in the data dictionary, along with the schema for that database.

A subschema is used in the following way. Usually, interaction with a network-type database is by one or more user-written programs, and each of these programs references the database via a particular subschema. Figure 14.13(a) illustrates this concept, in which several subschemas are defined for a particular database, and each subschema may be referenced by more than one program.

Figure 14.13
The interaction of user
programs with a
database (a) using
subschemas;
(b) without
subschemas.

(a)

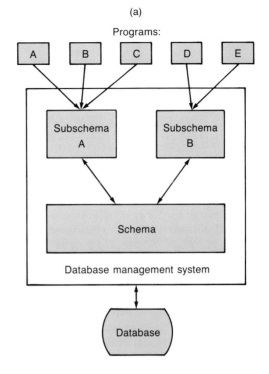

Each program accesses the database by reference to a particular
subschema, which in turn must indirectly reference the database
through the database schema

(b)

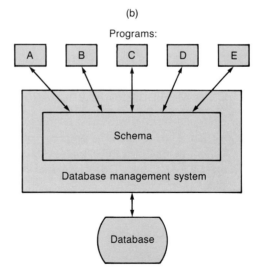

Subschema languages. The language used to define a database subschema must satisfy two criteria:

- It must be consistent with the schema definition for that database
- It must also be consistent with the language used by programs that reference it. For example, it would not make sense to define COBOL-type subfields within a subschema that was to be referenced by FORTRAN programs. In fact, the subschema language usually closely resembles the language of the referencing programs.

Subschema example. To illustrate these ideas, a subschema for the ZOO schema shown in figure 14.11 is shown in figure 14.14. We assume that programs that will access this subschema are written in COBOL. Therefore, the subschema language itself has something of a COBOL flavor.

It is useful to compare this subschema with the corresponding schema in figure 14.11. The subschema definition contains a USER portion, identifying valid passwords for the various parts of the database that are referenced with the sub-schema. However, the subschema defines only two record-types from the ZOO database, dealing with animals and their medical checkups.

Note that the structure of each record-type, as defined by the subschema, must agree with that of the original schema. For example, it would not make sense to define the field CHECK_DATE to be numeric, because data values for this field might include nonnumeric characters. The FILLER entry is standard COBOL syntax for data to be skipped.

Subschemas are by no means universally used. In fact, many database systems do not even recognize the subschema concept. Instead, each user-written program interacts with a database by referencing the schema directly in these systems, as shown in figure 14.13(b). With some DBMS's, this is accomplished by having programs refer directly to the database by name. The DBMS then automatically uses the schema for that database during all interactions between the program and the database.

Data Manipulation Languages

Every network DBMS must contain a method for manipulating database information. This includes the processes of data addition, deletion, and modification, as well as database reporting. As already mentioned, the commands used for these purposes by a DBMS are known collectively as its **data manipulation language.**

This section gives a general overview of the general characteristics of network-type data manipulation languages, with emphasis placed on those features common to most network DBMS's.

Figure 14.14

A sample subschema
for the schema of figure
14.11.

```
                    IDENTIFICATION SECTION

Database referenced is ZOO;

Subschema name is MEDICAL;

                       USER SECTION

User is ''MANAGER''
      Read access is (M)
      Write access is (M)

User is ''CLERK''
      Read access is (C)
      Write access is (C)

                      RECORDS SECTION

01      ANIMALS
        Read access is (M,C)
        Write access is (M)

        05 NAME            PIC x(15)
        05 FILLER          PIC x(20)
        05 ATTENDANT       PIC x(20)
        05 AGE             PIC Z( 3)

01      CHECKUPS
        Read access is (M,C)
        Write access is (M)

        05 ANIMAL__NAME  PIC x(15)
        05 DOCTOR__NAME  PIC x(20)
        05 CHECK__DATE   PIC x( 8)
        05 COMMENTS      PIC x(300)

                       SETS SECTION

Set name is MEDICAL
        Owner is ANIMALS
        Member is CHECKUPS
              Key is ANIMAL__NAME
```

Procedural nature of the language. Network-type DML's are fundamentally different from the type of query languages associated with relational database systems, which basically operate on a set at a time. In contrast, network DML's operate on the basis of a record at a time. That is, the languages are intrinsically procedural, and frequently many DML commands must be executed in order to carry out a particular database operation.

Each particular DML command has a specific purpose, usually relating to a single record, such as "Find a record," "Delete a record," and so on. Table 14.1 lists the most commonly-used types of DML commands, as well as examples for each type. Note that the syntax of these examples is representative only—each particular database system has its own special syntax.

Programs and DML commands. Normally, DML commands are contained within application programs written for the purpose of interacting with a database. In a sense, the DML commands are extensions of the programming language. Often, the commands are embedded within logical program constructs, such as loops, IF_THEN_ELSE structures, and so on.

The language in which application programs are written (in connection with a DBMS) is called a host language for that DBMS, and the part of the DBMS that performs the communication with the program is called the host language interface, which usually consists of a number of subroutines that are callable from application programs. A DBMS must contain a separate host language interface for each programming language with which it communicates.

The first host language for network DBMS's was COBOL, and virtually every network DBMS still supports a COBOL host language interface. In recent years, there has been a trend towards the use of newer languages, such as BASIC and Pascal, and many network systems now support several host language interfaces. In some of the following examples, COBOL is used as the host language. These examples should be comprehensible, even without any prior knowledge of COBOL. Only a smattering of the COBOL syntax is used, and with a little effort it is easy to uncover most of the meaning of each example.

Keeping track of position: CURRENCY. Because of the procedural nature of DML commands, the database system must keep track of various pieces of information relating to current database access with an application program. This information includes the following:

- The most recently accessed database record
- The most recently accessed record *of each type* in the database
- The most recently accessed record within each set

Table 14.1	Commonly Used Types of Record-Access Commands

Type of Record Access	Sample Syntax
Find a specific record, based on the value of a key	OBTAIN DIRECT CUSTOMERS RECORD FOR CUSTOMER_ID = "C2"
Find the next member record in a set occurrence	OBTAIN NEXT ORDERS RECORD WITHIN SET CUST_ORDERS
Find the previous member record in a set occurrence	OBTAIN PREVIOUS ORDERS RECORD WITHIN SET CUST_ORDERS
Find the owner record corresponding to a particular member record	OBTAIN OWNER RECORD OF SET CUST_ORDERS
Find the first or last record of a particular type, independent of any set membership	OBTAIN FIRST (LAST) ORDERS RECORD
Find the next record of a particular type, independent of any set membership	OBTAIN NEXT ORDERS RECORD
Add a new record to the database	STORE CUSTOMERS RECORD
Modify an existing database record	REPLACE ORDERS RECORD
Remove a record	REMOVE ORDERS RECORD

These various pieces of data are maintained by the DBMS in special locations called **currency indicators.** As each new record is accessed by a search command, the appropriate currency indicators are updated. The reasons for maintaining this information will become clear when we study the way in which DML commands operate within programs.

Program—DBMS communication. During the execution of an application program, a great deal of information sharing occurs between the program and the DBMS, including the following:

- **Database details.** In order for a program to interact successfully with a database, it must have access to various details concerning that database. For example, structural information concerning the various record-types and sets must be made available to the program. This information is supplied by the DBMS to the program, either by a database subschema, or by the schema itself.

- **Data transfer.** Database records may move from the database to the program, and vice versa. This data flow is in direct response to the various DML commands executed from within the program. When a record is retrieved by the program, it is copied into a work space, which is a portion of memory directly accessible to the program.

- **Operation status.** The DBMS maintains one or more **status indicators.** These are used to inform the program about the results of each database operation resulting from a DML command. For example, suppose that a particular command requests the retrieval of a specific record. There could be several possible outcomes of this search:

1. The record is located and copied to the program work space
2. An end-of-file is encountered, indicating the absence of the record
3. An end-of-set occurrence is reached, also indicating that the record is not in the database
4. Some other type of condition occurs that results in the record not being found.

The program can determine which of these outcomes actually occurred by reading the contents of the proper status indicator. The appropriate course of action can then be taken by the program.

DML Retrieval Commands

To illustrate the nature of DML commands, several of those listed in table 14.1 are discussed in this section. We begin with commands dealing with record retrieval, because the procedural nature of network DML's necessitates that a record must first be retrieved before *anything* can be done to it. The retrieval process involves the execution of one or more DML retrieval commands by an application program. When the desired record has been located by the DBMS, it may be copied into the program work space, where it can be manipulated by the program for any particular purpose (modification, deletion, etc.).

In some of the following examples, reference will be made to the database defined in figure 14.15. A sample group of records from this database is shown in figure 14.16. In the section following this one, some simple examples of program segments will be presented to show how some of the various commands can be used.

DML command: Find a specific record, based on the value of a KEY. This type of DML command is used to find a particular record. The field specified in the search must be declared as a key in the schema. For example, referring to figure 14.15, the CUSTOMERS description includes the clause, "Key is CUS-TOMER_NO." This permits any CUSTOMERS record to be directly accessed by specifying a particular value for the CUSTOMER_NO field. For example, the CUSTOMERS record with a CUSTOMER_NO of "C2" could be located with the following command (see table 14.1):

> OBTAIN DIRECT CUSTOMERS RECORD FOR
> CUSTOMER_ID = "C2"

Figure 14.15
Schema for the
database consisting of
CUSTOMERS and
ORDERS record-types.

```
Schema name is COMPANY

                        RECORDS SECTION

Record name is CUSTOMERS,

        NAME:                   CHAR (30),
        CUSTOMER_NO:            CHAR (10),
        ADDRESS:                CHAR (50),
        Key is CUSTOMER_NO,
        Duplicates not allowed;

Record name is ORDERS,

        ORDER_NO:               CHAR (10),
        CUST_NO:                CHAR (10),
        QUANTITY:               NUM  ( 3),
        ITEM:                   CHAR (15),
        ORDER_DATE:             CHAR ( 8);
        Key is ORDER_NO,
        Duplicates not allowed,
        Key is ITEM,
        Duplicates are allowed;

                         SETS SECTION

Set name is CUST_ORDERS
        Owner is CUSTOMERS
        Member is ORDERS
            Insertion is automatic
            Set selection is by value of CUSTOMER_NO in CUSTOMERS
```

Figure 14.16

A sample of records
from the COMPANY
database shown in
figure 14.15. Records
connected by solid
arrows form a single set
occurrence. Light,
broken lines indicate
the order in which
records can be
accessed sequentially,
independent of set
membership.

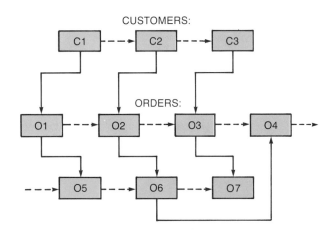

DML command: Find the next member record in a set occurrence. This type of DML access is used to locate successive members of the *current* set occurrence, that is, the one currently being accessed by the DBMS. For example, suppose that the CUSTOMERS record "C2" has been located by the command given in the previous example. As shown in figure 14.16, this record and all of its associated ORDERS records are connected into a set occurrence. Each of these ORDERS records can in turn be accessed with a command of the following form:

> OBTAIN NEXT ORDERS RECORD WITHIN SET CUST_ORDERS

Thus, the first execution of the above command would locate ORDERS record "O2." Subsequent OBTAIN NEXT commands would locate records "O6," then "O4."

DML command: Find the previous member record in a set occurrence. This is analogous to the OBTAIN NEXT type of DML command, except that the record accessed is the previous one in the set occurrence:

> OBTAIN PREVIOUS ORDERS RECORD WITHIN SET CUST_ORDERS

DML command: Find the owner record corresponding to a particular member record. Suppose that a particular record of a given type has been located, and that it is a member of a set occurrence. Often, it is desirable to access the owner record associated with that occurrence. For example, assume that a particular ORDERS has been retrieved with the following command:

> OBTAIN DIRECT ORDERS RECORD FOR ORDER_NO
> = "O3"

The CUSTOMERS record that owns the corresponding set occurrence may also be retrieved, using the following command:

> OBTAIN OWNER RECORD OF SET CUST_ORDERS

Notice that this command must specify the set (CUST_ORDERS). This is necessary because a record-type may belong to more than one set, and therefore a record may belong to more than one set occurrence.

DML command: Find the first or next record of a particular type, independent of any set membership. This type of command is used to navigate within the records of a certain type, without reference to membership to any particular set.

For example, all of the records within the ORDERS file could be scanned with the following commands:

```
OBTAIN FIRST ORDERS RECORD
OBTAIN NEXT ORDERS RECORD
OBTAIN NEXT ORDERS RECORD
            .
            .
            .
```

Referring to figure 14.16, the records would be accessed in the order "O1," "O2," and so on.

Retrieval Examples

In this section we present some simple retrieval examples to illustrate the way in which DML commands are implemented within user-written programs. These examples are written in COBOL, partially because of the English-like nature of the language. This helps to make the examples more comprehensible, even for those not familiar with the language. Also, in order to focus on general characteristics, these examples have been somewhat simplified, compared to actual COBOL programs. For the purposes of the following examples, the COMPANY database defined in figure 14.15 will again be used.

Example 1: Retrieving all orders corresponding to a given customer. As a first example, we present selected portions of a program for finding and listing all ORDERS records belonging to a particular customer. The program segments are shown in figure 14.17.

Lines 22–23 define the database to be referred to by the program. In actuality, a program might invoke a particular subschema of a database, rather than the actual schema itself.

Lines 25–35 define the details of the two record-types for the program. These must agree with the schema definitions of each record-type, with respect to both types and lengths of the element. For simplicity, element names within the program have been chosen to be identical to the corresponding schema names. In general, this need not be true.

Lines 25–35 also define work space. When a database record is retrieved, it is copied into the appropriate work space. From here, the record may be manipulated in any desired way by the program. Note that the concept of a work space is completely consistent with the record-at-a-time mode of data manipulation.

Lines 51–52 define variables to be used during the program execution. The field STATUS_IND is a status indicator maintained by the DBMS: its contents will indicate the results of each database manipulation.

Figure 14.17

Segments of a COBOL
program for searching a
database.

```
               "
               "
20.  DATA DIVISION
               "
               "
22.   SCHEMA SECTION
23.   INVOKE SCHEMA = ''COMPANY''
               "
               "
25.   01 CUSTOMERS
26.          05 NAME        PIC ×(30)
27.          05 CUSTOMER_NO PIC ×(10)
28.          05 ADDRESS     PIC ×(50)
29.
30.   01 ORDERS
31.          05 ORDER_NO    PIC ×(10)
32.          05 CUST_NO     PIC ×(10)
33.          05 QUANTITY    PIC Z( 3)
34.          05 ITEM        PIC ×(15)
35.          05 ORDER_DATE  PIC ×( 8)

               "
               "
               "

50.  WORKING-STORAGE SECTION

51.   01 CUST_ID            PIC ×(10)
52.   01 STATUS_IND         PIC Z( 1)
               "
               "
               "

75.  PROCEDURE DIVISION

76.   ACCEPT CUST_ID.
77.   OBTAIN DIRECT CUSTOMERS RECORD
78.          FOR CUSTOMER_ID = CUST_ID.
                     .
79.   IF    STATUS_IND = 0
80.   THEN
81.         PERFORM PRINT_CUSTOMER_RECORD.
82.         PERFORM GET_NEXT_ORDER
83.            UNTIL STATUS_IND <> 0
84.   ELSE
85.         PERFORM NO_GOT_CUST.

86.   RETURN.
```

These record
definitions must
agree with those
given in the
database schema

Read in customer
← ID-number
← Find the
CUSTOMERS
record
— Continue if the
record was
found
— Loop until flag
indicates that end
of set occurrence
reached

Figure 14.17
[*Continued*]

```
100.GET_NEXT_ORDER Section.

101.  OBTAIN NEXT ORDERS RECORD
102.         WITHIN SET CUST_ORDERS
103.  IF    STATUS_IND = 0
104.  THEN
105.         PERFORM PRINT_ORDER_RECORD.

106.         (End of GET_NEXT_ORDER section)

110.PRINT_CUSTOMFR_RECORD SECTION.

            (Prints current CUSTOMERS record)

150.PRINT_ORDER_RECORD Section.

            (Prints current ORDERS record)

200.END_OF_PROGRAM.
```

Whereas lines 20 thru 52 are concerned with *descriptive* information about records, fields, and so on, the remaining lines are concerned with program execution.

Line 76 reads the value of a customer identification number, possibly from an on-line user. The value read is stored in the variable CUST_ID. Line 77 instructs the DBMS to find the CUSTOMERS record whose CUSTOMER_ID value matches that of CUST_ID. If that record is located by the DBMS, it is copied into the CUSTOMERS work space.

Line 79 is a test to determine whether or not the CUSTOMERS record was found (corresponding to STATUS_IND = 0). If it was not, an error routine is called (lines 84–85). If the record was found, its contents are output (line 81). A program loop is then executed (lines 82–83), in which a search is made for all ORDERS records in the current set occurrence, which is defined by the last located CUSTOMERS record. Each time through this loop, the GET_NEXT_ORDER routine is called. This routine searches for the next ORDERS record in the set occurrence. The loop continues until a search fails to locate another record (STATUS_IND < > 0).

Lines 100–105 issue a search for the next ORDERS record (lines 101–102). If a record is retrieved, a call is made to another routine to output the record (line 105).

Notice in this example how the program and the database system complement each other: the program provides the search logic, and the DBMS provides the mechanisms for locating records as requested by the program. The DBMS also keeps track of which database records and set occurrences have been most recently accessed—information essential to the program logic. For example, the successful execution of each OBTAIN NEXT statement depends on the DBMS keeping track of which ORDERS record was most recently accessed. Moreover, the first execution of the OBTAIN NEXT statement presupposes that the DBMS has found the CUSTOMERS record.

Example 2: Obtaining CUSTOMER data for specific orders. In this example, we suppose that a program is to be supplied with a list of order numbers by a user, one at a time. For each order number, the program is to find and output details concerning the order and the corresponding customer. If data cannot be found for either an order or a customer, an appropriate error message is output. The executable statements for this program are shown in figure 14.18.

Line 51 executes a continuous loop, terminating when a zero value is input, signifying "End-of-data-input."

Lines 60–64 obtain the value of an order number from the user. If that value is nonzero, the procedure FIND_RECS is called, to locate the ORDERS record.

Lines 70–80 search for the specified ORDERS record, by using the OBTAIN DIRECT ORDERS RECORD command (lines 71–72). This command instructs the DBMS to retrieve the record corresponding to the order number value input by the user. The OBTAIN OWNER RECORD command (lines 75–76) causes the DBMS to retrieve the corresponding CUSTOMERS record. If either record cannot be located, an appropriate message is output (lines 79 and 80).

Notice that the logic of this example is formed by a doubly-nested IF_THEN_ELSE statement: if the ORDERS record is not found, the search for a CUSTOMERS record is omitted, and instead an error message is sent to the screen. On the other hand, if the ORDERS record is located, then it is output (line 74). The search for the CUSTOMERS record is then carried out (lines 75–76).

Data Modification

Data modification includes the processes of updating or removing existing database records, and adding new records. These processes are normally carried out by user-written programs, similar to those described earlier. In the following discussions and examples, the COMPANY database defined in figure 14.15 will be again used as a reference.

Adding New Records

Obviously, adding new records is a fundamental process of any database system. Moreover, when records are added they must often satisfy various constraints. With network DBMS's, many of these constraints may be specified in the database schema. For example, referring to the COMPANY database in figure 14.15, the following clause exists:

Key is CUSTOMER_NO, Duplicates not allowed

Figure 14.18
Parts of a program to
output data on
customers and orders.

```
                              "
                              "
                              "
50. PROCEDURE DIVISION.

51.   PERFORM KEEP_GOING UNTIL ORDER_NUMBER = 0.
52.   END.

60. KEEP_GOING SECTION.
61.   DISPLAY ''Please enter an order number:''
62.   ACCEPT URDER_NUMBER.
63.   IF      ORDER_NUMBER <> 0
64.   THEN    PERFORM FIND_RECS.
                              "
                              "
                              "
                              "



70. FIND_RECS SECTION.
71.   OBTAIN DIRECT ORDERS RECORD
72.           FOR ORDER_NO = ORDER NUMBER.

73.   IF      STATUS_IND = 0

74.   THEN   PERFORM PRINT_ORDER_RECORD,

75.   OBTAIN OWNER RECORD OF
76.           SET CUST_ORDERS,



77.   IF      STATUS_IND = 0
78.   THEN    PERFORM PRINT_CUST
               RECORD
79.   ELSE    DISPLAY ''No CUSTOMER record''


80.   ELSE    DISPLAY ''No such ORDER exists''.

90. PRINT_ORDER_RECORD SECTION.

    (Prints current ORDERS record)

100.PRINT_CUST_RECORD SECTION.

    (Prints current CUSTOMERS record)
```

This imposes the condition that no two CUSTOMERS records may have the same value in the CUSTOMER_NO field, and this will *automatically* be enforced by the DBMS.

Another constraint is imposed by the following clause in the COMPANY schema, in the SETS SECTION:

> Insertion is automatic

This clause involves the way in which ORDERS records are added to the database. It imposes the condition that when each new record is added, it will automatically be inserted into the correct set occurrence. The latter is defined to be that occurrence for which the owner (CUSTOMERS) record has the same CUSTOMER_NO value as the record being added. Furthermore, if no such set occurrence exists (there is no corresponding CUSTOMERS record), then the DBMS will not allow the addition of the ORDERS record to the database.

Automatic set membership. The preceding type of constraint is only one of many possibilities with regard to the membership of records in set occurrences. As we mentioned earlier, network DBMS's often allow a great deal of flexibility in this respect. For example, a clause such as "Insertion is manual" would allow the addition of an ORDERS record to the database, without it being inserted into a set occurrence. Many network DBMS's contain a variety of DML commands for moving records in and out of set occurrences under various conditions.[7]

Using programs to add records. With traditional network DML's, database records are added by a program. This is done as a two-step process:

- The record is constructed in a program work space, piece by piece
- After construction has been completed, the contents of the work space are copied to the database, using special DML commands

As an example, figure 14.19 illustrates a program segment for adding a new ORDERS record to the COMPANY database. In this figure, lines 71–75 build up the new record by adding data to the individual record fields within the ORDERS work space, defined by lines 30–35. Line 76 contains a DML command that instructs the DBMS to copy the contents of the work space into the database. The program also tests to determine whether the record insertion fails because of either of the following conditions: (1) no corresponding CUSTOMERS record exists in the database (lines 77–79), or (2) an ORDERS record with the same value of ORDER_NO already exists in the database (lines 80–82).

---

[7]We shall not discuss this subject further here, but it is treated in detail by many texts, including "Data Base Management Systems," A. F. Cardenas, Allyn & Bacon, Inc. (1985).

Figure 14.19
Program segments for
adding a new ORDERS
record to the
COMPANY database.

```
                                "
                                "
                                "
  20.   DATA DIVISION
                                "
                                "
                                "

  30.      01 ORDERS
  31.                05 ORDER_NO      PIC X(10)
  32.                05 CUST_NO       PIC X(10)
  33.                05 QUANTITY      PIC Z( 3)
  34.                05 ITEM          PIC X(15)
  35.                05 ORDER_DATE    PIC X( 8)
                                "
                                "
                                "


  70.   PROCEDURE DIVISION

  71.         MOVE ''0-3479-332''  TO ORDER_NO
  72.         MOVE ''H245-39266''  TO CUST_NO
  73.         MOVE    250          TO QUANTITY
  74.         MOVE ''FRIZBEE''      TO ITEM
  75.         MOVE ''05/25/84''    TO ORDER_DATE
  76.         STORE ORDERS RECORD

  77.         IF    STATUS_IND = 2
  78.         THEN  DISPLAY
  79.               ''ERROR: No customer record.''

  80.         IF    STATUS_IND = 3
  81.         THEN  DISPLAY
  82.               ''ERROR: Duplicate order no.''
                                "
                                "
                                "
```

Updating and Removing Records

Like record addition, the process of modifying a database record proceeds in several steps:

- The record of interest must be retrieved, that is, it must be found within the database and then copied into a program work space
- The appropriate record fields are then modified within the work space by the program as necessary
- The record is rewritten to the database with a special DML command

When several records are to undergo similar modifications, a program loop can often be used advantageously.

Figure 14.20
Program segment to
modify a group of
ORDERS records.

```
        "
        "
        "
        "

50. PROCEDURE DIVISION
51. ACCEPT CUST_IDENT, DATE

52. OBTAIN DIRECT CUSTOMERS
            RECORD
53.         FOR CUSTOMER_NO =
            CUST_IDENT
54. IF      STATUS_IND = 0
55. THEN    PERFORM OBTAIN_NEXT
56.             UNTIL STATUS_
                IND <> 0
57. ELSE    DISPLAY ''No such
            customer''.
58. END.


        "
        "


60. OBTAIN_NEXT SECTION.
61. OBTAIN NEXT ORDERS RECORD
62.         WITHIN SET CUST_ORDERS
63. IF      STATUS_IND = 0

64. THEN    MOVE ''08/22/84''
            TO ORDER_DATE,
65.         REPLACE ORDERS RECORD.
```

Example. Suppose that it has been discovered that several orders were received on a single day from a particular customer, but they were entered into the database using the wrong value for the ORDER_DATE field. These records must be found and the correct date substituted. The program segment shown in figure 14.20 performs this task as follows:

The program first inputs the customer identification number, corresponding to the ORDERS records to be modified (line 51). The correct value of ORDER_DATE is also input at the same time. The program then searches for the specified CUSTOMERS record (lines 52–53). If the record is found, the program performs a loop, searching for the ORDERS records that belong to the corresponding set (lines 55–56). Each time an ORDERS record is found it is brought into the work space, and the existing date is replaced with the correct one (lines 61–64). The record is then rewritten to the database (line 65), thus replacing the original copy.

As with previous examples, when a record is located as the result of an OBTAIN command, it is brought into the program work space. In addition, after the record has been updated, it is written back to the database, using the command REPLACE ORDERS RECORD. The special significance of this command is that it replaces the *most recently* accessed ORDERS record. Recall that the DBMS keeps track of the most recently accessed record of each type within the database, using currency indicators.

Deleting a record.   This process is similar to that of modifying an existing record:

- The record to be removed must be made the most recently accessed of its type, usually by a retrieval command that brings the record into the work space
- The record is then removed by a suitable DML command

For example, the following short program segment would input an identification value for a customer, access the record, and then remove it. The REMOVE CUSTOMERS RECORD command refers to the most recently accessed CUSTOMERS record.

```
ACCEPT IDENT
OBTAIN DIRECT CUSTOMERS RECORD FOR
      CUSTOMER_ID = IDENT
REMOVE CUSTOMERS RECORD
```

Nonprocedural Query and Report Languages

The first data manipulation languages used in conjunction with network-oriented DBMS's were procedural, as illustrated by previous examples. These languages have proven to be quite durable and even though many of them are several years old, they are still widely used. In part, this longevity is due to the flexibility provided by these languages. However, this flexibility is a double-edged sword. On the one hand, it gives the programmer complete control over all aspects of a database searching or updating process. On the other hand, this control is paid for in terms of the effort needed to generate the required programs.

In recent years, the use of relational database systems has been instrumental in spreading the popularity of nonprocedural languages such as SQL and QBE. Their success has been due largely to two factors. First, a simple query (or even a fairly complex one) can be generated ad hoc, and without the need to write any kind of program. The second reason for success is the fact that persons who are not data processing professionals can learn to generate significant queries in these languages. Languages such as SQL and QBE can be used by both data processing professionals and laypeople to serve a wide variety of searching and reporting needs, particularly in the *interactive* mode. Often, a spontaneous database query can be generated in minutes, producing results that could otherwise only be obtained by hours, or perhaps days, of programming.

Table 14.2	Relative Advantages of Conventional and Nonprocedural Query Languages

Conventional DML	Nonprocedural Query Language
Flexibility afforded by use of DML statements in conjunction with a programming language	Queries may be generated ad hoc
Minimal processing time required	Many types of queries may be written without the need for programs
Able to handle highly complex applications	Well suited to users with nontechnical backgrounds
Well suited to large batch-oriented processing	Well suited to interactive querying

As a natural consequence of these factors, nonprocedural query and reporting languages have found their way into the world of network-based DBMS's. Building this type of language to sit on top of a network DBMS is not as strange as it may seem at first. After all, a network-type database is merely a collection of records organized into files, in many respects similar to a relational-type database. The main difference between the two types of databases lies in the fact that a network database happens to have various pointers attached to the individual records, forming a variety of direct record connections. A nonprocedural language simply ignores these direct connections, searching the files just as it would an ordinary relational database.

This is not to imply that the days of procedural DML's are numbered. On the contrary, they continue to be a mainstay of network database systems. They have a decided advantage in the area of large, batch-oriented processes, in that they require considerably less processing time in comparison to nonprocedural equivalents. Furthermore, many applications are so complex that they simply cannot be accomplished with nonprocedural languages. It should be noted that many would disagree with this statement. In fact, at the time of this writing a controversy is flourishing over the issue of whether or not nonprocedural languages can effectively compete with their procedural counterparts in the large organization environment.

Table 14.2 summarizes the advantages of each type of query language.

Hierarchical Database Systems

One of the earliest approaches to database management followed the hierarchical database model, which was discussed earlier in this chapter. Hierarchical database systems restrict database structures to those conforming to the rules for hierarchies. This restriction results in the fact that any particular record may

Figure 14.21
A complex hierarchical
database structure. The
structure is purely
hierarchical because
each record-type is a
member of at most one
set.

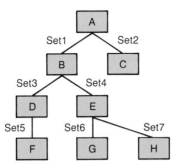

have at most one owner record (see figure 14.6(b)), and this severely limits the types of real-world systems that can be easily represented. (The stress is on the word *easily*, because with enough work and clever design, nearly any real-world system can be modelled with any type of DBMS.)

Examples of hierarchical databases are shown in figures 14.6 and 14.21. The SCHOOL database shown in the first of these figures is quite simple, while that in the other is a more complex example. These two illustrations represent the types of structures for which hierarchical DBMS's are well suited. However, even the simple ZOO database shown in figure 14.5 could not be easily implemented with a hierarchical DBMS.

Very few commercial database systems are based on the hierarchical approach (although the few that do exist are remarkably successful). These systems are of interest primarily because of the large number of existing installations of this type. They continue to survive because of the investment in programs, technical expertise, and hardware needed to support them. In many cases, the cost of shifting to a more sophisticated database system would be prohibitive. It is likely that during the course of his or her career, the data processing professional will run across a firmly entrenched hierarchical database system.

Languages

Each type of hierarchical DBMS has its own set of languages for database definition, querying, and reporting. In general, query and reporting languages are procedural; commands for these are embedded in programs written in a host language, typically COBOL or PL/I. However, nonprocedural languages have made significant inroads into the hierarchical database world. They offer the same types of advantages that were discussed for similar types of languages used with network DBMS's: increased database accessibility for the nonprofessional programmer, and reduced time necessary for the professional to develop a particular query/report or update application.[8]

---

[8]Hierarchical database systems tend to be quite complex, and a complete discussion of them goes beyond the scope of this text. A good overview of the subject is given in "An Introduction to Database Systems" (3d ed.), C.J. Date, Addison-Wesley Publishing Co. (1981).

Table 14.3	Typical Features of File Managers
	Relatively easy to use
	Each database consists of a single file
	Most functions are menu driven
	Fixed-length fields and records
	Allow numeric and character fields
	Easy and flexible querying and reporting

File Managers

These systems are popular primarily in the microcomputer area, where they are in fact one of the most popular types of data management systems. The following discussion is limited to microcomputer-based systems. We shall use the term *file manager* in our present discussions. This type of system is characterized by several common features, the first of which is that each database created with such a system consists of a single file. Because of this limitation, these systems are often compared to electronic file cabinets, and the types of applications that they can handle are limited.

Nevertheless, file managers are widely used because they are relatively inexpensive and reasonably simple to learn. They are designed for the nontechnical person who has very straightforward data-handling needs, and who wishes to expend a minimum of energy in order to be able to utilize computerized data management.

The major characteristics of this type of system are outlined in table 14.3, and described in this section. Because of the large number of file-managing systems in existence, generalizations made about them will probably have many exceptions.

Data Structures

For the most part, files managed by these systems have relatively simple structures. Each database usually consists of a single file, with the usual substructures of records and fields. Typically, the record structure consists of a fixed number of fields, each field being single-valued and fixed-length. The records themselves are therefore usually fixed-length as well. In general, this type of straightforward structure is popular because (1) it is easy for the user to comprehend, and (2) the file-handling software is comparatively easy to write. Some file managers are equipped for dealing with variable-length fields, and this is a very useful feature for certain types of applications. For example, many times it is useful to include a COMMENTS field as part of a record definition, and ideally this field should be variable-length to accommodate exactly whatever text needs to be stored.

File managers invariably allow fields to be defined as either numeric or alphanumeric. In addition, other data types are often allowed. These may include date, money, floating-point, fixed-point, logical, as well as others.

Data Definition, Manipulation, and Reporting

One of the common features of file managers is the ease with which they can be used. For example, the great majority of them are menu driven rather than command driven. That is, at each step in a session with a file manager, the user is given a set of choices, displayed on the computer screen. The action to be performed is chosen by the user from the menu. For example, the process of data definition often amounts to the user filling in a screen display that is built by the system to resemble a form, such as shown in figure 14.22. In this figure, text at the top of the form is created by the file manager. The user fills in the blank spaces with the names of the fields that (s)he wishes to define.

Many of the other functions, such as data entry and report generation, are often as easy to use as the process of data definition. The user is presented with a full-screen display of some type, and appropriate blank spaces are filled in as necessary. A typical data entry screen is shown in figure 14.23.

Figure 14.22
A typical data definition screen for a file manager. Shaded areas represent text written to the screen by the user.

FIELD NAME (20 characters max.)	FIELD TYPE C = CHARACTER N = NUMERIC	FIELD LENGTH (Max. no. of characters)
CLIENT-NAME	C	25
STREET	C	20
CITY	C	15
STATE	C	2
ZIP	N	5
AGE	N	2

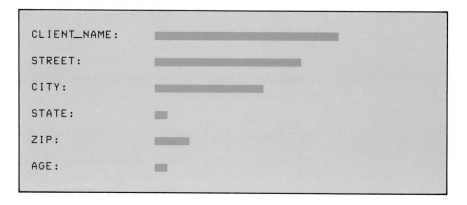

Figure 14.23
A typical data entry screen using a file manager. Shaded areas represent places where data may be entered by the user.

```
CLIENT_NAME: ██████████████████

STREET:      ███████████████

CITY:        ██████████

STATE:       █

ZIP:         ███

AGE:         █
```

Queries

Entering queries usually follows one of two formats. In the first, the user enters commandlike queries, similar to the style of the SQL language, but usually much more restricted in scope. Thus, a command such as LOCATE FOR NAME= "JONES, J." might be used to find a particular record. The other mode of query is again a process of filling in the blanks on a form generated by the file manager. This process is often similar to the style of QBE, discussed in chapter 11.

Reporting

The generation of reports is usually a very strong point of file managers. Users are given simple means by which a variety of different output formats can be produced. Often, the design of a report is accomplished by means of a full-screen display: the user moves the cursor around the screen, filling in titles and field names wherever desired. If several types of options exist, a HELP facility is often provided, by which the user is guided along by the system as much as needed.

Almost without exception, file managers can generate reports with records ordered in a specified manner. This is accomplished either by (1) a routine that sorts records according to a set of user-supplied criteria, or (2) one or more indexes that have been established by the user. Many file managers allow sorting on several fields simultaneously. Strangely enough, some systems that are called file managers have the facility for combining data from several files into a single report! It is not clear why they are not called database managers.

Summary of File Manager Features

In general, the types of available features vary considerably from one file manager to another. To help give an overall picture of the situation, table 14.4 summarizes the different features available on a large number of file managers. This data was derived from a study in which the characteristics of 43 different file

| Table 14.4 | Summary of File Manager Features |

Summary of File Manager Features

Feature	No. Systems Having Feature	Range of Values
Memory required (bytes)		64K–512K
Disks required		1–2
Menu driven	42	
Command driven	7	
Provides HELP screens	29	
Multiuser capability	6	
Maximum number of fields per record		9–Unlimited
Maximum field size (bytes)		24–Unlimited
Maximum record size (bytes)		1800–Unlimited
Maximum number of records per file		128–Unlimited
Allows full-screen editing	32	
Number of files displayed on a screen		1–Unlimited
Simulates paper forms on screen	30	
Maximum number of fields sorted at once		1–Unlimited
Ability to create indexes ad hoc	29	
Splits and merges file	31	
Multiple report formats	40	
Allows encryption	1	
Password access	11	
Maintains an activity log	5	
Price		$49–$975

Source: "Database Managers," PC Week Supplement, May 7, 1985. A total of 43 file management systems were surveyed.

managers were summarized. Clearly, there is a great variation of characteristics among systems, although there are some striking commonalities. For example, out of 43 systems, 42 are menu driven, 40 offer multiple report formats, and 29 or more offer HELP screens, full-screen editing, file merging and splitting, and indexing.

On the other hand, several characteristics often associated with larger database management systems are generally not supported by file managers. For example, only 6 out of the 43 systems support multiuser access, and only one supports data encryption. The particular mix of features indicated in the table exists primarily because file managers are generally designed for single-user, single-file applications. Consequently, many of the features common to large scale database systems are unnecessary. Furthermore, file managers are designed to run on machines with minimal memory and to be quite inexpensive, as table 14.4 also shows.

In summary, file management systems are extremely popular in the microcomputer field. They are relatively easy to use, offering a simple means by which information can be stored, manipulated, and retrieved. Their low cost makes them particularly attractive to the microcomputer user whose data-storage requirements are limited to single-file databases.

Text-Oriented Database Systems

In addition to the types of database systems that have been discussed so far, there exist a number of very specialized types of DBMS's, each of which is focused on a specific type of application. The most common of these are **text-oriented database systems.** The basic unit of data storage within this type of system is some arbitrary grouping of textual material. For example, a DBMS might be used to store a collection of word processing documents. Or, a database might consist of one or more entire books, journal articles, or perhaps an encyclopedia.

Obviously, database systems with this orientation must be characterized by variable-length fields and records. In fact many of them do not even use the terms *fields* or *records*. Instead terms such as *documents* or *fact sheets* are often substituted in order to emphasize the specific nature of the stored information.

Commercial Systems

Many commercial enterprises have become successful by installing enormous text-oriented databases on mainframe computers, then offering the use of these databases to the public. The user charges are normally proportional to the amount of time connected to the database. An individual can connect with one of these databases via an ordinary telephone line, and a search can then be conducted on those parts of the database that are of particular interest.

There are a great many commercial databases of this type, covering a wide range of topics. For example, Lockheed's Dialog system contains literally hundreds of different databases, encompassing a huge variety of subjects. The Dow Jones News/Retrieval Service is another example, offering information on a wide range of timely subjects.

Many specialized databases are also publicly available, dealing with subjects such as medicine and law. Typically, a database contains many thousands, perhaps even hundreds of thousands, of references dealing with the specific field. In some cases, a database contains only abstracts; others contain complete documents. A few of these DBMS's are menu driven and are readily accessible to individuals. Many, however, require the user to learn the query language. Also, because of the complexity of the subject matter involved, and the large amount of information to be searched, the successful and cost-effective use of some of these databases requires a modest amount of training.

Microcomputer Implementations

Until very recently, text-oriented databases were restricted to larger computers, due to the requirements of speed and data storage. However, because of the recent microcomputer developments in these areas, text database systems are beginning to emerge for the microcomputer market. With these systems, a user can create a database of virtually any type of textual information.

Typically, the unit of stored information is a document of some type (the definition of *document* is up to the user). Some DBMS's allow the definition of multiple variable-length fields within each document. With other systems, each document consists entirely of a single variable-length record, with no subdivision into fields permitted. In either case, the crucial issue is the ability to retrieve information rapidly and flexibly. Usually, this is done by means of various types of indexing.

With some database systems, when a user enters a document into a database, (s)he also enters a set of **keywords** for that document. These are entered into the **keyword index,** which is the basis for all retrievals.

Other types of database systems use nearly every word within every document to create an index. Words to be excluded from the index are contained in an *exclusion list*. This list usually contains the commonly used adjectives, pronouns, verbs, and so on, plus any other words that the user wishes to exclude.

The unit of retrievable text may be an entire document, or it may be a document subdivision such as a paragraph, depending on the particular system. Retrieval is accomplished by issuing search commands involving one or more user-specified words in various combinations. For example, suppose that a database consists of a group of document abstracts, and that the index consists of every word contained in all of these. Typical database searches might look like the following:

    (1) FIND FOR "BOATS"
    (2) FIND FOR "BOATS" AND "SAILING"
    (3) FIND FOR "BOATS" OR "SAILBOATS"

The first query would produce a list of every abstract containing the word "BOAT." The second would retrieve those abstracts containing both the words "BOAT" and "SAILING." The last query would retrieve abstracts that contained either "BOATS" or "SAILING."

Microcomputer text-oriented DBMS's have become increasingly popular for the storage and retrieval of references, such as books and journals. Often, each stored record consists of a short abstract of a particular reference, along with a set of keywords inserted into the index. This is particularly useful for those whose major interests require access to large amounts of information on a variety of subjects. In a sense, this type of database takes the place of a card file, but with the enormous advantage of highly complex cross-referencing.

At present, only a few text-oriented systems have penetrated the microcomputer market, although this situation is sure to change rapidly. Currently available systems include FACTFINDER, distributed by Forethought Inc., of Mountain View, California, and DAYFLO, by Dayflo Inc., Irvine, California, as well as others.

Graphics-Oriented Database Systems

A very recent development for microcomputers has been the use of graphics as part of database systems. The Apple Macintosh has been the basis for many of these innovations, which at present are merely in their infancy. For example, the HELIX database system uses the graphics capabilities of the Macintosh to help define relationships between different record-types. On the other hand, Telos Software's FILEVISION package integrates graphical images along with text into a single database.

The advancements of laser-optical disks will undoubtedly have a strong influence on future trends in database development. The ability to store thousands of megabits of information on a single surface will lead to databases with integrated text and images.

Summary

This chapter has summarized the various types of non-relational database systems that are currently in common use, both on mainframe machines and microcomputers. In addition to the types described here, there also exists a large number of special purpose database systems. Each of these is designed to meet the needs of very specific application. Although they technically come under the database management umbrella, they are not general purpose systems and therefore have not been discussed here.

The types of software systems described in this chapter fall naturally into two categories: those that manage single-file databases, and those capable of dealing with databases consisting of many files. The former are usually called file managers, although many other labels are also used, such as record managers, information managers, and so on.

File managers are well suited to the needs of nontechnically oriented users whose requirements can be met by single-file databases. These software packages are generally quite inexpensive and also user-friendly. Full-screen forms are often used for database definition, queries, and report generation.

The term *database system* generally refers to software packages that can manage multiple-file databases. These DBMS's are usually a large step up from file managers, in terms of the type of real-world situations for which information can be stored. In addition, they are typically considerably more complex than file managers, requiring a good deal of effort on the part of the user in order to achieve a reasonable level of competence.

Database systems are often categorized by model, that is, by the way in which information is structured. The relational and network models are the most common, and the hierarchical model is also the basis for a few commercial systems.

Within a network DBMS, a database is structured into fields, records, and files. Further structuring is also possible by defining sets, each of which consists of two files containing a one-to-many relationship. Within a set, related records are structurally connected, usually by means of pointers.

Several sets may be used to build complex data structures within a database. The power of these structures reveals itself in the speed with which groups of related records can be accessed, even though the records may be scattered over many different files.

Various types of network DBMS's exist, the most common being those that conform to some degree to the CODASYL DBTG guidelines. Each type of DBMS imposes restrictions on the types of network structures that are allowed. CODASYL DBMS's offer a high degree of flexibility in this respect, while some of other types may be quite restrictive.

Each network DBMS incorporates a database definition language (DDL) for defining the complete details of each database, called the schema. The DDL includes syntax for defining sets, as well as record-types, fields, constraints, and password protection. In addition, many network DBMS's incorporate a facility for defining subschemas, which allow several tailor-made user views to exist for a single database.

The traditional way to interact with a network DBMS is by the use of application programs, each of which contains embedded database manipulation language (DML) commands. Each program generally has a specific purpose, such as the generation of a report, the addition of records, and so on. Because of the procedural nature of a network DML, even the simplest database query requires the writing of a program. This built-in inhibiting factor has led to the use of nonprocedural languages with many network DBMS's. With these tools, a wide variety of queries and reports can be generated without the need for program writing.

Database management accounts for a sizeable fraction of computer applications, both on microcomputers and mainframes. Particularly with respect to micros, the field is witnessing a continued increase in the use of DBMS packages, as costs drop and availability of features grows. In all probability, new approaches to database management will continue to develop, and users will have a continued increase in the variety of database systems from which to choose.

The database field is mushrooming, and like most areas of computing, the end is nowhere in sight.

Chapter Review

Terminology

CODASYL DBMS
CODASYL DBTG
currency indicator
data manipulation language (DML)
file manager
hierarchical database model
hierarchical DBMS
keyword
keyword index
limited network
network

network database model
network DBMS
procedural language
schema
set
set membership
set occurrence
status indicator
subschema
text-oriented DBMS

Review Questions

1. Summarize the basic differences between a file manager and a database management system. Summarize the relative merits of each type of system.
2. What are the basic distinctions between network and hierarchical database systems?
3. What is the fundamental difference in data structures between relational and network DBMS's?
4. Why does a hierarchical structure not lend itself to representing a many-to-many relationship? Can this type of relationship in fact be represented by a hierarchical structure?
5. Explain why all hierarchical structures are a subset of simple networks.
6. Explain the significance of the "Set selection . ." and "Insertion . ." clauses in the network DDL.

Problems

1. Draw a simple diagram showing the levels of data structures that exist within a network database (files, etc.).
2. Suppose that a one-to-one relationship exists between two record-types A and B. Can a set be defined between them?

3. Modify the diagram shown in figure 14.5(b) so that from any particular ANIMALS record, both the CAGES and ATTENDANTS owner records may be found. What kind of data structure would this represent?

4. This problem refers to the ZOO database shown in figure 14.5(a). Suppose that the situation at the zoo changes, in that each animal is assigned *many* attendants. Redraw the figure to show the new relationships, and define the appropriate sets for this circumstance.

5. Suppose that the following rules apply to a particular zoo:

   - Each animal has one attendant
   - Each cage holds several animals
   - Each attendant is assigned to specific cages, rather than to specific animals

   Draw a data structure diagram similar to the one in figure 14.5(a), but showing the relationships dictated by the preceding rules.

6. This problem refers to the situation represented by the record-types shown in figure 14.6(a): each department has many instructors, and each instructor teaches many classes. Design a limited network structure to represent this situation.

7. Write down the schema for the database described in problem 5. Use the syntax shown in figure 14.11. Take particular care when developing the "Insertion is manual/automatic" clauses. Ignore any password entries.

8. Modify the schema developed in problem 7 to include the following protection scheme:

   - User DRONE is to have read-access to the CAGES and CLEANUPS record-types
   - User ATTNDT_MGR is to have read-access only to the ATTENDANT record-type
   - User MGR is to have unlimited access to the entire database

9. Consider the "Set name is MEDICAL" section in figure 14.11. Would it make sense to change the Insertion clause to "Insertion is manual"? Explain your answer.

10. Using syntax similar to that shown in figure 14.14, develop a subschema for the ZOO schema of figure 14.11 that would permit access to information relating only to cages and attendants. Which sets can be defined?

11. Using syntax similar to that shown in figure 14.14, develop a subschema for the zoo described in problem 5. This subschema should permit access to information relating only to cages and attendants. Which sets can be defined in this subschema?

12. Consider the following situation for a particular company:
    - The company has many customers
    - Each customer may submit many orders
    - Each order may contain many items

    a. Design suitable record-types to represent this situation. Your design should *exclude* repeating groups.
    b. Draw the data structure diagram for your design in (a), indicating the appropriate relationships and sets.
    c. Suppose that customer CUST1 has two orders: ORDER1 contains WIDGETS and GADGETS, and ORDER2 contains GADGETS and THINGIES. Draw the complete set occurrence for CUST1, similar to the diagram in figure 14.6(b).

13. Using any convenient programming language, write a program to output all of the CUSTOMERS records from the database shown in figure 14.15. Use the DML commands shown in table 14.1.

14. Using any convenient programming language and the DML commands shown in table 14.1, write a program to output selected data from the ZOO database shown in figure 14.7. Output is to consist *only* of those ANIMALS records meeting the following conditions:
    a. The animal's attendant is "Petum, O." and
    b. The animal lives either in cage A or cage B.

A Survey of Database Management Systems

This section contains a survey of commercially available database systems. This survey is by no means complete, as there are over two hundred systems presently available. Rather, the intent here is to present a representative sample of DBMS's, indicating costs in addition to a few of the major features.

The survey is broken into two parts: DBMS's for microcomputers, and DBMS's for larger machines. The first category is further divided into systems for the IBM PC and systems for the Apple Macintosh. The lists for the IBM PC and for the large computers are limited primarily to the more popular systems. However, an exception is made for the Macintosh: so few DBMS's are available for this machine that as many as possible have been included.

File-manager type of software is not presented here, since a compendium of microcomputer-based file managers was given in chapter 14. Also, a few types of computers have been neglected in this survey; in particular, those that do not enjoy a large audience. In addition, DBMS's that are specific to the CP/M operating system have been excluded. Although a wonderful operating system in its time, CP/M has become a victim to newer technology, and it will soon be an anachronism.

The information presented here is thought to be reasonably accurate. However, because the software market is highly volatile, particularly in the microcomputer area, it is quite probable that some of the information in the following tables will be out of date by the time this text has been published. This is particularly true with respect to prices. More complete listings are available from a variety of sources. Many publications, such as PC Week and InfoWorld, periodically issue extensive listings.[1,2] Also, various texts contain comprehensive lists.[3,4] These sources were used for some of the information presented in this appendix.

[1]"Database Management Software," PC Week supplement, Vol. 3, #17, April 1986.

[2]InfoWorld, 30 June 1986.

[3]"DataBase Management Systems," 2d ed., Alfonso Cardenas, Allyn & Bacon, Inc., 1985.

[4]"Database Design," 2d ed., G. Wiederhold, McGraw-Hill, 1983.

Database Systems for IBM PC's and Compatibles

The DBMS's included in this category are those specifically written for the IBM PC. Almost without exception, these systems will run on the IBM XT, and most of them will also work on the IBM AT. In addition, many of the computers generically known as "IBM-compatible" or "IBM clones" will run the majority of software specifically designed for the IBM machines. Because there are so many different brands of compatibles, the best statement that can be made is that most of the DBMS's for the IBM PC and XT will run on most of the clones.

Table A.1 lists the most common DBMS's currently enjoying popularity in the commercial market. A few general categorizations have been included, to give the reader some idea of system capabilities. By no means are these the only ways of judging the various packages, but space limitations prevent an exhaustive comparison of system characteristics.

In general, the following statements can be made, based on the data shown in table A.1:

- The majority of the DBMS's offer both command-driven and menu-driven modes of operation.
- Most systems offer the ability to restructure a database in a convenient manner. In other words, the user does not have to do a great deal of data manipulation involving unload/reload.
- As yet, only a few DBMS's offer multi-user capabilities. However, this situation is bound to change as local area networks become increasingly prevalent.
- Most single-user systems cost less than $700, and quite a few are less than $500. Multi-user systems are considerably more expensive.
- The majority of the systems offer some type of programming-language capability.
- With two exceptions, all of the systems claim to be relational. In fact, many of these DBMS's can access multiple files only with the help of application programs.
- One system is based on a free-form text mode. That is, the basic unit of data is a text string of arbitrary length.
- One system is based on the hierarchical model.

Database Systems for the IBM PC and Compatibles

Database System	Vendor	Type*	Required Hardware	Menu Driven	Command Driven	Easy File Redefine	Program Language	Password Protect	Multiuser	Special Features	Cost ($)
Aladin	Advanced Data Institute Inc., 8001 Fruitridge Rd., Sacramento, CA 95820	REL	192K, single disk drive	X	X	X	X	X			795
Paradox	Ansa Software, 1301 Shoreway Rd., Belmont, CA 94002	REL	512K	X	X	X	X	X		Query-by-example query language	695
Versaform XL 3.23	Applied Software Technology, 1350 Dell Ave., #206, Campbell, CA 95008	REL	192K	X	X		X				99
dBASE III	Ashton-Tate, 20102 Hamilton Ave., Torrance, CA 90502	REL	256K	X	X	X	X				495
dBASE III Plus	Ashton-Tate, 20102 Hamilton Ave., Torrance, CA 90502	REL	256K	X	X	X	X	X	X		695
OMNIS 3 Plus	Blyth Software, 2929 Campus Dr., Suite 425, San Mateo, CA 94403	REL		X	X				X		N/A

* REL: Relational
 HIE: Hierarchical
 TXT: Text-oriented

Database System	Vendor	Type*	Required Hardware	Menu Driven	Command Driven	Easy File Redefine	Program Language	Password Protect	Multi User	Special Features	Cost ($)
Reflex	Borland International, 4585 Scotts Valley Dr., Scotts Valley, CA 95066	REL	384K		X	X				Provides for graphical displays	100
Condor 3	Condor Computer Corp., 2051 S. State St., Ann Arbor, MI 48104	REL	128K, single disk drive	X	X	X	X				650
Revelation	Cosmos, 19530 Pacific Highway S., Suite 102, Seattle, WA 98188	REL	320K	X	X	X	X	X	X		950
Dataflex	Data Access Corp., 8525 S.W. 129th Terrace, Miami, FL 33156	REL	256K	X		X	X	X	X		1,250
DayFlo 1.2	DayFlo Software, 17701 Mitchell Ave. N., Irvine, CA 92714	TXT	320K, hard disk	X		X				Incorporates a text processor	495
FMS-Superbase	FMS Software Ltd., 54 N. Main St., Spring Valley, NY 10977	REL	128K	X	X	X	X				995
FoxBASE	Fox Software Inc., 27475 Holiday Lane, Perrysburg, OH 43551	REL	256K			X	X		X	$395 for single-user version	995
10-BASE	Fox Research Inc., 7005 Corporate Way, Dayton, OH 45459	REL	320K	X	X	X					495

Table A.1 [*Continued*]

Database System	Vendor	Type*	Required Hardware	MENU DRIVEN	COMMAND DRIVEN	EASY FILE REDEFINE	PROGRAM LANGUAGE	PASSWORD PROTECT	MULTIUSER	Special Features	Cost ($)
DDQuery	Gemini Information Systems, Box 5144, Englewood, CO 80155	REL	320K, hard disk	X	X	X		X	X		3,750
Cornerstone	Infocom, Inc., 125 Cambridge Park Dr., Cambridge, MA 02140	REL	256K	X	X	X					495
PC/Focus	Information Builders Inc., 1250 Broadway, New York, NY 10001	REL	512K, hard disk	X	X	X	X	X	X	$1,295 for single-user version	4,000
RAMIS II/VMPC	Martin Marietta Data Systems/Information, Technology Div., Box 2392, Princeton, NJ 08540	REL	512K, hard disk	X	X			X	X		1,395
MDBS III	Micro Data Base Systems Inc., Box 248, Lafayette, IN 47902	HIE	128K		X	X	X	X	X		5,000
Knowledgeman II	Micro Data Base Systems Inc., Box 248, Lafayette, IN 47902	REL	320K	X	X	X	X	X	X	$595 for single-user system	1,795
R:base 5000	Microrim, 3380 146th Place S.E., Bellevue, WA 98007	REL	320K, hard disk		X	X	X	X	X	$700 for single-user system	15,000

Table A.1 [*Continued*]

Database System	Vendor	Type*	Required Hardware	MENU DRIVEN	COMMAND DRIVEN	EASILY REFINED	PROGRAM LANGUAGE	PASSWORD PROTECT	MULTI USER	Special Features	Cost ($)
Infoscope	Microstuf Inc., 1000 Holcomb Woods Parkway, Suite 440, Roswell, GA 30076	REL	192K	X	X	X					225
Oracle	Oracle Corp., 2710 Sand Hill Rd., Menlo Park, CA 94025	REL	512K, hard disk	X	X	X	X	X			1,000
Power-base 2.2	PowerBase Systems/ Compuware, 32100 Telegraph Rd., Birmingham, MI 48010	REL	320K	X		X					349
Probase	Probase Group Inc., 1738 W. La Palma Ave., Anaheim, CA 92801	REL	256K, 1 disk drive	X	X	X	X	X	X	$395 for single-user version	692
Datastore: LAN	Software Connections Inc., 1435 Koll Circle, Suite 112, San Jose, CA 95112	REL	320K, hard disk	X				X	X		1,195
DataEase 2.12	Software Solutions Inc., 12 Cambridge Dr., Trumbull, CT 06611	REL	384K	X	X	X	X	X			600
Advanced DB Master	Stoneware Inc., 50 Belvedere St., San Rafael, CA 94901	REL	256K	X		X	X	X			495
dbMan-NET	VersaSoft Corp., 723 Seawood Way, San Jose, CA 95120	REL	256K, single disk drive		X	X	X	X	X		1,100

Database Systems for the Apple Macintosh

Table A.2 lists the systems currently known to exist for the Macintosh. Again, because the market is so highly volatile, there may be omissions from this table. Due to the small number of available systems, file-manager types have been included as well.

| Table A.2 | Database Systems for the Apple Macintosh |

Database System	Vendor	Type*	Required Hardware	Printers Supported	Cost ($)
dBASE MAC	Ashton-Tate, 20102 Hamilton Ave., Torrance, CA 90502	REL	N/A	N/A	N/A
OMNIS 3 Plus	Blyth Software, 2929 Campus Dr., Suite 425, San Mateo, CA 94403	REL	N/A	Any	495
Filemaker 1.0	Forethought, Inc., 1973 Landings Drive, Mountain View, CA 94043	FIL	128K, single disk drive	Imagewriter, Laserwriter	495
Factfinder	Forethought Inc., 1973 Landings Drive, Mountain View, CA 94043	TXT	128K, single disk drive	N/A	150
Habadex 2.0	Haba Systems Inc., 6711 Valjean Ave., Van Nuys, CA 91406	FIL	128K, single disk drive	Imagewriter	100
Ensemble 1.0	Hayden Software Corp. 1 Kendall Square, Cambridge, MA 02139	FIL	128K, single disk drive	Any	100
File 1.02	Microsoft Corp., 16011 N.E. 36th Way, Box 97017, Redmond, WA 98073	FIL	128K, single disk drive	Imagewriter, Laserwriter	195
Double Helix	Odesta Corp., 4084 Commercial Ave., Northbrook, IL 60062	GRF	512K, two disk drives	Any	495

* REL: Relational
FIL: File manager
GRF: Supports both graphical and textual data within a database
TXT: Text oriented

Table A.2 [*Continued*]

Database System	Vendor	Type*	Required Hardware	Printers Supported	Cost ($)
Overvue	Provue Development Corp, 222 22nd St., Huntington Beach, CA 92648	FIL	128K, single disk drive	Any	295
Interlace	Singular Software, 1340 Saratoga/Sunnyvale Rd., Suite 201, San Jose, CA 95129	REL	300K, single disk drive	Any	139
Business Filevision 1.0	Telos Software Corp., 3420 Ocean Park Blvd., Santa Monica, CA 90405	GRF	512K, double disk drives	Any	395

Note that two of the systems have the ability to incorporate graphical information into a database, while most of the rest are simple file managers. Also, due to the graphical orientation of the Macintosh, printer support is a major issue—three of the systems will support only the Apple Imagewriter, Laserwriter, or both. Finally, most of the systems are relatively inexpensive, compared to the median price of those DBMS's listed for the IBM PC in table A.1.

The Macintosh is becoming increasingly popular in the business world; many more database systems for this machine will undoubtedly become available in the near future.

Database Systems for Large Computers

Systems included in this category are those that run either on minicomputers or mainframes. Table A.3 lists the most popular DBMS's (this information is due primarily to Cardenas[3]), and the list is limited to the most popular systems. Consequently, a large number of DBMS's, most of which enjoy very limited audiences, do not appear in the table. Nevertheless, the group of DBMS's shown represents the vast majority of large-machine database users.

Based on the information in table A.3, the following observations can be made:

- Most DBMS's run on IBM equipment, although they may also run on other types as well.
- Unlike microcomputer DBMS's, a large number of these systems are either Network or CODASYL types (recall that CODASYL is a specific type of Network DBMS).
- Only two systems are based on the hierarchical model.

Large-Computer Database Systems: Network and Hierarchical

Name	Vendor	Type*	Required Hardware	Languages	Cost ($)
DMS-II	Burroughs	NET	Burroughs B1700-7800 series	COBOL, PL/1, Algol	400–1,100 per month; 14,000–39,000
Model 204	Computer Corporation of America	NET	IBM 360/370, 30XX, 43XX	COBOL, FORTRAN, PL/1, BAL	2,730–8,190 per month; 155,000–235,000
DMS-170	Control Data Corp.	COD	Cyber 70, 170, CDC 6000	COBOL, FORTRAN, Algol, Assembly	N/A
TOTAL	Cincom	NET	Many, including IBM 360/370, System 3 Burroughs 2500-4800, CDC 6000, Cyber 70-74, 170-175, DEC PDP-11, Honeywell 200,2000	COBOL, FORTRAN RPG II, Algol, Assembly, PL/1, BAL	500–1,500 per month; 15,000–40,000
IDMS	Cullinet Software	COD	IBM 360/370, 43XX, 30XX	COBOL, FORTRAN, PL/1	600–4,000 per month; 55,000–115,000
IDS-II DM-IV	Honeywell	NET	Honeywell H400, H60/6000	COBOL	900–1,600 per month
DBMS/10	Digital Equipment Corporation	COD	DEC PDP-10	COBOL, FORTRAN	N/A
IMS2, IMS/VS	IBM	HIE	IBM 360/370, Models 40, 145 & up, 43XX, 30XX	FORTRAN, COBOL, PL/1, BAL	950–3,700 per month
SYSTEM 2000	INTEL	HIE	Many, including IBM 360/370, 43XX, 30XX, Cyber 70, 170, CDC 6000, Univac 1100	COBOL, FORTRAN, PL/1, BAL	1,200–5,800 per month; 30,000–140,000
ADABAS	Software AG	NET	Many, including IBM 360/370, 30XX, SIEMENS 4004, Univac 9000, ICL System 4, DEC PDP-11	COBOL, FORTRAN, PL/1, BAL	2,500–5,000 per month; 40,000–132,000

* REL: Relational
  HIE: Hierarchical
  COD: CODASYL
  NET: Network

Table A.3 [*Continued*]

Name	Vendor	Type*	Required Hardware	Languages	Cost ($)
DMS 1100	Univac	COD	Univac 1100 series	COBOL, FORTRAN, PL/1	750 per month
SQL/DS	IBM	REL	IBM 370, 30XX, 43XX	COBOL, PL/1, Assembler	300 per month
Query-by-Example	IBM	REL	IBM 370, 30XX, 43XX	PL/1, APL	325 per month
ORACLE	Relational Software Inc.	REL	Many, including IBM 360/370, 43XX, 30XX, DEC PDP-11, VAX-11, DG MV8000, MV10000, Motorola-68000 based systems	COBOL, FORTRAN, PL/1, Pascal, BASIC, C	12,000–96,000
INGRES	Relational Technology Inc.	REL	DEC VAX-11, Motorola-68000 based systems	COBOL, FORTRAN, Pascal, BASIC, C	800–2,800 per month (on a 1–5 year basis); $30,000
RAMIS-II	Mathematica Products Group	REL	IBM 370, 30XX, 43XX	COBOL, FORTRAN, PL/1, BAL	40,000–172,000

- All of these systems support at least one host language, most support both FORTRAN and COBOL, and several support PL/1. Only two DBMS's support Pascal, BASIC, and C. These two DBMS's are relatively new to the large-computer arena.
- Compared to microcomputer systems, the costs of these DBMS's generally are enormously high. Most systems quote both a sale price and a monthly rental cost. Note that these cost figures are as of 1984, and presently they may be quite a bit different.

In general, these DBMS's are highly complex, expensive to maintain, and extremely time-consuming to master. Most of them are designed to support highly complex applications and concurrent access.

a

Alternate key See *candidate key.*

Application program A user-written program, used in conjuction with a DBMS.

Archive A copy of a database, stored permanently as part of a long-term record-keeping system. May be used for historical purposes, such as constructing audit trails.

ASCII An abbreviation for American Standard Code for Information Interchange, an industry-standard set of 8-bit codes for representing standard and special characters in machine-readable form.

Attribute (1) A particular quality associated with a conceptual entity-type. (2) The *column* of a relational table. Also, sometimes used interchangeably with the term *field.*

b

Backup A copy of a database. Used to assist in recovery, should a database be destroyed.

Batch program One that executes without on-line interaction with a user. See also *interactive program.*

Binary search A technique for rapidly locating a particular entry within a sorted list of data items.

Bit The smallest unit of data within a computer. It has two possible values: ON or OFF (0 or 1).

Bit map An array of bits, used to directly represent a many-to-many relationship. It is not commonly used.

Block The smallest unit of information that may be transferred to or from a magnetic disk or tape.

Block header Identifying information at the beginning of a block.

Boolean operator One of the following sets of operators: [**AND, OR, NOT**]. Used in constructing database queries.

Bucket A specific amount of secondary storage that is convenient to access as a unit. This is often a particular number of blocks, although it may also be a single block or track.

Byte A single character, stored in machine-readable form.

c

Candidate key A column of a relational table that could be the primary key. A table may have several candidate keys. Those that are not chosen as the primary key are called *alternate keys.*

Central processing unit (CPU) The area of the computer within which program instructions are executed. The CPU also controls movement of information between input and output devices and primary storage.

Chain A group of logically related records that are connected by sets of pointers. Records within a chain are directly accessible as a group, via the pointers.

Chain head A pointer that contains the address of the first record of a chain.

Clumping A tendency of records to be non-uniformly distributed within a hashed file.

CODASYL DBMS A database system that conforms to the standards set down by the CODASYL DBTG committee. The DBTG (DataBase Task Group) was formed as an arm of CODASYL (Committee On DAta SYstems and Languages) to establish a set of "modern" database standards. Most modern DBMS's do not conform to these standards.

Collision A situation in which the key values of two records produce the same disk address, when the keys are put through a hashing algorithm.

Column In relational database terminology, a field or attribute of a relational table.

Command-driven DBMS One that executes in response to commands entered by a user or an application program. See also *menu-driven DBMS.*

Complex network A data structure consisting of record-types or entity-types, among which exist *many-to-many relationships.*

Concatenated key A key consisting of two or more fields or columns.

Conceptual database model A conceptualized simplification of a real-world system; often the first design step in building a database.

Concurrency control The power exercised by a DBMS to resolve potential conflicts when several users concurrently access the same database information.

Concurrent access A situation in which several users simultaneously attempt to access the same database information.

Conditional dependency See *referential constraint.*

Constraint A restriction imposed on database information, usually due to particular characteristics of the real-world system represented by the database.

Control break Used in conjunction with report generation. Refers to special actions, such as sub-totaling, taken when the value of a particular field changes.

Control structure Used within a program for controlling the flow of operations.

Currency A special concept of CODASYL DBMS's. Refers to a group of pointers that indicate which parts of a database have been most recently accessed.

Cylinder A set of tracks, one per disk surface, that are all at the same radial position. The concept usually applies to hard-disk devices.

d

Database A set of organized data, under the control of a database management system. Most often, a database consists of one or more files of related information.

Database definition facility The part of a DBMS that establishes the structure of a new database by using the specifications written in the database definition language of the DBMS.

Database definition language (DDL) A language for defining the structure of a new database.

Database dictionary (1) The place where details about a database are stored. (2) A stand-alone software package, used to assist in the design, implementation, and use of complex databases.

Database implementation The building of a database structure within a particular DBMS. This usually follows after the development of conceptual and physical database designs.

Database management system (DBMS) A software package that gives controlled access to organized groups of data, for the purposes of searching, reporting, and modification.

Database model An idealization of a real-world system, used as a tool in designing a database. See also *conceptual database model* and *physical database model or design.*

Database restructuring The process of changing the design of an existing database.

Data consistency The concept whereby information within a database contains no internal inconsistencies, with respect to the real-world system that is represented.

Data definition language (DDL) A DBMS language used to define the details of a new database, including record-types, fields, etc.

Data independence A situation in which the physical structures of a database may be changed without impacting either (1) users' concepts of the database, or (2) associated application programs.

Data manipulation language (DML) The set of commands used to navigate through a database and to update database information. DML is primarily a CODASYL concept.

Data redundancy A situation in which information is duplicated unnecessarily within a database.

Data structure diagram A diagram that illustrates the structure of a database design, including record-types (or entity-types) and their relationships.

Data validation The process of checking input data for accuracy, done by testing the data against a set of pre-written rules.

DBMS See *database management system.*

Deadly embrace (deadlock) A situation in which two database users are competing for access to the same information; each user prevents the other from gaining access, and both are immobilized.

Decomposition The redesign of a table or file into two or more different tables or files, for the purpose of improving the overall database design.

Default value A value automatically supplied by a DBMS for a field in the absence of a user-supplied value.

Delimiter A special character used to separate values of adjacent fields. This character acts as an ''end-of-field'' mark.

Derived field or column One whose values are calculated from those of other fields. No data is actually stored for a derived field.

Determinant If each value of column A uniquely determines a value for column B, then column A is said to be a determinant of B.

Dictionary See *database dictionary*.

Direct-access device See *random-access device*.

Direct file One in which the disk address of a record is obtained directly by performing some type of computation on the record key.

Directory See *file directory*.

Disk access A single call to a disk, for the purpose of reading or writing a block of data.

Disk pack A set of removable disk platters; usually associated with disk drives for larger computers.

Distributed database One whose various pieces exist in different physical locations.

Distributed processing A situation in which various database users are located at different places, often far from the main computer. Each user works with his or her own terminal or microcomputer, which may perform local processing on data transmitted to or from the main computer.

Domain The range of values that may be taken on by a field or column.

Domain-compatible Refers to two different fields that have the same domain.

Doubly-linked chain A chain with both forward and reverse pointers.

e

Encryption Any scheme whose function is to protect information by transforming it into an unreadable form. A special *decryption key* must be used to restore the data to its original form.

End-of-block mark or gap A special code indicating the end of a block on a disk or tape.

End-of-file mark or gap A special code indicating the end of a data file.

End-user A person who uses a database as part of his or her work. This is the type of person for whom the database is built.

Entity-type A conceptual tool; it represents a class or group of similar real-world objects or events.

f

Fact That which can be represented by a database record or row.

Field Each database record consists of one or more fields, each of which contains a particular piece of data, such as a name or address. See also *attribute* and *column*.

File A collection of bits and/or bytes stored on a disk or tape. This could be a program or a group of data. A database file usually contains a group of similar records.

File directory A collection of information about a file, including the addresses of the various blocks making up the file.

File manager A relatively simple type of DBMS, in which each database consists of a single file.

File reorganization A process in which the various parts of a file are shifted around on a disk in order to eliminate unusable space.

Fixed-length records Refers to a file of records, all of which are the same length. Most database records are fixed length.

Footer The information appearing at the bottom of each page of a report.

Formatting The process of designing the physical layout of information to appear in a report.

Full-screen mode A situation in which a user may enter information only into selected parts of a screen. The rest of the screen contains descriptive information for the benefit of the user.

Functional dependency A situation in which there exists a direct relationship between values of two different record fields. See also *determinant*.

g

Gigabyte One thousand million (10^9) bytes.

Granularity The degree of fine-tuning that can be achieved when locking database resources (see also *record locking* and *resource locking*), or when utilizing password protection.

h

Hashed file A type of direct file.

Hashing The process of transforming a record key into a disk address. See also *direct file*.

Header The information appearing at the top of each page of a report. See also *block header*.

Hierarchical database model A generalized design concept in which record-types or entity-types are structured hierarchically. See also *hierarchical structure*.

Hierarchical DBMS One in which database structures may only be hierarchical. This is an archaic type of DBMS, very few of which have survived.

Hierarchical structure (hierarchy) One in which each child node or element may have at most one parent node or element.

Host language The language in which database-connected programs are written. These are ordinary languages, such as FORTRAN, COBOL, and Pascal.

Host-language interface The part of a DBMS that communicates with application programs written in an ordinary programming language.

i

Index A data structure permitting rapid access to records in a file. It contains values of record keys and record addresses, arranged for rapid searching.

Indexed file A file for which at least one index exists.

Indexed search A search for records, in which the search criteria involves fields that have been indexed. The corresponding indexes then allow rapid retrieval of the relevant records.

Indexed-sequential file See *ISAM file*.

Integrated package A software package that includes several major types of features, such as spreadsheeting, word processing, database management, graphics, and telecommunications.

Interactive A process in which a user communicates with a software package.

Interactive program A program whose flow is controlled by commands entered by a user as the program executes.

Interface The physical or logical connection between two software packages or pieces of hardware.

Intersection data A data field contained within an intersection entity-type.

Intersection entity-type One that is created during the process of transforming a many-to-many relationship into two one-to-many relationships.

ISAM (Indexed Sequential Access Method) file One that utilizes a specialized type of multi-level index. The index levels correspond to hardware subdivisions, such as tracks or cylinders.

j

Join The process of combining two relational tables into one, using a common column as the basis for combination.

k

Key A field or combination of fields that is used as a basis for locating records, such as via an index based on that field.

Keyword A text-oriented database record may be assigned several keywords. These become part of a *keyword index* that allows retrieval of the record on the basis of one or more of the keywords.

Kilobyte One thousand bytes.

l

Laser optical disk A storage medium in which information is encoded by physically altering the disk's surface with a laser beam. It has extremely high data-storage capacity.

Limited network A *network* type of database structure limited to two levels.

Linear addressing A type of direct file in which a linear correspondence exists between record keys and relative addresses.

Linked list See *chain*.

Local area network A situation in which a group of computers is connected together, usually by a simple cable, for the purposes of sharing resources and communicating with one another. The machines are usually located close to each other, usually within the same building.

m

Macro A group of commands contained within a file. The commands are executed simply by naming the file, as though it were itself a simple command.

Mainframe A general term applying to large computers. There is no clear division between mainframes and minicomputers.

Many-to-many relationship A type of relationship that exists between two record-types, entity-types, or sets of real-world objects.

Megabyte One million bytes.

Menu-driven DBMS One that executes in response to choices made by a user from various menus displayed by the DBMS. See also *command-driven DBMS*.

Modification anomaly A situation in which modifications to a database generate unexpected results, usually due to poor database design.

Modularization The dividing of a large process, such as a program, into several small and more manageable units.

Multilist A situation in which records of a file are interconnected by several chains, each one corresponding to a particular record field.

Multiply-occurring field or attribute See *repeating group*.

Multi-valued dependency A special type of functional dependency in which a particular value of a field may correspond to several values of another field.

n

Network database model A generalized design concept in which record-types or entity-types are structured into a network. See also *network structure.*

Network DBMS One in which database structures conform to the rules of the network database model. Often, the terms *DBTG DBMS* or *CODASYL DBMS* are used synonymously.

Network structure (network) One in which each child node or element may have many parent nodes or elements.

Node (1) A single member of a data structure. (2) A member of a computer network, such as a local area network.

Non-procedural language One in which commands express *what* is desired, but not *how* to obtain the results. Modern query languages and report-generator languages are non-procedural.

Normal forms If a relational table is in a particular *normal form,* it is known to have certain behavioral characteristics.

Normalization The process of transforming a relational table from one normal form to another, for the purpose of improving the table design.

o

One-to-many relationship A type of relationship that exists between two record-types, entity-types, or sets of real-world objects.

On-line storage Any data storage that is directly connected to the computer, such as a disk or tape.

Optional attribute (field) A field within a record or table that does not need to be given a value.

Overflow Records that for some reason cannot be written to their originally intended locations. They must instead be written to an **overflow area.**

p

Packing density In a hashed file, the ratio of (1) space utilized and (2) total space available.

Partial functional dependency A functional dependency in which the determinant is only part of the key of the relational table.

Password protection A system in which data and programs are accessible only to users with authorized passwords (special combinations of letters and numbers).

Physical database model or design A database design that corresponds to the particular DBMS on which the database will be implemented.

Physical disk address The precise place on a disk where a record is located.

Pointer A special field that contains the address of a record.

Primary key A field or combination of fields that uniquely identifies each record of a file.

Primary storage or memory That part of memory that is directly accessible to the CPU. An executing program resides in primary storage.

Prompt A message displayed on the terminal for the benefit of the user, usually requesting user action.

q

QBE (Query By Example) A type of query language in which a user generates a query by filling in blanks on a full-screen display.

Query A user request for a database search.

Query language The set of commands used to generate database queries. Often, commands for modifying a database are considered to be part of a query language.

r

Random-access device One capable of maintaining random access files.

Random-access file One in which any record may be directly accessed by specifying its address.

Range constraint A restriction on the values that may be taken on by a particular field. These values must either lie within a specified range, or be restricted to a group of pre-defined values.

Read-only access A situation in which a user may retrieve, but not modify, the contents of a database.

Read/write access A situation in which a user is permitted both to read and modify a database's contents.

Record The most common subdivision of a database file.

Recording density The number of bytes recorded per linear inch on a disk or tape.

Record key See *key.*

Record locking A situation in which a user issues a DBMS command that prevents any other user from gaining access to a record.

Record-type Refers to all records of a specific type, usually located within a single file.

Recursive relationship A situation in which there exist relationships among the records within a single file.

Referential constraint A requirement that a record of one type may exist within a database only if a corresponding record of another type also exists.

Referential integrity A situation in which a referential constraint has been successfully enforced within a database: with respect to that particular constraint, the database is consistent.

Relation See *table*.

Relational algebra A primitive type of non-procedural query language which forms the basis for many more sophisticated query languages.

Relational database model A generalized design concept in which information is divided into two-dimensional tables or relations.

Relational operator One of the following set: { =, < >, <=, >=, >, < }. These are used in constructing database queries.

Relationship An association that exists between records, entity-types, real-world objects, or other data items.

Relative address The number of the block where a record is written. Blocks within a file are often numbered sequentially.

Repeating group A field or attribute that may have several values. See also *singly-occurring field or attribute*.

Report writer A software package for constructing reports in response to user-generated input. This is often part of a DBMS.

Required field or column One that must be given a value for each record in the file or table.

Resource locking A situation in which a user issues a DBMS command that prevents any other user from gaining access to specific resources, such as a record or file.

Restore/rerun A method of recreating a database from a backup and a transaction log, in the event that the database is destroyed.

Restructuring See *database restructuring*.

Ring A type of chain in which the end is joined to the beginning by means of pointers.

Rollback A method of restoring a database to a consistent state by using a transaction log.

Rollforward See *restore/rerun*.

Rotational delay The time required for a magnetic disk to rotate so that a particular record or block is under the read/write head.

Row A relational database quantity, roughly equivalent to an ordinary record.

S

Schema A complete database description (hierarchical and network DBMS terminology).

Search conditions User-specified conditions that must be met by each record retrieved as the result of a query.

Search range The group of records to be searched as the result of a query.

Secondary index One that is based on any field(s) other than the primary key.

Secondary key A field or combination of fields, other than the primary key, used as a basis for locating records.

Secondary storage device Any medium, other than primary storage, used for storing information in machine-readable form.

Sector A physical subdivision of a disk, shaped like a pie wedge. Most commonly used with floppy disks.

Seek time The time required for the read/write head of a disk unit to move to the proper track position.

Sequential access A process in which the records of a file are accessed in order, beginning with the first one.

Sequential file A file in which sequential access is the only means of locating records.

Sequential search A file search in which records are sequentially accessed, for the purpose of retrieving those that satisfy a specific search.

Set A pair of record-types, between which there is a one-to-many relationship.

Simple network A data structure involving record-types or entity- types, in which the only type of relationship is *one-to-many*.

Singly-occurring field or attribute One which may contain only a single value. See also *repeating group*.

SQL (Structured Query Language) One of the most popular types of non-procedural query languages.

Standard output format A default report format chosen by a DBMS in the absence of user specifications.

Status indicator A variable whose value is set by a DBMS to indicate the result of the last database operation. Used in CODASYL database systems.

Structure diagram See *data structure diagram*.

Sub-schema A description of a subset of a database. Usually used by host-language programs in the CODASYL DBMS world.

Symbolic address Sometimes used in place of a physical or relative address within an index, in order to minimize the effort required to restructure a database.

Synonym An alternate name for a field or column name.

t

Table The basic structure of a relational database. It consists of a two-dimensional array of values, arranged in rows and columns.

Tape cassette A compact type of magnetic tape and enclosure, often used for storing database backups.

Text-oriented DBMS One in which the basic unit of storage is a variable amount of text, often a paragraph or a complete document.

Timesharing A situation in which several users simultaneously share the use of a computer and its resources.

Track A physical subdivision of a disk, namely, a narrow ring whose center is the middle of the disk.

Transaction All of the changes to a database that represent a single change in the corresponding real-world system.

Transaction log A file containing a sequential list of every interaction with a particular database. Essential for restoring a database following a wipeout.

Transitive functional dependency A dependency in which neither member is part of the key of the relational table.

Tree See *hierarchical structure.*

Tuple Relational database terminology for a table row.

u

Union-compatible Refers to two relational tables whose columns are pair-wise domain-compatible.

Unload/reload Part of the database restructuring process, involving the creation of temporary files for storing parts of the database.

User requirements The specific and projected needs of the end-users of a database.

User view See *view.*

v

Variable-length records Refers to a file whose records are not all the same length.

View A logical picture of a database that does not necessarily correspond to the actual physical database structure.

Virtual field or column See *derived field or column.*

w

Winchester technology A common type of hard-disk mechanism.

Word The smallest unit of information that can be directly accessed from primary storage.

significance of in relation design, 279

Keyword, 503

Language. *See also* Programming: languages; Query language
data definition (DDL), 329, 474
data manipulation (DML), 460, 480–482
fourth-generation, 342
nonprocedural, 328, 495–496

Laser optical disk, 71–74

Limited network, 472

Linear addressing methods, 107–109

Linked list, 204–205. *See also* Chain

Local area network, 404

Log. *See* Transaction log

Long-term data storage. *See* Archive

Loop, 448–450

Macro, 154

Magnetic-disk device, 51
built-in, 59
capacities, 54–58
comparison of various types, 60
current trends, 59
data-access modes, 65
floppy-disk, 52–56
hard-disk, 56–59
performance characteristics, 66
physical data layout (format), 60–64
for sequential access, 82–84

Magnetic-tape device, 67–68, 81
for database applications, 70
physical data layout (format), 69

Many-to-many relationship, 228, 305
decomposition of, 229–230, 267–268, 469–471

MDBS III, 473

Menu-driven system, 7

Micro Data Base Systems, Inc., 473

Model. *See* Database: model

Modification anomaly
description of, 285–286
source of, 286–287

Multi-file database, 178
programming for, 154
structures (*see* Structure)

Multilist, 429–430

Multiply-occurring
attribute, 219
field, 414–415

Multi-user system, 10, 19

Network, 443
complex, 443, 446–448
computer, 10
database management system, 274, 456, 458–459
classification of, 471–474
definition of, 465
languages for, 460
structures for, 459–460, 461–471
use of sets with, 460, 461–464
database model, 274
limited, 472
local-area, 404
simple (*see* Simple network)

Node, of tree structure, 438

Nonprocedural language, 328, 342, 495–496

Normal forms
the best, 294
Boyce-Codd, 296, 299
First, 282–284
Second, 288–290
Third, 290, 294
Fourth, 300, 303

Normalization, 220, 281–282, 306. *See also* Normal forms
combining tables, 303–304
when to split tables, 294–296, 299–300

NOT operator, 128

Occurrence of relationship, 183

One-to-many relationship, 182, 226–227
implicit in data, 305
representing with chains, 433–437

On-line data access, 60

OR operator, 127–128

Packing density, 112

Page header, 143

Partial functional dependency. *See* Functional dependency: partial

Password protection, 19, 376
examples of authorization methods, 378–380
programming for, 155
types of authorization, 377

Physical database design or model, 210
compared to conceptual model, 273

Planning for database design, 210–214

Pointer, 417
forward, 425
parent, 436–437
reverse, 425

Primary key, 85, 278

Primary storage, 10, 26, 50

Program-driven system, 8

Program examples, 163–171. *See also* Programming
with embedded SQL, 362–363
generating mailing labels, 164–166
for a two-file database, 196–203
for updating information, 167–169

Programming, 153
for database applications, 154–155
without database management, 2
languages
built-in, 157
for database applications, 156–158, 160–162
host-language interface, 156, 460
important qualities, 160–163
nonprocedural, 328
trends in, 157–159
for security, 155, 384

Projection, 344

QBE (Query By Example), 364–366

Qualifier, 358

Query. *See* Searching

APR 4 1989	DATE DUE	
5-18-90		
MAR 2 1 1995		
2-15-00		